Structured Finance

Structured Finance

Charles-Henri Larreur

WILEY

Library of Congress Cataloging-in-Publication Data is Available

ISBN: 978-1-119-37110-6 (paperback) ISBN 978-1-119-37128-1 (ePub)
ISBN: 978-1-119-37126-7 (ePDF) ISBN 978-1-119-38931-6 (Obook)

Cover Design: Wiley
Cover Image: © hunthomas/Shutterstock

Set in 10.5/13pt, STIXTwoText by SPi Global, Chennai, India.

SKY10088599_102224

To Tammy, Clémence, and Alexandre

Contents

Preface

STRUCTURED FINANCE (OR THE LIFE OF MY FRIEND DAVID)

David is my best friend. I met him a few years back in business school. We were in the same class and shared a background in history and political science as well as an interest in finance. Unlike me and many others in our class, David was not lured into banking by the prospect of a big pay check. He chose what looked like a boring option at the time, joining the management program of a major French retail company. It turned out to be a very clever move. While those of us who chose banking experienced at first hand one of the greatest economic crises of all time (2008) – and the frustrations of the regulatory clampdown that followed – David has enjoyed a brilliant career. He was sent to Italy to assist the local CEO with trade union negotiations; worked in Brazil for two years setting up a joint venture with a local partner; and lived in Singapore while helping to establish his firm in Asia. He now serves as head of corporate strategy, sitting on the company's executive committee.

David teases me when we talk about work. He tells me that his business is simple, where mine is incomprehensible. The recipe for making money in the retail business is easy: since supermarkets sell products at low prices, they have to buy products at *very* low prices. Margins are small but are offset by volume. Structured finance is the exact opposite: high profits but a business model that no one understands, even when they pretend they do.

What David says is partly true. Most people have a very limited understanding of my industry. Despite the profits it generates, structured finance is less well known than M&A or capital markets. And what little *is* known about structured finance has mostly to do with its role in bringing about the subprime crisis, leaving it associated with shady dealing, tax evasion, and accounting manipulation.

Far from being responsible for all of the planet's woes, structured finance is actually essential to the global economy. Most people benefit daily from it. There is nothing exotic about it. It is simply a set of techniques used to finance the companies and assets that are part of our everyday lives.

Take my friend David for instance. He ignores it, but structured financing is all around him.

A TYPICAL DAY IN THE LIFE OF MY FRIEND DAVID

David flies to New York regularly to meet the local management of his company's US subsidiary. He wakes up early, has breakfast and goes down to a car ordered on his smartphone. On his way to the airport, he passes the Seine River and the Eiffel Tower, making it out of the city in time to beat the morning traffic. He flies to New York on Delta, United, American, or Air France – whichever has the cheapest business-class ticket. After landing at JFK Airport, he hails a taxi to the office. When the workday is over, he heads to his hotel, usually the Hilton Midtown, a few blocks away from Rockefeller Center. He takes a shower and spends an hour making calls and answering emails. Then he takes another taxi to a fancy restaurant and has dinner with the local CEO or some key suppliers.

Most of the next day is spent at the office in back-to-back meetings with the local management team. There are intense discussions about all the typical aspects of a retail business: sales, margins, finance, supply chains, and HR. David then usually meets investment bankers to have their views on the US market and the strategic options available for his firm. I know, for instance, that a couple of years ago he spent a lot of time working on a potential acquisition of Safeway, a retailer with a strong foothold in the West. David unfortunately lost that deal, and Safeway was eventually acquired by another competitor, Albertsons.

When he has a minute, David calls his wife and speaks with his kids. They talk about school and the toys they want for Christmas or their birthdays. Almost always, they ask if he will take them to Disneyland Paris when he gets back.

The following day, David picks up a rental car at Hertz and drives to New Jersey or Connecticut to check on a few stores himself. One of them, in Newark, not too far from the Port of New York and New Jersey, where large ships from all over the world can be seen loading or unloading containers, is a worry for him. The supermarket has been struggling for years and, despite recent refurbishments, there has been no real sign of improvement. Its location is not the best: David will probably have to close it.

In Connecticut, however, business is good, especially in the south where his company's upscale grocery stores appeal to the large, affluent hedge fund community. The fresh products the stores offer are in line with the expectations and means of people who pay attention to what they eat. Customers here are also more eco-conscious than usual, an attitude reflected in the wind and solar farms that David passes on his drive.

On a day like this, David enjoys a simple lunch. If he had been with a colleague, he would have eaten in one of the cafés inside their stores. Alone, he chooses a fast food restaurant, ideally Burger King, a favorite from his childhood. In the afternoon, David goes back to Manhattan and tries, if he can, to squeeze in a drink or dinner with a friend. The next day, he checks out early from the hotel, using a Visa card or an American Express. He then goes back to the office and starts another round of meetings, this time mostly with suppliers.

A few hours later, David is back at the airport. He can finally relax. Comfortably seated on the plane, he enjoys a glass of wine, plugs his headphones into his cell phone and listens to classical music or David Bowie, his favorite singer. He checks the sports pages in the paper, paying extra attention to articles on motorsports and Formula One. Then he gets some rest and starts thinking about his weekend, wondering whether he will have enough time to take his Harley Davidson for a spin.

STRUCTURED FINANCE IS EVERYWHERE

To David, structured finance seems entirely remote from his daily routine, an obscure corner of the banking world that he associates mainly with economic disaster. He does not realize that structured finance is literally all around him. During his three-day stay in the United States, David unwittingly came across no fewer than 20 structured finance deals – highly complex transactions designed to optimize the financing of companies, specific projects, and services.

Securitization, certainly, has been misused to sell bad loans to gullible investors, but *Visa* and *American Express* (whose credit cards David travels with) use this technique to finance cash advances to their clients. It is also a perfect tool for funding intangible assets. *David Bowie's intellectual property rights* and the broadcast rights to *Formula One* were both financed through this instrument.

Securitization is not the only structured finance product that David came across. Companies that invest in expensive movable assets rely extensively on other types of structured solutions. All the airlines that David flies with (*Air France, Delta Airlines, American Airlines,* and *United Airlines*) finance the acquisition of their aircraft through structured transactions. The *shipping companies* that he passes at the Port of New York and New Jersey also use these methods to finance their vessels.

Infrastructure is also an important sector for structured finance. Many large assets like roads, airports, wind farms, and photovoltaic farms are funded through structured solutions. Even the telecom infrastructures that David relies on when he uses his phone are often funded this way. Structured finance has also brought to life more unconventional projects, like the *Eiffel Tower* and *Disneyland Paris*.

Finally, we cannot talk about structured finance without mentioning leveraged buyouts (LBOs). Since the 1970s, the number of private equity firms formed to execute LBOs has exploded, and some of the world's most recognizable brands have been reshaped by the LBO industry. They include *Hilton Hotels*, which puts David up on his trips to New York, *Hertz* where he picks up his rental car, *Burger King* where he eats lunch, and *Harley-Davidson*, which sold him his motorcycle.

Structured finance, then, is the great paradox of modern banking. Much maligned – with good reason – for its misuse before the crisis of 2008, it is also the beating heart of the global economy. It is everywhere. It has given us the Eiffel Tower, American Express, and many large infrastructure assets a point too often forgotten by business school professors, the financial press, and my friend David.

ABOUT THIS BOOK

Why a new book on structured finance? This is a question I have been asked quite often. To this question, my answer is simple: there are in fact not many books on the topic. The ones that I know are either too theoretical (to my taste at least) or too specialized. They generally deal with one sub-product of structured finance only and too rarely with the concept as the whole.

The ambition of this book is to offer readers a tour of the structured finance world. It is to present in a simple manner and with the help of case studies the four major structured finance techniques: (i) *leveraged buyouts*, (ii) *project finance*, (iii) *asset finance*, and (iv) *securitization*. The book will be divided into four parts and each of them will analyze in detail one of these instruments.

This book will not only describe each of these four techniques it will also highlight their commonalities and the reasons why we think they belong to the same family of products. Through 13 case studies and more than 500 examples of companies, the book will also offer a historical journey through the structured finance landscape. Our objective is not only to show how these techniques work but also to explain why financiers have come up with them and the reasons they have become so successful.

Introduction

A BRIEF HISTORY OF STRUCTURED FINANCE

The emergence of structured finance in the 1970s was a true revolution in the financial sector. It was probably the greatest shakeup in the money industry since the creation of organized and fluid stock exchanges in the seventeenth century.[1] If there is one day a Hall of Fame for financial innovations, structured finance will take its place among gold coins, hedge funds, central banks, and banknotes.

With the rise of structured finance, the banking industry has changed more drastically (for good and ill) during the past four decades than during the previous 300 years. In barely four decades, it has reshaped the world's largest banks and greatly increased the liquidity of financial markets. It has transformed banks from dull deposit-to-lend conduits with a staid management culture to money-making factories led by brash and colorful figures.

Investment banks now have large teams dedicated to structuring a wide array of deals for their clients. Most of them have entire departments focused on each of the four types of transactions analyzed in this book. These teams are sometimes even sub-divided by industry sector (telecommunications, energy, infrastructure, etc.). This gives them a deeper level of expertise to offer clients as well as the know-how to manage their own risks.

Large investment banks are today active at each stage of the structured finance process: identification of potential deals, arrangement, structuring, underwriting, syndication, and sometimes – at a later stage – refinancing.

Some corporations outside the finance industry, especially utility companies or players in the infrastructure market, have also developed a strong expertise in structured solutions. Some of them have specialized teams, and their level of sophistication is comparable, if not superior, to those of the shrewdest bankers. Companies involved in the development, construction and operation of renewable energy plants (the kind that built the windfarms David sees in Connecticut) are frequent users of structured

---

[1] There is little consensus amongst scholars as to when stocks were publicly traded for the first time. French historian Fernand Braudel has notably shown that the equivalent of what we would today call government bonds were already traded in Venice, Florence, and Genoa at the beginning of the fourteenth century. It is, however, safe to say that even though there may have been some organized and regulated trading activity before, the Amsterdam Stock Exchange – created in 1602 originally for dealing with the printed bonds and stocks of the Dutch East India Company – is widely seen as the first organized market place to offer a high level of liquidity for traders of bonds and securities.

financing. For them, structured finance is the norm, while traditional bonds and bank loans are the exception.

But why the sudden boom in structured transactions? Structured finance indeed spread quite rapidly, becoming the "the new big thing" in global finance in less than a decade. In just a few years, financiers had created a wide array of new products and established entire lines of business within banks. They had closed the first securitization deals and the first leveraged buyouts or LBOs (Revlon, Beatrice Foods, RJR Nabisco), invented project finance, and structured leasing transactions to finance entire aircraft fleets.

A complex mix of long-run trends in the banking sector and a shift in the broader context accounts for the speedy evolution of these new financing forms. The drivers of change are plenty but can be captured under three headings: (i) the rise of a new generation of uninhibited bankers, (ii) political and technological shifts, and (iii) rising demand for leverage from US and European companies.[2]

The Men

Although history books give credit to charismatic figures who alter the course of events, finance textbooks rarely do. In imparting their lessons about the optimal use of capital or the time value of money, they do not usually pause to mention the innovators behind these theories. And when they do, they focus on the academics who formalized them instead of the practitioners who used them in the real world – often well before they were ever expressed in a classroom.

The structured finance revolution cannot be understood without exploring the generational change playing out on Wall Street at that time. The men taking charge of banking in the 1970s were the first to carry with them no memory of the Great Depression. Born in the 1940s and just entering their 30s, they were for this reason probably more daring (or less prudent) than their seniors. In any case, they were more prone to financial audacity and less afraid of debt.

Among this group of young and ambitious financiers, some had enormous influence on the financial innovations of that period. At Bear Stearns, the two cousins Henry Kravis (b. 1944) and George Roberts (b. 1944), and their mentor Jerome Kohlberg,[3] structured the very first LBOs. At Drexel Burnham, Michael Milken (b. 1946) created the high yield market and, at Salomon Brothers, Lewis Ranieri (b. 1947) invented the concept of securitization. Far from Wall Street, in Los Angeles, Steven Hazy (b. 1946) founded in 1973 International Lease Finance Corporation, the first aircraft leasing company.

---

[2]As a reminder, leverage is the debt-to-equity ratio used to finance an asset, whether this asset is a company, an immovable property, or a financial asset. The higher it is, the greater the level of debt.
[3]The oldest banker in this list, Jerome Kohlberg, was born in 1925. He was only 30 years old when he joined Bear Stearns in 1955. He acted in a way as spiritual father to Henry Kravis and George Roberts with whom he founded KKR. He resigned in 1987 to found a new private equity firm, Kohlberg & Company. He passed away in 2008. His estimated net worth was $1.5 billion.

The Context

This wave of financial innovation was also partly conditioned by the evolution of the US banking regulation. The loosening of rules governing financial markets in the 1970s in many US states, and later at the federal level under Reagan, allowed easier structuring of certain debt products. It also gave banks the right to sell a wider range of financial instruments to insurance companies and pension funds, two types of investors which were, until that time, only buying stocks or corporate bonds.

Deregulation per se, was not the direct cause of these financial innovations. While most appeared around the mid-1970s, the liberalization of financial markets was more a child of the 1980s. Reaganomics only really took hold in 1982, when Ronald Reagan signed the Garn-St Germain Depository Institutions Act,[4] and the British "Big Bang" prepared by Margaret Thatcher only came into force in October 1986. Deregulation did not create structured finance but acted as a fertilizer, stimulating competition among banks and the development of new types of financial products.

The 1980s was also a period of profound changes in the IT sector. Companies began to give personal computers to their employees. Bankers gained powerful software tools previously unavailable. The spreadsheet program Lotus 1-2-3 appeared in 1983 and Microsoft Excel in 1987, allowing bankers to easily design the complex financial models which are at the very heart of structured finance. In 1983, Bloomberg LP launched its famous terminal, giving its users access to an unprecedented range of financial information. The generalization of this system would greatly favour the development of structured finance, allowing investment banks to better calibrate their products.

The Demand

No demand, no offer. Behind this truism lies one of the main factors of the rise of structured financing: banks, beginning in the 1970s, realized that demand was growing among their corporate clients for structured products.

Just as a new generation of bankers took power on Wall Street, a new wave of managers rose to positions of power in corporate America. And just like their counterparts in the banking sector, they were born after the Depression of the 1930s. And just like them, they proved less reluctant to use debt.

More importantly, structured finance offered solutions that met the particular corporate needs of the era. Because of the oil shock, for instance, and the attendant rise in energy prices, oil companies started digging in the North Sea, hoping to reduce their dependence on the Organization of the Petroleum Exporting Countries (OPEC). This involved massive and unprecedented investments for which they drew upon the financial engineering capabilities of banks.

---

[4]"This bill is the most important legislation for financial institutions in the last 50 years. [...] Now, this bill also represents the first step in our administration's comprehensive program of financial deregulation." Ronald Reagan on 15 October 1982 while signing the Garn-St Germain Depository Institutions Act.

Similar challenges spurred structured financing in other sectors. The sustained growth of demand for air transport from the 1970s forced banks and airlines to come up with the means to finance whole fleets of aircraft. Here again, structured finance was the only way to accommodate the need for large and recurring capital expenditures.

Similarly, from the 1990s onwards, thanks to deregulation and the withdrawal of governments from the direct funding of some public infrastructure, companies got involved more directly in the financing of new highways, airports, fiber-optic networks, etc. Once again, banks offered the structured solutions necessary to implement all this.

DEFINING STRUCTURED FINANCE

After this long introduction, it is probably time for a first definition of structured finance. Providing one is surprisingly difficult. There are indeed several definitions of the concept, none of which has achieved a consensus among bankers, scholars, or investment professionals.

To come up with a useful definition for this book, we will take things step by step. We will analyze the three main variants of the structured finance concept and finally settle on the definition we prefer.

> **First version**. Structured finance refers to all loans that are not "vanilla loans", i.e. plain and simple loans made by banks to their clients. These "vanilla loans" can be bullet (with the principal repaid at maturity) or amortizing (when principal is paid down over the life of the loan), but do not involve any twist and do not require any specific legal or financial engineering. The risk borne by the bank is solely and simply the credit risk of the company it has lent money to. According to this definition, structured finance comprises all the forms of funding that do not match the criteria of these vanilla loans.

This first definition underlines the complexity of structured finance and undoubtedly represents a solid first approach to the subject. It is unfortunately a little too vague and includes a wide array of financing types that do not have much in common. It is also a by-default definition, which is not likely to satisfy an audience as demanding as one that would take an interest in this book.

> **Second version**. Structured finance is a synonym of structured credit. It refers to the pooling and financing of financial assets through a dedicated company.

This definition, very popular among US scholars, strikes us as incomplete. Structured credit refers to a large sub-segment of structured finance (also called securitization) but does not capture the whole. Adopting this definition would mean neglecting the fact that structured credit transactions have a lot in common with other types of financing. So while the first definition of structured finance may be too broad, we believe that this second one is too narrow. Structured credit remains an important part of structured finance but the two concepts are not identical.[5]

Third version. Structured finance describes transactions in which funding is brought by lenders to a dedicated company (also known as a special purpose vehicle or SPV) created for the sole purpose of financing the acquisition of an asset or a group of assets (financial or physical assets). The repayment of the loan is linked only to the performance of the underlying assets, meaning that it depends on the income generated by the SPV. The lenders take a risk on these assets and have no recourse on the equity holders in the SPV.

This definition zeroes in on the fact that structured transactions are not set up to directly finance a company but rather a specific asset or a portfolio of clearly identified assets. This third definition is more precise than the first one but broader than the second. It excludes from the structured finance concept some similar arrangements that do not require the creation of a special purpose company (trade finance, for instance). Yet it encompasses structured credit (our second definition) and goes further by noting that structured finance can be used to finance a portfolio of financial assets, as well as real assets such as companies, equipment, or infrastructure projects.

As readers will probably have guessed, this book will focus on this third definition. We will explain in detail various types of financing. They will differ in their particulars, but each of them implies (i) the establishment of a SPV and (ii) a loan to this SPV without legal or financial recourse to the investors in the SPV.[6]

The four main financial techniques analyzed in this book are:

1. **Leverage buyout** (also known as LBO): one of the techniques commonly used to finance the acquisition of companies, especially when the buyer is an investment firm or an individual.
2. **Project finance**: a tool used to finance large infrastructure or energy projects.
3. **Asset finance**: the financing of investments in movable assets like aircraft or ships.
4. **Securitization**: the financing of portfolios of financial assets.

Each of these four techniques is – to some extent – a variation on the same structure. The details and subtleties may obviously vary from one deal to another but in each case an SPV is set up and financed by a mix of debt and equity with the sole purpose of acquiring an asset. The assets to be financed may differ (a company, an infrastructure, an aircraft, or a portfolio of securities) but all in all these four techniques are quite similar and could all be represented under the form of Figure I.1.

---

[5]Part IV of the book is dedicated to the analysis of structured credit.
[6]Note: the notions of special purpose vehicle (SPV), special purpose company (SPC), or special purpose entity (SPE) are all identical.

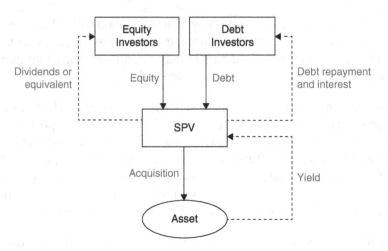

FIGURE I.1 Simplified diagram of a standard structured finance transaction

For the sake of clarity, we will in each chapter of this book refer back to this simplified structure. The idea is to underline the connections between these financing techniques and to show that they all belong to the same large family of products. This should also provide the opportunity to gradually highlight the similarities and differences between them.

Even if we perfectly understand that a reader may choose a targeted approach to this book and start from any given chapter (or simply focus on one part of the book only), we suggest – if possible – reading it from the start in the way in which it is presented here. This should enhance the reader's experience, since each chapter is not only an isolated description of one particular financial technique but also refers to concepts or elements mentioned elsewhere in the book.

WHY WAS STRUCTURED FINANCE SET UP?

There are many reasons why banks started to promote structured finance solutions to their clients. The first is obviously that structured finance products are lucrative per se. If a bank is able to capture the whole value chain for a single structured finance deal, there are not many areas of finance that can offer the same returns. The example of Michael Milken in the 1980s is striking. At one point, his single structured debt department at Drexel Burnham was earning more profits than any other US investment bank as a whole. (At the time, the other banks were generally not very active in this segment; needless to say, things changed rapidly after they saw the returns generated by Milken.)

The second reason is that structured finance can have a specific appeal to clients willing to optimize their capital structure. Structured finance is a set of techniques designed to put additional debt behind an asset. As such, it improves returns for equity holders. In an environment where companies are under pressure from shareholders to provide better returns, structured finance gives them tools to optimize their level of indebtedness.

The other reasons behind the success of structured finance are more technical and relate either to financial or regulatory specifics. If they seem a little abstract at this stage to readers without a strong background in finance, they should become less so over the course of this book. We will come back to these causes (five of them financial, one linked to regulation) in our conclusion and see how they apply to each specific type of structured finance deal.

Five Financial Reasons

From an equity investor perspective, setting up an SPV to acquire an asset (whatever this asset is) is a way to isolate risk. Debt is raised at the SPV level, and lenders have no recourse to the investor if the asset fails to perform. Other assets owned and controlled by the investor cannot be seized by lenders to repay the debt. It brings additional safety to investors, who can separate various investments into silos. Assets that are isolated this way are said to be "ring-fenced" (Reason 1).

By sizing the debt based on the cash flows generated by the SPV, lenders can offer a higher degree of leverage to their clients than if the same asset was mixed with lower performing assets. If the asset to be financed generates steady cash flows, it is preferable to isolate it in an SPV and take advantage of its credit quality by maximizing leverage (Reason 2).

Structured finance offers lenders direct exposure to risks they are comfortable with. Instead of funding a large corporation carrying out various businesses, including some they might find less attractive, lenders can simply finance an SPV which holds one specific asset. If they are comfortable with the credit quality of this asset, lenders would rather fund this asset than a mix of businesses (Reason 3).

Structured finance has also created entirely new investment opportunities for lenders and investors. They have access today to a range of products that did not exist before. In other words, structured finance attracts liquidity because it offers opportunities that cannot be found anywhere else (Reason 4).

These new products offer the whole spectrum of return/risk combinations. All types of debt and equity investors can find their niche. Depending on their risk appetite, investors can select the product that fits their needs most: senior debt, mezzanine, or equity (Reason 5).

One Regulatory Reason

The growing success of structured transactions over the last 40 years is not only due to financial reasons. The other main driver of their popularity is that they allow banks to optimize their balance sheets from a regulatory perspective.[7]

---

[7]We warn the readers in advance that the explanations they will be reading are complex. They are, however, essential to understanding the relevance of structured finance. We thank the readers in advance for their patience.

The concept of banking regulation originates in the Basel Accords, first signed in 1988, between the central banks of various countries and subsequently revised multiple times.[8] The Basel Accords aim to provide national regulatory bodies with tools to better control banks active in their countries. They are a set of non-binding recommendations that have been widely adopted by governments since the 2008 crisis.

Among the issues addressed by the Basel Accords is the desire to limit the risks taken by banks. After all, banks are institutions that – to a degree more than any other business – finance their activities with high levels of debt. Their borrowings are, for the most part, the cash sitting in the bank accounts of their customers.

A Primer on Banking Regulation

Given the large amount of money they receive from depositors, most banks are highly leveraged. Unlike traditional businesses, this borrowing capacity is almost unlimited. While the financial statements of any prospective borrower are closely scrutinized by the banker in charge of analyzing the loan request, very few depositors ever analyze the balance sheet of the institution where they deposit their savings. A bank can therefore in theory have an infinite debt-to-equity ratio. This would obviously pose a danger to clients, since any major loss suffered by a bank would directly impact the customers' deposits.

The Basel Accords aim to limit the capacity of banks to borrow money to prevent such a scenario from occurring. In simple terms, we could say that the Basel Accords require that for each loan granted to a client, a minimum portion of it should be financed by the bank's equity, i.e. with shareholders' contributions. As a reminder, these contributions are either direct (share capital) or indirect (retained earnings). Retained earnings are simply undistributed profits or, in other words, dividends surrendered by shareholders.

The main principle of the Basel Accords is to ensure that banks cannot fund the loans granted to their clients with customers' deposits only. Banks must maintain in their books a certain amount of capital so that any loss they might suffer could be absorbed by the shareholders without impacting lenders (i.e. the depositors). This minimum amount of capital is therefore often referred to as *capital buffer*.

A Weighted Approach to Risk

A dilemma lies behind this commendable principle nonetheless. When two banks (Bank 1 and Bank 2) each lend out $100 million to a client, they do not necessarily take the same level of risk. Bank 1 may, for instance, lend to Alphabet,[9] a company rated AA+ by Standard & Poor's (S&P), while Bank 2 lends to a start-up launched by two teenagers. Even if the project of the two young entrepreneurs is very promising, the

---

[8]Basel II was signed in 2004 and Basel III in 2010. New modifications to Basel III were introduced in 2016 and are sometimes referred to as Basel IV.
[9]Google parent company.

bank funding the start-up takes a much higher risk than the one lending to Alphabet. The amounts at stake are the same ($100 million) but Alphabet's likelihood of default is much lower than the start-up's. It would be nonsense if regulators were to require Bank 1 and Bank 2 to use the same amount of capital to fund their loans.

If banks had to finance every loan, whatever the underlying risk, with the same percentage of capital, they could be tempted to multiply dodgy loans. With the interest rates applicable to risky counterparties being significantly higher than the ones paid by investment-grade companies,[10] banks could prioritize loans with higher margins (hence risky) over safer prospects. For a given amount of capital, risky loans would indeed produce more revenues. This would lead to the exact opposite of what the Basel Accords aim for. Instead of creating safer banks, regulation would incentivize the opposite.

To avoid this pitfall, the Basel Accords stipulate that banks must for regulatory proposes convert each of their assets (i.e. loans, investments, guarantees, capital market instruments, etc.) into a Risk Weighted Asset or RWA, i.e. an asset whose nominal value is weighted according to its risk. The amount of capital set by the regulator to fund each asset is fixed as a percentage of the corresponding RWA. In other words, the amount of capital required from banks is not based on the nominal value of each asset but on the value of each asset weighted according to its intrinsic risk.

Let us take a numerical example. The Basel Accords indicate that the equivalent in RWA of a loan granted to a AA+ corporation like Alphabet is equal to 20% of the notional amount of the loan. If the loan is made to a non-rated company, this amount is equal to 100%. In short, for two loans, both equaling $100 million, regulators would assign a corresponding RWA of $20 million for a loan to Alphabet and the full $100 million for a loan to a start-up. Assuming that the required percentage of capital set by the regulator is 8%, a bank must mobilize at least $1.6 million of capital (8% x 20) when it lends $100 million to Alphabet. If it wants to lend the same amount to a start-up, it must use $8 million of capital (8% x $100 million), or five times more.

With this weighted approach to risk, regulators avoid the paradoxical situation mentioned earlier. In a system without RWA, in which the required capital amount to finance a loan would be calculated on a nominal basis, loans to start-ups would generate a profitability significantly higher than loans to investment-grade companies (because margins would be much higher). Thanks to the Basel framework, the profitability of the two loans is rebalanced. It is unfortunate for the two teenagers but all the better for the stability of the financial system.

Contribution of Structured Finance

An attentive reader might at this stage be wondering what the link is between banking regulation and structured finance. To keep things simple, we have for the moment assumed that RWAs are only a function of the borrowers' credit risk. Basel's regulatory

---

[10] As a reminder, the debt securities considered investment grade are securities with a rating of at least BBB- (S&P) or Baa3 (Moody's).

framework is in reality more complex. The amount of RWAs also depends on other factors such as potential additional guarantees. Specifically, if a bank lending to Alphabet obtains as part of the transaction a mortgage on the head office of the company, the amount of RWAs (which was $20 million) will be further reduced. The mortgage lowers the risk taken by the bank and decreases its potential loss. In case of bankruptcy of Alphabet, the bank can exercise its rights under the mortgage deed and recoup some of its losses through a sale of the building.

Even if we will see later that calculating the impact of a mortgage is not straightforward, we can assume at this stage that the amount of RWAs corresponding to a loan with a mortgage is equal to 20% of the same loan with no mortgage. In other words, the amount of RWAs corresponding to a $100m loan to Alphabet is reduced from $20 million to $4 million (20 x 20%). The bank needs as little as $320,000 (8% x $4 million) of its own equity to fund this loan, rather than $1.6 million.

TABLE I.1   Amount of Capital Required From a Bank to Fund a $100 million Loan (in $m)

Type of Loan	Loan Amount	Corresponding Risk Weighted Assets (RWA)	Capital (8% x RWA)
Loan to a non-rated company	100	100	8
Loan to Alphabet (rated AA+ by S&P and Aa2 by Moody's)	100	20	1.6
Mortgage loan to Alphabet	100	4	0.32

Table I.1 summarizes the impact in terms of RWAs and capital needs under the three scenarios discussed so far: a $100 million loan (i) to a non-rated company, (ii) to Alphabet, and (ii) to Alphabet with the benefit of a mortgage. The safer the loan, the less capital the bank has to use. This is in line with the objectives of the regulators. After all, the purpose of setting a minimum amount of capital to fund each loan is to create safer banks. It is not to discourage banks from doing business. If the risk of loss is minimal, then the bank should not be required to mobilize a lot of capital. There is obviously a thin line for the regulators to walk. They have to protect banks and depositors, but if they require too much capital, there is a risk that, all things being equal, margins will go up significantly. Banks' shareholders still need to receive a decent return for their investment and if a lot of equity is needed for each loan, they will ask for higher margins on these loans. That may slow down the development of small businesses.

Obtaining a mortgage when lending to a AA+ rated company may seem like a detail at first glance from a risk perspective. It is, however, essential from a regulatory perspective. It allows the bank to reduce the amount of capital allocated to the transaction. In our example, the bank saves $1.28 million (1.6 – 0.32) of capital by receiving the extra security. This capital can be allocated to other transactions, which will generate additional returns. In other words, thanks to a simple mortgage, the bank can dramatically improve its return on equity.

Structured finance transactions have in effect the same impact as this mortgage. They generally involve more leverage than plain vanilla loans but come most of the time with a package of additional securities or guarantees (called a security package). Depending on the transaction, this package can include pledges of shares, mortgages on properties, early repayment options, prepayment guarantees, etc. All things being equal, these elements reduce the amount of RWAs (and consequently capital) allocated to a deal. To put it simply, structured finance transactions allow banks to optimize their use of RWAs. This is one of the reasons for their growing success (Reason 6).[11]

Going into More Detail

As briefly mentioned earlier, the impact of a security package on the reduction in RWAs is not always easy to estimate. Without getting into the complexities of Basel II and III, the regulatory framework is such that banks are given some flexibility to assess the effect that a given security package can have in terms of risk (and therefore in terms of capital consumption).

The Basel Accords establish clearly the minimum impact that various securities like mortgages or guarantees can have on RWAs. Banks are by default bound to use this methodology, called the *standard approach*. However, if a bank can demonstrate based on its own historical data that the benefit of certain securities is greater than established in the Basel Accords, it can use its own data to calculate RWAs. The use of this method, called the *advanced approach*, is nonetheless subject to the approval of the local regulator.

Let us take an example:

Under the standard approach, a mortgage cuts RWAs by 80%, reducing by five times the amount of capital that a bank has to mobilize for a loan (from $1.6 million to $320,000 in the Alphabet example). From a conceptual point of view, this means regulators calculate that the risk of a loss for the bank is reduced by the same degree, five times.

Using extensive data culled from past transactions, a bank might argue that obtaining a mortgage has an even greater effect. It could, for instance, demonstrate to its local regulator that the risk of losses is reduced by six times rather than five. If the data is convincing, the regulator may grant to this bank the benefit of the advanced approach, in which case its RWAs and capital requirements would be reduced accordingly. All things being equal, it means that a mortgage loan is more beneficial for this bank than for banks using the standard approach.[12]

---

[11]Good news for readers: you have finished what is probably the most difficult part of the book. You deserve a medal if you have understood everything. In case of doubt, one just needs to understand that regulators require that banks fund each of their loans with a minimal portion of capital. Structured transactions often allow, one way or another, a reduction of this minimal portion. It consequently increases the profitability of the bank (as less capital is needed to finance a loan).
[12]Note to readers: obtaining the benefit of the advanced approach from a regulator is a very complex process.

This flexibility on the part of regulators may seem surprising at first, but the point is the same: to reduce risk. By dangling the possibility of lower capital requirements, regulators hope to prod banks into investing more in the right people and IT systems for monitoring their exposure. Banks may indeed be more willing to store and produce data on their business if this data can be used to optimize their use of capital. Through the advanced approach, the objective of the Basel Accords remains to create safer banks and more financial stability.

PART I

LEVERAGED BUYOUT (LBO)

An LBO or leveraged buyout refers to the acquisition of a company with a combination of equity and debt. It is a financial technique that slowly emerged at the beginning of the twentieth century. LBOs, however, have only really taken off since the early 1980s, around the same time as project finance, asset finance, and securitization.

Readers with a background in finance are generally more familiar with LBOs than with the other financing techniques analyzed in this book. LBOs are a topic that might have been encountered in previous reading or studied in a course related to business valuation or corporate finance.

Without ignoring the link between corporate finance and LBOs, we think of the LBO as primarily a financing technique. Debt is indeed used to finance the acquisition – via an SPV – of an asset that generates cash flow. LBOs are in this respect similar to the other structures that we will discuss in this book. The main difference is the nature of the asset that is financed. It is a company in the case of an LBO, rather than an infrastructure asset, as in *project finance* (Part II), a moveable asset, as in *asset finance* (Part III) or a portfolio of receivables, as in *securitization* (Part IV).

LBOs combine all the elements of structured transactions: (i) use of an SPV; (ii) recourse to financial leverage; and (iii) tax optimization. They tend to get more media attention than other structured finance techniques, probably due to the fact that some companies taken over via LBOs are extremely well known. It is easier to make headlines in the *Financial Times* with the acquisition of Burger King or Harley-Davidson than with the financing of a wind farm in Illinois or Colorado.

LBOs exemplify probably more than any other technique the series of financial revolutions addressed in this book. It is, therefore, only natural to start our journey with a plunge in the intricacies of leveraged buyouts. We hope that readers who are not familiar with the concept will discover its mysteries. For others, we hope that they will rediscover the spark – and the fun! – of this technique.

CHAPTER 1

What is an LBO?

1.1 THE MAIN FEATURES OF AN LBO

1.1.1 Definition

An LBO is an acquisition technique that allows an investor (also called a *sponsor*) to buy a target company using a large amount of debt. The buyout is structured using an intermediary company established for the sole purpose of acquiring the target company. That intermediary is an investment vehicle and does not have any employees. It is commonly referred to as an SPV (special purpose vehicle), SPC (special purpose company), or SPE (special purpose entity).

This SPV, which we will refer to here as the *holding company*, or *HoldCo*, is financed by debt and equity. The exact split between the two depends on the type of target company but also on market conditions at the time of the transaction. The equity is contributed by the buyer interested in the target company while the debt is provided by banks or investors who specialize in debt instruments.

Once taken over, the target company becomes a subsidiary of the HoldCo. The debt is repaid by the dividends paid by the target company. Here lies the magic of an LBO: a buyer can acquire a company while contributing only to a small part of the total amount of the target company value. The balance is supplied by lenders. Figure 1.1 represents a typical LBO structure.

1.1.2 Debt Sizing

Lenders in an LBO take the risk that the target company does not pay enough dividends to repay the debt. The loan provided to the HoldCo is said to be *non-recourse*, meaning that in case of default, lenders have no recourse to the sponsor. In other

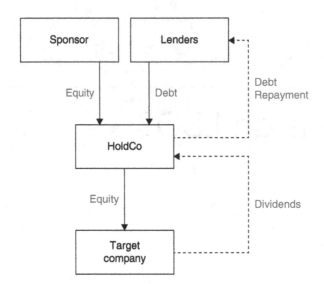

FIGURE 1.1   Simplified LBO Structure

words, lenders do not benefit from any guarantee nor any other type of credit protection from the equity investor. If the target company cannot pay dividends due to underperformance, lenders cannot go to the sponsor and ask for indemnification. Lenders generally only rely on a pledge of the shares of the HoldCo and the target company (a set of securities called a *security package*). These pledges can be exercised in case the HoldCo is unable to repay the debt. This allows lenders to take control of the companies and try to restructure the transaction or sell the target to repay their loan.

Given the risks, interest rates applicable to LBOs are usually higher than those of traditional corporate financing. To ensure that the target company will distribute enough dividends to repay the debt, lenders size their contribution based on the predicted profits or cash flow of the target company:

- For the acquisition of very small companies (turnover of a few million US$ or below), the total debt amount is usually expressed as a multiple of net profit.
- For larger acquisitions, the acceptable level of debt is expressed as a multiple of EBITDA (Earnings Before Interest, Tax, Depreciation and Amortization). EBITDA equals revenues minus operating costs. It is a measure of the operating profitability of a company regardless of its financial strategy, its tax position, or its investment policy. It is a very good indicator of the potential of a particular company and a pertinent reference to use when it comes to debt sizing in an LBO.

1.1.3   Various Types of LBOs

Behind the generic term of LBO, other acronyms are sometimes used to refer to some specific types of leveraged buyouts.

- An MBO (management buyout) is an LBO in which the management of the target company takes part in the buyout, alone or alongside another sponsor. MBOs are a very common form of LBO. They usually happen when:
  - the owner of a small or medium-sized enterprise (SME) retires and decides to sell his or her company to the managers who have worked with them for some time (typically their children or right-hand man);
  - a company is acquired by an LBO firm[1] that wants to retain existing managers. Many LBO firms can offer attractive packages in terms of stocks to key people in the target company. This is a way of aligning the managers' interests with their own interests. These key people are directly incentivized to help grow the company and ensure a successful LBO.
- An MBI (management buy-in) is an LBO in which the buyers did not work for the target company before the acquisition, but act as managers after the acquisition. MBIs are common when the founder of an SME retires and cannot find a new buyer among his or her employees. In this case, the company is put on the market and acquired by a buyer with no previous connection to the company. An MBI can be carried out by a manager alone, by a group of managers, or by one or several managers co-investing with an LBO firm.
- A BIMBO (buy-in management buyout) is a mix of the two previous approaches. It is a buyout in which existing managers and managers from outside the target company collaborate to buy out the target company. Here again, the buyout can be carried out by these managers alone or alongside an LBO firm. A BIMBO generally makes sense if the new managers bring expertise that the existing ones do not have but that is key to further developing the company.
- Finally, a *build-up* is an acquisition carried out by a company that is itself already under an LBO. The new target is in this case usually directly acquired by the original target by adding debt (and sometimes also equity) at the HoldCo level. A merger between the two companies can follow if this makes sense.

1.2 A THREE-STEP LEVERAGE

Contrary to what the reader might think at this stage, leveraged buyouts are not only financing structures. They are transactions implying a high level of tax optimization and that can only bear fruit if the strategy implemented by the new owner works. In other words, LBOs are said to be based on a triple leverage: *financial, tax,* and *managerial.*

---

[1]An LBO firm is an investment company specialized in the acquisition of companies via LBO. Its goal is to buy target companies, manage them, and sell them later at a profit. We will explain in detail in Chapter 2 how these investment firms operate.

1.2.1   Financial Leverage

Of the aforementioned three types of leverage, the financial kind is the easiest to grasp. It is defined as the use of debt to finance the acquisition of the target company. Debt gives more firepower to sponsors and allows them to increase the impact of their equity contribution. They can take control of a company while investing (relatively) little capital. Leverage is generally expressed as a multiple of the target company's EBITDA, as we mentioned before (4 x EBITDA, 5 x EBITDA, etc.).

Financial leverage is a fascinating tool. It boosts shareholders' returns when things go well but can also sting equity investors in case of a market turnaround – especially if debt levels are too high. The risks and rewards associated with financial leverage are pretty high. Sponsors do not have to commit a lot of capital to acquire a target but are exposed to the risk that there might not be enough dividends to service the debt. In other words, sponsors are not only exposed to the risk of the target company not performing; they are exposed to the risk of the target company not performing well enough. The history of LBOs is full of examples of target companies generating profits but of HoldCos incapable of repaying their debt.

1.2.2   Tax Leverage

Tax leverage is the second element that contributes to the performance of an LBO. This second leverage means that after the acquisition, the sum of the taxes paid by the HoldCo and the target company is lower than the amount of tax paid by the target independently before the acquisition.

With each country having its own tax rules, the precise impact of this leverage varies from one jurisdiction to another. It relies, however, on two tax provisions that exist in many countries: (i) the specific taxation system applicable to dividends, and (ii) the deductibility of interest.

1.2.2.1   Little to no Dividend Tax

Dividends paid by a company to its parent are in many countries taxed at a significantly lower rate than other revenues. They can sometimes even be tax exempt. This is mainly because dividends are paid from the after-tax profits of a company. In other words, they arise from profits that have already been taxed. It would make little sense to tax profits at the level of a subsidiary and tax them again when they are distributed under the form of dividends to a parent.

To avoid a double tax impact, many countries have introduced provisions limiting the taxation of dividends paid by a company to its parent. This limit can be integral (dividends are distributed free of tax) or partial (dividends are taxed at a lower rate or only a small percentage of the dividends are taxed).

There are sometimes more detailed rules about the applicability of this favorable tax treatment. The specifics obviously vary from one country to another: The parent company can, for instance, be required to own at least a minimal percentage of the subsidiary or commit to holding an equity interest in the company for a given period.

1.2.2.2   Tax Groups and Interest Deductibility

Many countries have designed specific tax provisions for companies belonging to the same group. These provisions generally allow them for tax purposes to pool all the financial results of the group's subsidiaries at the level of the parent company. This allows a group to offset the profits made by some of its subsidiaries with the losses of its non-performing entities. The concept of tax grouping can take many forms, depending on the tax system of the country where the group of companies is located. It can be optional or mandatory. It may require the parent to fully own the subsidiary or just a significant part of it.

In some countries where the concept of tax grouping does not exist, a company that has only one economic owner is treated as a flow-through entity. It is disregarded as an entity separate from its owner for tax purposes, so that the assets, liabilities, and activities of the subsidiary are treated as the assets, liabilities, and activities of its owner. This is conceptually slightly different from a tax grouping of companies but it has in essence the same financial consequence: a parent and its subsidiary are treated as one entity for tax purposes.

This provision is crucial for an LBO as the HoldCo taken independently is intrinsically a loss-making company for tax purposes. Its profit and loss statement is made up of dividends (non-taxable or almost, as explained above) and interests due on the acquisition debt (deductible for tax purposes). Conversely, with the target being an operating company, it is logically profitable for tax purposes. The possibility of merging the results of the HoldCo and the target for tax purposes means that the profits of the target are partly offset by the losses of the HoldCo. In other words, the total amount of tax paid after the acquisition is lower than when the target is a standalone company.

1.2.2.3   Alternatively, a Merger or a Debt Push Down

The buyer of a target company cannot always benefit from an optimal tax structure. This is notably the case in countries where the deductibility of interest by acquisition vehicles is limited or simply not allowed. If these limitations are too stringent, two alternative structures can be implemented: (i) a merger between the HoldCo and the target company, or (ii) a debt push down. These solutions are usually not implemented immediately after the takeover. They generally take place a few years after the acquisition, as they may otherwise be perceived as too aggressive by the tax authorities of the country where the deal is located.

A merger between the two entities may be a solution but raises questions from a financial and legal perspective.

From a financial standpoint, the merger may be complex if there are significant minority shareholders in the target company alongside the HoldCo. Since the buyer controls the HoldCo with a limited amount of capital only, the buyer can be significantly diluted after a merger. It has a lower share of capital in the target company than the HoldCo used to have.

In some countries, the merger between an operating company and a company with a large amount of debt can be seen as going against the interest of the target. There is a legal tension between what an owner (i.e. the HoldCo) has a right to do and the interest of the target company taken independently (as a standalone business). The feasibility of a merger depends on which country the merger takes place in, but it is generally necessary to demonstrate to national authorities that the newly formed company can sustain its debt.

As an alternative to a merger, a shareholder can consider a *debt push down*, i.e. the transfer of the debt from the HoldCo to the target. A debt push down is usually done by having the target reduce its capital or pay an exceptional dividend to the HoldCo. This payment is financed by a new loan taken out by the target. This allows the HoldCo to repay its debt. An independent expert is usually invited to show the tax authorities that the business of the target is capable of repaying the new loan.

1.2.3   Managerial Leverage

What is key to any LBO is the operating performance of the target company. Whatever the acquisition package or the audacity of the tax structure, an LBO cannot be a success unless the target company generates sufficient cash flow to service the debt and pay dividends to the new owners. An LBO is therefore not just a financial structure: it is a business adventure. The management of the target company has to find the right recipe to improve sales and profitability despite the additional pressure created by the large amount of debt raised by the HoldCo.

1.2.3.1   LBOs by Investment Firms

As already explained, LBOs are often structured with the involvement of managers. These managers can be in place prior to the buyout (MBO) or join only when the company is acquired (MBI or BIMBO). Managers are in both cases instrumental to the success of the transaction. LBOs promote the concept of manager-shareholders who become directly interested financially in the success of the target company.

In most companies, managers are mere employees of the firm they work for. These managers can have large responsibilities and make a lot of money but they still have shareholders to report to. Their own interests are not necessarily the same as the company they manage. They may favor short-term gains or view their position only as a means to a better job in a larger company. The situation is different in an LBO. The manager becomes a shareholder of the target company and is directly incentivized to focus on increasing its performance and valuation.

The management theory behind an LBO is that, all things being equal, the motivation of an entrepreneur – or at least a manager-shareholder – is higher than that of a traditional executive. Once a manager's personal wealth is directly indexed to the company's profits, he or she should work hard to increase the value of the target company. It is for this very reason that many LBO firms favor MBOs. They invite managers to invest alongside them to align shareholders' and managers' interests. Alternatively, LBO firms can also give the managers stocks or stock options.

The success of acquisitions by LBO firms is not only due to the incentive given to managers. LBO firms are experienced shareholders, they buy out a company with a strategy in mind. As majority owners, they have full latitude to implement their plans and choose the managers who will execute them. LBO firms can obviously make mistakes but they generally give a clear roadmap for the target company.

1.2.3.2 The Acquisition of an SME by an Individual Buyer

Managerial leverage takes a different form when the acquirer is an individual. In this case, the company changing hands is usually very small. It is sold by an entrepreneur who has put their money and their soul into the company. The acquirer does generally the same, meaning that both the buyer and the seller are financially and emotionally attached to the company.

That said, it could reasonably be assumed that a buyer who invests a large part of his savings in a new business is more committed to the success of his company than an owner who looks forward to selling his or her business and enjoying their retirement. A new manager, energized by a fresh start, brings new ideas, new methods and an attitude that can make a difference.

1.2.3.3 The Build-up

In a build-up the managerial effect is limited. In this scenario a company under an LBO acquires another company. Improved performance comes more from synergies between the two companies than from a change in management.

Examples of potential synergies include:

- increased investment and development capabilities
- sale of new products or services that could not have been developed before
- sharing of best practices between the two entities of the group
- reduced costs thanks to greater purchasing capabilities or strategies
- merger of the two companies' internal functions
- easier access to credit.

Case Study 1: The Harley-Davidson LBO (1981–1986)

The 1981 leveraged buyout of Harley-Davidson has all the ingredients of the perfect LBO. It almost looks like it had been done to be a case study for future MBA students. Structured at a time when leveraged buyouts were still a novelty, it combined all the features of a successful LBO: (i) audacious financial structuring, (ii) company turnaround, and (iii) entrepreneurial adventure.

The Birth of a Myth

The first Harley-Davidson was manufactured in Milwaukee in 1903 by Bill Harley and the brothers Arthur and Walter Davidson. Their prototype was imperfect (riders still had to pedal up slopes!) but this did not discourage the three friends. The trio achieved a reputation for being skilled mechanics and they soon started to sell motorcycles to friends, relatives, and neighbors. Their first factory was built in 1906 and the following year they were joined by William, the third of the Davidson brothers.

Walter Davidson – who was chosen as CEO of the company – convinced his three partners to focus on the production of powerful motorcycles. The objective was to win races to promote the brand and attract press coverage. The bet paid off. Harley-Davidson motorcycles performed well at these events and Walter Davidson won a few races himself. Company sales increased rapidly, and in 1908, Harley signed an agreement to supply the Detroit police department.

Four years later, Harley-Davidson was distributed by more than 200 retailers throughout the country. It had numerous contracts with local police forces and also secured major contracts with the US Army. The company sold 20,000 motorcycles to US forces in 1917 and supplied the army during World War II. The WTA model used by US soldiers during the liberation of France contributed significantly to the visibility of the brand in Europe.

Over the years Harley-Davidson slowly became an integral part of American culture. The brand became extremely popular. Its loyal customer base appreciated the sound of the engines, the rebellious image, and the distinctive design of the motorcycles. Actors like James Dean and Marlon Brando were faithful users and a movie like *Easy Rider* looks in retrospect like a TV commercial for Harley-Davidson.

In 1953, following the insolvency of its main competitor, Indian Motorcycle, Harley became the only motorcycle manufacturer in the US (compared to 110 when the company was founded). At that time, Harley-Davidson controlled more than 60% of the US motorbike market across all segments, small, medium, and high-powered.

The Problems

The 1960s were a period of intense change for Harley-Davidson. The company went public in 1965 with the double objective of raising capital for new investments and allowing the heirs of the founders to monetize their equity stake. Four years later, the entire company was acquired by AMF Group, a US conglomerate whose owner, Rodney Gott, was a die-hard Harley fan.

AMF Group unfortunately did not have a clear strategy for Harley. Despite heavy investments, the quality of the motorcycles started to deteriorate, hurting sales and damaging the brand. The drop in quality was all the more problematic as it coincided with the entrance of Japanese manufacturers into the US market. Harley-Davidson struggled to respond to the challenge. Japanese motorcycles simply had better designs and were more reliable.

When they entered the US market towards the end of the 1950s, Japanese brands like Honda, Yamaha, Suzuki, and Kawasaki were looked down upon by Harley-Davidson. Japanese manufacturers focused on small motorcycles and were not perceived as a threat by Harley's management. The brand had always specialized in high and medium-powered engines. Facing no competition in their segment, Japanese manufacturers started to swamp the market. Honda's turnover in the US rose from $500,000 in 1960 to $77 million in 1965.

From the 1970s, Japanese brands entered a second phase of development. They took advantage of customer loyalty acquired with their smaller machines to start competing directly in the medium and high-powered segments. Within a few years, Harley-Davidson lost its leadership in that category, first to Honda and then to Suzuki.

It seemed that nothing could reverse the decline of the brand. A joint venture with the Italian group Aermacchi to manufacture smaller motorcycles and the investment in new production lines were both blatant failures. The company became associated with low quality and production delays. A new marketing strategy, implemented to rejuvenate the image of Harley, only made things worse. In order to appeal to a larger pool of potential clients, the company moved away from its rebellious image and became more mainstream. This won few converts, while faithful customers were left bewildered. As difficulties multiplied, AMF Group hired Goldman Sachs to find a buyer for its subsidiary.

The LBO

Given the difficulties that Harley was facing, very few potential buyers were interested in the company. Many believed that its steady decline was unstoppable. After all, Harley-Davidson was an oddity. All the other US brands had long since disappeared. There was simply no room in this market for a company that manufactured motorcycles in the United States. No one could compete with Japanese products... Despite Goldman Sachs's intense marketing efforts, AMF did not receive a single offer for Harley.

(continued)

(*continued*)

In this context, the idea of an LBO begins to percolate. In 1981, the 13 top managers of Harley-Davidson, headed by CEO Vaughn Beals, decided to buy out the company themselves. After several months of difficult negotiations, Harley-Davidson was finally sold through an MBO to this group of managers. The company was valued at $81.5 million and 87% of this amount (a very aggressive ratio) was financed by a debt facility provided by Citibank.

CEO Vaughn Beals was an MIT graduate with previous experience in the aeronautics industry. He joined the group in 1977, but was never given the freedom to carry out his vision for Harley-Davidson by AMF. Vaughn Beals was nonetheless convinced that he could restructure the company and put it back on track. To celebrate the acquisition, he organized a motorcycle trip between New York and Milwaukee for the group's new shareholders. The impact on staff and retailers' morale was immediate. Some employees even took their bikes to join the new owners.

The Management, Post-LBO

Beals' first decision was to set a tour of a Honda factory for Harley's managers, engineers, and union representatives. They were all astonished by the cleanliness of the site. They also realized that production was less modern but better organized. The operating mode emphasized the *just in time* method. Motorcycles were produced only when ordered, which meant that stocks were limited and that new improvements could be added to existing models without delay.

The group of visitors was also very surprised to see that the morale of the employees was better and relations were less strained than in their own company. One detail stood out: the engineers knew all the workers by their first names. The Honda factory seemed superior in every aspect. Not only was the atmosphere much better than at Harley's but production figures were outstanding. Only 5% of the Japanese motorcycles did not pass the quality check at the end of the production line against 50% for Harley-Davidson.

Given the precarious situation, Vaughn Beals decided to act swiftly and introduced a series of radical changes to turn the company around. The Japanese methods observed at Honda were adopted and 50% of the workforce was laid off to adapt the cost base to the decline in production. Unions gave up a salary increase planned before the acquisition and remaining employees accepted a 9% pay cut.

In terms of the product itself, a new and more reliable engine was conceived by Harley-Davidson's engineers. It passed quality checks more easily, which allowed the company to achieve considerable savings. In parallel, the design of the motorcycles was entirely revamped. The objective was to differentiate Harley-Davidson from the competition. Chrome parts were made more visible and the mass marketing strategy was abandoned. The company reconnected with its roots and rebellious identity. Everywhere in the United States showrooms were refurbished to highlight the return to Harley's original positioning.

Back to the Stock Market

Thanks to these tough decisions and the adoption of Japanese methods, Harley-Davidson quickly regained market share. Turnover increased by 130% within five years and in 1985 the company was the new market leader ahead of Honda in the high-powered motorcycles segment. Brand image improved significantly, and Harley-Davidson became known once again for the quality and reliability of its products.

Despite these successes, Citibank decided unexpectedly in 1984 not to renew the facilities granted to finance the LBO. The bank feared that the cumulative effect of an ageing population and a lukewarm macroeconomic outlook might threaten Harley's recent recovery. Vaughn Beals found a new lender ready to replace the bank at the last minute: Heller Inc., a lending institution specialized in medium-sized companies.

Vaughn Beals and the other shareholders were deeply affected by Citibank's decision. They realized that the success of an LBO is fragile and depends largely on the availability of funds to secure a transaction. They decided, therefore, to monetize part of the value they had created and accelerate the return of Harley-Davidson to the public market. The initial public offering (IPO) was arranged in two steps. A first stake was introduced in June 1986 and a second in June 1987, on both occasions with a much higher valuation than that of its competitors.

CHAPTER 2

The Different Stakeholders

2.1 THE TARGET COMPANY

An LBO always begins with the search for a target. It is a time-consuming process that is generally animated by mergers and acquisition (M&A) departments of major investment banks. The role of these banks is to be at the crossroads of information and to be a constant link between potential sellers and interested buyers. On the one hand, they try to convince sellers that they can help them achieve a premium valuation, and on the other, they present these opportunities to well-known active buyers in the hope of arousing their interest. By doing so, they position themselves to advise the sale (sell-side mandate given by the seller) or the acquisition (buy-side mandate given by a potential buyer) of companies that are on the market. For smaller transactions, the market is usually animated by advisory boutiques specialized in M&A.

When it comes to buying companies, potential acquirers all have their own requirements. While individual buyers tend to look at companies active in sectors they know well, LBO firms define clear investment policies. These policies include several criteria, notably, the size, the sector, and the geography of their targets:

- *Size*: defined by turnover or EBITDA. Some investors focus on large acquisitions, others on small targets.
- *Sector*: some investors look at opportunities in one or several sectors only (retail, entertainment, healthcare, etc.).
- *Geography*: depending on their size, investors are active on an entire continent, a small group of countries, a single country, or even a region.

Although all of these buyers have different investment criteria, it is still possible to speak of an ideal LBO target in general terms. Given the nature of these transactions, buyers are always looking for a target that will generate a steady cash flow (to repay the debt) and offer growth perspectives (to increase the value of the target).

Readers should be warned here that the perfect target described in this chapter is a banker's fantasy; it exists only in books or MBA classes. The elements mentioned in what follows should be taken for what they are: a list of criteria that any potential LBO target can be measured against. No company will ever fit the definition perfectly.

2.1.1 Stable and Recurring Cash Flow

Given the financial leverage inherent in LBOs, ideal targets should primarily have the capacity to generate large, steady, and recurring cash flows. This feature gives comfort to lenders about the ability of the HoldCo to repay its debts. All things being equal, it also allows buyers to secure a higher amount of debt and boost their equity returns.

Companies that offer predictable and robust cash flows are highly sought after by potential acquirers. LBO firms are notably interested in companies that match the following five criteria: (i) established companies, (ii) operating in mature markets, (iii) ideally in a niche segment with limited competition, (iv) where demand is stable, and (v) alternatives are limited. Firms with a strong brand name and loyal customer base often fall into this category. Chains of specialized stores are always extremely popular targets for LBO firms. Table 2.1 shows how well-known restaurant chains have been particularly appealing to equity investors in the last 10 to 20 years. Readers are invited to benchmark these restaurant chains against the aforementioned five criteria.

Prior to any acquisition, LBO firms use financial models to test the sensitivity of the target's cash flows to variation in demand, notably in case of an economic downturn or a sharp increase in costs (iterations known as *stress tests*). The objective is to ascertain the capacity of the target to pay dividends in extreme conditions. These stress tests can be carried out by the LBO firm itself or by the M&A advisor hired for the deal.

2.1.2 Possibility of Improving Operating Processes

The perfect target company should ideally be a *sleeping beauty*, i.e. a company whose existing management team has been lazy and has partly neglected potential operating improvements. In other words, it should be possible for a motivated new buyer to increase the company's profits by focusing relentlessly on improving operating processes (e.g. optimization of supply chain, upgrading of production facilities, cost rationalization, better organization, etc.). The managerial leverage mentioned in Chapter 1 is most effective under these conditions. An experienced and properly incentivized management team should be able to track operating inefficiencies and improve profitability. Harley-Davidson (see case study 1) is a perfect example of an LBO in which success is due to the managers' ability to improve operating processes.

Burger King is also a good case study on this topic. With the support of its new shareholder, the fast food chain has been able to streamline internal processes, cut costs, and optimize its supply chain, leading to a sharp increase in EBITDA margin[1] (see Figure 2.1).

---

[1] EBITDA margin is calculated as follows: earnings before interest taxes depreciation and amortization divided by total revenues. It is a measure of a company's operating profitability as a percentage

TABLE 2.1   Ranking of the Largest Restaurant LBOs

Target	Buyer	Deal Value	Announcement Date
Burger King Worldwide	3G Capital	$4 billion	Sept. 2010
OSI Restaurant Partners (parent of Outback Steakhouse)	Catterton Partners, Bain Capital	$3.5 billion	Nov. 2006
Dunkin' brands	Carlyle Group, THL Partners, Bain Capital	$2.4 billion	Dec. 2005
CKE Restaurants (parent of Carl's Jr.)	Roark Capital	$1.7 billion	Nov. 2013
Burger King Worldwide	Goldman Sachs, TPG Capital, Bain Capital	$1.5 billion	July 2002
CEC Entertainment (parent of Chuck E. Cheese)	Apollo Global Management	$1.3 billion	Jan. 2014
Domino's Pizza	Bain Capital	$1.1 billion	Sept. 1998
P.F. Chang's China Bistro	Centerbridge Partners	$1.1 billion	May. 2012
CKE Restaurants (parent of Carl's Jr.)	Apollo Global Management	$1 billion	April 2010
Peet's Coffee & Tea	JAB Holding, BDT Capital	$1 billion	July 2012
Dave & Buster's	Oak Hill Capital Partners	$778 million	May 2010

Source: Standard & Poor's.

When 3G Capital bought out the company from TPG, Goldman Sachs, and Bain Capital in 2010, Burger King was valued at $4 billion (including $700 million of debt). The acquisition of the $3.3 billion equity portion was financed using roughly 50% of debt and 50% of equity, meaning that the total amount directly invested by 3G was $1.6 billion. Within two years, Burger King's EBITDA margin increased nearly 60%, allowing the company to pay a $393 million special dividend to its shareholders after

---

of its revenues. It is a very useful ratio to measure a firm's cost cutting efforts. The higher the EBITDA margin of a company, the lower that company's operating expenses in relation to revenues.

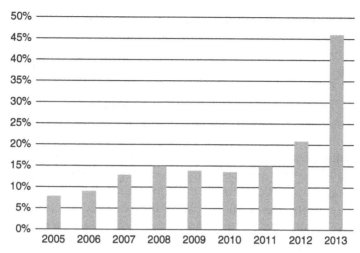

FIGURE 2.1   EBITDA Margin Burger King 2005–2013
Source: adapted from Francisco Souza Homem de Mello.

one year. In 2012, 3G sold 30% of its stake in the fast food chain to a special acquisition corporation (SPAC)[2] created by billionaire Nicolas Berggruen, Jarden's founder Martin Franklin, and Pershing Square Capital Management's founder Bill Ackman for $1.4 billion. Between this sale and the special dividend, 3G Capital had recouped in two years more than its original investment, still keeping 70% of its original position.

2.1.3   Growth Opportunities

Alongside profitability, growth is a buyer's main objective. Identifying ways to increase the top line is therefore a prerequisite before any acquisition. Growth can be achieved organically or via acquisitions.

2.1.3.1   Organic Growth

Organic growth can be achieved in a variety of ways: products or services can be added or improved, new marketing strategies can be implemented, or another category of customers can be targeted. An LBO firm acquiring a restaurant chain can, for instance, decide to open more restaurants in malls when the strategy so far had been to focus on city centers of large agglomerations only (or vice versa).

   Burger King is a prime example of a company that has been able to deliver organic growth since its takeover by 3G Capital. While many wondered if the price paid for the acquisition in 2010 was too high, Bernardo Hees, the new CEO named by the trio at the helm of 3G Capital (Jorge Paulo Lemann, Marcel Telles, and Beto Sicupira), was quick to implement changes in the restaurant chain to increase traffic in stores. Menus

---

[2]A Special Acquisition Corporation (SPAC) is a listed investment company.

were simplified, some recipes were modified, new breakfast foods, drinks, and coffee choices were added. The goal was to attract women and families, two categories of customers that Burger King had overlooked in the past. Unlike McDonald's, Burger King was in 2010 too dependent on its core base of young men. These customers had been particularly hit by unemployment since 2008, which had dramatically hurt Burger King's sales. 3G's strategy was to appeal to a larger group of customers and target customers who would be more prone to spending money on high-margin items such as coffees or fruit-flavored beverages. A similar strategy was pursued by Chuck E. Cheese after its acquisition by Apollo. The chain changed the layout and the design of its restaurants and added new menu options to encourage family dining.

Another organic growth option is to address a wider potential customer base. Private equity sponsors often dedicate part of their original investment in the target company to develop additional distribution channels or open new sales points. Burger King is again a good example of this. With the backing of its new shareholders, the company decided to enter the French market in 2012, 15 years after exiting the country.

3G did not choose France on a whim. Due to the lack of local competition in the fast food market, France is one of the most profitable countries for McDonald's. Out of the four largest McDonald's restaurants in the world in terms of turnover, three are located in France.[3] Interestingly, another company mentioned in Table 1.2 took aim at France for the same reasons. CKE Restaurants, parent of the hamburger restaurant chain Carl's Jr, opened its first restaurant there in 2018.

2.1.3.2   External Growth

External growth is another way to create value in an LBO. Build-ups allow a company to grow rapidly, which is extremely appealing to private equity firms given their investment horizon. If synergies are correctly identified and implemented, external growth can be a powerful shortcut to increase the valuation of a target.

US company K-III Communications Corporation, a publishing firm established in 1989 with the idea, right from the start, of expanding through external growth, is probably the most iconic example of a successive build-up. The K-III saga began in 1988 when several buyers, including KKR, entered a bidding war for Macmillan Group, a British publishing house founded in 1843. Competing with British mogul Robert Maxwell for control of the company, KKR partners understood that its value actually resided more in the exceptional quality of its management team than in its portfolio of books. So it eventually decided to withdraw its bid for Macmillan and instead poached three of its main directors, offering them the opportunity to build a rival publishing group through successive acquisitions. That was the beginning of K-III, a company that started off as nothing in 1989 and whose turnover reached $850 million in 1994 following 28 successive acquisitions for a total of $1.4 billion. Renamed Primedia in

---

[3] According to McDonald's, their largest restaurants in the world in terms of turnover are located (1) on the Champs Elysées in Paris, (2) in Disneyland Paris, (3) on Pushkin Square in Moscow, and (4) in the business district of La Défense near Paris.

1997 and then RenPath in 2013, K-III remained in KKR's portfolio for 22 years. Despite ambitious beginnings, the group fell victim to competition from the internet and the consequent reduction in budgets for print advertising. The company was sold off in 2011 to another LBO giant, TPG Capital.

A more recent (and successful) example of build-up is again to be found with Burger King. In August 2014, the US fast food chain announced its intention to acquire Tim Hortons Inc., Canada's largest quick-service restaurant chain known for its coffee and donuts. While the two chains would retain separate operations post-merger, the intention was to use Burger King's know-how in international markets to drive the expansion of Tim Hortons outside Canada. The day after the announcement of the acquisition, Burger King's market capitalization jumped by $2 billion, from $9.5 billion to $11.5 billion. Within a day, 3G (which had, remember, already sold off 30% of its stake in Burger King) saw its stake increase in value by $1.4 billion, an amount roughly equal to what they had invested when they bought out the company in 2010.

The agreement resulted in 3G holding a 51% stake in the new company (called Restaurant Brands International), Tim Hortons' existing shareholders owning 22%, and Burger King's other shareholders owning 27%. The new entity was based in Oakville, Canada – a country where the corporate tax rate was (at that time) lower than in the United States. By the end of April 2018, the market capitalization of Restaurant Brands International was $25 billion. In eight years, 3G Capital has transformed its original investment of $1.6 billion into a stake worth $12.5 billion.

2.1.4   Low Level of Net Long-term Debt

Given the high level of debt that a company has to repay after an LBO, buyers tend to look for targets that have an intrinsically low level of indebtedness. They avoid companies operating in sectors that require large and regular capital expenditures (or capex)[4] or targets that need to entirely replace ageing production lines or industrial facilities. Though LBO transactions take advantage of leverage, acquirers have to make sure that the target has sufficient cash flow to service its own debt plus the debt of the holding company. Consequently, if a target company is already highly indebted, the amount of debt available for the acquisition will be limited, capping for the buyer the multiplier effect of financial leverage. Banks or debt investors active in the LBO sector have the same approach. They analyze the leverage of a company as a whole and compare the EBITDA of the target to the sum of the company's own debt *and* the acquisition facility to ensure that the total leverage is sustainable over the long term.

The ideal target is typically not in a *capital intensive* sector, i.e. an industry requiring regular and heavy investments (steel production, car manufacturing, airline industry, etc.). These sectors have high fixed costs, and even a slight decrease in revenues can lead to significant operating losses, preventing the company from paying dividends.

---

[4]Capex (or capital expenditures) are funds used by a company to acquire or upgrade physical assets such as property, industrial buildings, or equipment. These expenditures include a wide range of outlays from purchasing a piece of equipment to building a factory.

2.1.5 Low Working Capital Requirement

The target company should ideally also have a low working capital requirement (WCR). WCR is the amount of cash needed by a company to conduct its day-to-day business. It is calculated as the sum of accounts receivable and inventory minus accounts payable. The higher the WCR, the higher the company's need for cash to finance its operating cycle.

There are only two ways to finance WCR: (i) by securing long-term liquidity (via additional equity or debt), or (ii) by using bank overdraft or short-term facilities. Whatever the option, banks are usually reluctant to finance LBOs of companies that have high working capital requirements. It inflates debt and puts the target under pressure. When the level of debt is already very high (which is the case in an LBO because of the acquisition facility), this is a risk that lenders are not willing to take.

In some cases, companies have a negative WCR. This means that their operating cycle does not need to be financed but, on the contrary, generates cash. This is the case, for example, at supermarkets or restaurant chains, for two main reasons: (i) suppliers are paid 30 days or more after delivery, while customers pay outright for services, and (ii) products are fresh, so inventory is limited. That is definitely another reason why these sectors appeal to LBO professionals (see Table 2.1, section 2.1.2).

That said, LBO firms can sometimes decide to invest in a company with a relatively high level of WCR, especially if they believe this is partially attributable to misman-agement. Tamping down working capital requirements – either through optimizing inventory management or the clients' or supplier's payment terms – is in this case a source of value creation. This is clearly a situation where a buyer identifies a possible opportunity for improvement of operating processes (see section 2.1.2).

2.1.6 Some Assets can be Collateralized (Ideally)

All things being equal, lenders prefer to finance the acquisition of targets whose assets have value that is independent of the company's business activities (offices, ware-houses, or trademarks, for instance). In negotiations over lending terms, banks always receive a pledge of the shares of the target company. This pledge is more valuable if some assets of the company retain value even when the target company becomes insolvent.

2.1.7 No Dirty Little Secrets

Buyers try to have access to a maximum of information on a target before making an offer to acquire it. They commonly perform due diligence (also referred to as DD), meaning that they verify all information shared by the seller on the company and the market it operates in. This due diligence covers, in theory, all aspects of the trans-action and includes financial, legal, technical, and commercial matters. Its objective is to ensure that the potential buyer will not have any unpleasant surprises after the acquisition closes.

Large buyers carry out this process with the help of an army of advisors.

- The *financial advisor* is a bank or an M&A boutique. Its role is to help the buyer finalize the valuation of the target company and to coordinate the interaction of all the other advisors. It ensures that all their input is taken into account when a price has to be shared with the seller.
- The *commercial advisor* is a consulting firm focused on strategic matters. It is typically one of the large management consulting firms (Boston Consulting Group, McKinsey & Company, Roland Berger Strategy Consultants, etc.) or one of their spin-offs. The role of this advisor is to confirm the commercial potential of the company, study the dynamics of its market, and analyze competitive intensity.
- If required, buyers can also hire a *technical advisor*. This technical advisor is a consulting firm specialized in the sector the company operates in. Its objective is to assess the quality of the existing assets (machinery or production lines, for instance) and to identify potential technical risks and, possibly, the costs associated with these risks.
- The role of the *legal advisor* is to check the major contracts the company is a party to and verify the main regulations applicable to the sector the target operates in. This legal advisor will also be in charge of negotiating the deal documentation if an offer is made and accepted by the seller.
- An *audit firm* is hired to analyze the target's financial statements. And finally, a *tax advisor* can also give its views on the fiscal aspects of the deal or on the target's tax returns.

When transactions are smaller and buyers are individuals, acquirers are obviously less reliant on advisors. They have to carry part of the due diligence themselves to reduce costs and fees paid to consultants. Individuals will still typically hire a law firm and an auditor (or an accountant), but often avoid spending on other types of advisors or limit their scope of work. For very small transactions (the ones led by individual buyers), the due diligence is limited to the bare minimum as the cost of the DD can represent a substantial share of the amount that the buyer is ready to invest. If a buyer has, for instance, $500,000 to invest in an acquisition, it does not make sense to spend more than $50,000 on due diligence (already 10% of the investment!). As a consequence, an individual buyer may be more exposed than a large investment firm to an unpleasant surprise after an acquisition.

Whatever the size of the deal, buyers always require a liability guarantee from the seller, i.e. a document in which the seller agrees to be liable for the consequence (financial, tax, legal, etc.) of any action taken when it was still the owner of the target. If the transaction takes place between two individuals, it is usually advisable to have the liability guarantee counter-guaranteed by a bank.

2.1.8 People Matter

2.1.8.1 A Top-notch Management Team

For an LBO firm, it is much easier to keep a company's management team rather than appoint a new one. Past managers know the business inside out and, if they are properly incentivized, they are usually able to deliver the growth that professional investors are looking for.

One of the most important decisions that an LBO firm has to make prior to an acquisition is to decide how many managers will become shareholders in the target company. It is a difficult choice. If there are too many, the buyer runs the risk that managers who have the most influence on the business are not sufficiently incentivized and decide to leave the company. If, on the contrary, some key managers are left out of the scheme, tensions can emerge and have negative effects on the company's general performance.

If the target is smaller and the acquisition is made by an individual buyer without the support of an investment firm, this person must ensure that the staff will not leave the company despite the change of ownership. This buyer might therefore also structure a stock option scheme to incentivize the key people within the company.

2.1.8.2 Change of Culture

Beyond a change of mentality at the top of the company, highly successful LBOs are able to promote the emergence of a new work ethic among the entire staff of the target company. The mindset of employees is key to a firm's performance and constant attention to detail has an extremely positive impact on the profitability of a company.

Some very large investment firms are particularly well known for focusing on culture. 3G Capital has implemented comprehensive trainee programs in all the companies it has acquired. The firm's leaders believe in training people regularly and have based their management style on a mix of approaches developed by Goldman Sachs and General Electric. People constantly receive feedback from their managers and are rated annually. The bottom 10% employees are usually fired. 3G's management style has become so famous that it has been nicknamed the "3G way" and has even inspired a book.[5] The style is ruthless but promotes meritocracy, a concept that 3G's founders believe is too often talked about but never implemented. In an interview in 2013, Marcel Telles, one of 3G's founding partners, said the firm was looking for boring companies with strong brands that do not attract talented people. Bringing in the talent is the recipe for turning the company around.

---

[5]Souza Homem de Mello. F. (2015) *The 3G Way: An introduction to the management style of the trio who's taken over some of the most important icons of American capitalism.* 10x Books.

2.2   BUYERS

2.2.1   Private Equity Firms

2.2.1.1   Private Equity Sponsors

Most LBO acquisitions are made by investment firms (also called *private equity (PE) sponsors*). Their objective is to (i) acquire a company with a high level of financial leverage, (ii) develop it, and then (iii) sell it off or get it listed on the stock exchange with a profit after three to eight years.[6]

2.2.1.2   The Origins of LBOs

The first LBO funds were structured in the United States at the end of the 1970s. KKR, the pioneering firm in this domain, was established in 1976. However, even before they created KKR – and while they were still working for Bear Stearns – KKR's founding partners, namely Jerome Kohlberg, Henry Kravis, and George Roberts, had already made a foray into the world of LBOs.

While running Bear Stearns's corporate finance department in the 1960s and 1970s, Kohlberg arranged several successful LBOs, described back then as *bootstrap investments*. The acquisition of Orkin Exterminating Company by Rollins in 1964, in which Bear Stearns arranged and funded the acquisition, is widely regarded today as the first major LBO.

In the following years, Kohlberg expanded his activities and hired the two cousins Henry Kravis and George Roberts. The newly formed trio completed a series of LBOs, including notably Stern Metals (1965), Incom (1971), Cobblers Industries (1971), and Boren Clay (1973). The equity for these acquisitions came from external buyers but also from limited partnerships set up by the group for the sole purpose of buying out companies.

The rapid growth of this activity meant that the three bankers spent more and more time arranging and structuring LBOs and less and less on other M&A business. In the early 1970s, Kravis was forced to act as interim CEO of one of the companies acquired via LBO, creating a conflict with his duties at Bear Stearns. Similar situations multiplied and, by the mid-1970s, it became obvious that the trio could not pursue their jobs as M&A bankers and their investment activities at the same time.

After Cy Lewis, the legendary managing partner of Bear Stearns,[7] rejected their proposal to set up a dedicated in-house investment vehicle, Kohlberg, Kravis, and Roberts decided to leave Bear Stearns and establish their own venture, KKR. In 1977 they completed their first buyout, with equity coming from First Chicago Bank

---

[6]We will see at the end of this chapter that the scope of private equity is larger than just LBO. Consequently, if private equity firms are not all focused on LBO, investment firms active in the LBO space are nonetheless all private equity firms.

[7]Managing Partner of Bear Stearns from 1949 to 1978, Cy Lewis transformed Bear Stearns into a Wall Street powerhouse. He was a well-known workaholic and passed away during his retirement party.

and the Hillman Company, the investment vehicle of Henry Hillman, an American billionaire who made his fortune in the chemical industry.

Initially, the three partners focused on companies facing succession-related issues. Their ideal target was a firm whose owner:

- wished to retire
- had no designated successor
- did not wish to sell his company to a rival against whom he had competed all his life
- was not able to float his firm on the stock exchange due to its relatively limited size.

After several successful transactions, KKR convinced the Oregon State Public Employees Retirement Fund (i.e. the pension fund of civil servants of the State of Oregon) to finance the acquisition of US supermarket chain Fred Meyer, in 1981. This transaction was a major breakthrough for KKR as they identified their first large recurring equity investor. This deal was also a turning point for the whole LBO industry. Pension funds were, at that time, mostly exposed to public stocks and investment-grade bonds. This investment marked the beginning of a new trend that would see pension funds deploying more and more capital in the private equity segment. Pension funds are today one of the largest investors in the LBO sector.

Other clever financiers were quick to emulate KKR's strategy: Bain Capital and Advent were founded in 1984, Blackstone in 1985, Carlyle in 1987, and Apollo in 1990. In Europe the LBO market emerged around the same time: Cinven was created in 1977, Permira in 1985, BC Partners in 1986, and 3i in 1987.

2.2.1.3 LBO Firms vs. LBO Funds

Every LBO firm has its own investment strategy. Acquisitions are, however, not made directly by the firm, but via a fund set up by the LBO firm with the sole purpose of buying out companies. LBO firms are sometimes improperly referred to as funds but are, in fact, management companies that raise money from private or institutional investors (insurance companies, sovereign wealth funds, pension funds, university endowments, family offices,[8] etc.) through a separate entity (i.e. a fund) to proceed with acquisitions. Figure 2.2 represents a typical LBO fund structure.

As a general rule the LBO firm is the fund's *general partner* (or *GP*), while investors contributing to the fund are *limited partners* (or *LPs*). Limited partners are passive investors. They only contribute to the fund with the aim of generating a profit. The general partner usually makes only a modest investment in the fund (a few percentage

---

[8]A family office is a company whose purpose is to manage the assets of very wealthy families. There are single family offices, dedicated to one family only (and owned by this family) and multifamily offices, which manage the wealth of several families (generally owned by independent partners).

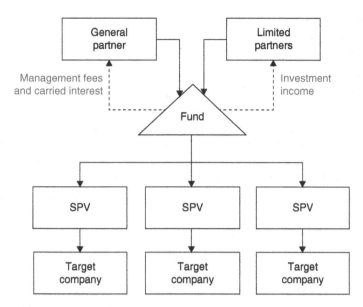

FIGURE 2.2 Fund Structure in the LBO Sector

points). Its role is more complex than the limited partners' and its obligations cover a wide spectrum of responsibilities, including:

- Establishing the fund and designing its strategy. The fund is always set up with a specific positioning in terms of:
  - companies it is looking for (size, sector and geography)
  - maturity (the number of years during which the fund will be active before the money is returned to investors)
  - size (the amount that the private equity sponsor wants to raise for the fund: $500 million, $1 billion, etc.).
- Identifying investors. When they want to launch a new fund, private equity sponsors present their project to a wide range of potential investors. They travel to major financial centers to promote the track record of their previous funds and their ambitions for the next one. This process, called a *road show*, can be done with the help of an advisory boutique or an investment bank that is responsible for introducing investors to the LBO firm.
- Selecting target companies. Once the fund has been set up and investors have been identified, the investment firm can look for companies to buy out. Targets are sought through existing contacts or with the help of banks or M&A boutiques.
- Structuring the acquisition. In parallel with the M&A process itself, the PE firm has to coordinate with the lenders who will fund the acquisition of the target. This is done in most cases by the same team inside the company. In very large PE firms, however, the investment department (selecting targets) and

the debt or capital market team (structuring the debt package) are completely separate. The LBO firm can also have an advisor for this task. This can be the same bank as the one acting as M&A advisor or a different one.

- Making investments. LPs do not invest money in the fund on day one; that would not make financial sense. Instead LPs commit to invest a certain amount in the fund and to wire this money to the fund when the target companies are acquired. When a company is bought out, the managing partner issues a capital call requiring limited partners who have committed to the fund to transfer their money. If an investor has committed to invest 10% of the total size of the fund, they will be required to fund 10% of each acquisition.
- Managing the fund's participation. Once an investment is made, the role of the managing partner is to actively contribute to the growth of the target company. Each stake that a fund has in a company is monitored by an investment professional working for the PE sponsor. This person generally serves on the board of directors of the target company.
- Selling the target companies. After a few years, the investment firm must find a new buyer for each target. For large transactions, an M&A advisor is almost always hired to coordinate the sale process.

2.2.1.4   Profit Sharing between LPs and LBO Firms

Under a typical LBO fund structure, the limited partners, who are passive investors, receive an investment income derived from the performance of the fund. This performance is the sum of the profits generated by all the fund's investments. The LBO firm – which has only contributed a small amount to the fund – receives *management fees* and *carried interest*.

To perform all its duties as general partner, the private equity firm receives annual *management fees*, calculated as a predefined percentage of the capital committed by the LPs (generally 2%). The precise calculation of the management fees varies from one private equity firm to the next. The level of management fees generally decreases once all the capital committed by the limited partners has been deployed.

In addition to fees, investment firms collect a portion of the fund's profits above a certain level of performance. This remuneration, called *carried interest,* is usually equal to 20% (*carry level*) of all sums received by the LPs above a predetermined return (*carry hurdle*). The carry hurdle varies depending on the type of investments targeted by the fund and the countries in which the investments take place. The carry hurdle is obviously higher in emerging countries than in Europe or the United States.

2.2.1.5   Fund's Lifetime

A fund usually has a lifetime of 10 years. After that period the fund is unwound and the money is returned to investors. This 10-year period is divided into two phases. The first five years are generally called the investment period. It is during this period that companies are acquired by the fund. The second phase is a divestment period. Companies bought out during the first phase are sold before the fund is unwound. The fund by-laws usually allow, under certain conditions, an extension of the lifetime of the fund. This way, the general manager has some flexibility to sell a company at a later stage if market conditions are unfavorable at the end of the original 10-year period (or if a company is going through a difficult stretch that might complicate a sale).

LBO firms usually raise a new fund every four to five years. This timing coincides with the end of the investment period of the previous fund. It ensures that an LBO firm is always active in the market.

The investment strategy of a fund is usually in line with the DNA of the private equity sponsor acting as general partner. If the LBO firm is extremely specialized, the fund will be too. Some private equity firms look at one sector only. This is the case, for instance of Roark Capital in the United States, well known for its investments in restaurant chains and retail businesses based on a franchise model. It is also the strategy of Lion Capital in the United Kingdom (active in the retail segment only), Antin Infrastructure Partners in France (active in the infrastructure sector), and many others.

Very large investment firms like KKR, Carlyle, Blackstone, or Ardian have several funds to deploy simultaneously. These funds do not compete with each other and all have generally a distinct strategies and sectoral focus. There is, for instance, a fund dedicated to large LBOs, another one focused on energy assets, a third one dedicated to technology and media, etc. The split may also be geographical, with a fund aimed at investments in North America and another in Europe.

2.2.1.6 Performance Targets

Private equity firms only buy out a company if they believe that they can obtain a return in line with a predetermined target. Given the high level of leverage and the risk involved in an LBO transaction, this target is usually around 20% per year, a figure highlighted by the LBO firm during the road show that accompanies the launch of the fund.

A fund makes a certain number of investments, and the overall return that flows to investors is therefore the weighted average of the returns made with each acquisition, minus the fees paid to the general partner. Achieving the target return is key for the long-term credibility of the management company, as the performance of a fund determines the ability of a private equity sponsor to launch the next one.

2.2.2 Individual Buyers

Although LBOs arranged by investment firms garner most of the attention, a large portion of buyouts are done by individuals. As already mentioned, these transactions typically involve the sale of a company by an owner wishing to retire. The buyers are often the children of the owner or an executive of the company, but outside managers are also sometimes involved. There are many corporate executives who, after a career in a large organization, use part of their savings to buy out an SME and start an entrepreneurial adventure. These LBOs vary in size from less than $1 million to more than $10 million. The bulk of these transactions involve personal contributions ranging between $100,000 and $500,000. For acquisitions of larger SMEs, it is not uncommon for the buyer to solicit the support of a local investment firm.

Acquisitions by individuals are different from buyouts by funds. Private equity sponsors only look for a financial capital gain. Their objective is to resell the target after a few years (three to eight), making sure that in between they accomplish enough from an operating point of view to increase the value of the company. An individual buyer has a different approach, looking generally primarily for an entrepreneurial adventure. That involves developing a company, but disposing of it rapidly is rarely part of the business plan. Long-term growth is the goal. Having said that, these investors are statistically more open to selling their company than entrepreneurs who have developed their businesses from scratch. This may be explained by the fact that an individual buyer performing an LBO is usually emotionally less attached to a company than someone who has set up their own venture.

2.3 LENDERS

2.3.1 Basic Concepts

2.3.1.1 Sizing

As mentioned earlier,[9] LBO debt is sized based on the EBITDA of the target company. The leverage involved in an LBO is therefore generally expressed as a multiple of EBITDA (four times, five times, etc.). The use of this metric allows lenders to compare transactions. All things being equal, resilient and mature businesses should be able to support a higher leverage than cyclical ones. That said, the level of debt available for a specific deal depends also on market conditions at the time of the transaction. Deals structured before the 2008 crisis were obviously more leveraged than transactions done in the early 2010s.

The acquisition debt is sized considering the net debt of the target company itself. In other words, what financiers measure is the total net indebtedness of the group formed by the HoldCo and the target company. The total leverage of a transaction is therefore the sum of the acquisition debt and the loans taken out by the target company minus the cash available at the target company level. If, for instance, the acceptable level of debt for a transaction is 5 x EBITDA and the total net debt of the target company is equal to 1 x EBITDA, the acquisition facility will be equal to 4 x EBITDA.

2.3.1.2 Debt Structure

The debt structure of an LBO depends on the size of the target company. Smaller deals consist mainly of one tranche of debt arranged by a small group of lenders. For larger

---

[9]Chapter 1, section 1.2.1.

acquisitions, it is not uncommon to see several tranches of debt. The senior tranche is repaid in priority but bears a lower interest rate than the junior tranche.

The debt structure in an LBO depends also on the location of the deal. Although they have many similarities, debt instruments are not exactly the same in Europe and the United States. Banks are still active lenders in continental Europe, while the US market is mostly dominated by debt funds. The United Kingdom stands between continental Europe and the United States but increasingly resembles the US market.

2.3.2 Term Loans

2.3.2.1 How Does it Work?

Traditionally, most of the acquisition debt for an LBO is provided in the form of a term loan (also called senior loan). This debt is generally secured by a pledge on the shares of the HoldCo and the target company. If an LBO requires several tranches of debt, this term loan ranks senior to the other tranches. This seniority means that this loan has priority in terms of repayment.

The senior debt can sometimes itself be divided into several tranches:

- A Term Loan A (or TLA) amortizes totally or partly and usually has a maturity of five to seven years.
- A Term Loan B (or TLB) is a bullet, interest-only loan. Its maturity is generally around seven years.
- In some rarer cases, a Term Loan C (or TLC) is structured. The TLC is a bullet loan that has a longer maturity than the TLB.

These various tranches rank *pari passu*, meaning that they have the same seniority and the same right to repayment. Each tranche bears, nonetheless, a different interest rate. A bullet loan is riskier than an amortizing loan. If it exists, tranche C pays the higher interest rate as it is bullet and has a longer maturity than the other tranches.

Smaller deals have only an amortizing loan, while larger transactions can be financed by the combination of a TLA and a TLB. When market conditions are favorable, a TLB can also be structured without TLA. In this case, all the senior debt tranche is bullet. The use of TLBs is attractive for private equity sponsors because there is no principal repayment. Even if interest rates are higher, the debt service is lower, which improves the investor's internal rate of return (IRR).

2.3.2.2 Covenants

Covenants are a form of legal protection used by lenders in loan agreements. They are commitments of the borrower to perform or refrain from some action. A breach in these covenants triggers sanctions for the borrower. These sanctions can go as far as obligating the borrower to repay the loan in advance (see section 2.3.2.3).

Covenants are usually divided into two categories: affirmative and negative covenants.

- Affirmative covenants are actions that the borrower must perform. Examples of affirmative covenants include sharing financial statements with lenders, complying with applicable laws, etc.
- Negative covenants include activities that the HoldCo is barred from. In an LBO, the most common negative covenants are:
  - the commitment not to use the proceeds of the loan to finance anything else aside from the acquisition of the target company
  - the commitment not to take any additional loans without the prior unanimous consent of the lenders.

Some lawyers sometimes discern a third category of covenants, that of financial covenants (although they are generally drafted as a negative or affirmative covenant). The most common financial covenant is the obligation for the group of companies that comprises the HoldCo and the target company to maintain its net debt to EBITDA below a predetermined ratio, commonly known as the *leverage ratio*.

The leverage ratio is widely used by lenders in LBOs to assess the ability of the target company to meet its financial obligations (discussed earlier). The level of net debt of the structure is compared to the EBITDA generated by the target company. All things being equal, it measures the number of years needed by the target company to repay the debt.

The leverage ratio is often a covenant in an LBO. Above a certain predetermined ratio, the margin applicable to the acquisition debt can increase to reflect the additional risk taken by the lenders. If the leverage ratio is too high, it can also trigger the obligation for the borrower to repay the loan in advance.

2.3.2.3   Events of Default

An event of default is a predefined circumstance where lenders have the right to demand the early repayment of the loan. The events of default are clearly spelled out in loan documentation. They include, notably, the inability of the HoldCo to pay on time any amount due to the lenders under the loan.

Events of default are, however, not limited to the insolvency or bankruptcy of the SPV. As stated already, the breach of a covenant can trigger an event of default. If, for instance, the leverage ratio increases above a certain level or if the HoldCo takes steps that are forbidden under the loan agreement (using its funds to acquire properties unrelated to the transaction, for instance), lenders can request immediate repayment of the loan. If the loan cannot be repaid, lenders can exercise their pledge on the shares of the target and take control of the company.

2.3.2.4   Cov-lite Structures

Many LBOs are arranged today using covenant-lite (or cov-lite) structures. Cov-lite loans contain fewer restrictions than traditional LBO loans, meaning that they usually have a very limited number of covenants. They notably often exclude any kind of leverage ratio.

Cov-lite loans give a lot of flexibility to borrowers, as they drastically limit the scenarios under which the lenders can require repayment of the loan or exercise their rights under the security package.[10] Cov-lite loans usually proliferate in a bull market. They were the norm before the 2008 crisis and have been back in fashion since the mid-2010s. The acquisition of Hilton Hotels by Blackstone in 2007 is a famous example of LBO structured with a cov-lite loan (see case study 4).

2.3.2.5 Banking Pools

The size of the target company is one of the main drivers of the senior debt structure. Small acquisitions are generally funded by a few lenders working jointly with the sponsor. In this case, the arrangement and structuring of the debt is defined as a *club deal*. The acquisition facility for these transactions consists generally of one tranche of senior debt at the HoldCo level.

For larger deals, debt is often structured via an *underwriting*, meaning that one (or several) lenders commit to provide the debt but aim to sell it later (partly or totally) to other lenders. Underwritings are particularly useful for transactions that require a large amount of debt. Sponsors use underwritings to avoid negotiating the terms of the acquisition debt with many lenders. They can instead discuss the transaction with a selected number of parties (one to three generally). Underwritings are more costly than club deals as the underwriters want to be paid for the service and the additional risk. They allow, however, for a simpler and swifter negotiation process.[11]

2.3.2.6 Non-bank Investors

When they underwrite a deal, banks do not only distribute the acquisition debt to other banks. They can sell the loan to non-bank investors specialized in leveraged loans, i.e. in loans with a non-investment grade rating. Most of these investors are CLOs (*collateralized loan obligations*) or CDOs (*collateralized debt obligations*). CLOs and CDOs represent now the vast majority of the volume invested in LBO debt. We will detail how they operate in Part IV of this book (on securitization).

The growing role of these non-bank investors is partly the consequence of the regulatory constraints under which banks operate. We have explained in the Introduction that banks have to finance part of their loans with capital coming from shareholders. This share of capital depends on the risk of the loan granted by the bank. The riskier the loan, the more capital a bank has to mobilize.

Given that LBO loans are generally non-investment grade,[12] they usually translate into very high risk weighted assets (RWAs).[13] They are therefore costly for banks in

---

[10]See Chapter 1, section 1.1.2.

[11]See Appendix B (Syndication and Club Deals) for more information on club deals and underwritings.

[12]Or equivalent to non-investment grade as they are not always officially rated by rating agencies.

[13]See definition in the Introduction.

terms of capital. In many cases, the RWA equivalent of an LBO loan is even greater than its nominal value (meaning its weighting is greater than 100%). Even if leveraged loans pay very well, it is in many cases uneconomical for banks to keep them on their books, as they require a lot of capital. Despite the high margin, the return on capital for the bank will be low.

For these reasons, banks instead sell their LBO loans to investors like CLOs, which do not have the same regulatory constraints. When it comes to large LBOs, the role of banks nowadays is, in many cases, to arrange, underwrite, and then distribute the loan. Save for some specific transactions (small ones or very strategic ones), banks rarely keep LBO loans on their books.

The growing role of non-bank investors in the LBO space has also had an impact on LBO structures. Given that these investors have a lot of funds to deploy and relatively limited teams, they prefer to invest in bullet loans rather than amortizing loans (so that they do not have to reinvest funds constantly). This means that TLBs are getting more popular and that many deals are now structured without TLAs.

2.3.2.7   Other Credit Facilities

In addition to the debt provided at the HoldCo level, the target company also needs loans to carry on its business. If these facilities pre-date the acquisition, they are repaid and restructured by the owner. The objective is to align all lenders (at HoldCo and target levels) so that there is no conflict of interest between HoldCo and company lenders.

The main ancillary facilities structured in an LBO are:

- A *revolving credit facility* (or RCF) is a credit line at target level that can be drawn any time by the company (this line works like a credit card). It can be used to finance the working capital needs of the firm or any other unexpected expense. It is the backbone of the company's day-to-day activity.
- A specific *capex facility* may be added at company level in case the firm needs to make an investment to upgrade its equipment.
- An *acquisition facility* (provided at HoldCo level) can also be structured in case the owners' plans for the target company include a build-up strategy.

These various credit lines are provided by banks, usually by those that have structured the acquisition debt. They can nonetheless also be offered by banks that want to develop a relationship with the target company. CLOs do not provide these facilities because these credit lines are not necessarily drawn. Given their need to provide returns for investors, CLOs want to invest in loans that are fully drawn.

2.3.3   Subordinated Debt

Subordinated debt is debt which ranks below the senior debt with respect to claim on earnings or assets. It is also called junior debt. Several forms of subordinated debt can be included in an LBO. There is usually no junior debt for small LBOs.

2.3.3.1 Second Lien

Some LBOs include a debt instrument called *second lien*. Second lien debt is a tranche of debt that has equal payment rights to the senior debt but has subordinated rights to any collateral given by the borrower to the lenders. In other words, second lien lenders generally benefit from second ranking pledges over the shares of the HoldCo and the target company.

In case of termination of the transaction following an event of default, the second lien lenders can receive the proceeds of the sale of the assets pledged to secure the loan (often shares of the target), but only after the senior lenders have been entirely repaid. Second lien debt can be considered on paper as an additional tranche of senior debt but is in practice a junior debt instrument.

2.3.3.2 Mezzanine Debt

Mezzanine debt is a tranche of debt that is junior to the senior debt but senior to the equity. It is a hybrid type of financing that sits midway between debt and equity. Mezzanine debt is a bullet loan, with proceeds flowing from a mix of:

– interest payments during the transaction
– capitalized interest (paid at maturity or when the transaction is refinanced), called PIK (*payment in kind*)
– *warrants* on the equity of the company. Warrants are an option for the mezzanine lender to be paid interest in a predefined percentage of equity of the company. Financially, it is extremely attractive if the valuation of the company has increased from the date of the LBO to the exit.

The use of mezzanine debt is a good way to add leverage in an LBO without putting pressure on the senior lenders' risk profile. Mezzanine lenders are debt funds that can also generally invest in second lien debt. Mezzanine debt and second lien debt are generally mutually exclusive.

2.3.3.3 High-yield Bonds

The junior tranche of debt in an LBO can also take the form of bonds issued by the HoldCo or by an additional SPV situated between the HoldCo and the sponsor. These *high-yield bonds* are sometimes colloquially called *junk bonds*. They were popularized in the United States in the 1980s by Michael Milken, the star bond trader of Drexel Burnham Lambert.[14] High-yield bonds are rated as non-investment grade by rating agencies.

As a reminder, ratings issued by the three main credit rating agencies (Moody's, S&P, and Fitch Ratings) range from AAA (or equivalent) for debts with a near certainty of repayment, to D (or equivalent) for defaulting securities. Securities

---

[14]See case study 2.

with a rating of BBB– or above qualify as investment grade. Non-investment grade instruments are rated BB+ or below.

High-yield bonds are different from mezzanine debt in two ways: (i) they are rated instruments, and (ii) they do not contain PIK or warrants; they only pay a high interest rate. High-yield bonds are used for sizable transactions when there is a need to tap a large pool of liquidity. Below a certain amount (c. $500 million), the need for rating, and therefore high-yield bonds, is limited.[15]

Depending how they are structured, high-yield bonds are often legally referred to as *subordinated notes* or *senior unsecured notes*. The expression *senior notes* to describe these bonds can be misleading. The instrument is indeed a junior one. It is only referred to as senior because it is issued by an SPV which sits above the HoldCo in the acquisition structure. This SPV having raised no other debt, the notes are senior from the SPV perspective. When considering the whole deal, however, they rank junior to the senior debt.

2.3.4   Unitranche Debt

2.3.4.1   What is it?

Unitranche is a debt instrument offered as an alternative to the senior and mezzanine debt duo. It has grown significantly in popularity since its debut in the mid-1990s thanks to its simplicity: sponsors have only one loan agreement to negotiate instead of two. Unitranche is non-amortizing and generally has a maturity of five years. Its pricing is a sort of weighted average of senior and mezzanine debt. It often mimics coupon features of mezzanine debt with a mix of (i) cash interest paid during the transaction, (ii) PIK paid at maturity, and (iii) warrants. Unitranche is nowadays by far the most popular debt instrument for medium-sized LBOs.

Unitranche is not provided by banks. It is a product offered by funds specializing in private debt (also called *direct lenders*). These funds are in essence very similar to the funds used by private equity firms to perform LBOs. They are set up by an investment firm and funded by limited partners, which are a mix of insurance companies, pension funds, sovereign wealth funds, and family offices. The main difference between a debt fund and an equity fund is the return expected by the LPs (lower for debt funds) and the investment policy (investment in debt instead of equity). Debt funds providing unitranche are also generally active in the mezzanine and second lien space.

The companies managing these credit funds are very often the same as those who manage equity funds (Apollo, Ardian, Bain Capital, Carlyle, etc.) although some players focus solely or mainly on debt products (Alcentra or Ares Management, for instance). To avoid conflict of interests, firms that have both equity and debt funds can usually not invest in the same company as both shareholder and lender.

---

[15]Many debt investors can only invest in securities that are rated. They can therefore not invest in mezzanine tranches, which are rarely rated. For this reason, when the transactions are small, the junior debt takes the form of mezzanine. For large transactions, the junior debt is structured as high-yield bonds.

2.3.4.2 Bifurcated Unitranche

The LBO market has seen in the last few years an increasing number of transactions in which direct lenders have cooperated with banks. In this scenario, the unitranche is sliced in two. The senior part of the unitranche (generally an amount below 2 x EBITDA) is taken by a bank while the junior portion is funded by a debt fund. Interests payable under the senior part of the unitranche (called *first-out*) are obviously lower than those due on the junior part (called *last-out*). Although the unitranche is split into two, there is only one loan agreement with the HoldCo. Flows and payments are regulated by a separate agreement that is only discussed between the debt fund and the bank. This type of structure is known as a *bifurcated unitranche*.

Structuring a bifurcated unitranche is a way to entice a bank into participating in the deal at the target level. The bank taking part in the unitranche is often the bank that provides the RCF, the capex line, and the acquisition line. The amount of these ancillary facilities is generally small and banks may be reluctant to provide them (they have a whole deal to analyze but would only perceive limited revenues). Adding the junior part of a unitranche to this package makes the deal more sizable for the bank. The fact that this debt tranche is small in size relative to the EBITDA means also that the loan is not too risky and does not consume a lot of capital.

Case Study 2: Michael Milken and the Birth of the High-Yield Bond Market

Michael Milken is undoubtedly one of the most famous financiers in history. Very few bankers have so deeply impacted the structure of financial markets. He has played a central role in the development of leveraged buyouts and is still known today as the father of the high-yield bond market.

Drexel Burnham Lambert

Milken was born in California in 1946. He studied economics and finance at Berkeley before completing his MBA at Wharton. He then joined Drexel Firestone, a small investment bank with a prestigious past but which had long been in the shadow of the Goldmans and Morgan Stanleys.

Drexel & Company was created in Philadelphia in 1838 by Francis Martin Drexel. On the death of his father, Francis's son, Anthony, reorganized the company and entered into a new partnership with John Pierpont Morgan. Together they founded Drexel, Morgan & Co, an institution that became one of the most powerful firms on Wall Street. After Drexel's death in 1893, Morgan changed the name of the company to... JP Morgan & Co, the bank behind what it is known today as JP Morgan Chase.

(continued)

(continued)

The Drexel patronym being available after this change of name, former employees of Drexel, Morgan & Co decided to buy the rights to use it and launch their own investment bank. Despite this prestigious lineage, the new Drexel was never in a position to compete with the best. The company struggled and was constantly in search for new partners to keep it afloat. In 1970 the tire manufacturer Firestone was called to rescue the bank (which changed its name to Drexel Firestone). Three years later, the firm was taken over by Burnham & Company, a second tier Wall Street broker looking to expand in the corporate finance segment and drawn by the prestige of the Drexel name. Finally, as part of its extension strategy in the US market, Belgian holding company Groupe Bruxelles Lambert took a minority stake in the bank in 1976, giving birth to Drexel Burnham Lambert.[16]

At that time, the company was still only a very small investment bank. In 1986, though, 10 years after its creation, Drexel Burnham Lambert became – thanks to Michael Milken – the most profitable investment bank on Wall Street.[17]

Milken's Vision

During his time at Berkeley, Michael Milken discovered the work of Walter Braddock Hickman, an economist and central banker who spent a lot of time researching debt markets. Through empirical studies backed by an impressive amount of data, Hickman demonstrated in a book published in 1958[18] that the risk-adjusted return offered by non-investment grade (or high-yield) bonds is better than the risk-adjusted return of investment grade bonds. In other words, this means that even if high-yield bonds are intrinsically riskier than investment grade bonds, the additional risk is more than compensated by the delta in margin.

In the mid-1950s, the high-yield market was still extremely small. It consisted only of *fallen angels*, i.e. bonds originally issued with an investment grade rating but which had been downgraded by rating agencies after their issuers ran into problems. Bonds in this market traded at high discounts compared with their face value. This discount reflected, obviously, the additional risk, but Hickman showed that from a financial perspective the discount was greater than it should be.

Hickman explained this situation by the fact that many investors in the traditional bond market (insurance companies, savings banks, pension funds, etc.) have investment guidelines that prevent them from holding on to their book bonds

---

[16]Groupe Bruxelles Lambert is a Belgian holding company listed on Euronext. It is one of the largest market capitalizations in Belgium.

[17]On the basis of Annual Reports published on 31 December 1986.

[18]Corporate bond quality investor experience. New York: Princeton University Press, 1958.

which have slipped below a non-investment grade rating. In other words, if the rating of a bond falls below BBB-, they have to sell it (hence the term *junk bonds*). For Hickman, this explains why junk bonds trade with such a high discount: not only are they riskier than investment grade bonds, but a lot of traditional buyers are not allowed to invest in them. This reduces the liquidity available and drags their price down.

Drawing on Hickman's work, Milken concluded that the junk bond market is full of opportunities. A bond downgraded below investment grade is not necessarily doomed to default. The downgrade only indicates that the risk of default has increased. If bought at the right price, junk bonds can generate substantial gains for investors, sometimes significantly more than stocks. And unlike stocks, a bond's return is only conditioned upon the ability of the borrower to repay the bond when due. Profits for the investor are not linked to the growth prospects of the company, the performance of the firm against its peers, market conditions, a country's tax policy, etc. They depend solely on two factors: (i) the difference between the bond's acquisition price and its issue price, and (ii) the ability of the company to generate enough cash flow to repay its debt.

The Initial Years

Milken first joined Drexel as a bond analyst. He was recommended by one of his Wharton professors and instantly impressed everyone at the firm with his work ethic and attention to detail. Milken was known not to take the subway in the morning because he did not want to run into people he knew and waste his time chitchatting. He preferred to take the bus where he could quietly read company financial statements, with a miner's lamp on his forehead when it was too dark.

Milken was quickly frustrated by his job as research analyst. He wanted to take advantage of the inefficiencies he saw in the market and offered to start a junk bond trading desk. His proposal was turned down, and he was about to leave to study for a PhD when Drexel Firestone merged with Burnham & Co. Convinced by the potential of the young man, Tubby Burnham – who was also a Wharton alumnus – gave him some capital to launch a trading desk. The initial years were spectacular: Milken generated annual returns of more than 100% on his junk bond portfolio.

Where most investors only saw risk, Milken perceived the risk-adjusted yield. He was the best trader at Drexel and a young rising star on Wall Street. When Drexel Burnham became Drexel Burnham Lambert, he was already one of the most powerful bankers in the firm. He was 30 years old and his annual salary was estimated at $5 million.

Milken's aura was such that he was able to move back to California in 1978 with the blessing of Drexel's shareholders. He brought his whole team with him

(continued)

(*continued*)

and recreated an entire trading floor in Los Angeles, focused almost exclusively on junk bonds. From LA, Milken ran his business independently from his bosses. It was a win-win situation. Milken made billions for Drexel and could in return spend more time in his home town with his family, especially his father who had been diagnosed with cancer.

The Birth of the High-yield Bond Market

The turning point of Milken's junk bond revolution happened in April 1977, when he arranged for Texas International, a small oil exploration company, one of the first ever high-yield bond issuances. The transaction was small, raising only $30 million, but it was a landmark deal for the industry. Whereas junk bonds were until then only *fallen angels*, this was one of the first times that a company issued a bond that was non-investment grade from the start.

Drexel Burnham Lambert quickly became the undisputed leader of high-yield bond issuances. It ranked number one in league tables for more than 10 years in a row, with a market share ranging each year from 40% to 70%. Milken and his team were the junk bond one-stop shop. They did everything related to the product: they convinced companies to issue high-yield bonds, structured the issuances, placed the bonds with investors, and ensured the liquidity of these bonds in the secondary market.

The period was ideal for high-yield issuances. The double effect of the second oil shock (1979) and the savings and loans crisis (1985) severely restricted the amount of debt available to middle-sized companies. With banks reluctant to lend, issuing high-yield bonds was for many of them the only way to obtain financing.

The nature of the junk bond market changed dramatically over the period. While it was until then reserved for bonds downgraded by rating agencies, it became, thanks to Milken, the new home of non-investment grade bonds issued by small and high growth companies. According to Milken, these companies were too small or too risky to be correctly assessed by S&P or Moody's. And yet they represented fantastic investment opportunities: they operated in segments of business that had fantastic growth prospects and their debt paid a high coupon.

Milken arranged at that time high-yield bond issuances for companies that would later become household names, including CNN and the Murdoch Group in the media sector, and Wynn Resorts in the gambling industry. The perception of non-investment grade bonds changed drastically within a few years and the expression *junk bonds* was gradually supplanted by the term *high-yield bonds*.

The Emergence of LBOs

The birth of the high-yield bond market contributed directly to the development of LBOs. By offering new financing solutions to sub-investment grade borrowers, Milken opened the door to LBOs and other highly leveraged transactions. It is not a coincidence that so many private equity firms sprang up between the late 1970s and the early 1990s. Leon Black himself, the founder of Apollo, worked at Drexel with Milken from 1977 to 1990.

Thanks to his knack for arranging outsized transactions, Milken became the preferred point of contact for all LBO firms. He also worked with corporate raiders, those financiers who try to buy out listed companies through hostile takeovers. Milken financed some of the biggest deals ever clinched. He supported Ronald Perelman's 1985 hostile bid for the takeover of cosmetics giant Revlon. He also arranged the bond issuance for the buyout of RJR Nabisco by KKR in 1989, the largest LBO in history.[19]

Drexel at the time had very few competitors in the LBO segment. Most of the clients of other investment banks were established companies and potential targets for the raiders. These banks faced a potential conflict of interest if they backed the firms that end up acquiring companies they work closely with. Drexel took advantage of this situation and built from scratch an M&A franchise whose focus was to arrange LBOs and to feed Milken's high-yield department. Though not a managing partner at Drexel, Milken was incontestably the most prominent figure at the bank. The whole firm was organized around him.

The Most Influential Banker since JP Morgan

Milken was not only the star of Drexel he was at the time the most revered figure in the US financial industry. While his counterparts in rival investment banks earned between $2 million and $7 million in 1987, Milken's package that year reached $550 million, the fattest salary ever paid on Wall Street. Such an astounding level of compensation stemmed from his original salary negotiations. In 1974, while he was still a young analyst looking for an opportunity to trade, Milken got Teddy Burnham to pay him a fixed percentage of all the profits he would generate for the firm. Back then Drexel was a small bank, and nobody could have imagined that this 28-year-old man would one day have such an impact on financial markets.

Milken is clearly one of the fathers of what has become known as financial disintermediation, in which companies obtain funding directly from financial markets without having to rely on bank loans. The high-yield bonds he arranged in the late 1970s showed that there was a way for many companies, even small ones, to obtain financing. Thanks to Milken, most institutional investors shifted part of their portfolios into high-yield instruments and made capital available to a large number of companies that would not otherwise have had access to capital.

(continued)

---

[19]RJR Nabisco remained the largest LBO in history until the takeover of HCA Healthcare (a US healthcare facility company) in June 2006. Corrected by inflation, it undoubtedly continues to be the most important LBO transaction ever made.

(*continued*)

Milken was also indirectly behind the development of the LBO sector. Without his ability to channel large amounts of money from investors into the high-yield space, it would have taken more time for this market to emerge. By making LBOs and raids on large firms possible, Milken also contributed to the reshuffle of US capitalism. Under the pressure of hostile takeovers, large companies gradually changed their corporate structure, switching from a conglomerate-based paradigm to a business model in which companies focus on one type of activity only and give priority to creating value for shareholders.

For all these reasons, Milken had a deep influence on the way the US financial system evolved from the mid-1970s. His role in the development of the high-yield market has had a lasting impact on the financial industry. He was a gifted financier and undoubtedly the most influential banker since John Pierpont Morgan, the man who built JP Morgan and saved the US banking system from bankruptcy in 1907, playing the role of a Federal Reserve, which did not yet exist.

The Decline

The year 1986 marks the beginning of Milken's decline. The famous raider Ivan Boesky (inspiration for the character Gordon Gekko played by Michael Douglas in Oliver Stone's *Wall Street*[20]) was arrested that year for insider trading. To reduce his sentence, he made a deal with the US authorities and provided compromising information on Milken and Drexel.

A three-year double investigation – from the Security Exchange Commission (SEC), the US Stock Exchange watchdog, and the Attorney for the Southern District of New York, a certain Rudolph Giuliani – concluded that Milken and his teams had routinely engaged in insider trading. They had repeatedly purchased in their own name stocks of listed companies against which they were confidentially preparing takeover bids on behalf of clients.

The investigators also discovered that Milken had regularly taken advantage of his dominant position in the market to knowingly misprice bond issuances and charge clients higher fees and margins than they should have paid, given their risk profile. In parallel, the investigation demonstrated that Milken, his brother, and some of their colleagues had secretly set up several investment vehicles to acquire for their own profit some of these mispriced bonds. To make things worse, Milken's best clients (i.e. the fund managers buying the high-yield bonds he arranged) were regularly invited to invest personally in these secret vehicles.

---

[20] Ivan Boesky notably said "greed is good" in a graduation speech he gave at Berkeley Hass Business School in 1986, a sentence that is Gekko's motto in the film.

Milken was finally sentenced to 10 years in prison. He also had to pay a fine of $600 million and damages to various investors for a total of $1.1 billion. Drexel Burnham Lambert negotiated in parallel an agreement with the SEC. The bank had to pay a record fine and sell some of its activities. A few months later, Drexel was in the red. It looked for new investors but its tarnished reputation and the fear of other legal liabilities limited the enthusiasm of potential buyers. Unable to face its debt obligations, the firm declared bankruptcy in February 1990.

Epilogue

Michael Milken's sentence was later reduced to two years for good behavior and cooperating against others accused of insider trading. Though banned for life from the financial industry, he spent only a total of 22 months in prison. Diagnosed with cancer a few weeks after he was released, he managed to survive and today devotes most of his huge fortune to cancer research, philanthropy, and the promotion of access to education.

After years of lobbying to successive US presidents, Milken was finally pardoned by Donald Trump on 18 February 2020. Although his ban on working in the financial industry was not lifted, his positive influence on the financing of US companies has been officially recognized. The White House statement describes him as *"one of America's greatest financiers"* and explains that *"his innovative work greatly expanded access to capital for emerging companies [and] has helped create entire industries, such as wireless communication and cable television"*. Seen as scandalous by some or natural by others, this pardon is ironically due to the diplomatic talents of Rudolph Giuliani, Donald Trump's personal attorney, who – after putting Milken in jail in the 1990s – became a good friend of his after he was also diagnosed with cancer.

Case Study 3: Malcolm Glazer and the Manchester United LBO

Although the takeover of Manchester United by Malcolm Glazer is still controversial – especially among fans – it is also an impressive acquisition story. Glazer saw the financial potential of the club, whose value has increased dramatically over the past 10 years. He has shown that owning a football club can be a lucrative activity, and not just a billionaires' hobby.

Manchester United

Manchester United Football Club was formed in 1878 as Newton Heath LYR Football Club. Its players were employees of the Lancashire and Yorkshire Railway

(continued)

(*continued*)

working at the Newton Heath depot. They started off playing against the football teams of other railway companies and joined the first division of the national football league in 1892. The team was unfortunately relegated soon after to the second division. The club struggled for some years and nearly went bankrupt in 1901. It was saved by John Henry Davies, a local brewer, who renamed the club Manchester United in 1902.

By that time, Manchester United was known as a "yo-yo" club, a team regularly promoted and relegated, never playing in the first division for long but always fighting for promotion when in the second division. On the death of John Henry Davies in 1927, the club again faced financial difficulties and was saved by British businessman James Gibson in 1931.

In October 1945, as league football was about to resume, Gibson appointed a young Scottish retired footballer, Matt Busby, as the club's manager and gave him full control over the selection and training of players. Busby's arrival was greeted with skepticism at the club due to his youth and the fact that he played for United's arch rivals Liverpool and Manchester City. His appointment was nonetheless a resounding success, with the club winning the English league three times in the 1950s.

In 1958, tragedy struck and the club lost eight players in a dramatic airplane crash. Matt Busby himself was injured and out of action for months. Despite the accident, he was able to rebuild a team around young players like Denis Law and George Best. Together they wrote a new chapter of United's history. They won the league twice, in 1965 and 1967, and eventually the European Cup in 1968, a first for an English club.

Off the pitch, Manchester United faced changes. After the death of Gibson in 1951, Louis Edwards slowly emerged as a new leading figure. He bought shares from the Gibson children and took a seat on the Board of Directors in 1958. He was appointed chairman in 1965 and became majority shareholder five years later. On his death in 1980, his son Martin took over the club.

Although he remained chairman until 2000, Martin Edwards was never a popular figure with the fans, partly because he entertained over the years several offers from would-be buyers. Media tycoon Robert Maxwell bid £10 million in 1984 and property magnate Michael Knighton £20 million in 1989. In both cases, the sale fell through but the situation angered the fans, who blamed Edwards for being more interested in cashing in than in supporting the club. In 1998, BskyB Corp's Robert Murdoch made a £623-million bid, an offer ultimately accepted by the board but blocked by the UK Monopolies and Mergers Commission. Again, the flirtation with a sale exasperated the fans.

In the meantime, Edwards took steps to improve the team. He appointed Alex Ferguson as manager in 1986 and backed him despite a difficult start. In 1991, the club was floated on the London Stock Exchange, giving it the cash to attract players on the transfer market and sign better talent.

After several bleak years on the pitch in the 1970s, Ferguson's appointment did eventually bring stability to the club. From 1992 to 2003, Manchester won the league 8 times in 11 years, making Ferguson the most successful coach in United's history. The club again became one of the most respected teams in Europe. They won the UEFA Cup Winners' Cup in 1991 against Barcelona and their second Champions' League in 1999 after a thrilling game against Bayern Munich in the final.

In the early 2000s, however, tensions began to emerge between Ferguson and the two largest shareholders of the club, Irish magnates John Magnier and John Patrick McManus. Magnier and McManus tried to have Ferguson removed but other shareholders decided to back him. After weeks of tension, it was decided that the board would look for new anchor investors to bring stability to the club.

2003–2005: The Glazer Takeover

American businessman Malcolm Glazer, owner of the NFL's[21] Tampa Bay Buccaneers, was the first to show interest in investing in Manchester United. He was familiar with sport business ventures and had been looking into investing in European football for quite some time. Glazer led the Buccaneers to a Super Bowl victory in 2003 and was confident he could achieve the same level of success in the English Premier League.

The acquisition of Manchester United was done in successive steps. In March 2003, Glazer bought 2.9% of the club through Red Football Limited, a personal holding company set up specifically to invest in the club. He increased his stake to over 3% in September and then to almost 9% in October.

Rumors about a possible takeover started to surface in 2004 when Glazer raised his stake to more than 16% and then to 28%. After a few months of negotiations, Glazer finally reached an agreement in May 2005 with Magnier and McManus to acquire their shares in United. Glazer then bought out other significant smaller shareholders, bringing his stake to 75.7%, just above the 75% threshold that allowed him to delist the club. He obtained full control of United shortly after. Based on the price offered to the final minority shareholders, the club was valued at £790 million, a 26% increase compared with the price offered by BSkyB seven years earlier.

A big chunk of the money Glazer used to acquire United came in the form of loans taken by his holding company, Red Football Limited. Roughly £560 million was borrowed to finance the acquisition of the club, including £270 million of PIK loans provided by three US hedge funds: Citadel, Och-Ziff Capital Management,

(continued)

---

[21] The National Football League (NFL) is the name of the professional American football league in the United States.

(*continued*)

and Perry Capital. Rates on the PIK loans were set at 14.25% but rose to 16.25% if the ratio net debt-to-EBITDA of the Manchester United Group exceeded a five-times multiple. The rest of the debt took the form of a senior loan paying a lower rate but secured by Manchester United's assets, including primarily the brand and the Old Trafford stadium. Given significant interest payments, many believed that United's takeover would endanger the club. Fans especially feared that the club's cash flow would be redirected to repay the acquisition debt rather than attracting football talent.

Although it was a novelty in Europe at the time, acquiring a sports team via an LBO was a common structure in the United States. Although financial arrangements behind sport franchises are rarely disclosed, some transactions are known to have relied on the use of financial leverage. In the 1980s, several baseball teams were acquired via LBO, notably the Seattle Mariners for which Jeff Smulyan paid $76 million in 1989 (split between $41 million of equity and $35 million of debt). Similar transactions also occurred in the NFL. In 1999, Dan Snyder acquired the Washington Redskins for $800 million, including a $340-million acquisition facility and a $155-million loan secured by the stadium.

On the Pitch

Despite the expectations of many football pundits, Glazer decided to limit changes in United's day-to-day business. The club kept its CEO, David Gill, and more importantly its manager, Sir Alex Ferguson.[22] Despite heavy investment by other teams, notably Chelsea and its new owner Roman Abramovich, Manchester United remained the top team in England. The club won the Premier League three times in a row from 2007 to 2009. They also won another European cup in 2008 (against Chelsea), reached the finals twice (in 2009 and 2011), and won the Premier League again in 2011 and 2013.

The following years were more complicated for United. Ferguson's retirement in 2013 after 27 years had a deep impact on the club. David Moyes, Ferguson's successor, was sacked after nine months in charge due to a series of poor results. The two following managers, Louis Van Gaal and Jose Mourinho, did not see the end of their contracts either. Despite enjoying success in national cups and in Europe, neither of them was able to help United win the league.

Investment Rationale

Contrary to the perception of some fans, Glazer did not acquire Manchester United on a whim. He made a very rational investment and had no intention of damaging

---

[22]Ferguson was knighted in 1999 after his team managed to win the European Cup, the Premier League and the FA Cup in the same year.

the club by underinvesting in the team. He was a business sport expert and was convinced that European football clubs were undervalued compared with US sport franchises. Notably, TV rights and sponsorship deals were nowhere near where they should be.

Glazer purchased the Tampa Bay Buccaneers in 1995 for $192 million, the highest sale price for a professional sport franchise up to that point. In the 10 years that followed (between his acquisition of the Buccaneers and his takeover of Manchester United), the six transactions involving NFL teams all closed for bigger sums, ranging from $194 million for the Seattle Seahawks in 1994 to $800 million for the Washington Redskins in 1999 (see Table 2.2). The last four transactions signed before Glazer bought out Manchester United closed for amounts between $545 million and $635 million, roughly three times the price paid for the Buccaneers.

TABLE 2.2   Transactions involving NFL franchises since Glazer's acquisition of Tampa Bay Buccaneers in 1995

NFL Team	Buyer	Year	Value
Tampa Bay Buccaneers	Malcolm Glazer	1995	$192m
Seattle Seahawks	Paul Allen	1997	$194m
Washington Redskins	Dan Snyder	1999	$800m
New York Jets	Woody Johnson	2000	$635m
Atlanta Falcons	Arthur Blank	2002	$545m
Baltimore Ravens	Steve Bisciotti	2004	$600m
Minnesota Vikings	Zygi Wilf	2005	$600m
Miami Dolphins	Stephen Ross	2008	$1.1bn
St. Louis/Los Angeles Rams[23]	Stan Kroenke	2010	$700m
Jacksonville Jaguars	Shad Khan	2012	$770m
Cleveland Browns	Jimmy Haslam	2012	$1.1bn
Buffalo Bills	Terry & Kim Pegula	2014	$1.4bn
Carolina Panthers	David Tepper	2018	$2.2bn

Source: Forbes, NFL.

The increase in value of NFL franchises is primarily due to the rising value of TV rights for American football. These rights had for a long time been shared more

(continued)

---

[23]The Rams played in Saint Louis when acquired by Kroenke in 2010, but were relocated to Los Angeles in 2015 where they had played from 1946 to 1994.

(continued)

or less equally between the three main broadcast channels in the United States: ABC, CBS, and NBC. The arrival of newcomers like ESPN, Fox, and TNT at the end of the 1980s disrupted the status quo. Competition led to a fierce battle among networks, driving TV rights up to the benefit of players and franchise owners.

After 38 years of airing the NFL, CBS lost their rights to Fox Networks in 1993. Fox offered a then-record $1.58 billion over the 1993–1997 period. Four years later, CBS got back in the game and agreed to pay $4 billion over eight years for the 1998–2005 period, this time edging out NBC for the right to broadcast NFL games.

In the following years, the competition between channels continued to up the value of TV rights, which climbed from $420 million per year in the 1980s (all channels included) to more than $3 billion for the 2006–2013 period and more than $5 billion for the 2014–2021 period, driving up the value of NFL teams. Comparing Table 2.2 and Figure 2.3, it is clear that both the 1998–2005 and 2006–2013 TV deals coincided with a rise in value of NFL teams (from less than $200 million on average before 1998 to $540–$800 million after, and more than $1.1 billion after 2006).

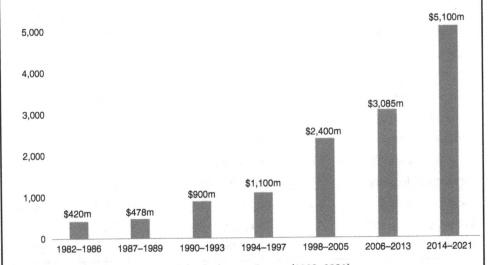

FIGURE 2.3 Value of NFL TV Rights in $m per Season (1982–2021)
Source: LA Times and New York Times.

TV rights are obviously not the sole value driver of an NFL franchise. A team's acquisition price may also be affected by tangible assets like stadium capacity, ticket prices, and sponsorship deals, and also intangibles, like the popularity of the team or the number of bidders during the acquisition process. That said, TV rights for the NFL being split equally among all teams, it is the biggest factor driving up the value of NFL franchises.

More generally, a rise in TV rights is the cornerstone of the general increase in team revenues. Higher TV rights have forced TV channels to promote games more heavily, which has given more visibility to the NFL. As a consequence, audiences have increased, paving the way for a rise in other revenues, notably sponsorship deals and ticketing.

Premier League TV Rights

When he took over Manchester United, Malcolm Glazer was convinced that TV rights for football in England would go up. He noted that the same trends were at work in Europe in 2005 as in the US 10 years before: new channels were springing up while overall demand for entertainment programs was growing.

Glazer also noted that unlike American football, football is a global product. It is played everywhere and has, therefore, the potential to reach an extremely wide audience. While the NFL is a sport mostly followed in the US, football can potentially be followed by billions of viewers.

When Glazer bought out Manchester United, domestic TV rights for the Premier League for the seasons 2004–2007 were £341 million per year. These rights have increased exponentially ever since, reaching £1.712 billion per year for the seasons 2016–2019 (see Figure 2.4).

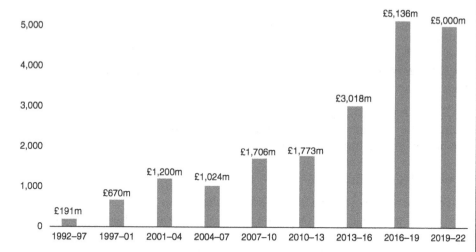

FIGURE 2.4 Domestic Premier League TV Rights in £m per Period (1992–2022)
Source: author.

The amounts shown in Figure 2.4 do not include overseas TV rights. These are sold separately in each country and have also increased spectacularly between 1992 and 2022. They were only £40 million for the 1992–1997 period and have jumped to £4.35 billion for the 2019–2022 period, representing an amount almost equal to the domestic TV rights (see Figure 2.5). It is interesting to note that while domestic TV rights have been multiplied by five between the Glazer takeover and the 2019–2022 period (from £1.02 billion to £5 billion), overseas TV rights have been multiplied

(continued)

(continued)

by more than 12 (from £325 million to £4.35 billion). This clearly validates Glazer's intuition on the international potential of English football.

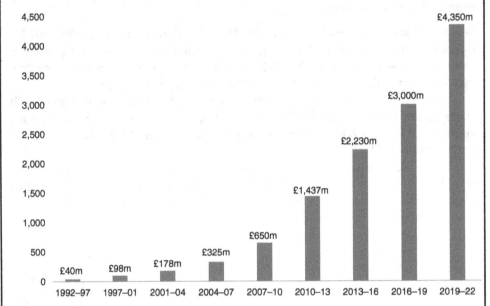

FIGURE 2.5 Overseas Premier League TV Rights in £m per Period (1992–2022)
Source: author.

In addition to these revenues, a team like Manchester United also receives a share in the TV rights paid by channels to broadcast European competitions like the prestigious Champions League.

Sponsorship and Ticketing

To generate more revenue, Glazer also worked on improving United's sponsorship deals. In 2005, the club's jersey sponsor, the UK phone company Vodafone, paid £9 million a year. Worried – like many – by United's growing debt, Vodafone terminated the deal two years early in 2006. US insurer AIG took over and agreed to pay the club £14 million a year until 2010. AIG was then replaced by Aon for an even bigger amount: £20 million per season for four years. In 2015, Chevrolet decided to pay £361 million for a seven-year contract – i.e. more than £50 million a year – while Aon agreed to pay £120 million over eight years (£15 million a year) to sponsor United's training ground and kit. Within 10 years, the amount paid by sponsors to advertise on Manchester's jersey went from £9 million to £65 million.

In parallel, Adidas signed a 10-year deal with Manchester United worth £750 million from 2015–2016 onwards to replace Nike, becoming the club's official jersey provider. This deal made Manchester United's the most valuable jersey in football at the time, before the deal signed between Nike and France's national team (€45 million per year). Figure 2.6 shows the 10 most expensive club jersey deals in football.

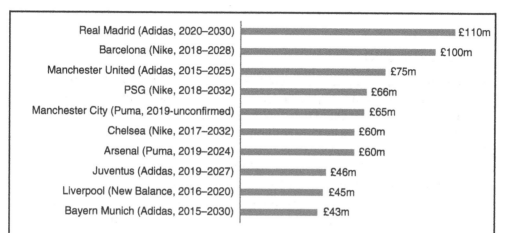

FIGURE 2.6 The 10 Most Expensive Jerseys in Club Football (Amounts in £m per Season) Source: author.

Manchester United's ticketing strategy was also optimized. Prices rose sharply after the takeover. Between 2006 and 2009, a season ticket in the East Stand Upper Tier at Old Trafford increased by almost 30%, from £494 to £665. Combined with an extension of the stadium,[24] bringing the number of seats from 68,000 to 76,000, this strategy generated substantial additional revenues for the club (see Figure 2.7).

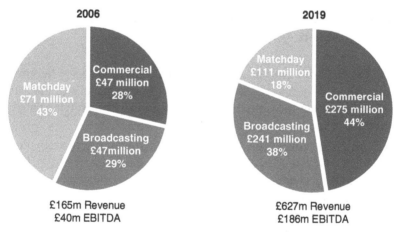

FIGURE 2.7 Manchester United Revenues in 2006 and 2019 Source: Manchester United.

(continued)

---

[24]The extension of the stadium was decided before the takeover.

(*continued*)

Refinancing and IPO

Despite success on the pitch post acquisition, Manchester United's growing debt was a source of concern for fans. Given the large outstanding PIK loans with high interest rates, the total indebtedness of Red Football increased even after the acquisition and peaked at nearly £778 million at the end of 2009 (vs. £560 million in 2005).

In January 2010, the club announced its plan to raise two new seven-year bonds to pay back its existing debt. One GBP tranche was issued with a coupon of 8.75% for £250 million, while a USD tranche was issued with a coupon of 8.375% for $425 million. This refinancing at a lower cost was made possible by an increase in EBITDA, which rose from £40 million to more than £100 million over the period.

In 2012, 10% of the club was listed on the New York Stock Exchange (NYSE) at an overall valuation of £1.47 billion, more than double the price paid by Glazer to acquire the club seven years earlier. The proceeds were split between a dividend payment and a partial repayment of the acquisition debt. Two years later, following Glazer's death, his six sons sold another 5% of the club on the NYSE at a 38% premium over the 2012 listing, valuing Manchester United at more than £2 billion.

Epilogue

In many ways the acquisition of Manchester United is a by-the-book LBO and a lesson for PE investors:

- *Lesson 1*: Glazer bought a company operating in a sector he knew well and whose dynamics he was familiar with. He was able to identify market trends other investors had not seen, namely the growing value of TV rights and sponsorship deals.
- *Lesson 2*: Once in charge, he kept the same management team, i.e. David Gill as CEO and Alex Ferguson as team manager. The duo had been extremely successful under the previous ownership and the likelihood of finding better professionals was slim. Manchester United was able to win the Premier League five times between 2005 and 2013 and the Champions League once in 2008. Since Gill and Ferguson's departures in 2013, the club has been less successful (no league titles) showing how important key people are in a company.
- *Lesson 3*: Once the situation of the club stabilized, its debt was refinanced at a lower rate, creating value for shareholders.
- *Lesson 4*: The club was eventually partially listed, a mechanism used by investors willing to monetize part of their investment while keeping control over the company they have acquired.

CHAPTER 3

The LBO Process

3.1 THE SALE PROCESS

The sale process of a company varies depending on its size and the seller's strategy. Private companies of interest to major private equity firms are generally auctioned. An M&A advisor is hired by the seller to coordinate the process, approach potential buyers, maximize the price, and ensure a swift execution of the deal.

The auction's schedule is precisely monitored. It starts at a certain date and is meant to end at a fixed date as well. All the steps in between are organized based on a pre-determined calendar. This method ensures equal treatment among bidders and puts pressure on them to put forward their best offer.

It is, however, not always possible to auction a company. A shareholder (whether it is an entrepreneur or a firm) may decide not to disclose openly that it wants to the sell the company it controls. An open sale process can indeed unsettle employees, clients or suppliers, and hurt the company's profits.

It is also possible for a company to be sold without ever being put up for sale. A bidder can make an unsolicited offer to the board of directors of the company (or to its shareholders) and start discussions if the offer raises some interest. *Public to private* transactions are a prime example of LBOs starting without any organized sale process. They are transactions aimed at taking a listed company private. Famous examples of public-to-private transactions include Manchester United (case study 3) and Hilton Hotels (case study 4).

Very small companies that can be of interest for individual buyers are also usually difficult to auction. Potential acquirers cannot be identified in advance, which makes it complicated to stick to a precise timeline. The company is in this case simply put on sale through an arranger whose role is to find the right buyer at the right price.

3.1.1 Preliminary Analysis

An LBO starts with a phase of preliminary analysis during which potential investors assess whether buying out the company is a good opportunity or not. If an advisor has been hired to coordinate the sale process, the first interactions often take place in two steps.

First, a very brief presentation of the target (teaser) is sent to the parties identified as potential buyers by the advisor. This document usually includes an overview of the company in terms of sector, size, product or services, turnover, and growth potential. The form of the teaser varies depending on the size of the company or the strategy of the seller. It can be a few bullet points in an email or a few pages in a PowerPoint presentation. The document can reveal the name of the company (especially if it is obvious, given the company description or market gossip) or not if the seller wants to keep things confidential.

Second, when a potential buyer takes interest, they sign a confidentiality agreement (also called a *Non-Disclosure Agreement* or NDA). Through this document they request additional information on the target while committing not to disclose it. The document containing the additional information is called an info-memo (information memorandum or IM). It is a comprehensive document prepared by the seller's advisor that includes a lot of confidential data on the company: profits, margins, profitability by division, detailed market analysis, information on the workforce, etc. When necessary, additional memos are prepared by specialized advisors on top of the IM. These memos can be useful in addressing some of the potential issues that may be raised during the sale process (e.g. a specific technical report can be drafted by an engineering firm if the company has factories, or an environmental report if chemicals are used during the production process). The documents shared by the seller can also include a business plan (prepared by the seller's advisor) and a potential valuation of the company based on this business plan.

Once they have signed the NDA, potential buyers analyze the opportunity in the light of their own investment strategies. If they consider the company a fit with their investment criteria (size, sector, profitability, growth potential), they dedicate resources to the deal. Large buyers hire their own consultants: M&A, legal, and possibly technical and commercial advisors, but also accountants or tax specialists.

The precise next steps of the process may vary, but a meeting with the management of the target company is usually organized. If the company is auctioned, the seller's advisor arranges meetings with the parties that have signed the NDA and expressed interest in buying out the target. Active, well-known lenders in the LBO market are also generally invited to meet with the management, especially for large transactions. Lenders can in this way directly form their own view of the target and start their analysis of the deal early in the process. They can then possibly back one (or several) buyer(s). This phase is called the *education process*. Its purpose is to allow all potential interested parties to get to know the target better.

If the sale is not organized through an auction the meeting with management can take different forms. For small transactions between individuals it can even be spread out over one or two days and include site or factory visits so that the buyer gets a full picture of a potential acquisition. Banks are not invited and are contacted directly by buyers. In any case, auction or not, a meeting with the company's management should help potential buyers form a more precise view of the company and its growth potential.

3.1.2 Valuation

Valuing the target is a key step in the LBO process. This is done in accordance with orthodox financial techniques. Readers who are particularly interested in this topic may consult any number of books dedicated to corporate valuation. In this section, we simply try to outline the generally accepted methods for valuing a company.

For the sake of simplicity, we can assume that there are only two ways of valuing a company: the *intrinsic* method or the *comparative* one. There is nothing surprising here, this is how people evaluate almost everything they buy. We all determine whether a product is expensive or not by comparing its price to the need that this product fulfils (intrinsic method). We also compare this price against the price of products that have similar properties (comparative method).

3.1.2.1 Comparative Method

The comparative method is the more intuitive one. It is close to the method used to value residential real estate. It consists simply in (i) looking at the price of recent similar transactions, (ii) identifying an easy method to benchmark these deals (in real estate this would typically be the average price per m^2), and (iii) thereby deducing the potential value of the target.

This method is perfectly valid, but for the fact that there is less data available on M&A transactions than real estate deals. This is due partly to the liquidity and the depth of the real estate market and partly to the fact that real estate transactions are in many countries registered with notaries or local authorities that then compute the data and distribute reliable statistics to a wide audience.

When it comes to using this valuation method, sellers and buyers have first to identify similar firms that have been sold recently. They then analyze all these deals one by one and divide each sale price by specific performance criteria (turnover, EBITDA, etc.). From there, they calculate an average for the sector and use the figures to negotiate a price for the target. If the parties discover, for instance, that comparable companies were sold in the last three years for, on average, 10 times their EBITDA, they will apply this multiple to the EBITDA of the target to calculate its enterprise value (or EV). For this reason this comparative calculation technique is known in finance as the *multiples approach.*

This method is, in reality, slightly more complex as parties can always legitimately argue over which previous transactions are similar enough to include in the benchmarking. Every company has its own particular characteristics, and the game between buyer and seller will be to highlight or minimize these differences, based on their interest.

Once again, an analogy can be drawn between the multiples approach and the method used to value property. If the average real estate price in a city is $5,000 per m², it does not mean that every property in the city will be sold based on this multiple. The average will include renovated apartments in the city center as well as decrepit buildings on the outskirts. There may indeed be major deviations from the average, where some properties go for $10,000 per m² while others do not exceed $2,000 per m². In real estate these deviations arise from the condition of the property or its location. In the case of a company, factors such as recent growth or Return on Invested Capital (ROIC)[1] will influence the sale price.

One of the most important questions when using the multiples approach is which measure of performance to multiply. One critical point to note is the connection between the criterion to be used as a reference and the concept of EV. Since EV equals equity value *plus* net debt, multiples should be calculated using performance criteria relevant to all stakeholders (both stock and debt holders). Therefore, the relevant criterion must be computed *before* interest expense. An EV/Net Income multiple is, for instance, meaningless because the numerator applies to shareholders and creditors, but the denominator accrues only to shareholders. For this reason, there are three main reference criteria that can be used to value a company: EBITDA, EBIT, and turnover.

The most common criteria used in the multiples approach is EBITDA. As has already been explained, EBITDA (Earnings Before Interest, Taxes, Depreciation and Amortization) is the balance between a company's income and its operating costs. It gives an indication of the profitability of a firm without taking into consideration its financial strategy, its tax position, or its investment policy. It is as such an important measure of the potential of a particular business. There are, however, limitations to using EBITDA as a reference criterion. EBITDA is calculated before depreciation and thus ignores capital expenditures that may be necessary to sustain the business. From a theoretical point of view, focusing only on EBITDA to value a firm would imply that a company can stay in business forever without making any investment. Warren Buffett is for this reason very skeptical about the use of EBITDA to value a company. He once famously illustrated his thinking: *"Does management think the tooth fairy pays for capital expenditures?"*

EBIT (or *Earnings Before Interest and Taxes*) is also sometimes used as a reference criterion in the multiples approach. Unlike EBITDA, EBIT is calculated after the depreciation of assets used by a company in its production cycle. That being said, depreciation is only a proxy for capital expenditures. Some assets that have been acquired by a company for a long time may already have been fully depreciated.

---

[1] ROIC is the operating profit after tax relative to the entire amount invested by the shareholders and lenders. For those who like formulae, ROIC = net operating profit/(total of the company's own funds + net debt – available cash). Please note that the concept of ROIC is strictly similar to the concept of ROCE (Return on Capital Employed).

Replacing them would come at a cost that EBIT does not capture. As an alternative, bankers may use EBITDA – Capex as a reference multiple.

The EV of a target company can also be calculated based on other multiples. Turnover may suffice if a target is loss-making or if a large number of companies included in the sample used to calculate the multiple are not profitable. That is often the case of targets that are start-ups or operate in a very cyclical business. But since the LBO industry is generally focused on mature companies that generate strong cash flows, turnover multiples are rarely used in LBOs.

Once the EV has been calculated, the company's net debt is deducted to find the equity value of the company. This equity value is in theory the amount that the potential buyer has to pay to acquire the company.

3.1.2.2 Intrinsic Method

The intrinsic approach, also known as the *Discounted Cash Flow (DCF)* method, is slightly more complex. Its starting point is to acknowledge that from a theoretical standpoint the value of a firm is equal to the sum of the cash flows that it generates in the long run. These cash flows have to be calculated and added up to arrive at an enterprise value for the target.

Users of this method perform their analysis in two steps:

- First, they first determine the cash flows to be generated by the company over time. To do so, some assumptions have to be made. These assumptions include growth in turnover, costs, capex, inflation, taxes, etc.
- Second, once the expected future cash flows are known, the present value of these future flows has to be calculated. Future cash flows must be discounted because getting $100 is not the same as getting $100 in the future. This concept is known as the *time value of money*. Money available at the present time has more value because there is no risk involved and because it has earning capacity.

The rate used to convert future cash flow into today's money is called the *discount rate*. From a theoretical point of view, this discount rate is the rate at which an investor is ready to abandon a given sum now in order to earn a higher sum in the future. If an investor has $100 but is ready to make a certain investment to earn at least $110 in one year, the discount rate is 10%.

What then is the discount rate applicable when valuing the future cash flows of a company? In theory, a company's objective is to generate cash flows which are ultimately shared between lenders and shareholders. If we refer to the earlier example – in which we defined the concept of discount rate – it means that the rate applicable to convert future cash flows is the weighted average of the earning expectations of the company's lenders and shareholders. In other words, the discount rate to be used is the weighted average cost of capital needed by the company to carry on its business. In financial theory, this cost is known as the *Weighted Average Cost of Capital (WACC)*.

To calculate the WACC of a target, the potential buyer must know the target's cost of debt and cost of equity. The cost of debt is relatively straightforward to find. It is the after-tax margin due on the loans taken out by the company.[2] The cost of equity is more complicated. It is the return that the company must deliver to its shareholders. This return is a cost from the company's perspective, because if it fails to deliver it, shareholders will sell their shares and the value of the company will drop. Put differently, the cost of equity is the amount that a company must invest and spend to maintain a certain share price and distribute dividends.

Let us take a numerical example. If a company, operating in a country where the corporate tax rate is 30%, has $70 million of debt yielding 3% and $40 million of equity from investors expecting a 15% return, the WACC of this company is equal to:

$$70/(70+40) \times 3\% \times (1-30\%) + 40/(70+40) \times 15\% = 6.79\%.$$

In the context of valuing a company, this WACC can be used as the rate at which to discount future cash flows, converting them into today's money. If the WACC of the company is 6.79%, each future flow must be divided by $(1+6.79\%)^{\wedge n}$, n being the number of years into the future when the cash flow will actually occur. The value of the company is equal to the sum of all its discounted future cash flows.

3.1.2.3   Determining the Offer Price

In practice, the valuation of a target and the determination of the offer price are two different exercises. While private equity sponsors use the two methods mentioned above to understand the valuation of a company, the price of their offer is often set as follows:

- They first model the future financial flows that the target can generate over their investment horizon (approximately 5 years) by making a certain number of growth and cost assumptions.
- They anticipate an exit multiple at this date. In other words, they set a theoretical valuation of the target in 5 years as a function of a multiple (usually EBIT or EBITDA, as indicated above).
- They subtract from this theoretical valuation the amount of debt they think the LBO could support at that date. The result is the equity valuation of the target (i.e. what the buyer will obtain from the sale of the company in five years).
- Finally, considering the return objectives of their fund, they are able to find out, from this equity valuation in 5 years, the amount they are ready to invest today to acquire the target.

3.1.3   Letter of Intent

When a buyer confirms their interest in the target, they do so through a letter of intent (LOI). The LOI is a non-binding document in which the buyer declares to the seller

---

[2]Interests are tax deductible, so the real cost of debt for the company is the after-tax margin.

that, based on the information available at this stage, they are interested in buying out the target. The LOI is often referred to as a *Non-Binding Offer* or NBO.

An LOI usually includes the following elements:

- The terms of the transaction: an LOI can be a proposal to buy the entire company or only a subsidiary or activity. Certain assets of the company can be excluded from the offer.
- The proposed acquisition price: the NBO sets out the valuation of the company by the buyer. It also includes the assumptions that have been used. The price proposed at this stage is always subject to new information, which the potential buyer will have access to in the next phase.
- The payment structure: the potential buyer explains how it plans to pay the purchase price. Will it be paid at the time of signing or will a portion of the payment be deferred? The LOI also indicates how much of the price will be financed by equity and by debt. The potential buyer has at this stage already held discussion with lenders. If some of them have expressed interest in financing the acquisition, the buyer asks them to draft a support letter in which they explain what type of leverage they can provide.
- The extent of the due diligence:[3] the NBO includes the list of elements that the buyer wishes to specifically verify in the next phase of the sale process. This list includes access to financia statements, legal information on the company, potential industrial reports, etc.
- The transaction schedule: if no precise schedule has been shared by the seller's advisor in the previous phase, the buyer generally proposes one to the seller. It indicates notably how much time is needed for due diligence and for executing the deal.
- Non-compete clause: the potential buyer may require that the seller does not invest in the same sector as the company being sold for a certain period of time. If so, a non-compete clause has geographical and time limits.
- Exclusivity: a buyer may ask the seller for an exclusive negotiation period during which the latter cannot discuss the sale of the target with other buyers. This exclusivity is not necessarily possible, especially during an auction process in which the seller wants to select several bidders for the next phase.

If the sale process is organized through an auction, the seller usually receives several non-binding offers. It then has to decide how many bidders are selected for the next phase. Only two to four bidders are generally invited to continue talks. This is to maintain some competitive pressure while indicating progress. Having too many bidders in the next phase may discourage buyers, who may lose interest if they feel competition for the target is too intense.

---

[3]See Chapter 2, section 2.1.7.

3.1.4   Due Diligence

The bidders who are still in the race after the NBO are invited to the due diligence phase. They have access during this stage to a wide range of information on the company. Their objective is to confirm the assumptions taken during the valuation phase and shared in the LOI.

As explained in Chapter 2, section 2.1.7, due diligence is an investigation that covers all aspects of the company: operational management, financial statements, legal contracts with clients or suppliers, lists of customers, etc. In this effort, the potential buyer is supported by a team of advisors consisting mainly of bankers, accountants, and lawyers. A bidder can also require the help of other professionals: strategy consultants, environmental specialists, or tax experts, etc. These advisors have sometimes already supported the bidder in the pre-NBO phase.

The seller and their advisor provide during this phase all the support needed by the bidders. They generally prepare a due diligence package that includes all the information that potential buyers could require on the company. Specific technical reports pertaining to the situation of the target can be included in this package. These reports can deal with the quality of the company's industrial equipment, its R&D policy, its capex needs, etc.

If they are still interested in buying out the target, bidders are invited to submit a binding offer at the end of this phase. They can confirm the price included in the NBO or propose a new one. Explanations are usually included if the price has been lowered.

3.1.5   Structuring and Closing

While they prepare their NBO, bidders discuss with lenders how to structure and fund the acquisition. These discussions can be held by the bidder or via an advisor (who can, as already mentioned, be the bank acting as M&A advisor or another bank). Lenders are asked to provide the terms and conditions under which they would be willing to finance the deal. Typically, they share the following information:

- the maximum total leverage accepted
- the percentage of the facility that the lender is willing to finance (including underwriting amount)
- the loan profile (partly amortizing or not)
- the margin and upfront fees
- the covenants.

If the sale process is competitive, the same lender can be invited to support several bidders at the same time. In this case, it allocates different teams to the analysis of each bid. These teams (called *trees*) are not allowed to communicate on the deal and the bidding strategy of their client. Some bidders require that a lender supports them on an exclusive basis to avoid any potential information leakage. However, lenders may be reluctant to provide exclusivity, since it means they will be shut out of the deal if their bidder is not selected.

Once a bidder is chosen, the buyer and the seller enter into a phase of exclusive negotiations called *exclusivity period*. They finalize the deal and negotiate the share purchase agreement (SPA), i.e. the legal document through which ownership of the target is transferred from the seller to the buyer. In parallel, the buyer finalizes the signing and closing of the acquisition debt with the lenders.

3.1.6   After the Acquisition

3.1.6.1   Private Equity Firms

Buyers do not stop working once they have acquired a target. Their focus shifts toward priorities such as strategy and operating performance. Reporting tools are implemented or improved in order to closely monitor the *Key Performance Indicators* (KPIs) of the company and the impact of the change in strategy.

KPIs are quantifiable elements defined by the company and used to measure progress against final objectives. These KPIs can relate to a wide range of tasks. They can be financial (growth in revenue, improvement in margin, etc.), operational (average hours spent on after-sales service, time needed to perform a certain function, etc.), or linked to commercial strategy (number of new clients, average amount spent per client, etc.). KPIs are set based on the issues identified by the new shareholder. They are followed closely during the whole life of the LBO.

A private equity firm is not responsible for the day-to-day business of the company it controls. It acts, in theory, as a professional shareholder in charge of determining strategy and selecting the executives who will implement it. Typically one or several employees of the LBO company sit on the target's board of directors, providing support to the CEO and his or her team.

Contacts between the private equity firm and the target company's CEO are ideally not limited to board meetings but happen on a regular basis, so that the CEO feels backed by the shareholders. A strong relation between the CEO and the private equity firm is key to the success of an LBO. Christopher Nassetta, who was appointed CEO of Hilton Hotels after its takeover by Blackstone, said he would have never been able to turn the company around had he not been able to count on the full support of his chairman, Jonathan Gray, who was also Global Head of real estate at Blackstone (see case study 4).

Some private equity firms are known to relentlessly focus on rolling out a business plan and improving the operating performance of the companies they acquire. Brazilian firm 3G, for instance, focuses on efficiency, with methods inspired by Vicente Falconi, a Brazilian management consultant and professor at the University of Belo Horizonte, who has done extensive research on the way Toyota came out of nowhere to become the largest car manufacturer in the world.

3G is also obsessed with cost, inspired by Bob Fifer (the author of a little-known book called *Double Your Profits in Six Months or Less*, which 3G founders have repeatedly distributed among their executives). Unlike in many companies, where spending plans are simply based on last year's costs, Fifer promotes an approach called Zero Based Budget (ZBB). In this method, each manager has to justify foreseen expenses based on clearly defined needs and not on what happened in the previous year. It forces the whole company to reevaluate its needs every year and makes it harder for managers to increase costs without a reason. The founders of 3G give the zero-based approach credit for stripping out non-strategic expenses that do not directly contribute to the company's top or bottom lines (travel expenses, layers of middle management, etc.), keeping only those that have a clear impact on the company's profitability (R&D, marketing, branding, etc.).

3.1.6.2   Individual Buyers

The financial structuring of a takeover is just the first step in the adventure for an individual buying out a company. Once the LBO is executed, the buyer has to lead the company and implement the changes identified as necessary before the buyout. This approach is not so different from that of a private equity fund, although they cannot rely (because of the expense) on an army of consultants to define and track KPIs. In the Harley-Davidson example (case study 1), we saw that Vaughn Beals decided to focus on diminishing the number of motorcycles that did not pass quality tests at the end of the production line. Improving this KPI meant less cost for the company and better client satisfaction.

3.2   EXIT STRATEGIES

Individual investors buying out a (generally small) company usually do it because they want to own, manage, and develop a business. For them it is an exciting challenge that shares a lot of commonalities with the life of an entrepreneur. They want to be their own boss, have fun, and make a living out of it. They usually do not have short-term exit strategies in mind, although they may be open to attractive offers. With some exceptions, they only sell the company when they retire.

Private equity firms have a different approach. They buy a company with the intention of reselling it after a few years. Their investment horizon is generally between three and eight years. The sale may however be delayed, (i) if market conditions are not optimal during that period, or (ii) if the company is not performing well and needs time to be put back on track.

3.2.1   Initial Public Offering

An initial public offering (IPO or public offering) is the process of selling shares of a private company to the public. This is organized via a stock exchange on which the shares of the company are subsequently listed and freely tradable. Exits via IPOs are seen as the holy grail of private equity. They embody a by-the-book LBO in which a buyer has taken over a sluggish business and turned it into a profitable company that can be publicly listed. The perfect example is Harley-Davidson, as discussed earlier.

Exits via IPO easily make headlines and capture the imagination. Many case studies on LBOs are written on deals ending with a public offering, and this book is no exception. Case studies 1 and 2 on Harley-Davidson and Manchester United both include an IPO. Such exits are not actually that frequent, though. They are only possible for companies that are large enough to attract the interest of public investors. And even so, they are not necessarily the preferred exit route. Table 3.1 shows the top 10 private equity exits announced in 2016. Only three involved a public offering.

IPOs are more complicated to organize than a straight sale to a private equity firm or a competitor. They are more regulated and more uncertain. Public markets being more volatile, there is also a greater risk that the exit is delayed. In practical terms, IPOs are only considered if the valuation of the target company is substantially more attractive to the seller. This can be the case for very large companies that are out of reach for many buyers.

Given the uncertainties of an IPO, LBO firms contemplating a public offering for a portfolio company often engage in a *dual-track process*. This means that they pursue in parallel a potential IPO and an M&A exit. This strategy allows pressure to be put on potential buyers while making sure they have a fallback position. The sale to a buyer generally takes priority if they receive a good offer or if the IPO proves too difficult for whatever reason.

IPOs generally imply that the exit is done gradually. It is technically impossible for a private equity firm to sell all its shares at once on the stock market (except if it only owns a minority stake). In other words, a private equity firm generally remains a shareholder of the target company after the IPO. This was the case in the Hilton Hotels LBO. It took five years from the IPO in 2013 for Blackstone to totally exit the deal (see case study 4).

Given the need for a gradual exit, choosing an IPO may be a strategic choice. It is a way for the sponsor to partly monetize an investment while remaining a shareholder of the target company. This strategy makes sense if the LBO firm believes that more value can be created in the short to medium term. Remaining a shareholder is a way to capture some of this future value creation.

3.2.2 Sale

3.2.2.1 To a Company

The sale of a target company to another firm is a more common exit than an IPO. Buyers are usually direct or indirect competitors of the target company. They can also be clients or suppliers. This type of buyer is referred to as a strategic buyer. They want to expand their business and capture synergies between their activities and those of the target. In 2011, for instance, the financial software company Fidelity National Information Services (FIS) acquired its competitor Sungard from a group of seven

TABLE 3.1 Top 10 Private Equity Exits Announced in 2016[4]

Date	Company	Value ($bn)	Seller	Deal Type	Buyer
9 June 2016	Dong Energy A/S[5]	$15.0	Goldman Sachs Capital Partners	IPO	—
25 Feb. 2016	Sharp Corporation (66.06%)	$8.0	Japan Industrial Solutions	Strategic	Foxconn
7 Sept. 2016	Formula One World Championship Ltd	$7.9	CVC	Strategic	Liberty Media
5 May 2016	MultiPlan, Inc.	$7.5	Partners Group, Starr Investment Holdings	Secondary	Hellman & Friedman, GIC and Leonard Green & Partners
5 Sept. 2016	Quironsalud	$6.4	CVC	Strategic	Fresenius
25 May 2016	US Foods Holding Corp.	$5.1	KKR, Clayton Dubilier & Rice	IPO	—
12 June 2016	Blue Coat Systems	$4.7	Bain Capital	Strategic	Symantec
23 Sept. 2016	Nets A/S	$4.5	Advent International Corp. Bain Capital, ATP Private Equity Partners	IPO	—
28 June 2016	Change Healthcare	$4.0	Blackstone, Hellman & Friedman	Strategic	McKesson
7 Aug. 2016	Mattress Firm	$3.9	JW Childs Associates[6]	Strategic	Steinhoff

Source: adapted from EY.

private equity firms that had jointly bought out Sungard in 2005 in what was, at that time, the second largest LBO in history after RJR Nabisco.[7]

Private equity firms can also decide to split up the various operations of a company and sell them separately to various buyers. KKR pursued this strategy for the iconic

---

[4]In the table, "Strategic" means a sale to a company while "Secondary" refers to a sale to another LBO firm.

[5]Now known as Ørsted.

[6]Rebranded to Prospect Hill Growth Partners in 2019.

[7]The seven private equity firms were Bain Capital, Blackstone, Goldman Sachs Capital Partners, KKR, Providence Equity Partners, Silver Lake, and TPG Capital.

RJR Nabisco deal. Nabisco's UK operations were sold to French company BSN (now Danone), its line of Chinese canned food was sold to Yeo Hip Seng (a Singaporean drink company), and Del Monte Foods was sold to a consortium of private equity firms and Japanese soy sauce producer Kikkoman.

From the point of view of financial theory, the fact that a target firm is acquired by an LBO firm before it is ultimately sold off to a natural acquirer (i.e. a competitor) speaks to the advantages of private versus public ownership. Unlike public companies, private firms do not have to publish quarterly results. Their shareholders can focus on long-term value creation and make drastic decisions even if it means less profit in the short term. Private equity firms fill a gap. They can buy companies that need total reorganization, transform them radically and sell them to more traditional buyers.

3.2.2.2   To Another Private Equity Firm

The sale of the target company to another private equity firm (or *financial* buyer) is also a potential exit route. It means that after a first LBO, the target company will go through a second buyout with another sponsor. This second transaction is called secondary LBO. In the early days of private equity, an exit of this type was associated with a failed buyout. It gave the impression that the first private equity firm had not been able to manage it well enough to attract interest on public markets or from a strategic buyer. Today, a sale to another LBO firm has become an extremely common exit option. It is no longer associated with any negative connotation. There are so many private equity firms with so much capital to deploy that secondary (or tertiary...) LBOs have become an exit option like others.

Private equity firms have deep pockets but are also reliable counterparties. Unlike other potential acquirers, they buy companies regularly and know how to analyze a target, negotiate a deal, and close a transaction. Given the high degree of leverage that LBO firms rely on, a market environment with low interest rates and attractive lending terms tends to put private equity firms in pole position among potential buyers. They can pay multiples that strategic investors may find difficult to match.

Compared with traditional buyers, private equity firms do not face the same pressure to create synergies between their existing business and the companies they acquire. Their only focus is to optimize the performance of the target. In that sense, making an investment decision is easier for them. Private equity firms are also usually less likely to be constrained by antitrust laws – unless they are very specialized – so they have more freedom than corporate buyers to position themselves for an acquisition.

Companies under an LBO represent attractive targets for other private equity firms. They have demonstrated that their business model is compatible with a leveraged buyout. Private equity firms can also assume that the management team is used to working with a demanding shareholder. In addition, after a successful LBO, these managers are generally open to a secondary LBO. They know that they will have more freedom under a private equity firm than with a strategic buyer. They also know that they are likely to remain shareholders of the company, which can be extremely lucrative.

Some companies have famously passed from one private equity firm to another. In the United States, healthcare service firm MultiPlan Inc. is a well-known example, having undergone four LBOs since 2006. Carlyle and Welsh, Carson, Anderson & Stowe (WCAS) acquired the company in 2006 and tripled their money when they sold it to BC Partners and Silver Lake in 2010. In 2014, MultiPlan was sold to Swiss private equity firm Partners Group and Starr Insurance Group for an enterprise value of $4.4 billion. Two years later, the company was sold again to a consortium of Hellman & Friedman, GIC, and Leonard Green & Partners for $7.5 bilion (see Table 3.1).

In Europe, French company Picard Surgelés, a firm specialized in the manufacturing and distribution of frozen products, is probably the most iconic example of a company going from one LBO to the next. Bought from the Carrefour group (the French equivalent of Walmart) by Candover in 2001, the company was then sold in 2004 to BC Partners, which subsquently sold it to Lion Capital in 2010. A partial exit to a strategic buyer was arranged in 2015, when Swiss company Aryzta, an industrial baker also specialized in the production of frozen products, acquired 49% of Picard Surgelés. Aryzta has since then sold most of its stake but Lion Capital still remains the majority shareholder.

3.2.3 Dividend Recapitalization

Dividend recapitalization (or *dividend recap*) allows a private equity firm to monetize its investment without selling its stake in the target company. This technique consists of refinancing an LBO with more debt at the HoldCo level to pay out an extraordinary dividend to shareholder(s). In the absence of real exit options, a dividend recap is an alternative used by LBO firms to generate immediate return and boost their IRR.

3.2.3.1 How Does it Work?

If a company under an LBO performs well, the deal's total leverage (calculated as Net Debt/EBITDA) should decrease over time. This is the logical consequence of two factors:

1. the company's EBITDA increases year after year due to better operating performance, and
2. the nominal value of the company's net debt decreases after a few years if the acquisition debt is partly (or totally) amortizing.

As a result (and just to take a simple example), the leverage of an LBO could in theory go from five times EBITDA at the date of the acquisition to three times EBITDA a few years later. All things being equal, the transaction is at this point underleveraged. If there were indeed lenders willing to provide leverage of five times EBITDA when the target was acquired, there is no reason to believe that lenders would not be willing to accept the same leverage a few years later, especially if the target company has performed well.

This situation means that in our example, the private equity firm controlling the target can take additional debt at the Holdco level for an amount equal to two times EBITDA. This additional debt is injected through a refinancing of the company (i.e. existing lenders are repaid via a new facility). The difference between the former and the new debt is used to pay out a dividend to the LBO firm.

Dividend recaps are used in the following situations:

- Market conditions do not allow for a sale of the target company nor an IPO.
- The seller cannot find a buyer at an acceptable price.
- The target company is performing very well and is hitting performance benchmarks ahead of schedule. The private equity firm controlling the target company has, however, no intention of selling. It believes that there is still value to be created and chooses to proceed with a dividend recap to partly monetize the work that has already been done. If the company's EBITDA has improved dramatically over the first two years of ownership, why wait for a sale in another two to three years to generate a return?

3.2.3.2 Constraints

Lenders do not always welcome dividend recaps, as they are used to pay special dividends to shareholders rather than finance the target company. In other words, they involve lenders taking additional risk to generate a better IRR for an LBO firm. So dividend recaps can typically only happen when the target company has performed very well. They also generally occur when markets are buoyant and financing conditions extremely favorable. It comes as no surprise that 2007 was a record year for dividend recaps. After a slowdown between 2008 and 2012, they have come back into fashion as markets have improved. Some observers see dividend recaps as a sign that markets are overheating.

In some countries, dividend recaps may hit legal barriers. It is a technique that is sometimes perceived as going against a company's own corporate interests, aimed only at paying a special dividend to shareholders. As a consequence, some countries have implemented restrictions on dividend recaps. In the European Union (EU), Article 30 of the Alternative Investment Fund Managers Directive (AIFMD) imposes restrictions on distributions (which includes dividends and interest on shares), capital reductions, share redemptions, or share repurchases by EU-incorporated portfolio companies during the first two years following acquisition of control by a fund managed by an asset manager located in the EU or established outside the EU but actively marketing its fund to EU investors.

3.3 LBO AND PRIVATE EQUITY

It is not possible to fully analyze leveraged buyouts without mentioning some of the other financial arrangements they are often associated with. LBOs belong to a subset of finance known as private equity, i.e. the part of finance that deals with the valuation and ownership of unlisted companies. Although they form a large proportion of private equity transactions, LBOs are not the only financial structures that involve a change of ownership among private companies.

The private equity world revolves around three techniques: (i) venture capital, (ii) growth capital, and (iii) LBOs. While these three forms of financing have some commonalities, it is important to point out the differences between them, if only to better understand the specificities of LBO structures.

3.3.1 Focus on Venture Capital and Growth Capital

3.3.1.1 Venture Capital

Venture capital is the activity of investing capital, generally as a minority shareholder, in early-stage and promising companies to give them the means of developing rapidly. The ultimate objective of the investors is to resell their stake at a profit after a few years.

Sequoia Capital's investment in Google is probably one of the most famous examples. The Silicon Valley-based firm acquired 10% of Google for $12.5 million in 1999. Five years later, in 2004, when Google was IPOed, Sequoia Capital received 23.9 million shares at a price of $85, the equivalent of more than $2 billion, or more than 162 times their initial investment.

Venture capital allows entrepreneurs to finance the development of their company by selling part of their equity to an external investor. For early-stage firms with no or limited profits and therefore no access to bank loans or debt capital markets, an equity injection from a new investor is often the only way to fund new investments. Venture capitalists take on the risk of financing these early-stage companies because they hope the firm will be able to grow thanks to this investment. This growth should improve the valuation of the company and consequently allow venture capitalists to sell their stake at a profit to another investor.

Given the high level of risk associated with investing in an early-stage company with a limited track record, venture capitalists tend to spread their investments. They know that for one clever find – a Google – there will be numerous less successful ventures. Having said that, top venture capital firms usually provide more than funds to the companies they invest in. They offer marketing advice, technical expertise, and access to a network of professionals. Investing in early-stage companies is not a lottery. Some firms have an impressive track record. Besides its investment in Google, Sequoia Capital has also, for instance, funded companies such as Apple, Yahoo, Cisco, Electronic Arts, YouTube, PayPal, LinkedIn, and WhatsApp.

Another well-known player in the field, Kleiner Perkins, has funded companies like Amazon, AOL, Compaq, Google, Airbnb, Spotify, and Uber. Other successful venture capital firms include Benchmark (with investments in Dropbox, Snapchat, and Instagram), Greylock Partners (Airbnb, Facebook, LinkedIn, Dropbox), and Accel (Facebook, Dropbox, Spotify).

3.3.1.2 Venture Capital Firms

The way large venture capital firms operate is similar to LBO firms.[8] They set up funds in which they act as general partners and raise money from various investors acting as limited partners. Each fund has a precise scope and is established for a predetermined number of years. The role of the venture capital firm is to identify the companies that the fund will invest in, negotiate the acquisitions, close the transactions, and organize the exits. Exactly like their LBO counterparts, GPs in venture capital perceive (i) management fees based on the amounts committed or invested by LPs and (ii) carried interest if they deliver to their LPs an IRR above a certain hurdle.

3.3.1.3 Several Rounds

Successful start-ups may need several rounds of equity investments before generating sustainable profits. Just as money invested by founders may not be enough to develop the company, the investment made by an early-stage venture capital firm may not be sufficient to cover the needs of the start-up for a long period of time. In this case, the company may raise additional equity, sometimes through several rounds. Nowadays, in the highly codified world of venture capital, each equity raising round has a specific name and a specific purpose.

The main differences between these successive equity raising rounds are:

- the maturity levels of the companies they are meant to fund
- the purpose of raising capital
- the type of investors involved in the equity round.

Funding rounds begin with a *seed capital* phase, followed with an A, B, and C funding round.

The *seed round* provides the company with the funds needed to start the business, develop a prototype, and possibly hire the first employees, etc. It is often a very informal round and the source of capital may include funds from the founders, friends and family money, or investments by angel investors (wealthy individuals who invest in start-up companies). Valuations at this round are subjective and strongly tied to the background of the founders, the sector, and estimated capital needs. Equity raised at this stage is usually limited to avoid diluting the founders.

Series A is the first institutional round. Valuations are based on the progress made by the company since its seed round. At this stage, the company's business model is usually more precisely defined than during the previous round. Capital raised during this phase is used to optimize the product and possibly hire additional talent. Amounts raised during series A rounds can amount to several million US dollars.

---

[8]See Chapter 2, section 2.2.1.

Series B is usually much larger financing than previous rounds. Companies that reach this stage have generally already found their niche. They have a clear business model, and their objective is to obtain funds necessary to build a fully operational business. Investors active in series A and B rounds are usually traditional venture capital firms such as Sequoia, Greylock, Accel, etc. (see section 3.3.1.1).

Series C round is meant to perfect a product and scale it up. This later stage financing is usually designed to bring the business to profitability. Funds raised during this round are also used to develop new products or services and, sometimes, finance acquisitions. Investors active in this round are typically different than those participating in previous rounds. They are usually referred to as growth capital firms rather than venture capital firms (see section 3.3.1.5 on growth capital).

3.3.1.4   History of Venture Capital

Investing in new and promising ventures is an activity that wealthy families have performed since well before the appearance of modern finance. Historians have found examples of venture capital-type transactions in Ancient Greece. Without going too far back, some authors describe the funding of Christopher Columbus's expedition in 1492 as one of the first modern venture capital deals in history. There are indeed all the ingredients of an exciting venture capital story: an entrepreneur (Christopher Columbus) with an innovative project (to reach India by a new route) is looking for money (to equip three ships) from people capable of providing funding (Isabella I of Castile and Ferdinand II of Aragon) and is ready to relinquish a part of his potential profits to his backers (9/10 in this case). There is even a contract documenting this agreement (the "Capitulations of Santa Fe").

Until the end of World War II, however, most of the players active in the field of venture capital were wealthy private individuals or families (although no one used the term "venture capital" at the time). In Florence during the Renaissance, for instance, bankers like the Medici or the Frescobaldi funded many trading businesses and ventures proposed by third parties. In the first half of the twentieth century, the Rockefeller and Vanderbilt families in the United States and the Wallenberg family in Sweden also participated in various entrepreneurial projects.

The origins of modern venture capital date back to the period after World War II. In 1946, the Frenchman Georges Doriot,[9] "the father of venture capitalism", established the first self-styled venture capital firm, American Research & Development Corporation (ARDC). The purpose of ARDC was to provide capital to entrepreneurial ventures developed by US soldiers returning from Europe. It was the first venture capital investor to operate like a true firm. ARDC raised money from a variety of sources, rather than one wealthy family or individual. It also had a portfolio approach, bundling all of its investments into a single fund. ARDC's most successful deal was

---

[9] Georges Doriot emigrated to the United States to pursue an MBA at Harvard Business School (HBS). He later became a professor at HBS before creating INSEAD in 1957 in Fontainebleau, France, with two of his former students, Claude Janssen and Olivier Giscard d'Estaing.

their investment in Digital Equipment Corporation (DEC) in 1957. In the 1960s, DEC became one of the largest computer companies in the United States, allowing ARDC to exit its investment through an IPO in 1966.

The development of venture capital as an asset class really emerged in the 1970s with the development of personal computers. The possibility of individual computer ownership meant that all businesses linked to this industry (video games, semiconductors, computer manufacturing, etc.) had the potential to scale up rapidly. Capital was automatically drawn to venture firms. Don Valentine created Sequoia Capital in 1972 in Menlo Park, California. The exact same year in the exact same city, Eugene Kleiner and Tom Perkins, two former Hewlett-Packard executives, founded Kleiner Perkins.

3.3.1.5 Growth Capital

Growth capital is another – less well known – subset of private equity, aimed primarily at financing profitable or at least cash-flow generating companies. These firms have typically passed the start-up phase and have usually found their niche or business model. Unlike venture capital, growth capital is not used to kick start a company. It is meant to fund a logical extension or an addition to an existing venture. These businesses are more mature than venture capital funded companies but do not generate sufficient cash flows to fund major expansions without additional equity.

Growth investments usually take the form of a minority interest. They can be structured as ordinary or preferred stock but generally do not grant controlling rights to investors. If structured as preferred stock, these investments give a preference right when it comes to dividend distributions. A right does not mean that the dividend payment is automatic but that the company must pay dividends on preferred shares (set at a pre-agreed level in deal documentation) before they pay dividends on common shares. Preferred stock is usually non-voting and ranks senior to ordinary shares in case of liquidation of the company. Additional structuring mechanisms usually allow the convertibility of preferred stock into common stock or give the company the right to call the preferred stock at a pre-agreed price.

Firms relying on growth capital are usually still founder-owned. They may have already raised equity from venture capital firms, but this is by no means a prerequisite for an investment. Some companies go through all the stages of capital raising (seed round, series A, series B, etc.) while some can grow their business without the support of venture capital money and raise additional equity only when they need to scale up their business.

Growth capital players typically start investing at the series C round, when companies need cash to fuel growth and achieve or consolidate profitability. Equity raising rounds after series C are less codified; the logical next step is typically either an IPO or sale to a strategic buyer. However, with the need of certain companies to achieve a rapid international scale to dominate a market, rounds after series C are becoming more common, especially in the technology sector. Facebook, for instance, took several rounds of additional private equity money after its series C round and before its IPO.

Table 3.2 shows Airbnb's funding rounds between its creation in 2009 and its *series F* round in March 2017. A wide range of investors backed the company during this period: angel investors (Ashton Kutcher, Jeff Bezos), venture capital firms (Andreessen Horowitz, Greylock, Sequoia, etc.), growth capital firms (Capital G, TCV, TPG Growth, etc.), and diversified holding companies (Groupe Arnault[10]). Airbnb also raised debt in June 2016 after settling its business model.

TABLE 3.2 Airbnb Funding Rounds, from Seed Money to Growth Capital (2009–2017)

Date	Transaction Name	Amount Raised (USD)	Number of Investors	Selected Investors	Pre-money Valuation (USD)
Jan. 2009	Seed round	20k	1	Y Combinator	—
Apr. 2009	Seed round	600k	2	Sequoia Capital, Y Ventures	—
Nov. 2010	Series A	7.2m	9	Ashton Kutcher, General Catalyst, Greylock Partners, Y Ventures, Sequoia Capital	—
July 2011	Series B	112m	9	Andreessen Horowitz, Ashton Kutcher, Jeff Bezos, Sequoia Capital	1.2bn
Oct. 2013	Series C	200m	5	Ashton Kutcher, Founders Fund, Sequoia Capital	2.3bn
Apr. 2014	Series D	475m	7	Sequoia Capital, Andreessen Horowitz, TPG Growth, Sequoia Capital	9.5bn
June 2015	Series E-1	1.5bn	15	Fidelity Investments, General Atlantic, Groupe Arnault, Kleiner Perkins, Hillhouse Capital Group, Sequoia Capital	24bn
Nov. 2015	Series E-2	100m	1	FirstMark Capital	24.5bn
June 2016	Debt Financing	1bn	4	Bank of America, Citigroup, JP Morgan, Morgan Stanley,	NA
Sept. 2016	Series F	555.5m	6	Capital G, TCV	29.4bn
Mar. 2017	Series F	447.8m	5	Capital G, TCV	30bn

Source: Craft, Crunchbase.

---

[10]Groupe Arnault is the personal holding company of Bernard Arnaud, the founder of LVMH.

The growth capital industry is organized exactly like venture capital. Firms specialized in the sector structure funds in which external investors act as limited partners. They also usually provide more than just financial support. They offer advice, experience, and potentially technical expertise. They can also help management teams and founders get ready for an IPO. IVP, for instance, one of the largest growth capital firms in the United States, has IPOed roughly 25% of the companies they have invested in. Other growth capital firms include Capital G, Alphabet's growth equity investment fund, and TCV, known for (i) making its first investment in Netflix in 1999, when the company was still a DVD-by-mail operation, and (ii) recapitalizing the company after the dot-com bubble burst (and before it entirely switched its business model to streaming).

3.3.1.6 Growth Capital vs. Venture Capital

The line between late venture capital and early growth capital is not always as clear as detailed here. Some investors can be active in both segments and venture capital firms present at early-stage investments generally reinvest in the following rounds if they believe that the company they are backing is on the right track. Sequoia Capital backed Airbnb from seed round to series E (see Table 3.2). Nonetheless, from an investor's perspective, the main difference is that growth capital firms focus on investing in companies that are profitable (or approaching profitability) whereas venture capitalists look at early stage companies. Table 3.3 summarizes the main differences between the two approaches.

TABLE 3.3 Growth Capital vs. Venture Capital

	Venture Capital	**Growth Capital**
Investment target	Early stage start-up companies	Late stage start-up (or mature) companies
Ownership of the target company at the time of investment	Founder(s) owned	Founder(s) owned. With or without prior institutional investment
Nature of investment	Minority non-control interest	Minority non-control interest
Investment amount	Hundreds of thousands of dollars to several million dollars	Generally above ten million dollars (and up to several hundred million)
Leverage of the investor's investment	No	No
Sizing of the investment amount	Based on product development costs	Based on a plan to achieve or strengthen profitability
Investment thesis	Disruptive innovation	Ability to scale up
Target's cash flow	Generally negative	Positive (or almost)

(continued)

TABLE 3.3   (*continued*)

	Venture Capital	Growth Capital
Risk level	Extremely high	Significant
Sectors	Mainly technology and healthcare	Wide range of sectors
Exit	Sale to a strategic, another financial investor, or IPO	Sale to a strategic, another financial investor, or IPO
Example of active players	Accel, Andreessen Horowitz, Benchmark, Founders Fund, Greylock Partners, Kleiner Perkins, Sequoia Capital	General Atlantic, IVP, JMI Equity, Kleiner Perkins, Summit Partners, TCV, TPG Growth

3.3.2   LBO Compared with Venture Capital and Growth Capital

Although LBOs are part of the same private equity family as venture capital and growth capital, they are probably more a distant cousin than an older brother. Compared to venture and growth capital, LBOs have several distinctive characteristics:

- LBOs are an acquisition finance technique and not a financing method. While venture capital and growth capital provide companies with resources to finance their expansion, an LBO involves the acquisition of an equity stake. In other words, venture capital and growth capital finance company development, whereas LBOs finance acquisitions.
- LBOs are a recent technique. They sprung up in the late 1970s, whereas venture capital and growth capital are very old financial instruments. Though formalized only recently, both concepts are long-standing. Wealthy individuals investing in other people's businesses to help them grow in return for a share of the profits, existed in ancient times and during the Middle Ages.
- LBOs involve a change in ownership of the target company. While venture or growth capitalists usually take minority stakes alongside existing investors, LBO firms tend to go for full control of the company – albeit this control is sometimes exercised jointly with a co-investor.
- In an LBO, the equity investment in the target company is partly financed by debt. This leverage is supposed to boost the investors' returns. In venture or growth capital, the acquisition of shareholding interests by funds or angel investors is financed with equity only. The return on investment for venture capital or growth investors is only linked to the capacity of the underlying business to generate profits. It does not benefit from financial leverage.
- While venture and growth capital provide funds to relatively young companies, LBOs favor target companies operating in mature markets and with a strong track record. Strong and steady cash flows are needed to convince lenders to provide an acquisition facility.

- An LBO can involve a change of management, notably in case of an MBI or a build-up. Venture and growth capitalists do not want to change the management teams of the companies they invest in.
- Finally, an LBO investor buys a company to control it and implement the business plan they have designed. On the other hand, a venture or growth capitalist generally cannot (and does not want to) impose their own views: they are investing in the company because they believe in the business plan proposed by the management team.

Case Study 4: Hilton Hotels LBO, the Most Profitable Private Equity Deal Ever

When he bought The Mobley hotel in Cisco, Texas, in 1919 for $40,000, Conrad Hilton could have not imagined that his small venture would someday grow into one of the biggest hotel chains in the world. Among bankers and financiers, though, Hilton Hotels is more than a successful hotel brand; it is an iconic private equity deal. After a first IPO in 1970, the company was taken over by Blackstone in 2007, and six years later became the most profitable deal in LBO history.

Hilton Hotels

Hilton Hotels was established in 1948. Its purpose was to unite in one legal entity all the various hotels bought by Conrad Hilton since the acquisition of the Mobley hotel. In 1964, after 16 years of remarkable growth in the United States and abroad, the decision was made to spin off Hilton's international business and focus on the US market. In 1971, the firm consolidated its position in its home market and acquired International Leisure Company, a Las Vegas-based hotel chain whose chief assets were the Flamingo and the International casinos. The transaction was financed via an IPO in 1970.

Although Hilton Hotels became the first casino operator listed on the New York Stock Exchange, from a financial perspective it was conservatively run. Conrad Hilton and his son Bannon, who took over the group in the 1970s, were both reluctant to rely on debt. They had been scarred by the Great Depression and shied away from financial audacity.

Bannon Hilton was replaced in 1996 by Stephen Bollenbach, a former chief financial officer at The Walt Disney Company. The new CEO led Hilton Hotels on a new journey, marked by a series of large acquisitions. The advent of low interest rates and friendly financing conditions in the late 1990s enabled the group

(continued)

(continued)

to acquire brands including Embassy Suites, Doubletree, Hampton Inn, Homewood Suites, Bally's, and Caesars. In 2005, Hilton Hotels bought back its former international business for $5.7 billion and sold its casinos to Harrah's Entertainment, a company eventually acquired via LBO by Apollo and TPG Capital in October 2006.

Hilton outgrew all its main competitors between 1996 and 2007, adding more than 350,000 rooms to its portfolio. The company went from being the seventh to the fourth largest hotel group worldwide by room numbers. This impressive growth was accompanied by a substantial improvement in EBITDA. Hilton outperformed all its peers over the period, demonstrating that revenue growth can be combined with increasing profitability. However, this growth was mainly financed by debt and in December 2005, after the acquisition of its international business, Hilton's debt fell into junk bond territory, its rating cut by Moody's from Baa3 to Ba2.

LBO Frenzy

The market crash of the early 2000s, after the collapse of the tech bubble, prompted the Federal Reserve to cut interest rates and keep them low for an extended period. This decision led to a stretch of extremely cheap money, at least compared to previous years. Businesses relying on financial leverage benefited logically from this new monetary policy. Private equity firms notably had more fire power to acquire companies. They started looking at targets that once seemed out of reach. In July 2006, KKR, Bain and Merrill Lynch took over the Hospital Corporation of America for $32.7 billion, overtaking the previous record-breaking deal, KKR's $31.1 billion buyout of RJR Nabisco in 1989. In the space of just over a year, this new record was eclipsed twice, first by Blackstone's buyout of Equity Office Properties (EOP) ($38.9 billion) and then by a KKR-led buyout of Energy Future Holdings ($44.4 billion).

The list of the largest LBOs in history (Table 3.4) shows how buoyant the LBO market was at the time. In less than two years, from November 2005 to October 2007, 12 of the 15 largest LBOs in history were structured. The only other deals to make that list are (i) RJR Nabisco in 1988, and the acquisitions of (ii) Dell by Silver Lake and Michael Dell, and (iii) of Heinz by 3G Capital and Berkshire Hathaway, both in February 2013. The acquisition of Hilton Hotels by Blackstone in July 2007 was one of the very last jumbo deals of this frantic period.

TABLE 3.4 The 15 Largest LBOs in History

Company	Sponsor	Deal Value (in $bn)	Date
Energy Future Holdings (TXU)	KKR, TPG Capital, Goldman Sachs Capital Partners	44.4	Feb. 2007
EOP	Blackstone	38.9	Jan. 2007
Hospital Corporation of America Healthcare	Bain Capital, KKR & Merrill Lynch	32.7	July 2006
RJR Nabisco	KKR	31.1	Oct. 1988
First Data	KKR	29	Apr. 2007
Harrah's Entertainment[11]	Apollo, TPG Capital	31	Oct. 2006
Alltel	TPG Capital, Goldman Sachs Capital Partners	27	May 2007
Hilton Hotels	Blackstone	26	July 2007
Clear Channel	KKR, Bain Capital and Thomas H. Lee Partners	25.7	Oct. 2007
Alliance Boots	KKR	24.8	May 2007
Dell	Silver Lake Partners, Michael Dell	24.4	Feb. 2013
Heinz	3G Capital, Berkshire Hathaway	23	Feb. 2013
Archstone-Smith	Tishman Speyer, Lehman Brothers	22.2	Oct. 2007
Kinder Morgan	Carlyle, Goldman Sachs Capital Partners, Riverstone	22	Aug. 2006
Georgia Pacific	Koch Industries	21	Jan. 2006

(continued)

---

[11] The company was renamed Caesars Entertainment Corporation in 2010.

(*continued*)

Blackstone

Blackstone was founded in 1985 by two ex-Lehman Brothers bankers, Peter George Peterson, the former CEO, and Stephen Schwarzman, the former head of M&A. Established originally as an advisory boutique, Blackstone[12] had emerged by 2007 as the largest private equity firm in the world. It had at that time a total of $79 billion in assets under management (AUM), a figure significantly higher than its main competitors Carlyle ($59 billion), Bain Capital ($40 billion), KKR, or TPG ($30 billion each). Active in many segments of private equity, the firm had developed a particular expertise in the real estate sector through investments in amusement parks, hospitality companies, and Real Estate Investment Trusts (REIT) – a type of company that owns and operates income-producing real estate.

The year 2007 was an important one for Blackstone, Hilton LBO aside. The firm closed in January what was at the time the largest LBO in history. It acquired EOP, a company that managed rental buildings, for close to $39 billion. A few months later, in June, Blackstone launched its own IPO, a first among private equity companies. The firm listed a 12.3% stake that valued Blackstone at $39 billion. The two founding partners, each with roughly 20% each in the company, were instantly ranked by Forbes among the richest people in the United States.

Blackstone and its Interest in Hilton

While all of this was happening in the background, Blackstone was sketching the plans for a takeover of Hilton Hotels, which when combined with its existing hotel portfolio would end up making it the operator of the largest number of hotel rooms in the world. Blackstone had already established a reputation for applying operational changes and investing capital in order to turn around underperforming businesses in the hospitality industry. In the four years leading up to the Hilton deal, Blackstone had taken over Extended Stay America, Prime Hospitality, Boca Resorts, Wyndham Hotels & Resorts, La Quinta Inns & Suites, and the hotel REIT MeriStar Hospitality.

Blackstone was considered a top player in the real estate sector. The firm had launched eight funds focused on real estate since 1994, including two specifically dedicated to its international operations. During a two-year period between 2006 and 2007, Blackstone took advantage of the low interest rate environment and the strong appetite of investors for the asset class to raise three new major real estate funds – one for Europe denominated in euros in 2006, and two in US dollars:

---

[12]The name Blackstone is derived from the names of the two founders. Schwarz means black in German while Peter comes from the Greek word petra, which can be translated as stone in English.

Blackstone Real Estate Partners V ($10.9 billion) and Blackstone Real Estate Partners VI ($5.25 billion). At the time, only Morgan Stanley and Lone Star were playing in the same league (Table 3.5).

TABLE 3.5   Top Five Real Estate Funds Raised During the 2005–2008 Period

Asset Manager	Fund	Vintage	Fund Size
Lone Star Funds	Lone Star Fund VI	2008	$7.5bn
Blackstone	Blackstone Real Estate Partners VI	2007	$10.9bn
Morgan Stanley	Morgan Stanley Real Estate Fund VI Intl.	2007	$8bn
Blackstone	Blackstone Real Estate Partners V	2006	$5.2bn
Lone Star Funds	Lone Star Fund V	2005	$5bn

Source: Blackstone, Loan Star Funds and Ludovic Phalippou.

Blackstone started courting Hilton in August 2006 but took more than a year to strike a deal. The deal finally offered a healthy 40% premium at $46.50 per share, compared with a market value of $33. Despite Hilton's healthy recent performance, it was an offer the company's board found hard to refuse. Shareholders also knew that Hilton would struggle to continue growing at the same pace. The group's ambitious expansion plans needed a substantial cash infusion, and Blackstone came in with the necessary financial muscle.

An Aggressive Capital Structure

Blackstone ended up paying $26.5 billion for the company. The deal, though large in its own right, was not outrageous for the time. Four bigger LBOs had already been announced in the first six months of 2007: TXU, EOPs, First Data, and Alltel. As shown in Table 3.6, valuation and debt levels were nonetheless clearly on the high side. Hilton's EBITDA amounted to $1.68 billion at the time of acquisition. With a total debt of $20.4 billion, the deal's leverage represented a multiple of more than 12 times EBITDA.

TABLE 3.6   Hilton Hotels LBO Capital Structure

	Amount	Percentage	EBITDA Multiple
Equity	$5.7	21.5%	—
Term Loan B	$14	53%	—
Senior Unsecured Notes	$6.8	25.5%	—
Total Debt	$20.8	78.5%	12.4
Total sources of funds	**$26.5**	**100%**	**15.8**

Source: adapted from Dawoon Chung and Ludovic Phalippou.

(continued)

(*continued*)

Equity for the deal came through Blackstone's two most recent US funds, Blackstone Real Estate Partners V and Blackstone Real Estate Partners VI. The debt was raised from various banks, hedge funds, and real estate debt investors. At 12.4 times EBITDA, the debt level was particularly high, though several recent deals had also closed with double-digit net debt-to-EBITDA ratios. The debt was split into two tranches: (i) a senior loan of $14 billion at a margin of 2.75%, and (ii) senior unsecured notes for $6.8 billion at a margin of 4.91%.[13] Jonathan Gray, Global Head of Real Estate at Blackstone and the driving force behind the deal, managed to secure the whole debt package at cov-lite,[14] a typical feature of LBOs during this period.

The Financial Crisis

The 2008 financial crisis was extremely bad news for the hospitality industry. Companies and households cut their travel budgets and hotel revenues dried up globally. Hilton – which was extremely leveraged – was particularly hit. Its earnings dropped sharply, but thanks to the cov-lite structure, lenders were not able to call their debt or take control of the company. This gave Hilton the much-needed flexibility to continue pushing forward with its expansion strategy.

In 2009, Blackstone wrote down the value of its equity in the business by 70%. The following year, lenders agreed to restructure the debt and take a loss to ease the pressure on Hilton. Total outstanding debt was reduced from $20 billion to $16 billion. In the meantime, Blackstone pumped in another $819 million to buy back $1.8 billion of junior debt at a 54% discount.

Blackstone's decision to reinvest in the business was driven by the need to restructure the company's debt and allow some lenders to exit the transaction. It was also a show of confidence in the investment. At that time, Blackstone still needed to invest a substantial part of the $10.9 billion Blackstone Real Estate Partners VI fund (see Table 3.4). The decision seemed bold but was, after all, an investment in quality real estate at the very low point of the cycle.

Hilton's Strategy under Blackstone

Hilton had grown a lot since Stephen Bollenbach took over as CEO in 1996, but Blackstone thought it still looked more like a holding company with a collection of disparate assets than a true integrated global business. The firm believed that Hilton Hotels lacked a hard-driving organization and was too fragmented across various divisions.

---

[13]Despite being referred to as senior, senior unsecured notes are a form of junior debt. See Chapter 2, section 2.3.3.3 on high-yield bonds, if needed.

[14]See Chapter 2, section 2.3.2.4, for more information on cov-lite structures. Cov-lite structures are typical of a bull market in which liquidity is abundant and many lenders chase the same opportunities.

One of Blackstone's first moves after the takeover was to replace Bollenbach with a new CEO, Christopher Nassetta. Nassetta was the former CEO of Host Hotels & Resorts, a company that doubled its size in the space of a decade under his management. With the backing of Blackstone – and despite the crisis – Nassetta made a series of decisions that would transform Hilton. He reset the company culture to a more goal-oriented approach and moved Hilton's headquarters out of Beverly Hills, California, to Mclean, Virginia. This move allowed Hilton to operate from a cheaper and better connected hub, enabling the group to operate more efficiently.

With Blackstone's blessing, Nassetta implemented a strategy with four pillars:

1. *A capital light model*: Although the company continued to grow, it pulled back on debt-fueled acquisitions. Post-buyout, 99% of the growth in hotel rooms came via franchising. This strategy allowed Hilton to grow its portfolio by 36% with little or no increase in debt. It also allowed the group to expand rapidly into emerging markets without a major capital injection.
2. *Internationalization*: In the wake of the buy-back of Hilton International (made before the LBO), the company continued to invest massively outside the United States. In China, for instance, the group went from 6 to 171 hotels between 2007 and 2013.
3. *Branding*: Nassetta re-energized Hilton's iconic brand and better positioned each of the group's subsidiaries. The company focused particularly on the expansion of its two luxury brands, Conrad and Waldorf Astoria, into key international markets.
4. *Technology*: By 2013, customers could check into the hotels using phones, tablets, or computers, and Hilton put an extensive loyalty program in place that allowed customers to take advantage of all Hilton brands under one loyalty umbrella.

Nassetta describes his first years at Hilton as the toughest period of his life. With the support of Stephen Schwarzman and Jonathan Gray he was nonetheless able to transform the sprawling giant. Within a few years, Hilton became a leaner company with stronger brands and a larger non-US client base.

Exit Strategies

By 2013, financial markets had recovered from the 2008 crisis. After six years of hard work it seemed like the right timing for Blackstone to monetize its investment. The firm considered three strategies for its exit: (i) a trade sale to a competitor, (ii) putting Hilton up for a secondary buyout, or (iii) going for an IPO. Blackstone disregarded the first two solutions. Although markets were in better shape than in 2008, Gray and Nassetta believed that a strategic buyer would not pay enough of a premium for synergies. In parallel, Hilton's large debt, at a time when LBO leverage

(continued)

(continued)

was back to more reasonable levels, made the company a relatively unattractive option for a secondary buyout.

In light of these factors, an IPO looked like the right exit path. The S&P 500 was back at its October 2007 levels and there had been substantial recent IPO activity, with 112 new listings in the first three quarters of 2013. Twenty-two of those IPOs were companies operating in the real estate sector. Blackstone itself had raised $565 million through an IPO of Extended Stay America. The market was bullish again and the private equity firm had faith in Hilton's capacity to attract investors.

In December 2013, Hilton went public again. The company raised $2.34 billion for 11.8% of its capital, giving Hilton Hotels an equity valuation of $19.7 billion. Adding the $14 billion of debt the company still had at that time, Hilton Hotels had an enterprise value of $33.7 billion (compared with an enterprise value of $26 billion in 2007). More impressively, Blackstone only invested $5.6 billion of equity in buying Hilton out, making this the most profitable LBO in history.

The IPO was only the first step of Blackstone's exit. It continuously sold shares through 2014 and cut its stake to less than 50% in 2015. It then sold 25% of Hilton to China's HNA Group for $6.5 billion in October 2016, implying an equity value of $26 billion (4.6 times Blackstone's initial investment!) and leaving HNA as Hilton's largest shareholder. Blackstone sold its final 5.8% stake in Hilton in May 2018, ending an 11-year investment.

Epilogue

Hilton's success in fighting back from the lows of a global financial crisis into a booming, profitable world leader is a dream scenario for private equity specialists. The firm could not have achieved such impressive returns without making ample use of the cov-lite leverage terms available at the time and opportunistically buying back debt. But Blackstone maintains that it never lost faith in the investment... Whatever the case, some hard facts cannot be changed. Hilton is an impressive investment story. It is safe to say that the deal has catapulted Jonathan Gray and Christopher Nassetta into LBO legends.

Summary

LBOs: What Have We Learnt?

- A leveraged buyout or LBO is a financing technique that allows an investor to buy a target company without having to commit a lot of capital. The acquisition is accomplished via an SPV, also called a holding company or HoldCo. This HoldCo is financed with equity (coming from the investor) and debt.

- The acquisition debt is repaid with the dividends paid by the target to the HoldCo. It is therefore important for the success of the LBO that the company taken over is able to distribute dividends. Leverage buyouts are only possible for mature companies generating steady and recurring cash flows.

- An LBO is also a tax structure. It creates a tax shield for the new owner because interest on the acquisition debt is deductible, while the dividends received by the HoldCo are tax-free. All in all, it means that from a tax perspective, the group of companies consisting of the HoldCo, plus the target, pays jointly less tax than the target would on a stand-alone basis.

- The success of an LBO also relies on the full commitment of the company's managers. These managers are directly interested in the success of the company, either because they are themselves the buyer of the target or because the buyer has awarded them with some of the company's shares. This gives them a strong incentive to improve the company's valuation.

- LBOs can be performed by individuals willing to buy out a company or by investment companies called LBO firms. These firms are specialized in acquiring companies via LBO. They raise funds from third-party investors (pension funds, insurance companies, etc.) to buy out companies, operate them for a few years, and divest them at a profit.

- This exit generally takes the form of a sale to a strategic buyer, another LBO firm, or an IPO. The profit on the exit (if any) is shared between the LBO firm and its third-party investors.

- The debt necessary for the acquisition of a target company can be provided by banks or lenders specialized in leveraged loans. The debt is sometimes divided in several tranches. In this case, the senior debt is repaid before the junior debt but bears a lower interest rate. Debt instruments used to finance leveraged buyouts are generally non-investment grade.

PART II

PROJECT FINANCE

Project finance is a financing technique designed for large infrastructure and energy projects. Project finance is probably the least controversial of all the structures analysed in this book. Its objective is to allow the construction of projects that require significant upfront costs and have long-term economic lives. Such projects, like hospitals, roads, or energy plants, mostly belong to the social or economic infrastructure sectors, which provide basic services that are beneficial to a large number of people. For the critics of structured finance, LBOs are an easier target than project finance.

Experts believe that the first project finance transaction was structured in England towards the end of the thirteenth century. In 1299, King Edward I and his bankers, the Florentine family Frescobaldi, signed an agreement to finance mining interests in Devonshire. The Frescobaldi were at that time one of the richest and most powerful families in Europe. They owned banks across the whole continent and had stakes in many businesses. They were also very close to many royal families, to whom they lent large amounts of money to finance wars and business ventures.

Without any money to fund the development of newly discovered silver mines, Edward I agreed with the Frescobaldis to let them finance the construction of the whole mining infrastructure. In exchange, they would receive all the income derived from the operation of the project for one year. The Italians, however, had no recourse to the Crown if their profits turned out to be lower than the investments made. At the end of this one-year period, the infrastructure had to be handed over to the Kingdom of England, which could then operate it for its own benefit.

Despite this medieval example, project finance remained a rarely used technique for a very long time. In economies largely dominated by agriculture, the construction of infrastructure (and the need for project finance) was extremely limited. Things started to change after the first Industrial Revolution. The Suez Canal and the Eiffel Tower, for instance, two of the most iconic projects of the nineteenth century, were financed via a project finance structure.

CHAPTER 4

The ABC of Project Finance

4.1 DEFINITION

4.1.1 The Purpose of Project Finance

The purpose of project finance is to finance the construction and operation of large-scale public or private infrastructure projects. The cases mentioned in the Introduction to Part II (silver mines, the Eiffel Tower, the Suez Canal) all fall into this category. The construction of Disneyland Paris, one of the case studies analyzed later in the book (case study 6), is also a prime example of giant infrastructure financed via a project finance structure.

Project finance is used worldwide to finance all types of infrastructure assets: highways, railways, ports, airports, wind or solar farms, wastewater treatment plants, desalination plants, hospitals, schools, stadiums, fiber networks, telecom towers, etc. These assets all have in common:

- a high construction cost
- a relatively long construction period
- a project lifetime spanning over several decades.

4.1.2 Financing the Construction of Infrastructure with Non-recourse Debt

Project finance is not only defined by the type of assets it finances, it is also characterized by a set of rules common to all project finance structures. A more detailed definition of project finance could therefore be: "... the financing of an infrastructure project through non-recourse debt granted to an SPV, established by one or several corporate or financial shareholders for the sole purpose of constructing and operating this infrastructure. Debt and equity used to finance the project are paid back from the cash flow generated by the project only".

A simplified project finance structure is represented in Figure 4.1. In this example, a SPV (or project company) is established by a shareholder (or *sponsor*) for the sole purpose of building a highway commissioned by a government. The SPV is financed by a mix of debt and equity and uses these funds to fund the construction of the highway. Once the asset is fully built, the project starts generating cash flow. This cash flow (which is, in this example, the sum of the toll payments and potential subsidies) is used to pay for the operation and maintenance of the highway and to repay the debt. If the SPV has enough cash after these payments, dividends are distributed to the sponsor.

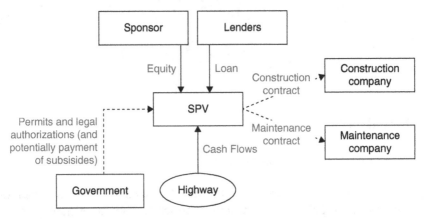

FIGURE 4.1   Simplified Diagram of a Project Finance Structure

To elaborate on this simple structure and definition:

1. The SPV is established by a shareholder (the *sponsor*) that has an economic interest in the development of the project. In our example, for instance, the sponsor could be a major construction company. There are sometimes several sponsors jointly backing the same project. Sponsors can also be investment companies specialized in infrastructure. In this case, the sponsor is referred to as a *financial* sponsor – as opposed to an *industrial* sponsor when the company behind the project is an industrial company. Financial and industrial sponsors sometimes team up to develop or own infrastructures together.

2. The SPV is established for the sole purpose of the project. It can generally not perform the construction and operation of the project on its own. These activities are outsourced to other companies, including sometimes the sponsors themselves, or specialized subsidiaries of the sponsors. In Figure 4.1, for example, the sponsor that has invested in the project could also be directly or indirectly responsible for the construction and maintenance of the highway.

3. Project finance is a bespoke financial technique. Each transaction is analyzed and structured separately. Lenders finance the SPV and the SPV only. They have no legal or financial recourse to the shareholders of the project company.

Project debt is said to be *non-recourse*. If, in our example, the highway does not generate enough cash flow to repay the debt, lenders cannot go after the construction company. Lenders forego the right to any and all claims on the other assets of the sponsors. In return, they generally obtain a pledge on the shares of the SPV and (if legally possible) a mortgage on the infrastructure itself.

4. If the lenders have no recourse to the sponsors, this implies that the loan has to be repaid solely through the cash flow generated by the project. Debt sizing is strictly based on the potential revenues of the SPV. An extremely detailed analysis of the project has to be carried out by the lenders to ensure that the infrastructure can be built and will generate sufficient cash flow.

5. As a result of the absence of recourse to the sponsors, contractors (suppliers, entities in charge of the construction or the operation, etc.) have strict contractual obligations towards the SPV. These obligations generally include financial guarantees so that the SPV can have a financial recourse to them in case it is proven that any issue with the project (delay in construction, underperformance, etc.) is directly attributable to a contractor not meeting its obligations.

6. Project finance can broadly be divided into three phases:

   – A first phase, called the *development phase,* during which the sponsors work to obtain all the permits and necessary legal, administrative, and regulatory authorizations to build the project. Costs associated with this phase are usually financed by equity only.

   – A second phase, called the *construction phase,* during which the non-recourse financing is structured. Loans as well as the remainder of the equity are drawn to pay for the construction of the infrastructure.

   – A third phase, called the *operational phase,* during which the SPV can start selling the output of the goods or services produced by the project. Cash flow generated by the project is used to (i) pay for the operation and maintenance (O&M) costs, (ii) repay the debt, and (iii) distribute dividends.

4.2   WHY CHOOSE A PROJECT FINANCE STRUCTURE

4.2.1   Two Different Options to Finance Infrastructure Assets

Infrastructure projects are not all financed through project finance structures. A sponsor developing a project always has to choose between two main financing options:

   – it can either raise debt at corporate level to develop the project directly on its balance sheet (corporate financing), or
   – it can fund the project via a special purpose vehicle whose role is to raise funds to finance the construction of the infrastructure (project financing).

In the first option (corporate financing), banks lend directly to the sponsor so that the sponsor can develop and construct the project. The repayment of the loan is linked to the ability of the sponsor to generate cash flow. Lenders are in the same position as the other creditors to the sponsor. Their loan is repaid as long as the sponsor is solvent. Repayment of the loan is due even if the project taken independently is a financial failure. Inversely, if the project is successful and the sponsor goes bankrupt anyway as a result of its other activities, the lenders who signed on to fund the successful project are not in any preferred position. They face the turmoil of the sponsor's bankruptcy like any other creditor.

In the second option (project financing), the repayment of the debt raised by the SPV is solely based on the cash flow generated by the project. Lenders have no recourse to the sponsor's other assets. Lenders face a project risk. The repayment of their loan is not impacted by the profitability of the other businesses of the sponsor. If the project is a failure, their loan will not be repaid even if the sponsor is hugely profitable thanks to its other activities.

4.2.2 Advantages of the Project Finance Option

4.2.2.1 Isolating Risks

For a sponsor, the use of a project finance structure with an intermediary SPV makes it possible to transfer all legal and financial risks to another entity. The SPV is established under the form of a limited liability company so that the shareholder's liability is limited to its capital contribution. In other words, if the project fails, the sponsor is not required to repay the debt raised by the SPV. The SPV is said to be *bankruptcy remote*, meaning that a bankruptcy of the SPV has little impact on the sponsor. The sponsor's maximum loss is limited to its equity investment in the project company. If, on the contrary, the sponsor decides to finance the project through corporate financing, the sponsor has to continue servicing the debt incurred in connection with the project irrespective of the way the project pans out. Lenders have in this case *full recourse* on the sponsor.

4.2.2.2 Optimizing Leverage

Using a project finance structure is also a way to increase the total amount of debt raised in connection with infrastructure. Lenders to a project company size their loan based on the cash flow generated by the project. If this cash flow is steady and predictable, lenders can be aggressive in terms of leverage, especially if the project company benefits from a long-term purchase agreement with a company or a government-controlled entity with an excellent credit rating. It is not uncommon to see projects financed with 80% debt.

In the case of corporate financing, banks will not only analyze the cash flow generated by the project; they will analyze the whole revenue structure of the sponsor. If some other businesses of the sponsor are more volatile and less predictable, it will negatively affect the ability of the sponsor to raise debt. In this case, the total amount of debt available to finance the project may be higher through a project finance structure than via corporate debt.

Obviously, if the sponsor has an excellent credit rating and project costs are very limited compared to the size of the sponsor's balance sheet, structuring the debt as a non-recourse loan will not positively impact the maximum available leverage. The sponsor may in this case be able to finance the entirety of the project through corporate financing.

4.2.2.3   Extending Debt Maturity

If a project offers sufficiently a predictable and steady cash flow, lenders specialized in project finance can usually offer financing solutions with very long maturities, sometimes for periods exceeding 20 years. The average maturity of project finance solutions is far greater than most of the instruments marketed by banks or institutional lenders for general financing purposes. Revolving Credit Facilities for investment grade companies have on average a maturity of 5+1+1 years, whereas bond issuances with maturities over 10 to 15 years are usually quite rare (they obviously become more common when market conditions improve, but in this case, appetite for project finance increases as well, consequently extending maturities for project finance debt).

4.2.2.4   Ideal Solution for Consortiums

Financing a project through a project finance structure is common when several sponsors want to participate together in a project. Establishing an SPV to secure debt at the project company level means that the cost of debt will be linked to the creditworthiness of the project. This cost will be the same for all shareholders. When each co-sponsor raises corporate debt individually to fund its stake in the project, sponsors pay a credit spread that depends on their individual credit rating. There may be huge differences in terms of cost if some sponsors are large investment-grade companies and others are not. Structuring project financing is a solution to put all shareholders on the same-level playing field and align interests between them.

4.2.2.5   Ideal Solution for Financial Sponsors

As has already been explained, sponsors can be either (i) construction or infrastructure companies (in which case they are referred to as *industrial sponsors*), or (ii) financial investors specialized in investing in infrastructure or energy assets (i.e. *financial sponsors*). These financial sponsors are not so different from the LBO firms discussed in Chapter 3. Their organization is very similar. Their objective is to raise funds from limited partners through dedicated investment vehicles and invest this cash in operating companies. The main difference is that investment companies specialized in infrastructure target only investment in project companies or companies holding infrastructure assets, while LBO firms have a broader investment spectrum. Infrastructure investment companies also generally have a longer investment period and can hold an asset for a period of 10 to 15 years – as opposed to five to seven years for traditional LBO firms. Finally, given that infrastructure investment companies usually invest in companies with steady and predictable cash flow, they target a lower IRR than LBO firms.

Unlike industrial sponsors, financial sponsors do not have the option to raise funding at corporate level. Their structure is such that the size of the investment company is rather limited. The equity used to invest in projects comes from funds that are separate legal entities. For these financial sponsors, the only option available to finance an infrastructure project is to use a project finance structure, whereby the SPV in which the financial sponsor has a stake raises non-recourse debt.

4.2.2.6   Only Solution for Small or Medium-size Sponsors

It is not uncommon that a sponsor is simply too small to access sufficient long-term liquidity for a large infrastructure project. In this situation, project finance is the only solution for moving forward. Independent power producers (IPP) specialized in renewables fall generally into this category. These companies develop wind and solar farms and their objective is to build a power plant connected to the grid and capable of producing energy. They usually do so by signing long-term contracts with publicly regulated entities that will in the end distribute the electricity. For lenders, financing a wind or solar farm with the certainty of collecting revenues from a government-owned institution is easier than directly financing an IPP, which can be in some cases an extremely small company.

4.3   CONSTRAINTS OF THE PROJECT FINANCE STRUCTURE

Despite the aforementioned advantages, the use of a project finance structure does not come without drawbacks as compared to corporate financing:

- Lenders being at risk on the project itself, carry out a thorough analysis of the project. They require a lot of information and ask for technical, legal, tax, and financial due diligence. These reports have to be prepared and drafted by consultants and specialized firms, adding costs, time, and complexity to the transaction.
- The contractual arrangement (which we will analyze in more detail later) is very complex. The number of parties involved in a project finance transaction can be significant, which naturally slows down the negotiation process. A project finance transaction can easily take several months to structure, whereas a corporate loan is a matter of weeks.
- The project monitoring cost is generally very high: lenders have important technical, financial, and legal monitoring requirements and have to dedicate whole teams to actively follow the transaction until it fully amortizes.
- Because of the additional risks borne by lenders – high leverage, long maturity, and no recourse to the sponsors – financing costs can be higher than those of a corporate financing, especially if the sponsor is investment grade.

Given these disadvantages, the use of project financing is generally limited to very large projects. It does not make sense for a sponsor to enter into a long negotiation process and incur heavy transaction costs if the asset to be financed is limited in size (unless the sponsor itself has no other choice, which can be the case, as explained earlier, if the sponsor is too small and does not have access to bank loans). Lenders share the same approach. Since each transaction requires a deep level of analysis, they would rather focus on a large deal than on a small transaction. Small transactions are therefore usually quite difficult to finance via project finance debt.

4.4   HOW TO CHOOSE BETWEEN CORPORATE AND PROJECT FINANCING

Since projects can be financed through an SPV or by using corporate debt, sponsors have two financing options to choose from. They have to decide ahead of constructing a project which route they want to follow. Although project finance is the path chosen in most cases, some small-size or standardized projects are regularly handled through corporate financing. Some large companies with excellent credit ratings sometimes also choose corporate financing to benefit from simplicity and a cheaper cost of debt. Table 4.1 presents the respective merits of both techniques.

TABLE 4.1   Key Differences between Corporate Financing and Project Financing

	Corporate Financing to the Sponsor	Project Financing to the SPV
Risk taken by the lenders	Capacity of the sponsor to generate cash flow	Capacity of the project to generate cash flow
Risk analysis by the lenders	Analysis of the sponsor's financial statements	Thorough analysis of the project from all angles (technical, financial, tax, and legal)
Available if	Sponsor has a minimum size and a good credit rating	Project analysis shows that the infrastructure is bankable on a standalone basis
Debt sizing	Based on the sponsor's metrics and its ability to repay debt	Based on the project cash flow. A buffer is calculated to ensure that, even in case of underperformance, project cash flow will be higher than debt repayment
Maturity	Rarely more than 7 to 10 years for investment grade names (depending on market conditions and liquidity available at that date)	Very long maturity can be contemplated if the lifespan of the project and the predictability of future cash flow so allows (generally between 15 and 25 years and sometimes over 30 years)
Margin	Based on sponsor's credit quality	Based on the predictability of the project cash flow and the credit quality of the project's users
Risk for the sponsor	Debt repayments are due even in case of project failure	Financial risk limited to its investment in the project company
Structuring	Limited: loan and bond issuances' documentations are traditionally very standard	Complex, time consuming, and costly
Security package available to the lenders	None: the bank is an unsecured creditor to the sponsor. If the financing is granted to a subsidiary of the sponsor, a corporate guarantee is offered by the main entity of the group, ensuring that lenders take a credit risk on the sponsor and not on the subsidiary	Lenders have a pledge on the shares of the SPV (they can also have a mortgage on the infrastructure itself).[1] They have no recourse to the sponsor(s) but can repossess the SPV (or the infrastructure) in case of default
Best suited for	Small projects and/or situations where the sponsor has an excellent credit rating and wants to take advantage of this rating and retain flexibility	Large infrastructure projects, especially when: (i) sponsors want to limit their exposure to a specific project; or (ii) several sponsors are involved in the project; or (iii) the sponsor is a financial sponsor; or (iv) the sponsor cannot finance the project otherwise given the limited size of its balance sheet

---

[1]If it is legally possible. In some projects awarded after public tender, the SPV is only the economic owner of the infrastructure. The legal ownership remains with the public entity that has awarded the project, meaning that the SPV cannot pledge it in favor of lenders. It can only pledge its own shares.

Case Study 5: The Construction of the Eiffel Tower

When he presented his design of a 300-metre-high metallic tower in the centre of Paris in 1886 Gustave Eiffel was already a well-established engineer and successful entrepreneur. He had built bridges all across Europe and conceived parts of well-known buildings in Europe and the United States. His most famous achievement was the Statue of Liberty. While the sculpture itself was designed by Frédéric Bartholdi, the metallic framework inside was entirely conceived by Eiffel.

The tower that Eiffel had in mind was revolutionary. It would be the tallest monument in the world. Eiffel had been working on the concept since 1884 and wanted to build it for the World Exposition of 1889, an event meant to commemorate the centenary of the French Revolution. Eiffel did everything in his power to make sure that his project would be chosen by the organizers of the event. He had meetings with politicians, bought ads in newspapers, and met regularly with Edouard Lockroy, the President of the Organizing Committee of the Exposition. After two years of intense lobbying, he finally convinced Lockroy to launch a tender for building a modern monument in the centre of Paris.

The tender was flagrantly biased. Owing to his close relationship with Lockroy, Eiffel influenced the drafting of the tender notification. The specifications were such that they matched almost perfectly what Eiffel had in mind. And to make sure that Eiffel was chosen, contenders had only 18 days to present their responses. Eiffel, who had been refining his concept for more than two years, won easily.[2]

The Concession Agreement

On 8 July 1887, a little over a year after the selection of the project, Gustave Eiffel, Edouard Lockroy, and representatives of the French government signed a tripartite agreement specifying details with regard to the location, financing, and operation of the project. As per this 12-page deed,[3] it was agreed that the tower would be located in Paris's seventh district along the River Seine. Eiffel took personal responsibility for designing, constructing, and funding the project. In return, the city of Paris, as the legal owner of the tower, granted him the right to use and operate the asset for a 20-year period.

(continued)

---

[2]This technique is well known to firms responding to tenders. They try to convince the public authority issuing the tender to require the project to have some technical specifications that favor their company over the others. Many countries nowadays have laws to regulate lobbying and restrict these behaviors.

[3]This number deserves to be highlighted in the context of modern project finance agreements that often take up several hundred pages.

(continued)

Eiffel was also entitled to receive state aid totaling 1.5 million francs. The grant was to be paid in three installments of 500,000 francs each. The payment milestones were the completion of the first, second, and third floors. In other words, Eiffel benefitted from government subsidies but had to start the construction of the tower with private funds. The government would support the project but only after notable progress had been made.

In exchange for these subsidies, Eiffel agreed to cap the fees charged to visitors. Although the term was not in use at the time, the agreement signed by the parties was similar to what is known today as a concession agreement: a private entity was in charge of building and operating a piece of infrastructure and received the revenues generated by the infrastructure for a certain period of time, subject to some basic rules imposed by the public authority which allowed the construction to go forward.

Initial Difficulties

The construction of the tower was to be done by Eiffel's company, *Les Etablissements Eiffel*. It estimated the project's total cost at 6.6 million francs, with 6.5 million for construction and 100,000 in legal and structuring fees. Eiffel had therefore, to raise 5.1 million on top of the 1.5 million in subsidies. Although he was constructing what is today the most famous monument in Paris, Eiffel struggled to find partners. Building a 300-metre-high metal structure in the center of Paris was considered extremely risky from a technical point of view.

Eiffel hired a financial advisor to convince banks to finance the project. The role of this expert was to demonstrate that the concept of a tower in the middle of Paris could be profitable. The advisor built what was, for the time, an extremely sophisticated financial model. He looked into how many tourists on average visited prominent monuments in Paris and abroad, deducing from these figures how many people the tower might attract. Based on expected growth and inflation targets, he extrapolated the number of visits for the next 20 years, considering seasonality, weather conditions, and the difference between weekends and week days. The advisor's calculations revealed that over 20 years the net present value of the project's operating cash flow was well over 5.1 million francs.

Thanks to this analysis, three banks finally agreed to finance the tower: Société Générale, the Franco-Egyptian Bank, and Crédit Industriel et Commercial (CIC). The deal was signed in July 1888, two months after the completion of the first floor. In the meantime, Eiffel himself financed the first phase of construction.

Financial Structure

In exchange for investing in the project, the three banks required from Eiffel that he transfer all the rights and obligations related to the construction and operation of the tower to the *Société de la Tour* Eiffel (STE),[4] a special purpose company established for the sole purpose of building and managing the project. The share capital of STE was divided between two classes of shares:

(i) 10,200 redeemable ordinary shares with a face value of 500 francs each (i.e. a total of 5.1 million francs), and

(ii) 10,200 founders shares with no face value.

Both categories of shares offered the same rights to dividends. Dividend distribution on both classes of shares could nonetheless only occur when holders of the redeemable ordinary shares had entirely recouped their initial investment (i.e. 500 francs per share). These redeemable shares were subscribed half by Eiffel (5,100 shares) and half by the banks (5,100 shares), meaning that Eiffel and the banks had each invested 2.55 million francs. The total capital contribution by the shareholders was equal to 5.1 million francs. Table 4.2 summarizes the sources and uses of funds of the project.

TABLE 4.2 Sources and Uses of Funds in French Francs

Sources of Funds		Uses of Funds	
Subsidies	1,500,000	Construction Cost	6,500,000
Redeemable shares (G. Eiffel)	2,550,000	Legal and advisory fees	100,000
Redeemable shares (Banks)	2,550,000		
Founders shares	–		
Total	6,600,000	Total	6,600,000

Source: Michel Lyonnet du Moutier *L'aventure de la Tour Eiffel*.

The founders shares had no face value. Their owner did not contribute to the capital of STE. Their only purpose was to allow dividend distribution to their holders. They were all allotted to Eiffel (10,200 shares). Once the ordinary shares had been entirely paid back, there was no difference between the two classes of shares. Figure 4.2 summarizes the financing structure behind the Eiffel Tower.

According to the agreement between Eiffel and the lenders, banks had the option of buying 25% of the redeemable ordinary shares for 500 francs per share up to four months after the end of the World Exposition. They also had to sell 25% of the remaining redeemable ordinary shares – held by Eiffel – through a public

(continued)

---

[4] Eiffel Tower Company in English.

(*continued*)

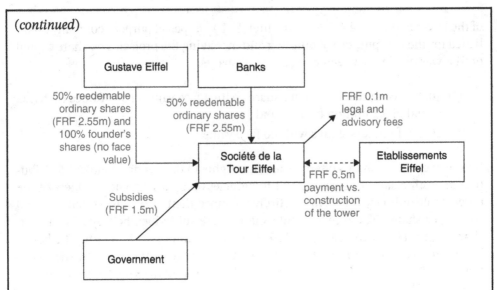

FIGURE 4.2   Financing Structure of The Eiffel Tower
Source: Michel Lyonnet du Moutier *L'aventure de la Tour Eiffel*. Michel.

offering. As remuneration for their service, they obtained 45% of the founders' shares and a commission of 125,000 francs. All the parties could then freely hold or sell their shares. Figure 4.3 shows the shareholding structure of the Eiffel Tower once the construction was finished.

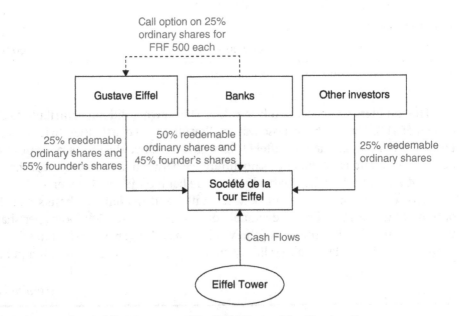

FIGURE 4.3   Shareholding Structure of The Eiffel Tower After Construction
Source: Michel Lyonnet du Moutier, *L'aventure de la Tour Eiffel*.

After Construction

The construction of the Eiffel Tower is an example of industrial efficiency. It was completed without any mishap within the planned budget and in record time, within 10 days of the original schedule. The pace for construction workers was intense but Eiffel avoided a strike by granting a substantial salary increase to employees. The raise was made possible thanks to savings generated through the optimization of construction processes in the factory where the tower was assembled.

The success of the construction was a financial boon for Eiffel and the banks. On their first day of listing, STE shares touched a high of 770 francs and soared to over 1,000 francs a few weeks later. Even though visits remained below expectations, revenues during the World Exposition generated a total profit of 5.6 million francs, triggering the full repayment of the redeemable ordinary shares and allowing a dividend distribution of 500,000 francs to shareholders.

Although the total profit made by Eiffel on this project is not precisely known, it turned out to be an extremely lucrative deal. But it was also the beginning of a less successful period. Hired as a contractor to design and build the Panama Canal, he was embroiled in a corruption scandal. Sentenced to two years in prison, he was finally acquitted on appeal. Eiffel remained deeply affected by this ordeal and decided shortly after to retire from his own company and focus on scientific research.

Epilogue

The tower's financial performance after the World Exposition remained rather disappointing, but in 1910 Eiffel succeeded in obtaining an extension of the concession period for another 70 years. Benefiting from the growth of mass tourism during the twentieth century, the tower slowly became a focal point for tourists visiting Paris. STE developed into a profitable business and in 1980 the tower attracted the appetite of new bidders when the concession was renewed.

From that date, the operation of the tower was transferred to a new company, the *Société Nouvelle d'Exploitation de la Tour Eiffel* (SNETE; New Operating Company of the Eiffel Tower), 30% of which was owned by the City of Paris and the remaining 70% by a holding company controlled by the City of Paris (40%) and a financial partner (60%). Since 2006, the concessionaire of the Eiffel Tower has been the *Société d'Exploitation de la Tour Eiffel* (SETE; Operating Company of the Eiffel Tower). The company was originally set up as a subsidiary of the City of Paris (with a 60% stake) and several partners from the private sector, including EDF, Unibail-Rodamco, Eiffage, and LVMH (40%). In 2015, the shares held by private partners were transferred to public entities. The tower is run today as a fully independent business. It does not benefit from any subsidy and attracts more than 6 million paying visitors every year, making it one of the most profitable monuments in the world.

CHAPTER 5

The Main Parties to Project Financing

5.1 DIFFERENT TYPES OF PROJECTS

Project finance structures are obviously not all the same. A highway that leaves the project company exposed to traffic risk and uncertain cash flow cannot be financed like a wind farm that benefits from a long-term power purchase agreement (PPA) from an investment-grade utility company. The degree of certainty concerning projected revenues determines the structure, the amount of leverage, the cost, and the maturity of the debt secured by the project company.

In finance, projects are often classified based on the origin of their cash flow. Three main categories are commonly identified:

1. Projects with long-term purchase contracts in which the SPV sells its output (or service) for a long period to an identified buyer.
2. Projects with traffic or merchant risk, in which the project company sells its output (or service) directly in the market.
3. Projects in which the SPV receives fixed rental payments from a public entity to build and manage infrastructure used to offer a public service. These projects are generally referred to as Public–Private Partnerships (PPPs).

5.1.1 Projects with Long-term Purchase Contracts

Some projects benefit from long-term purchase contracts for the output (or service) they produce. These contracts (called *offtake* contracts) are usually signed for a long period of time (c. 20 years), giving sponsors and banks high visibility on future cash flow. These projects constitute a large part of the infrastructures financed through non-recourse debt.

5.1.1.1 How Does it Work?

Projects of this kind are common in the energy sector. To entice power producers to generate clean energy and build large wind or solar farms, governments throughout the world often offer long-term PPAs to renewable energy producers. These contracts come with a fixed price, generally indexed to inflation, guaranteeing to the project company that 100% of the energy output will be purchased at a given price for a very long period. Such PPAs offer renewable energy producers a high level of visibility on the future revenues of the project company, which is supposed to encourage the construction of renewable energy projects.

The risk analysis of an energy project benefiting from a long-term PPA is greatly simplified. Neither the sponsor(s) nor the lenders have to make assumptions about the long-term movements of energy prices. They analyze instead the creditworthiness of the counterparty buying the output over the contract period. For energy projects, this counterparty is often the government or the local national utility company of the country where the project is built. In the energy sector, these PPAs often take the form of Contracts for Difference (CfD), meaning that the project company sells energy on the spot market but benefits at the same time from a top-up payment made by the national utility company or the government if market prices are lower than the price guaranteed when the project was awarded. Inversely, if market prices are higher than the guaranteed price, the project company has to pay the difference between the market price and the CfD price to the national utility company or government.

PPAs are not necessarily signed with government entities. They can be agreed between a corporate willing to secure a given supply (electricity, gas, oil, etc.) at a given price for a long period of time and a project company that is selling the desired output. These private (or corporate) PPAs are often signed when private players have strong energy needs or are in a country where the energy supply is expensive or unreliable. Companies that want to use only clean energy can also sign corporate PPAs with project companies operating wind or solar farms. Google is a well-known example, having signed numerous private PPAs in the United States, Chile, Europe, and Asia to provide clean energy to its data centers.

Long-term purchase agreements reduce but do not eliminate risks. Between one wind farm selling its output on the market and another benefiting from a long-term PPA, the main difference is that market risk has been replaced by a counterparty risk. All the other risks remain unchanged. Notably, sponsors and lenders in both cases face (i) a construction risk (there is no cash flow if the project cannot be built), and (ii) a resource risk (if there is no wind, a wind farm will not generate revenues even if it has a great PPA attached).

5.1.1.2 Financing a Project Benefiting from a Long-term Purchase Agreement

If the creditworthiness of the offtaker is acceptable, having a long-term purchase agreement allows the project company to secure long-term financing. Assuming the other risks are correctly mitigated, the SPV could, for instance, raise an 18-year, fully amortizing loan if the project benefits from a 20-year offtake contract. This two-year difference is known as a *tail* and plays the role of a buffer in case other risks limit the capacity of the project to generate cash flow during the initial debt repayment period. In the case of a wind farm, for instance, even if the offtaker is an investment-grade company, lenders are exposed to the risk of there being very little wind for a year or two. In this case, the SPV could not generate electricity, which consequently would limit its capacity to generate revenue and repay the loan. Having a tail allows lenders to restructure the debt and extend its maturity while still benefiting from a bankable PPA.

In some cases, lenders are willing to accept a *negative tail*, meaning that the debt maturity is longer than the purchase contract. This is possible when it is known that the infrastructure has a life expectancy greater than the offtake contract. Lenders assume in that case that the project will still be able to produce and sell an output (whatever it is – electricity, gas, etc.) even after the end of the original purchase agreement. This negative tail does not exceed a few years. The risk is mitigated by the fact that the debt has at this stage already significantly amortized, ensuring that the credit exposure of the lenders is limited compared to the project's cash flow. Having a negative tail is obviously only possible if the SPV does not have to automatically hand over the infrastructure to the government or a government-owned entity at the end of the original contract (which can be the case in some countries).

5.1.2   Projects with Traffic or Merchant Risk

5.1.2.1   Definition

Projects exposed to traffic or merchant risks are those which do not benefit from a long-term offtake contract. These projects have to sell their output or service directly on the market. The Eiffel Tower, analyzed in case study 5, is an example of this kind. Its revenues are directly linked to the number of visits.

- *Projects with traffic risk:* toll roads are a typical example of projects exposed to traffic risk. Revenues are linked to the numbers of paying customers. If potential users prefer to take the train or use a public road, the project company may not generate enough cash to repay its debt. Projects in the port or airport sectors also generally come with traffic risk. Revenues are linked to the shipping companies or airlines that pay a fee for the use of the infrastructure.
- *Projects with merchant risk:* energy projects that do not benefit from a PPA are exposed to merchant risk. The project company has to sell its output (gas, oil, electricity) directly on the market. Revenues of the SPV can be extremely volatile.

5.1.2.2   A Higher Level of Risk than Projects Benefiting from Offtake Agreements

Projects exposed to merchant or traffic risk are riskier than projects benefiting from PPAs and consequently are more difficult to finance. Lenders must take a view on the potential revenues of the asset and understand whether and how much customers are ready to pay for the goods or services produced by the project. All things being equal, projects exposed to merchant or traffic risk are usually less leveraged than projects benefiting from long-term offtake agreements. The margin on the loan is generally higher and the maturity of the debt shorter. These projects are also riskier from an equity perspective. Sponsors investing in this type of assets usually require a higher IRR than investors taking an equity position in a project benefiting from a long-term PPA.

Projects with merchant risk require the input of experts to determine how market prices may evolve in the future. This is a difficult exercise and many lenders are cautious about financing such projects. Others agree to lend but generally require a higher amount of equity and a more conservative financing structure to make sure there is a sufficient buffer to absorb the impact of very low revenues (see Chapter 6).

Lenders analyzing projects with traffic risk have to understand the value of the service provided by the infrastructure. In the case of a toll road, for instance, they have to measure the gains for customers in terms of time and convenience compared to the other options available (free roads, train, etc.) and determine if users would be ready to pay the price proposed by the sponsors. Banks usually work with consultants to perform this analysis. Various traffic scenarios are envisaged to test the resilience of the infrastructure and its leverage capacity.

5.1.2.3 Subsidies

Governments that grant the right to build projects exposed to traffic or merchant risk can offer subsidies to minimize the risks for the private sector. Back in the day, the Eiffel Tower benefited from an 1.5-million-franc grant from the French government (see case study 5). These subsidies reduce the total cost of the infrastructure and make it easier for the project to reach its breakeven point. Paying subsidies is a way to attract more players to participate in the construction of infrastructure, while leaving a large part of the risk to the private sector.

Subsidies can be paid either during the construction period (like the Eiffel Tower) or during the operational phase. In the latter case, payments occur only if the infrastructure is properly built and adequately performing, decreasing the risk for the government involved. In this situation, however, the risk is higher for the private sector. The timing of the subsidies (if any) can therefore impact the appetite of some players to participate in a project.

5.1.2.4 Projects Partly Exposed to Merchant Risk

In some cases, an SPV is only partly exposed to merchant risk. The project company has an offtake agreement to sell a part of its output (or service) at a fixed price over a long period and is exposed to market risk for the sale of the remainder of its output. This can often be the case in the energy sector. A wind or solar farm can sell part of its output to a client via a corporate PPA and the rest directly in the energy market. Whatever the scenario, lenders are generally able to offer more leverage to the project company when there is more certainty over the future cash flows of the SPV.

5.1.3   PPPs

There is no real consensus around the definition of PPP. Some scholars believe that PPP refers to all legal agreements between the private and the public sectors that aim at building, financing, and operating infrastructure. Others think the concept is defined by the nature of the revenue generated by the project company. Consequently, they tend to differentiate between a *concession* (where revenues come directly from end users) and PPP (where rentals are paid by a public entity). This is the approach we follow in this book.

5.1.3.1   Concessions: a Historical Approach

The idea of roping in the private sector to develop, finance, build, and operate public infrastructures is not recent. It is almost as old as the very notion of project finance. The development of silver mines in Devonshire in 1299 – discussed in the Introduction to Part II – shows that cooperation between governments and the private sector dates back centuries. In this example, the private sector (i.e. the Frescobaldis) financed the construction and obtained the right to receive all revenues of the project for a year before returning the installation to the king (Edward I of England). Such a legal structure ensured that the government did not disburse money to finance key public infrastructure. The legal agreement pertaining to the construction of the Eiffel Tower (case study 5) is not so different. Gustave Eiffel and the banks did indeed finance an asset that belongs to the city of Paris. They were, in exchange, entitled to receive all revenue generated by the project for 20 years.

This type of cooperation between governments (or public bodies) and the private sector is usually referred to as a *concession*. According to a concession contract, the private sector is given the right to develop, finance, build, operate, and maintain a piece of infrastructure by a public authority. In return, the entity in charge of the project is entitled to retain all (or a large part of) the revenue generated by the infrastructure for a given period of time; one year in the case of the Devonshire mines, 20 years for the Eiffel Tower. Concession contracts are relevant for regulated public infrastructure but do not only apply to new infrastructure. They can be used to finance the renovation, improvement, or extension of existing assets.

Concession agreements expose the concessionaire (i.e. the owner of the concession granted by the public authority) to the performance risk of the infrastructure it has to build or renovate, and operate. There are sometimes subsidies involved, but since the aim of the concession is to transfer costs and risks from the public to the private sector, the amount of these subsidies is typically limited.

5.1.3.2   PPPs: from the United Kingdom to the Rest of the World

The abbreviation PPP is relatively new, referring to infrastructure projects built using a specific set of contracts and remuneration established in the United Kingdom in 1992 through a program called the Private Finance Initiative (PFI). The ambition of this program was to provide a legal and financial framework for partnerships between the public and private sectors in the field of infrastructure. Several countries have since adopted a similar framework, and although details may vary depending on the jurisdiction, these specific legal arrangements are defined as PPPs.

PPPs may seem similar to concessions, but the model offers much greater scope for possible partnerships with the private sector. In a traditional concession system, sponsors and lenders financing the project take a real performance risk. The SPV offers a service or a product to end-customers who are free to use it or not, whether this is a highway (competing with rail and other transit options) or a water concession (competing with bottled water and subject to fluctuations in use). In a PPP, direct users of the infrastructure and clients of the infrastructure are not the same. The users are individual people, while the clients paying for the asset are governments or local public authorities.

A classic example of a PPP is the delegation of the construction and operation of a hospital to a private consortium. As in any project financing, the construction of the infrastructure is done by an SPV, which has subcontracted this obligation to companies specialized in this field. Once the project is completely built, the SPV takes charge of all non-medical activities of the hospital: security, catering, maintenance, cleanliness, etc. In exchange for these services, the government or the local authority pays rent to the project company. These rents are used by the project company to (i) pay for the operation of non-medical services of the hospital, and (ii) repay the debt contracted to finance construction. Any upside is distributed to the sponsors. All the medical elements of the hospital (choice and selection of personnel, health services provided, etc.) are outside the scope of the agreement and remain under the control of the government or the local authority.

PPP structures are obviously not meant to finance hospitals only. They can be used to build a large number of assets including schools, universities, prisons, court houses, tramways, stadiums, roads, etc. PPPs mostly cover social infrastructure projects that are used by a government or a public entity to provide a basic public service like health, education, or justice.

Revenues received by the SPV in a PPP are collected from the government or the local public authority that uses the infrastructure to provide non-commercial services to citizens. This is one of the main differences from a concession, in which it is the end user who pays for using the service provided by the infrastructure.

Rent payments made by a government or a public authority in a PPP are called *availability payments*. An availability payment is a payment for performance, irrespective of demand. In other words, as long as the infrastructure built by the SPV is fully available and can be used without any restriction by the public, the rent is due to the SPV (regardless of whether the infrastructure is used by the public entity or not).

To ensure that the infrastructure is well conceived, correctly operated, and professionally maintained, availability payments are indexed to certain performance criteria. They are set at a certain level between the public authority and the project company but are reduced if the usability of the infrastructure is unsatisfactory. The PPP contract indicates, for instance, that availability payments are to be decreased in case of poor maintenance of equipment, defective material, security issues, lack of cleanliness, etc.

The objective of a PPP is to allow the transfer to the private sector of the construction and the operation of core public infrastructure. The idea is that while the duty of the public sector is to provide services like education, public transportation, and justice to citizens, it is not necessarily its role to build, operate, and maintain the assets that help public authorities offer these services. PPPs simply aim at taking advantage of the efficiency of the private sector in the fields of construction and operation.

Following the success of the British experience and the need to control public expenditure, many countries have taken steps to adopt in their own legal systems a model similar to the PFI. The PPP framework is now used worldwide. South Africa, Australia, Brazil, Belgium, France, Germany, Italy, Ireland, the Netherlands, and many others have financed metro projects, railways, schools, hospitals, prisons, etc. using this legal and financial technique.

5.1.3.3   Financing PPPs

PPPs are traditionally seen by lenders as the safest type of project finance. Construction is often quite easy and cash flow is not exposed to market risk. They depend only on (i) the creditworthiness of the public counterparty, and (ii) the ability of the project company to provide a high level of service to the infrastructure so that availability payments are made in full. For lenders, it means that the risk is much lower than for traditional concessions, especially if the companies in charge of the operation of the infrastructure on behalf of the SPV are top-notch players in their field.

For all these reasons, PPPs are financed with relatively less equity than other types of projects. In Western Europe, gearings can be in the region of 90/10[1] if the counterparty making the availability payments is rated single A or above. The cost of debt is also very low and the maturity of the loans quite long. In emerging markets where ratings of public entities are traditionally lower and where construction risks are perceived as higher, structures are obviously less aggressive: gearing is lower, debt maturity is shorter, and margins are more expensive.

5.1.3.4   Legal Forms of PPPs

The legal forms of PPPs vary from one country to another. They are generally structured as BOT contracts, i.e. Build, Operate, and Transfer agreements, whereby the ownership of the infrastructure remains with the public sector while the financing, construction, and operation of the asset is under the supervision of the private sector. At the end of the PPP period, the infrastructure is transferred to the public sector. A new PPP can be signed at that time, whereby the new private party either commits to financing an extension or renovation of the infrastructure or simply receives a

---

[1] Meaning that the project company is financed with 10% equity and 90% debt.

fee from the public authority in exchange for the operation of the project for a given period of time.

In some countries, PPPs are structured as BOOT contracts, i.e. Build, Own, Operate, and Transfer agreements. They are, in essence, very similar to BOT contracts save for the fact that legal ownership of the infrastructure belongs to the SPV during the PPP period. The main consequence is that with a BOOT the SPV can offer lenders a pledge on the infrastructure itself, which is not possible under a BOT, where lenders receive only a pledge on the shares of the SPV.[2]

In some cases, a PPP is structured as a BOO (Build, Own, Operate) agreement, meaning that the SPV does not have to transfer back to the public sector the infrastructure it has built and financed. BOO contracts are extremely common for concessions and widely used for mobile phone and fiber networks. Even if they seem very favorable to the private sector, BOO contracts are a way for the public sector to avoid taking back old assets or infrastructures that may become obsolete in the future.

5.2 SPONSORS

The sponsors are the shareholders of the SPV. They provide equity to the project and are the first to suffer financially if the project fails. As mentioned earlier, there are two categories of sponsors: industrial and financial.

5.2.1 Industrial Sponsors

Industrial sponsors are those that have a real business activity beyond investing in infrastructure projects. Investing may be a large part of their business model, but it is not the only one. In the energy sector, for instance, power producers may invest equity in SPVs to finance the construction of wind or solar farms, but their task is not limited to these financial investments. They perform a lot of industrial activities around the life of the project:

- they identify and secure land to build and develop the project
- perform studies to make sure there is enough wind or solar radiation
- design the project and its specifications
- secure a bankable PPA
- oversee the construction of the project
- operate and maintain the project once it is built.

Industrial sponsors are to be found in many projects. Their objective is to create value through various channels and investment is only one of them. In our aforementioned example, for instance, the energy company makes a profit through

---

[2]See Chapter 4 section 4.4, Table 4.1 "Security Package Available to the Lenders".

the dividends paid by the project company but also through the operation of the project. A large part of the value creation in this case is achieved through the development of the project and not through the mere equity investment, something only an industrial sponsor can do.

That said, the development of the concession system in many parts of the world has changed the business model of many sponsors. The French company Vinci, for instance, founded in 1899, was originally a construction company. It is now an integrated business including construction but also a concessions division, most notably in the highway and airport sectors. Vinci today operates more than 4,300 kilometers of highways in France and has obtained the concession of many airports, in France (Lyon, Nantes, etc.) and abroad (Belgrade, Lisbon, Porto, Santiago de Chile, Salvador de Bahia, Osaka, Kobe, etc.). In 2019, the net income of Vinci's concession business represented 69% of the group's total (€2.255 billion of €3.260 billion),[3] meaning that the concession business is now more than twice as profitable as the historical construction business.[4]

Vinci is not the only firm that has evolved this way. Many companies involved in the construction of infrastructure projects nowadays have developed a concession or investment division (ACS in Spain, Atlantia in Italy, Eiffage in France, etc.). Three main reasons explain this major trend. Firstly, investing in infrastructure is a lucrative business per se, as the example of Vinci demonstrates. Secondly, being active in the concession business is a way to secure contracts for the construction division. A consortium with Vinci as equity investor obviously bids for concessions with Vinci as a contractor for the construction. Finally, consortiums are sometimes reluctant to select suppliers that are not fully committed to the project. Having all major subcontractors investing in a project company is a way to align the interests of shareholders and suppliers. In other words, equity investors prefer to select as subcontractor a company that believes in the project and is ready to take equity risk. This is especially true when projects are large and can be extremely profitable for a subcontractor.

Having major suppliers taking an equity position is also a way to ensure that prices proposed by the subcontractors to the project company will be competitive. If a supplier can receive dividends once the project is operating, it is more incentivized to put together a competitive offer than if its remuneration is only the margin on the supply contract.

This trend is notable in the offshore wind sector in Europe. Some companies specializing in marine engineering, which are responsible for installing the foundations for the mast, wind turbines, and electric cables, have taken stakes in projects in which they have participated. The Dutch company Van Oord, for instance, has invested equity in the 600MW Gemini wind farm in the Netherlands, while one of its competitors, the Belgian company DEME, has taken a stake directly or indirectly in several projects, including Merkur in Germany and Rentel, C-Power, and Seamade in Belgium. Wind turbine manufacturers have in some cases adopted a similar strategy. General Electric has invested in the Merkur offshore wind farm to which it was

---

[3] Source: Vinci annual report 2019.
[4] In terms of operating profits, not return on capital employed, obviously.

supplying 66 turbines, and Siemens has taken a stake in the Veja Mate project in Germany, which is equipped with 67 Siemens turbines.

5.2.2   Financial Sponsors

5.2.2.1   Definition

Financial sponsors are investment companies that invest equity in infrastructure assets. They do not perform any industrial tasks related to the projects they invest in. Their only purpose is to generate a profit from their investment. As already explained, their logic and organization are similar to private equity firms specialized in leveraged buyouts. The main difference is that instead of investing in shares of companies acquired via LBOs, they buy shares of companies holding infrastructure assets. Given the resilience and the lower volatility of the sector, they traditionally target a lower IRR than investment firms specialized in LBOs.

Financial sponsors active in the infrastructure field are rather recent. Macquarie, one of the pioneers in this segment, started investing in the sector at the end of the twentieth century. Ardian, the largest European private equity player, began its infrastructure activity in 2005, while Carlyle launched its first infrastructure fund in 2006.

Many of the historic private equity players now have funds focused on infrastructure (and entire teams in charge of deploying and managing these funds). The asset class is very popular, and capital available in the sector has grown steadily over the last 10 years. KKR, for instance, closed its first infrastructure fund in 2012 at $1 billion, its second in 2015 at $3.1 billion, and its third in 2018 at $7.4 billion. The interest of private equity firms for the sector is largely due to the fact that infrastructure appeals to their limited partners. As an asset class, infrastructure offers the opportunity to lock in stable yield with low volatility over a long period, two features that long-term investors like pension funds, insurance companies, or sovereign wealth funds are seeking desperately.

5.2.2.2   A Growing Competition between Financial Sponsors

The interest in this asset class is such that infrastructure investment firms now face direct competition from investors who had traditionally only invested in their funds as limited partners. Indeed, some of these players believe there is no reason to pay fees to an investment company when taking a stake in a wind farm that benefits from a long-term and bankable PPA. In this case it is true that a specialized infrastructure investment firm adds little value; the SPV is on autopilot and relies on the experience of an energy company for the operation of the project.

Some insurance companies, pension funds, or sovereign wealth funds now compete directly with private equity firms specialized in infrastructure. They have set up in-house investment vehicles and look actively at investment opportunities in the infrastructure sector. Consequently, the landscape of financial sponsors looking at the asset class is now extremely diverse: private equity firms specialized in infrastructure, traditional LBO firms that have developed an infrastructure expertise and launched funds focused on the asset class, conventional asset managers, pension funds, sovereign wealth funds, and insurance companies.

Private equity firms have adapted to this new competition by slightly shifting their investment focus. While they were previously investing heavily in assets with stable and predictable cash flow, they now look for assets that are more complex and infrastructures that need to be actively managed. In other words – and at the risk of over simplifying – they have abandoned PPPs and other projects with long-term offtake agreements, ceding the field to less sophisticated or more conservative investors (i.e. their former LPs), concentrating instead on infrastructure assets with multiple clients and/or a certain level of traffic or merchant risk. A lot of them also now invest directly in private utility companies, which are more diversified than one single project but are exposed to the same kind of risks.

5.2.2.3 Financial and Industrial Sponsors Work Together

Financial and industrial sponsors often invest alongside each other. The case of Heathrow Airport, for instance (see Table 5.1), shows that a wide variety of investors can hold an asset in common. Amongst seven shareholders, one is an industrial sponsor (Ferrovial), and six are financial investors: two pension funds, three sovereign wealth funds, and one infrastructure fund. Heathrow being a trophy asset[5] with limited downside (it is hard to imagine Heathrow having no traffic for an extended period of time[6]) but also limited upside (air traffic congestion), it is a natural investment opportunity for conservative investors like pension funds and sovereign wealth

TABLE 5.1 Shareholding of Heathrow Airport Holdings Limited

Shareholder	Type of Investor	Stake
Ferrovial	Construction and concession company	25.00%
Qatar Investment Authority	Sovereign wealth fund	20.00%
Caisse de dépôt et placement du Québec (CDPQ)	Pension fund	12.62%
Government of Singapore Investment Corporation (GIC)	Sovereign wealth fund	11.20%
Alinda Capital Partners	Infrastructure investment company	11.18%
China Investment Corporation	Sovereign wealth fund	10.00%
Universities Superannuation Scheme (USS)	Pension fund	10.00%

Source: Heathrow Airport (as of December 2020).

---

[5]A trophy asset is an extremely well-known infrastructure that some investors may want to have in their portfolio not only because of its financial value, but also because of its prestige.
[6]Extreme situations like the Covid-19 crisis are exceptional and (hopefully) only transitory.

funds. It is not surprising to see that there is only one infrastructure investment firm with a limited stake (11.18%) amongst the shareholders.

5.2.3   Greenfield and Brownfield Investments

Even though investment in infrastructure is a long-term play, investors holding stakes in project companies are like any other shareholder: they sometimes sell their participation if they believe that it makes sense. M&A activity in the field of infrastructure is driven by the divergent strategies of the various types of sponsors, and by their respective risk appetite.

Financial sponsors do not usually take part in the development phase of a project (apart from a few exceptions like Macquarie or Meridiam, for instance). Permits and licenses have not yet been obtained, and the risk of the project not succeeding or not even starting is very high. This phase is generally funded by industrial sponsors only. This is a type of risk they know well.

After legal authorizations have been obtained and preliminary studies demonstrate the potential and feasibility of the project, it is possible to obtain financing and start construction of the infrastructure. This construction phase is still dominated by industrial players but, in some cases, they sell part of their equity to financial sponsors – notably for mature asset classes (renewable energy) and in countries where the construction risk is deemed particularly low (Europe, North America). Selling part of the equity at this point is a way for the industrial sponsors to lock in some of the value created during the development phase. Assets under construction are commonly referred to as *greenfield* assets.

Once the infrastructure is operational (referred to as *brownfield* assets), financial investors become natural potential buyers. The project is perceived as de-risked and it is not rare to see entire assets sold to financial sponsors. If the maintenance of the infrastructure has been contractually transferred to an experienced player, there is indeed no real need for a financial player to take part along with the industrial company. In the renewable energy sector, where most of the solar or wind farms are backed by long-term PPAs with creditworthy counterparties, many assets change hands once they have a decent operating track record. They are usually sold, either partly or entirely, by industrial players to financial sponsors. The example of Heathrow (Table 5.1) shows, nonetheless, that for complex assets it is preferable that an experienced industrial sponsor remains an anchor investor in the project.

Finally, some projects are referred to as *yellowfield*, meaning that they sit somewhere between greenfield or brownfield assets. These are projects that are already partly operating but are also still partly under construction. This can be the case, for instance, with a fiber network that has been deployed but is being extended. Brownfield assets that need a lot of capex to be renovated are sometimes also referred to as yellowfield, highlighting the need for future investment and the associated risk. Given that they already generate cash flow, yellowfield assets often attract the interest of financial sponsors.

M&A activity in the infrastructure sector is also driven by the very nature of infrastructure investment companies. These firms manage funds that have a predefined lifespan (usually 10 or 15 years). When a fund reaches the end of its life cycle, the investment firm that manages the fund liquidates the assets that the fund still holds in order to pay returns to limited partners. These regular sales trigger a constant flow of M&A transactions and it is typical to see infrastructure assets going from one financial sponsor to another.

5.2.4   Stock Exchange Listing

5.2.4.1   Listing of Infrastructure Companies

Large infrastructure assets are also sometimes publicly listed. Because of their size and the diversity of their revenue sources, airports are particularly attractive candidates for this shareholding structure. Sydney Airport and Fraport (Frankfurt airport) are listed on the Sydney and Frankfurt stock exchanges, respectively. However, these are more traditional companies with infrastructure features than mere project companies. Fraport, for instance, operates and owns a portfolio of airports throughout the world: Frankfurt, Saint-Petersburg, Cleveland, Baltimore, Lima, Fortaleza, Porto Alegre, Delhi, etc.

The business model and the financial structure of these companies show that there is sometimes a thin line between traditional project finance and corporate financing. Even though the two financing instruments are different (see Chapter 4, section 4.4), there is obviously a grey area in between where loans have some characteristics of both instruments. Companies like Fraport have a very stable revenue source because they are truly infrastructure businesses. In parallel, however, they have an expansion strategy that goes beyond the original asset (in this case the Frankfurt airport), exposing their shareholders to a higher level of risk. As a consequence, investors looking for assets like Fraport (whether they are listed or not) will usually require a higher IRR than investors taking control of a wind farm benefiting from a long-term PPA.

5.2.4.2   Listing of Infrastructure Funds

The listing of infrastructure assets can also be done indirectly, meaning that it is the financial vehicle controlling the asset that is publicly listed. Macquarie Infrastructure & Real Assets (MIRA), one of the largest infrastructure investment companies in the world, manages four funds that are publicly listed (see Table 5.2).

TABLE 5.2   Publicly Listed Funds Managed by MIRA

Public Fund	Type of Assets Held	Place of Quotation
Atlas Arteria	Four major toll roads in France (2), the United States, and Germany	Australian Securities Exchange (ASX)
Macquarie Infrastructure Corporation	Portfolio of US infrastructure assets in energy generation, storage, and distribution	New York Stock Exchange (NYSE)

TABLE 5.2 (*continued*)

Public Fund	Type of Assets Held	Place of Quotation
Macquarie Korea Infrastructure Fund	Portfolio of toll roads and bridges in South Korea	Korea Exchange (KRX)
FIBRA Macquarie México	Real estate investment trust investing in industrial, office, and retail property in Mexico	Bolsa Mexicana de Valores (BMV)

Source: Macquarie Infrastructure and Real Assets.

5.2.4.3 Yieldcos

A yieldco is a type of listed company active in the field of renewable energy. It is an investment vehicle established by a renewable energy developer to hold its operating assets. In a traditional yieldco structure, a renewable energy developer transfers its portfolio of operating projects to the yieldco, while keeping its development business and its portfolio of assets under development. A yieldco is listed but the developer that has established the yieldco retains a significant minority stake.

The establishment of a yieldco enables renewable energy developers to partly monetize their existing portfolio of operating projects. This is a way for them to finance the construction of new projects without having to raise additional equity that would dilute their existing shareholders. By selling operating projects backed by long-term PPAs, they offer an investment opportunity to investors with a low risk profile who favor yield over growth (hence the term yieldco).

An important element of the yieldco structure is that the yieldco and the developer have an agreement regarding the future projects that will be built by the developer. In a traditional yieldco structure, new renewable projects are developed and built by the renewable company owning a stake in the yieldco. Once a project has reached completion, the yieldco is invited to buy it. The yieldco has no obligation to acquire every project. It only has a right of first offer (commonly referred to as *Rofo*) over the assets built by the developer.

This *Rofo* is an important element for investors. They are not only investing in operating projects; they are also buying privileged access to a portfolio of future assets. The fact that this access comes in the form of a Rofo and not an obligation to buy reduces potential risks. They know that they will not overpay for these projects. At the same time, if the yieldco decides to buy a project, it has to pay market price. The cash that is not used by the yieldco to purchase new projects is distributed to shareholders. Figure 5.1 represents a simplified yieldco structure.

The logic behind a yieldco is that equity investors backing energy developers and those looking to finance the operations of renewable assets are not taking the same risk and not targeting the same IRR. Valuations of integrated operators specialized both in the development and ownership of renewable assets can therefore be driven down by the high-risk level of the development business. Separating the two activities (i.e. development of projects and ownership of operating assets) should lead to

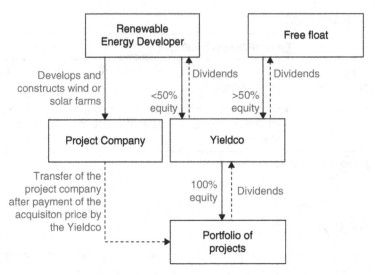

FIGURE 5.1   Simplified Yieldco Structure

an optimal valuation of both legs of the business. Yieldcos were an extremely popular type of financing vehicle during the early and mid-2010s. Many developers in North America and Europe set up yieldcos between 2013 and 2015, as shown in Table 5.3.

A yieldco is also partly an accounting arbitrage. Listing the majority of a yieldco enables a developer to deconsolidate the debt raised at the SPV level for each transaction.

- When a developer has full control over an SPV, the SPV is consolidated onto the developer's financials.
- When a developer transfers the full ownership of its operating projects to a yieldco, the yieldco becomes the controlling shareholder of the SPVs. It consolidates the SPVs and their debt.
- However, if the developer only retains a significant influence[7] over the yieldco, it does not have to consolidate the yieldco, it only recognizes its pro-rata share of the yieldco's net profit following the *equity method* of accounting.

A developer can therefore hugely reduce its level of debt by selling its operating assets to a yieldco and yet keeping a share of the profits generated at the SPV level.

Let us take a numerical example to illustrate this accounting arbitrage:

- If a developer owns an SPV financed with $20 million of equity and $80 million of debt that generates a net income of $1 million over the course of a year,

---

[7]Note that there are several rules that define significant influence such as equity interest, voting rights, influence on the board, etc.

TABLE 5.3 List of the Main Yieldcos' IPOs

Yieldco	Energy Developer	Type of Assets	IPO	Amounts Raised
NRG Yield[8]	NRG Energy	Solar, wind, thermal, and conventional	July 2013, NYSE	$840m
TransAlta Renewables	TransAlta Corporation	Wind and hydropower	August 2013, Toronto Stock Exchange (TSX)	C$346m
Pattern Energy	Pattern Development	Wind[9]	October 2013, NASDAQ and Toronto Stock Exchange (TSX)	$938m
Abengoa Yield[10]	Abengoa	Solar, wind, and conventional	June 2014, NASDAQ	$829m
NextEra Energy Partners	NextEra Energy	Solar and wind	June 2014, NYSE	$406m
TerraForm Power	SunEdison	Solar (US assets)	July 2014, NASDAQ	$500m
Saeta Yield	ACS	Solar and wind	Feb. 2015, Bolsa de Madrid (BME)	€852m
8point3	First Solar and SunPower	Solar	June 2015, NASDAQ	$420m
TerraForm Global	SunEdison	Solar (non-US assets)	July 2015, NASDAQ	$675m

Source: HSBC, Agefi Hebdo.

the developer recognizes both the SPV's income and its debt in its consolidated financial statements (respectively $1 million and $80 million).

- Let us assume now that the developer sells 100% of its stake in the SPV for $20 million to a yieldco that it does not control but in which it has a 40% interest. The developer must then apply the equity method to account for this 40%.
- If the project company is the only asset of the yieldco, the developer records as a non-current asset its original investment of $8 million in the yieldco (40% x $20 million). At year-end, it adds 40% of $1 million to this value and records in parallel an income of $400,000. Compared to the original scenario, the developer has now erased $80 million of debt but still keeps in its books 40% of the net income of the SPV.

---

[8] Changed its name to Clearway Energy on 31 August 2018.
[9] Pattern Energy was a pure player in wind energy at the time of its IPO. It has later expanded into solar energy projects.
[10] Changed its name to Atlantica Yield on 7 January 2016.

The concept of a yieldco raises several questions, however:

- Issue (1) *conflict of interest*. Even if a yieldco is an independent company and only has a right and not an obligation to acquire projects from the developer, it is still buying assets from a shareholder – which may cause conflicts of interest. To ensure that a yieldco is not overpaying for its assets, yieldcos have special valuation committees that verify that the yieldco buys assets at the right price. These valuation committees are mandated by the Board of Directors of the yieldco to protect the yieldco's interest. Despite the protection offered by this contractual framework, many specialists have argued that the yieldco model is flawed from a compliance perspective.
- Issue (2) *dependence on the anchor shareholder*. Being at the same time affiliates and captive clients of renewable energy developers, yieldcos are not mere renewable investment vehicles. Their shareholders have to accept that the yieldco they invest in is part of a larger group. For instance, the bankruptcies of Abengoa and SunEdison, two companies that had set up yieldcos (see Table 5.3), had a negative impact on the stock price of their captive yieldcos.
- Issue (3) *a conflict between yield and growth*. A yieldco is not only providing yield to shareholders. Since it has the option to buy operating projects from the developer, a yieldco is also a growth platform. To acquire these assets, a yieldco has to raise capital on a regular basis, as the cash received from projects and not distributed to shareholders is not sufficient. If the price of renewable assets on the market keeps increasing (which has happened since the end of the 2000s due to a better understanding of the risks and an appetite for green investment), the yieldco is not in a position to provide the same yield to investors. Each capital increase triggers a dilution of existing shareholders and a fall in the stock price.

Given these challenges, the market has shown less appetite for yieldcos since 2015, especially following the aforementioned bankruptcies. Integrated players, active in the development, ownership, and maintenance of renewable energy projects, have been back in fashion since then. Neoen, one the largest independent European renewable players, for instance, was one of Euronext's largest IPOs in 2018, with €638 million raised for a 24% stake.

Yieldcos in the meantime have attracted interest from infrastructure funds, probably because their DNA is more compatible with the investment logic of private investors looking for long-term yield. Out of the nine yieldcos listed in Table 5.3, five were delisted by 2020: Brookfield Renewable Partners, the renewable arm of Brookfield acquired TerraForm Power, TerraForm Global and Saeta Yield, 8point3 was acquired by Swiss investment fund Capital Dynamics, and Pattern Energy by Canadian Pension Plan Investment Board (CPPIB).

5.2.5   Infrastructure-like Assets

5.2.5.1   Definition

Given the flow of liquidity now available in the infrastructure sector, investors' yields and IRRs have come under constant pressure. To cope with this situation, some financial sponsors, especially infrastructure investment firms, have stretched the definition of infrastructure to bid for assets that are less coveted by their peers. While these investors always look for long-term real assets with high barriers to entry that operate in the sectors of transportation, energy, telecommunications, and social infrastructure, they have wandered outside the scope of what is traditionally seen as infrastructure (i.e. PPPs, wind or solar farms, highways, airports, ports, etc.).

The French infrastructure investment firm Antin Investment Partners probably epitomizes this evolution. The company acquired and sold Westerleigh, the second largest private operator and developer of crematoria and cemeteries in the UK. In 2015, it acquired Amedes, one of the leading platforms for medical diagnostics in Germany, and the following year Inicea, the leading private operator dedicated to psychiatric care in France. While these businesses are far outside the traditional definition of infrastructure, they are all (i) long-term real assets, (ii) with public service features, (iii) that operate – usually because of regulation – in oligopolistic markets. These types of assets are usually referred to as *infrastructure-like* (or more commonly *infra-like*) assets.

5.2.5.2   Financing of Infra-like Assets

The financing structure of infra-like assets often look more like an LBO than a typical project finance. Debt is usually raised for five to seven years at the HoldCo level to fund the acquisition of the equity of the target company. Loans in infra-like acquisitions tend, however, to pay a lower margin than traditional LBO debt. The specific features of these companies (high barriers to entry, long-term visibility on cash flow) limit risk, allowing lenders to be more aggressive in terms of price. Given the specificities of the infra-like asset class and its positioning between infrastructure assets and regular companies, it is not uncommon to see traditional LBO firms and infrastructure funds bidding for the same assets.

5.3   LENDERS

5.3.1   Banks

5.3.1.1   Leading Banks in Project Finance

Banks do the bulk of the lending in project finance. All major institutions have departments that specialize in this type of transaction. Banks that operate in both the corporate and the retail sectors have a competitive advantage in this field. Their access to liquidity through their retail networks gives them the ability to provide long-term funding more easily than competitors that operate only in the investment banking segment. Table 5.4 shows the 2019 project debt league table, ranking banks based on the amounts lent in project finance and the number of deals closed. All the institutions in this table have a strong retail business coupled with good project finance structuring capabilities.

TABLE 5.4   2019 Global Project Debt League Table

Rank	Company Name	Value (m$)	Deals
1	SMBC	19.988	134
2	MUFG Bank	14.910	127
3	Mizuho Bank	14.460	75
4	Santander	11.779	165
5	BNP Paribas	10.755	96
6	State Bank of India	10.725	22
7	Crédit Agricole CIB	8.790	89
8	ING	8.204	87
9	Société Générale	7.023	81
10	Natixis	6.524	70

Source: Dealogic.

Global project debt league tables should not overshadow the fact that project finance is in many ways a local business. Banks with cheap access to euros will be, for instance, more competitive in the Eurozone than their peers. The same goes for Canadian banks in Canada, Australian banks in Australia, etc. Japanese banks are an exception. Given the competitiveness of their home market and the weak long-term interest rates in Japanese Yen, lending abroad is a good trade-off for them.

Basel III regulations are creating difficulties for banks active in the project finance market. For a transaction of a given amount and a given credit rating, RWAs and capital consumption increase significantly with loan maturity. Offering competitive pricing on long-term financing is extremely complicated for some of them, especially if they do not benefit from Basel's advanced approach in the project finance space. Some banks have now totally disappeared from the project finance business and most of the others find it difficult to lend over more than 20 or 25 years.[11]

To accommodate increased capital consumption when maturities extend, banks usually include margin step-ups in their loans, meaning that the initial margin increases regularly by a few basis points. For instance, a loan can pay 200bps for the first five years, 215bps for the following three years, 230bps for the next three years, etc. Margin step-ups are meant to encourage refinancing and reduce the effective maturity of a loan. This benefits banks because shorter loans mean lower RWAs for

---

[11] The concepts of the Basel Accords and RWAs are defined in the Introduction to this book.

them. In case the loan is not refinanced after a few years (due, say, to unfavorable market conditions), the bank benefits at least from an increase in margin, which partly compensates the increase in RWAs.

5.3.1.2   What Types of Loans Do They Offer?

Banks can offer different types of loans to project companies: (i) fully amortizing loans, (ii) hard mini-perms, and (iii) soft mini-perms.

(i) Fully amortizing loans are traditional project finance loans that amortize down to zero over the life of a project. The maturity of these loans is based on the revenue scheme of the project company. If the SPV sells its output via a 20-year PPA with a creditworthy counterparty, for instance, the loan can cover the construction period +18 years (or more). In this case, the loan is drawn progressively during the construction period and repaid over 18 years as shown in Figure 5.2. Fully amortizing loans are common to finance PPPs in developed economies or assets that benefit from long-term contracted revenues.

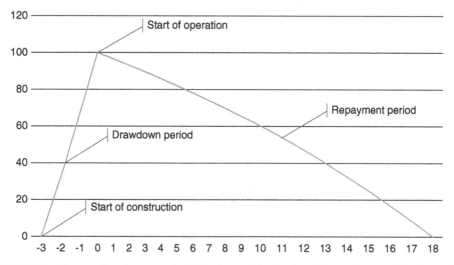

FIGURE 5.2   Outstanding Amount of a Fully Amortizing Project Finance Loan with a Maturity of Construction Period (of 3 years) +18 years

(ii) If it is not possible for banks to offer long-term debt (given the risk of the project or the lack of long-term liquidity in a currency), banks can offer hard mini-perms. A hard mini-perm is a loan with a maturity of usually 7 to 10 years with a balloon repayment at the end. The debt profile is sculpted over a fully amortizing long-term loan, but after 7 to 10 years a full repayment of the outstanding amount of the loan is due (cf. Figure 5.3). In other words, the SPV must refinance the loan at or before maturity. If it fails to do so, the project company defaults.

(iii) Finally, banks can also offer soft mini-perms. A soft mini-perm is similar to a hard mini-perm in the sense that a balloon repayment is expected by the banks

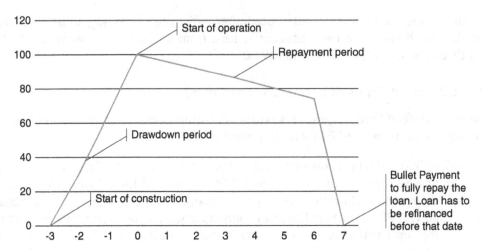

FIGURE 5.3   Outstanding Amount of a Hard Mini-perm with a Maturity of Construction Period Seven Years

after an original period of 7 to 10 years. Unlike a hard mini-perm, though, the repayment is not mandatory after this period. The SPV can keep the loan but there are generally significant margin step-ups. The sponsor is also usually not allowed to receive dividends after this original period: all the project's cash flows are devoted to the repayment of the loan (a mechanism known as a *cash sweep*). A soft mini-perm is meant to incentivize sponsors to refinance the loan after the original period. But it is more flexible than a hard mini-perm, as lenders cannot require the repayment of the loan after this original period.

5.3.1.3   Junior Loans

In addition to the aforementioned main project finance loans, some banks can provide facilities that rank junior to these loans but senior to equity. This type of additional facility is called a *junior loan* (the main project loan in this case is referred to as a *senior loan*). Having a junior loan allows sponsors to increase leverage (and improve their IRR) while keeping the level of risks unchanged for senior lenders.

Including a junior facility is only possible for large projects, as this tranche has to be sizeable enough to (i) compensate for the costs associated with the additional complexity, and (ii) incentivize potential junior lenders to analyze the opportunity (lenders do not mobilize teams to work on a deal if it is too small; they prefer to focus on large transactions; it represents the same amount of work but more potential revenues). The junior loan (usually) has a shorter maturity than the senior loan and (always) pays higher margin.

5.3.2   Infrastructure Debt Funds

5.3.2.1   New Players in the Infrastructure Space

Infrastructure debt funds are relatively new players in the field of project finance. They are investment vehicles that provide long-term debt to infrastructure and energy projects. The structure of these funds is similar to the setup of the funds managed by private equity firms: an investment company acts as manager and GP of the funds, while long-term investors, such as pension funds or insurance companies, act as LPs. The main difference with the funds that we have seen so far is that these funds invest in infrastructure debt and not in equity.

The growing success of these funds since the early 2010s coincides with both (i) the emergence of infrastructure as an asset class and (ii) the difficulties faced by banks following the subprime crisis. At that time, many banks were reassessing their priorities and questioning the wisdom of providing long-term debt when most of their funding (deposits) is short term. Regulation did not help. The more stringent capital-consumption rules applicable to long-term debt was making it more difficult for banks to provide project finance loans.

Given this change in paradigm, investors sitting on long-term money have taken the opportunity to actively look at this asset class. Infrastructure debt funds provide attractive investment opportunities to long-term investors. Project debt offers stable yields over a long period with low correlation to the economic cycle or other asset classes. Compared to equity investments, debt investments provide a lower return but a higher level of capital protection, an appealing mix for conservative investors.

5.3.2.2 Regulatory Background

While banking regulation makes it more difficult for banks to lend long term, regulatory rules applicable to insurance companies set a strong incentive for insurers to invest in infrastructure debt. Notably, insurance companies need to match their investment horizon with the maturity of their liabilities. So infrastructure debt – which is by nature very long term – represents an ideal investment opportunity for these players. This is especially true for life insurers, which have the longest liabilities among insurance companies.

In Europe, the regulation of insurance companies is set by a collection of rules called Solvency II, applicable since 1 January 2016. It requires insurance companies to fund part of their investments with equity and not only with premiums paid by the insured. This minimal amount of equity is called *capital charge*. The approach is, in essence, similar to the rules that Basel III sets out for banks, according to which loans provided by banks also have a defined capital charge (see the Introduction to this book). Under Solvency II, infrastructure debt has a lower capital charge compared with corporate credits with a similar rating and duration. This provides a strong incentive for insurance companies to invest in the asset class.[12]

For all these reasons, infrastructure debt funds can generally offer longer tenors than banks. Most of them can go well over 30 years, which many banks cannot do. However, these debt funds are probably more conservative and some are reluctant to take construction risk. They generally prefer to finance brownfield assets. When they are involved in greenfield projects, they sometimes demand a guarantee during the

---

[12]The lower capital charge imposed on insurers for infrastructure debt (compared with other debt instruments) exists as well for equity investment (compared with other equity investments). This is one of the reasons why insurance companies are also heavily invested in the equity of infrastructure or project companies.

construction phase. This guarantee is usually provided by a bank that is comfortable with the risk. Alternatively, the protection offered to the debt fund by the bank can be structured as a put option. The fund lends to the project company but has a put option on a bank (for which it obviously has to pay) that it can exercise if there is an issue with the project during construction.

Infrastructure debt funds can also be reluctant to finance long construction periods because they want to quickly deploy the capital of their LPs. They ideally want to have their loans drawn in one shot and not progressively (which is the case during the construction of infrastructure, as loans are drawn gradually to pay for successive steps of the construction). Although these funds are becoming more and more flexible and can now accommodate short construction periods – and take more construction risk – they are still more active in the financing of brownfield assets than greenfield ones.

Infrastructure debt funds are not only active in long-term debt; some asset managers also deploy funds dedicated to investments with shorter maturities and higher yields. These funds generally target debt opportunities in the infra-like space or investments in junior loans raised by traditional project companies. Investors in these types of debt funds are mainly property and casualty (P&C) insurers, i.e. insurers that have shorter liabilities than life insurers. P&C insurers usually look for maturities ranging from 5 to 15 years maximum.

5.3.2.3   Who are These Funds?

Unsurprisingly, many of the top asset managers in the field of infrastructure debt are affiliated with insurance or reinsurance companies (e.g. Allianz Global Investors, Aviva Investors, AXA-IM, Legal & General IM, M&G Investment,[13] MEAG[14]). The other leaders in the sector are traditional asset managers or infrastructure specialists (AMP Capital, BlackRock, IFM, Macquarie, etc.). The focus of infrastructure debt funds may vary but most of them target investment in OECD countries – which is quite logical for vehicles offering a high level of capital protection to their LPs.[15]

5.3.3   Project Bonds

Project bonds are another source of liquidity in project finance. They are issued by a project company and acquired by investors who get repaid only through the cash flow generated by the project. Project bonds differ from other sources of project debt as follows:

- Project bonds must be rated. An investment-grade rating is usually targeted as investors are extremely conservative. Most of them cannot invest in

---

[13] A subsidiary of US insurance group Prudential.
[14] A Munich Re company.
[15] The OECD is the Organization for Economic Co-operation and Development, an international organization whose goal is to promote the development of market economy. OECD members are the world's most developed countries (with a few exceptions).

non-investment grade papers. Depending on the transaction and the legal characteristics of the issuance, two or even three ratings may be needed. The bank in charge of the bond issuance coordinates the rating process.

- Insurance companies constitute the bulk of the investor base. They are buy-and-hold investors looking to invest in long-term instruments. Insurance companies active in infrastructure debt can have several investment vehicles. Some are dedicated to investments in project debt (as discussed earlier), others only invest in project bonds.
- Due to the regulation applicable to insurance companies (see section 5.3.2 on infrastructure debt funds), project bonds can have a very long maturity. They are ideal for financing infrastructure assets that enjoy long-term concessions or offtake contracts. Some investors have, nonetheless, a mandate to look at junior bonds. These bonds have a shorter maturity and usually come with a sub-investment grade rating. For the reasons we have already explained, investment in junior bonds are more suited to P&C insurers.
- Project bonds are especially appealing in the case of big projects. Investors have deep pockets but limited teams. They tend to favor large investments.
- Bonds pay a fixed coupon. The interest due is not defined as a margin plus a reference rate. The coupon is fixed throughout the life of the project. Unlike project debt, project bonds do not include margin step-ups.
- Project bonds include a make-whole provision in case of early repayment. A make-whole provision is a clause whereby the issuer has to pay to the lender an amount equal to the present value of all the coupons that the investor will forgo in case of early prepayment. Given this feature, project bonds are generally not meant to be refinanced before maturity. They are truly long-term financing instruments.
- The integral value of the bonds is usually drawn on the day of the issuance. So they are not the ideal instrument for greenfield projects, where debt is typically drawn gradually as construction progresses. Project bonds are better suited to refinance brownfield projects. That said, there are solutions to structure project bonds with delayed draw mechanisms where funds are made available over time to match the construction payment schedule. In any case, project bonds are better suited to brownfield assets. The risks associated with the construction of a project are, indeed, rarely compatible with an investment grade rating.

5.3.4 Development Finance Institutions

Development Finance Institutions (DFIs) are another source of liquidity in project finance. While debt funds and investors in project bonds focus mainly on assets in the best rated OECD countries, DFIs can support projects in frontier or emerging markets.

5.3.4.1 Definition

DFIs are financial institutions owned and controlled by sovereign states. Their purpose is to support economic development by providing funding to projects and companies that cannot attract enough private capital. DFIs can be *bilateral* (owned by one government) or *multilateral* (owned jointly by several governments).

The strategy and the scope of DFIs varies but they all share the same objective of supporting and fostering economic development. DFIs provide corporate loans to local companies and are extremely active in project finance (on the debt and sometimes on the equity side). DFIs can also offer guarantees or technical assistance. It is not rare to have several DFIs working together, whether this is to structure a corporate or a project finance loan.

Bilateral DFIs invest and lend according to the guidelines of their sole shareholder. They are generally active outside their country of origin and are an essential tool to serve their government's foreign development and cooperation policy. Some bilateral DFIs (but not all) only invest if a company if their country acts as a sponsor or provides a part of the equipment used for the project. Bilateral DFIs are also to some extent an element of soft power, and all the governments of the largest economies in the world have their own DFIs: Canada (FinDev), the United States (OPIC), France (Proparco), Germany (DEG), the United Kingdom (CDC Group), China (China Development Bank), Japan (JBIC), etc.

5.3.4.2   Multilateral Development Banks

Multilateral development banks (MDBs or multilaterals) are DFIs owned and controlled by several sovereign states. The most famous and largest MDB is the World Bank Group. It has 189 members. Its main goal is to reduce poverty and promote economic development. It consists of five institutions, each with a different set of objectives. Two of them are active in the project finance space: the International Finance Corporation (IFC) provides loans to private projects, while the Multilateral Investment Guarantee Agency (MIGA) offers political risk insurance (i.e. guarantees) to investors and lenders.

The other MDBs have a regional focus and generally only finance projects in one specific region. The list of these MDBs is long. It includes, inter alia, the African Development Bank (AFDB), the Asian Development Bank (ADB), the Asian Infrastructure Investment Bank (AIIB), the European Investment Bank (EIB), the Inter-American Development Bank (IDB), etc. A regional multilateral institution is generally not solely sponsored by countries of that region. Along with African countries, for instance, the United States, China, and many European countries are members of the ADB. Because they benefit from the support of their shareholders, MDBs enjoy excellent credit ratings – which allows them to raise rather cheap funding from banks and capital markets to finance their investments.

Membership of a regional development bank is motivated by the desire to support economic development but also by the ambition to have some kind of influence in that region. Given this political dimension, there is sometimes some competition between institutions. The creation of AIIB in 2013 (while there was already a regional Asian bank, i.e. the ADB) was proposed by China and is seen by many as a way for China to have a greater influence in the Asia-Pacific region and promote projects in which Chinese companies play a role. While most European countries are members of the AIIB, the United States is not.

5.3.4.3 MDBs in Project Finance

MDBs play a very important role in project finance. Financing basic infrastructure is at the heart of their mission, and they are very active in emerging markets. In other countries, they focus more on financing innovative projects or infrastructure using technologies that are not entirely mature. The EIB, for instance, is active in Europe in financing floating offshore wind projects – an energy source that is still in its infancy.

MDBs are always faced with the contradiction that they must bring added value (i.e. demonstrate that their involvement in funding projects and companies satisfies a need not met by private markets) while ensuring financial sustainability (they are banks, not NGOs). This situation can create tensions internally but also with some private competitors; MDBs are sometimes criticized for investing in projects that could have attracted private capital.

5.3.4.4 Preferred Creditor Status

Given the high risk involved in their projects, the IFC and other major multilaterals have suffered surprisingly limited losses historically. This is partly because they benefit de facto from a *preferred creditor status*. This status is not recognized legally but is in practice the consequence of the very nature of major MDBs: they are supranational financial institutions owned by sovereign states. The IFC, for example, benefits from the backing of more than 180 countries. Missing a payment on an IFC loan might mean political pressure on the defaulting project or company and, potentially, political isolation for the country where it happened.

The preferred creditor status of the IFC has been confirmed by events on several occasions. IFC loans were notably excluded from the restructuring of Russian government debt in 1998, as well as the moratorium on foreign debt repayment imposed by Argentina in 2001.

5.3.4.5 A/B Loans

The IFC and other major MDBs take advantage of their preferred creditor status to share part of their credit exposure with other institutions. When the IFC structures a transaction and provides a loan to a project, it keeps part of the loan for its own account (*A loan*) and distributes the rest to other lenders (*B loan*).

In terms of legal documentation, a loan agreement is signed between the IFC and the borrower while the other lenders sign a participation agreement with the IFC. Their participation is known to the borrower but the IFC remains in the driving seat and is the lender of record. This ensures that other lenders fully benefit from the advantages of the A/B loan structure. The participants in the B loan benefit de facto from preferred creditor status. In the earlier examples (Russia and Argentina), B loans as well as A loans were excluded from any restructuring or default. The IFC commits in any case to allocating repayments under the A/B loan structure on a pro rata basis. In the case of a default, both loans would be affected equally.

Given the preferred creditor status, B loans are given a preferential treatment from a regulatory perspective under the Basel framework. All major credit rating agencies (Fitch Ratings, Moody's, and S&P) also recognize this status in their analysis.

5.3.5   Export Credit Agencies

5.3.5.1   Definition

Export Credit Agencies (ECAs) are a source of liquidity that is also, to a certain extent, under the supervision of governments. ECAs are financial entities owned and controlled by or operating on behalf of a government. Their role is to support the export of equipment and services. ECAs exist in many countries: EDC in Canada, Sinosure in China, BPI France in France, Euler Hermes in Germany, SACE in Italy, United Kingdom Export Finance in the UK, US Ex-Im Bank in the United States, etc.[16]

The support of an ECA can take two distinctive forms: (i) a direct loan to an importer buying services or equipment produced in the country of the ECA, or (ii) a guarantee given to the importer's banks. These mechanisms are referred to in the first case as a *buyer credit* and in the latter as a *buyer credit cover*.[17] Depending on their internal guidelines and setup, some ECAs prefer to lend directly, while others prefer to offer guarantees to commercial lenders. Some ECAs can do both.

ECAs are very active in infrastructure finance. They lend or offer guarantees to banks providing debt to project companies purchasing equipment produced in their countries. They are involved in many projects in which a large underlying export contract exists, and not only in emerging markets. Wind renewable projects sometimes benefit from loans covered by the ECA of the country where the turbines are manufactured. For instance, EKF, the Danish ECA, has supported many projects relying on Vestas wind turbines, a brand of turbines manufactured in Denmark.

The involvement of an ECA can be key to securing export contracts. Large and complex projects or projects in emerging markets often fail to attract enough liquidity from private financial institutions. The role of an ECA is to increase the liquidity available to buyers and to facilitate exports. ECAs are also particularly useful when liquidity is scarce, as was the case after the 2008 financial crisis or during the European sovereign debt crisis.

---

[16] Just to name a few. A large number of countries (and not only the most industrialized nations) have their own export credit agency. There are many other ECAs: Atradius in the Netherlands, CESCE in Spain, Credendo in Belgium, EKF in Denmark, EKN in Sweden, GIEK in Norway, K-Sure and Kexim in South Korea, Nippon Export and Investment Insurance (NEXI) in Japan, etc.

[17] ECAs also provide other types of solutions to facilitate export. These products are less relevant to project finance and are not described here.

Figure 5.4 represents a project finance structure in which an ECA is involved through a buyer credit cover. The diagram is similar to the traditional project finance structure save for the presence of the ECA. The ECA guarantees the lenders the repayment of the loan provided to the project company. In exchange, the ECA receives a premium like any insurance company. The premium is paid by the borrower, in this case the SPV.

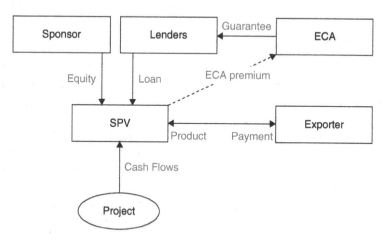

FIGURE 5.4 Simplified Project Finance Structure with ECA Cover

The decision to support an export contract is taken by an ECA based on a mix of criteria:

- the level of risk involved
- the importance of the contract in terms of employment for the exporter
- the strategic fit of the project with the economic development goals set by the government supervising the ECA and, in some cases,
- other political or geopolitical considerations.

5.3.5.2 Rules Applicable to ECAs

ECAs are not free to offer any type of guarantee at any price. They operate within a framework set by the OECD called the *OECD Consensus* (or simply the *Consensus*). The purpose of the Consensus is to create a level playing field among exporters. This arrangement between countries sets limits on what ECAs can actually do in terms of support to their national exporters. This framework is to be considered more of a gentlemen's agreement between countries than a set of binding rules.

The main applicable constraints for ECAs according the Consensus are the following:

- They have to charge a minimum premium and/or interest rates.
- They cannot lend or guarantee a loan beyond a maximum maturity. This limit is 14 years (plus construction period) but can go up to 18 years (plus construction period) in the case of renewable energy projects.

  – There is a maximum amount that they can finance or cover. ECAs usually lend or cover up to 85% of an eligible contract value.[18]

In addition to this general framework, each ECA has its own set of rules and credit guidelines. The goal of an ECA is to promote the export of goods and services of a country but this objective cannot jeopardize the balance sheet of the institution. ECAs have credit limits and credit committees like any other lender or credit insurer.

5.3.5.3   Example

In practice, projects in which ECAs are involved have generally two tranches of debt: one ECA-backed tranche and one tranche of commercial debt (i.e. a normal tranche of debt provided by private lenders). This dual tranche structure can be found in wind energy projects, for instance. The acquisition of turbines can benefit from an ECA cover, while the project costs linked to the construction of the farm are not covered (there is no export, since the construction is done locally). In this situation, the ECA tranche is sized according to the acquisition value of the turbines. It is equal to a maximum of 85% of this value (referred to as the 'eligible value'). The rest of the debt is provided by commercial banks, which do not benefit from a cover. Both tranches are pari passu, meaning that they have the same seniority and the same right to repayment.

To illustrate this concept, we can take the example of a wind project whose total cost is $150 million split as $100 million for the turbines and $50 million for the rest (construction and other costs). If the turbines are imported and benefit from an ECA cover, the SPV will seek to secure $85 million of ECA-backed debt (85% x $100 million). Assuming that lenders will require an equity buffer of 20% (i.e. $30 million), the total amount of commercial debt to be raised for the project is equal to $35 million (150 − 85 − 30 = 35). This non ECA-backed debt tranche is called a *clean tranche*.

While the value of the ECA-backed tranche is $85 million, it does not mean that the ECA guarantees the repayment of 100% of this amount. Depending on their internal rules, some ECAs can require lenders to take what is called a *residual risk*. When they cover project finance loans, ECAs often invite lenders which benefit from the ECA cover to take a 5% (or 10%[19]) residual risk. In other words, the ECA covered tranche will be equal to $85 million but banks will only benefit from the ECA cover up to 95% (or 90%), i.e. $80.75 million (or $76.5 million). The amount of residual risk is in this case equal to $4.25 million (or $8.5 million). Although this residual amount is limited compared to the size of the ECA tranche, its existence is a way for ECAs to test the appetite of commercial banks for the underlying risk. If banks are not able to take a 5% or 10% residual risk, why would an ECA accept to cover this loan? Table 5.5 summarizes this simple example.

---

[18]ECAs are obviously entirely free to finance or cover a lower percentage of the export contract. The percentage is defined by the ECA's credit committee.
[19]Or more. It is the ECA's decision to set the amount of residual risk that commercial lenders must accept.

TABLE 5.5 Simplified Overview of a PF Financing Structure with an ECA Cover

Sources of Funds	Amount
ECA covered loan	$85m
Amount benefiting from the cover (95%)	$80.75m
Residual risk (5%)	$4.25m
Commercial loan (clean tranche)	$35m
Sponsors	$30m
Total project cost	**$150m**

5.3.5.4   Advantages of ECAs

ECAs offer directly (when they lend), or indirectly (when they provide a cover), additional liquidity in the project finance market. This liquidity is generally relatively cheap given the strong credit ratings of the governments that control the major ECAs. Two situations exist:

- If the loan is directly provided by the ECA, this ECA benefits generally from the funding costs of the local government. This funding cost is usually very low if the government has an excellent credit rating.
- When a bank lends to a project company but benefits in parallel from an ECA guarantee, the bank is taking a risk on this ECA (save for the residual risk). The margin of the loan is adapted to the credit rating of this ECA, which is in line with the credit rating of the controlling government.

Benefiting from an ECA cover is also precious for banks in the light of the Basel regulations. RWAs applicable to ECA-backed loans are calculated by banks based on the OECD credit risk classifications. The OECD classifies country risk from 0 to 7, with 0 being the best rating. According to Basel regulations, loans backed by ECAs controlled by governments of countries rated 0 or 1 by the OECD have no weighting. In other words, a loan covered by an ECA controlled by one of the most industrialized governments translates into zero RWAs. This is obviously extremely attractive for banks as it means that ECA-backed loans do not consume regulatory capital. This explains the competitive pricing that banks can offer on ECA tranches.

5.3.5.5   Structuring Options

Although they are sometimes seen by sponsors as quite bureaucratic, the relative rigidity of ECAs should not be exaggerated. Considering the risks they accept and the constraints they have (i.e. the Consensus), ECAs remain very helpful. From a structuring point of view, they offer various options. Several ECA tranches can be structured jointly – each covering the acquisition of different equipment – and an ECA tranche can also be structured in combination with a tranche of debt provided by a DFI. The construction of the Ichthys LNG terminal[21] in Australia, the largest project financing ever closed, required the involvement of eight ECAs (some lending directly to the project company, some others covering a loan) and 24 commercial banks. Table 5.6 shows the source of funds of the Ichthys project.

TABLE 5.6   Initial Project Financing of the Ichthys LNG Terminal[20]

Sources of Funds	Amount
ECAs direct loans	$5.8bn
JBIC (Japan)	
Kexim (South Korea)	
Export Finance & Insurance Corporation (EPIC), (Australia)	
ECA covered loans	$5.4bn
NEXI (Japan)	
Kexim (South Korea)	
K-Sure (South Korea)	
Atradius (the Netherlands)	
Euler Hermes (Germany)	
BPI France (France)	
Commercial loans	$4.8bn
Total lenders	$16.0bn
Sponsors	$4.0bn
Total project cost	**$20.0bn**

Source: INPEX, Total.

ECAs can also offer credit covers for project bonds. As part of the financing of the Walney extension offshore wind farm, an asset owned jointly by Ørsted and a consortium of PFA and PKA (two leading Danish pension funds), rated project bonds were issued to a group of investors consisting of Aviva Investors, BlackRock, Legal & General IM, and Macquarie. EKF provided a 16-year guarantee of more than £300 million to cover one of the tranches of the bond.

5.4   THE ROLE OF PUBLIC AUTHORITIES

Public authorities play a key role in the field of project finance. They notably set the rules applicable to PPPs and concessions. They are also responsible for organizing tenders to select the private investors and operators of these infrastructures.

---

[20]The Ichthys LNG terminal was subsequently refinanced in 2020. What is shown here is the initial financing, structured in 2012.
[21]An LNG terminal is a facility for regasifying the liquefied natural gas (LNG) shipped in by LNG tankers from production zones.

5.4.1 Framework

Governments are obviously in charge of voting on the laws that are applicable to project finance. Each country has its own PPP and concession framework and has drawn lines between what has to be funded by public entities and what can be financed by the private sector. Given the long-term nature of infrastructure projects, the stability of the legal framework is a key element in attracting investors. Governments of OECD countries are usually aware of that and tend to minimize legal changes, or do so after taking time to interact with various infrastructure stakeholders.

Public entities have a role at each step of a project, especially during the development and construction phases. They grant sponsors the necessary legal authorizations to build the infrastructure: construction permits, environmental licenses, etc. Laws also regulate the interaction between citizens and project companies. It is always possible for residents to oppose the construction of new infrastructure: for example, a citizen may argue that their well-being is harmed by the presence of a project in their neighborhood. Judicial systems are designed – more or less successfully – to find a balance between the need for infrastructure and the well-being of citizens living close by. In many countries, the right to appeal against the construction of a project is strictly limited, ensuring that decisions can be made quickly – another assurance for equity investors.

5.4.2 Public Tenders

Governments or public authorities organize public tenders to select which sponsors will be allowed to finance and operate infrastructure. These tenders are designed to select the most qualified party for the project based on a set of criteria defined by the government or the public authority. Tenders are generally divided into two phases:

- A first phase, called the *pre-qualification phase*, is a period during which sponsors present their technical and financial credentials and any relevant experience. Sponsors can bid alone or in consortiums. Only parties selected at the end of this phase are allowed to receive the final tender conditions and participate in the next phase.
- The second phase, the *bid phase*, is the period in which sponsors prepare and present their final offers to the tendering authority. A preferred bidder is selected at the end of this phase. This preferred bidder will be in charge of building and operating the infrastructure.

This two-phase process usually ensures that only prequalified companies or consortiums present a bid for the project. This is a way for public authorities to eliminate inexperienced sponsors early in the process and limit participation in the second phase to qualified players.

Selection criteria for a bid are usually twofold: (i) the quality of the technical offer and (ii) the price. In a traditional tender, a certain number of points are attributed to each bidder for both criteria. The candidate with the highest number of points in total is declared the preferred bidder.

(i) The definition of the quality of the technical offer obviously varies from one project to another. In some tenders, the design of the infrastructure is key, in others the environmental footprint of the project must be limited. Bidders may also be required to demonstrate that their project will not disturb economic activity in the region. In offshore wind, for instance, bidders are often required to show that they have considered the potential impact of the offshore wind farm on the activity of fishermen and that they have found ways to mitigate this impact.

(ii) The definition of a competitive price is more consistent. For a PPP, for instance, the price is the sum of availability payments required by the candidate to build and operate the project (the lower, the better). For a concession, it can be the level of subsidies or the price levels that the project company intends to charge to the users (here again, the lower, the better).

Case Study 6: The Near Bankruptcy of Disneyland Paris[22]

When Disney CEO Michael Eisner officially announced his intention to build a theme park near Paris in 1985, there was every reason to believe that the project would be a resounding success. Eight years later, and only one year after its opening, the park was about to go bankrupt. The executives of The Walt Disney Company were left with the toughest decision of their careers: abandon their ambitions in Europe or inject additional equity into a fragile project.

Beyond the drama attached to such an iconic project, the destiny of Disneyland Paris illustrates the vicissitudes of project financing, demonstrating (i) just how complex it can be to forecast cash flow in the absence of a fixed-price offtake contract or reliable comparisons, as well as (ii) the appeal of non-recourse financing as a means of reducing risk for sponsors.

The Genesis of the Project

A pioneer of the animation industry, The Walt Disney Company ventured into the theme park business in the 1950s. By the time Michael Eisner announced his plans for Paris, the entertainment company was already operating three other parks, two in the United States and one in Japan. Disneyland Park opened in California in 1955

---

[22]The park has changed name several times since it opened in 1992. For the sake of clarity, we will only be using the name that prevails today: Disneyland Paris.

and Walt Disney World in Florida in 1971. The first park outside the United States opened in 1983 in Tokyo.

Western Europe had been on the map of the group for a very long time. The aura of the Disney brand in the region was strong and profits generated by its cartoons in Europe had historically been higher than in North America. The Walt Disney Company had high expectations for its new park, hoping to replicate its success in the United States and Japan.

The new town of Marne-la-Vallée to the east of Paris was chosen as the site in 1985 after a thorough selection process in which no fewer than 40 places across five different countries were carefully scrutinized. Marne-la-Vallée narrowly outcompeted a site near Barcelona; despite very good weather, Catalonia was viewed as less strategically appealing. Paris seemed a better option thanks to its large population, its central location in Europe, and the constant flow of tourists already attracted by the French capital.

Project Calibration

When they started planning in earnest, Disney executives made a paradoxical observation: although each of their three parks had been a commercial success, Disney had never found the formula to maximize profits.

- In California, the land area being too small, Disney was not able to construct sufficient hotel accommodation to welcome visitors. A large part of the revenues that Disney could have captured itself went to hotels built opportunistically by hotel chains in the surrounding area.
- While planning its park in Florida, The Walt Disney Company was probably overly conservative, underestimating demand and investing too little in hotels. Once again, surrounding hotel companies were the ones to benefit from the windfall of a Disney park.
- Finally, in Japan, the construction and operation of the project was passed on to a local partner to limit risks. Disney received only royalties. Here again, the huge success of the park redounded only partly to Disney's benefit.

The Walt Disney Company was not short of ambition for its European project. To avoid the frustration of the US and Japanese experiences, Disney executives made two important decisions. They would operate the park without a local partner and include a huge hotel complex in the project. The total construction cost was estimated at $4.4 billion – more than three times the amount paid to build the Tokyo park. This was by far the largest investment in Disney's history.

(*continued*)

(*continued*)

The Japanese project was a key reference. Built a few years before, it was the first park outside the United States. It was also wildly successful. The number of visitors each year exceeded the most optimistic predictions and by the late 1980s, it was drawing 15 million visits a year – more than either US park. Disney's local partner, Oriental Land Company, had constructed the park and was the operator. The $1.1-billion long-term loan they had taken to build it, had been – against all odds – fully repaid in three years.[23]

Master Agreement with the French Government

The battle between Paris and Barcelona to host the park ended up as a political fight between the French and Spanish governments. Both realized the value of a Disney theme park in terms of jobs and committed to provide direct and indirect support. Spain proposed the larger subsidies, but France offered better logistical support and more rail and road connections.

The final partnership agreement between Disney and the French government was signed in 1987, after two years of negotiations. In this document, the French government agreed to the following:

- the sale of land for the park at a price 30% below market
- the construction of a metro station, a bus station, parking lots for visitors, and a road link from the park to the motorway
- loans to a total value of FRF 4.8 billion[24] at the rate of 7.85% (lower than that applicable to French government bonds at that time)
- the use of a VAT rate of 5.5% on all products sold in the park, including those that are usually subject to a higher rate.

In exchange for these advantages, The Walt Disney Company committed to the following:

- guaranteeing a minimum of traffic on public transportation in the direction of the park – if this level was not achieved, Disney had to compensate the French government
- opening of one attraction within the park that showcased French culture

---

[23]Oriental Land Company (OLC) was established jointly by railway operator Keisei Electric, real estate promoter Mitsui Fudosan, and the Chiba prefecture. OLC is still today the owner and operator of Tokyo Disney Resort.
[24]The Euro did not exist yet at that time.

- no construction of another Disney theme park within 800 kilometers of Marne-la-Vallée for a certain period of time
- retention of a significant share of control over the project for at least five years.

Financing Structure[25]

The choice of the park's financial structure was hotly debated among Disney's executives. The plan was originally to simply raise debt and equity at the corporate level to fund the construction of the project. Disney's advisors, however, suggested financing with a project finance structure as the wiser option. The use of project finance would isolate the park from Disney's balance sheet. It would also allow Disney to raise additional equity at the level of the project rather than the group, a step aimed at avoiding any dilution for Disney's existing shareholders.

The structure selected by Disney relied on an SPC set up with the sole purpose of building and operating the park and hotels. The SPC – Euro Disneyland SCA (or Euro Disney) – had total control over the project. Its role was to set the park's strategy and to select and remunerate employees. The SPC also received payments from customers, repaid the project debt, and distributed royalties to Disney for the use of the brand and the know-how deployed in the park. An important point: royalties were indexed to turnover and not profits.

Disney controled 49% of the SPC. The rest of the equity was raised through an IPO organized simultaneously in London and Paris. Completed in November 1989, three years before the opening of the park, this IPO was one of the largest ever for a company without a track record. Despite the lack of revenues, future operating risks, and a long construction period, the IPO was more than 10 times oversubscribed.

The SPC also raised two tranches of 20-year non-recourse debt. BNP[26] led a syndicate of 39 banks and provided a loan to allow for construction. A second group of 30 banks led by Indosuez funded the hotel component of the project (cf. Figure 5.5).

Although construction costs ran higher than expected, investors cheered the park's opening in April 1992. Shares soared to 165 French francs, more than twice the IPO price (72 francs). In October 1992, Michael Eisner was even appointed Knight of the Legion of Honour, the highest French order of merit, by the then prime minister, Pierre Bérégovoy.

(continued)

---

[25]The structure as described here has been deliberately simplified in the interests of readability.
[26]BNP and Paribas were back then, two separate entities. They merged in 2000 to form BNP Paribas.

(continued)

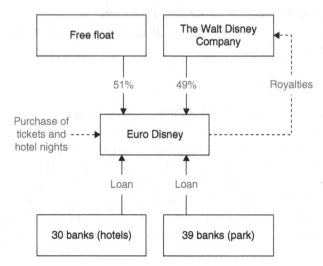

FIGURE 5.5   Simplified Financing Structure of Disneyland Paris
Source: adapted from J. D. Finnerty (2007) *Project Financing, Asset-based Financial Engineering.*
Hoboken NJ: Wiley.

The Debt Issue

Despite the initial enthusiasm, it quickly emerged that the project had been improperly sized. Revenues were barely enough to cover costs. The park recorded a loss of $900 million in 1993 for its first full financial year. Disneyland Paris was no longer in a position to pay its debt and in November 1993 its share price fell to 11 francs.

The hotel portion of the project in particular was underperforming. Rooms were perceived to be too expensive and tourists preferred to sleep in a hotel in Paris rather than stay in the park. This was a major break from past experience. Visitors in Florida and California usually organized a special family trip to see the park. In France, they took the opportunity to see the park while visiting Paris. Tourists went to the park to please their kids, but they wanted to sightsee in Paris in the evening.

It also soon dawned on executives that they had mistimed the opening of the park. Europe was going through the worst economic crisis since World War II. France entered a recession in 1993 and unemployment rose in many European countries. The situation was exacerbated by France's monetary policy. The imperative to keep inflation under control drove up the French franc, increasing prices for foreigners and discouraging potential tourists who might otherwise have visited the park.

Errors in the Design of the Project

The park itself was also not quite in line with the expectations of French and European visitors. The climate was the first major issue. Disneyland Paris followed the design of the other Disney parks, but it was much colder in Paris than in California, Florida, or Tokyo. The attractions were not adapted to the winter. Turnover at the park fell sharply in the autumn when the days got cooler.

Attendance during the week was another problem. Disney was expecting that parents would take a day off and have their kids miss a day of school to visit the park during the week – as is the case in the United States. This was not really part of French culture. On average, kids have more holidays in the summer than in the United States and parents are more reluctant to let them miss school during the year. The French park was empty during the week and then extremely busy on weekends, which fueled the frustration of parents who had to queue for a long time, sometimes in the cold.

Catering was another source of disappointment, both at breakfast and lunch. Disney was not expecting that French customers would want breakfast at the park. But with most clients declining to stay overnight, they wanted to have an early start and eat when they arrived. The lack of options for breakfast was a source of frustration, but lunches were also an issue. The non-alcohol policy in force in the park when it opened was incomprehensible for many European visitors.

While the success of the park in Tokyo was one of the major drivers behind the opening of Disneyland Paris, it was also the main reason why the park was so far from expectations in Europe. Disney executives were fully aware of cultural differences and the need to adapt to local tastes. In Japan, they even thought about dedicating a portion of the park to the world of Samurais (Samurailand) instead of cowboys (Frontierland). But they were convinced by their Japanese partner to resist the desire to "localize" the attractions. Oriental Land Company was sure that the Disney universe was well known to Japanese visitors, and that the park would be more successful if it looked like an authentic American experience. In Tokyo, the only concessions to the Japanese culture are the presence of a sushi restaurant and the kimonos worn by Mickey and Minnie on New Year's Day. Given the success of the park in Japan and the historic popularity of Disney's cartoons in Europe, it was understandable that Disney would try to replicate in Paris what had worked in Tokyo.

Restructuring

Faced with so many difficulties, Disney's management was forced to act. Ticket and hotel prices were lowered and partnerships were signed with tourist agencies and tour operators to bring in new visitors. Attractions were also redesigned for winter use. The park adapted the food to local taste and started selling alcohol (wine and beer) in some restaurants.

(continued)

(continued)

In this context, rumors started to spread that the park would close. This was not actually an option for Disney. The company had gone too far to step back at this point. Restructuring the whole project was the only option. Crisis talks between Disney, Disneyland Paris, and the park's creditors resulted in an agreement that included:

- a major capital increase in which Disney would take a leading role
- a waiver[27] of 18 months' interest payment by the banks
- a postponement of the principal repayment by three years,
- the cancellation by Disney of several hundred million of receivables due from Euro Disneyland SCA
- a waiver of all royalty payments due to Disney for five years, and
- a sharp reduction of royalty payments after that.

The restructuring was accepted by lenders in June 1994. In parallel, Saudi prince Al-Waleed took a 10% stake in Euro Disney, becoming the second largest shareholder of the park after Disney itself.

Epilogue

While the agreement gave Disneyland Paris some temporary breathing space, troubles resurfaced eight years later in 2002, when Disneyland Paris opened its second park, The Walt Disney Studio, a complex of attractions adjacent to the first park. This massive investment put Disneyland Paris in trouble for a second time and in February 2004 a new agreement was struck with creditors to restructure the debt.

The same recipe was applied: debt restructuring, a cut in royalty payments, and a capital increase. A few years later in 2014, amid renewed difficulties, Disney subscribed to a third equity increase. In 2017, Disney finally decided to take full control of the project, offering to buy out the remaining shareholders. It marked the end of an ill-fated adventure in project finance – and, paradoxically, one that resulted in one of Europe's main tourist attractions.

---

[27] A waiver is a consent to give up a right. In this specific case, the lenders agreed not to receive interest payments for 18 months although they had a contractual right to them in the loan agreement.

CHAPTER 6

Project Finance Structuring

6.1 PRELIMINARY ANALYSIS OF THE PROJECT

Project finance presents a number of risks. It involves the triple challenge of funding a company (i) without a track record, (ii) that requires heavy investment, and (iii) that – given the construction period – will not be in a position to generate cash flow immediately.

Project finance and LBOs share some obvious similarities. Both structures are meant to finance an asset (a company or infrastructure) via an SPV with a mix of debt and equity. Debt repayment and investor returns stem solely from the cash flow generated by this asset. In both cases, lenders have no recourse to the sponsors in case the SPV defaults. They have to size their loan based on the ability of the asset to generate revenues.

Nonetheless, these two financing structures differ in one major respect: project finance is generally not meant to finance an asset that is already operating (except brownfield transactions). Its purpose is to enable the construction of an asset. Lenders are therefore exposed to construction risk. This is what sets project finance apart from the other techniques analyzed in this book, including asset finance and securitization. For this reason, project finance requires detailed due diligence before any investment decision is made. All potential risks have to be identified and lenders have to make sure that in each case a solution is implemented to properly mitigate the risk.

6.1.1 Construction Risk

Construction risk is defined as the sum of all the risks that can delay or prevent the construction of a project or significantly push up its total cost. To minimize these risks, lenders never commit to finance a project before the SPV has obtained all the necessary building permits. They also generally rely on a technical advisor (called lenders' technical advisor or LTA) to identify the peculiarities of the project. This advisor ascertains that the project is technically viable and that the construction can take place seamlessly within the budget presented by the sponsors.[1]

Construction risk is also minimized by subcontracting the construction of projects to reputable companies with a strong track record in that field. These firms usually also provide a certain number of guarantees through their standard construction contracts. They usually agree to bear cost overruns and to indemnify their clients in case of significant delays or defects in the construction. Lenders and sponsors pay close attention not only to the track record of the construction company but also to its credit quality. This may be an important point if indemnities have to be paid to the SPV in case of delays or defects in the construction.

Sponsors tend to limit the number of counterparties they contract with. They often rely on contracts covering jointly engineering, procurement, and construction (EPC). Through an EPC contract, a project company transfers to a contractor the full responsibility of building the project. The contractor takes charge of the design, procurement, construction, commissioning, and the handing over of the infrastructure to the project company. By having only one EPC contract with a major firm instead of a multitude of contracts for each of the elements of construction, sponsors minimize construction risk. They improve the efficiency of the construction process and avoid the risk that a minor supplier will underperform or go bankrupt during the construction. This risk is instead transferred to the EPC contractor.

For large and complex projects, it is not uncommon to have a consortium of companies in charge of the EPC rather than one single contractor only. In that case, the EPC contract must state that the entities in charge of the EPC are jointly and severally liable to the SPV.

6.1.2   Resource Risk

The economic viability of a project sometimes depends on the presence of natural resources. This is especially true for projects in the mining or oil and gas sectors. Sponsors and lenders must ensure that the current reserves enable the project to be viable over the long term. Specialized engineers and independent geologists are responsible for assessing the probable availability of resources, both in terms of quantity and accessibility. Sponsors conduct a first analysis themselves (or through mandated experts), but lenders generally require a second expert opinion. Lenders usually take a base case with an x% certainty over the stock and run sensitivities based on probable downside scenarios.

Resource risk also exists for projects in the renewable energy space. Wind and irradiation studies are carried out by experts during the development phase. They are

---

[1]In practice, the LTA is mandated by the project company before the banks are selected. The LTA prepares a report that is shared with prospective lenders. Lenders use the conclusions of this report to make their investment decision.

shared with lenders when the financing is structured. Studies are ideally performed over several years to ensure that the data collected truly reflects the typical weather conditions of the place where the project is located.

6.1.3   Credit Risk

The credit risk borne by lenders in project financing depends on various factors:

- *Origin of the project cash flow*: As mentioned in Chapter 5, section 5.1, the nature of a project and the origin of its cash flow have a direct impact on the risk taken by the lenders. A PPP in which an SPV receives availability payments from the German government has very little in common with a highway concession fully exposed to traffic risk. In the PPP case, lenders accept the risk of a counterparty rated AAA by S&P and Aaa by Moody's.[2] In the case of a concession, the analysis is more complex. Lenders must get familiar with the other transportation options available and understand the gain in terms of time and comfort provided by the new highway.
- *Leverage of the structure*: Lenders adapt the leverage to the quality and the certainty of the cash flow. All things being equal, PPPs with AAA counterparties are more leveraged than projects exposed to merchant/traffic risk or projects in emerging markets.
- *Strategic importance of the project*: The risk that lenders are exposed to is also a function of the importance of the project for the sponsor. Although project finance is non-recourse, sponsors can always decide to recapitalize an SPV in case of underperformance. The restructuring of Disneyland Paris after tough beginnings (see case study 6) occurred because The Walt Disney Company did not want to abandon such a symbolic project. Lenders had no legal recourse on The Walt Disney Company, but Disney was too exposed reputation-wise to let the project go. Similar situations can also be found in PPPs. A public authority, for instance, would rather agree on restructuring a non-performing project than run the risk of operational disruption.
- *Nature of the securities provided to the lenders*: Lenders usually insist on a security package that includes a pledge on the shares of the SPV. In case of default, they can exercise their rights, take control of the SPV and sell the company to a third party to pay off the debt. The quality of the infrastructure is an additional element of comfort for lenders. Some projects are more liquid than others. In the UK, for instance, the M6 toll road was sold in June 2017 to IFM after the original lenders took control of the asset from Macquarie in December 2013 following a default.

---

[2]Credit rating of the Federal Republic of Germany as of September 2020.

6.1.4   Market Risk

Some projects (notably in the energy sector) are by nature exposed to market risk. The product they sell (gas, oil, power, etc.) is freely tradable and its price can vary greatly over time. This market risk hurts the capacity of an SPV to secure long-term financing. It may even prevent sponsors from securing project debt, which means that the asset will not be built or must be financed via a corporate loan.

To minimize (or neutralize) this risk, sponsors can negotiate long-term offtake contracts with potential clients. Through this type of contract, an SPV sells all or part of its output at a predetermined price over a long period. One or several offtake contracts can be signed to partly or totally offset this market risk. Long-term offtake contracts with creditworthy counterparties generally enable a project company to secure long-term funding.

As already explained in Chapter 5, many governments have chosen to eliminate market risk for project companies to develop renewable energy sources like wind or solar farms. They offer *feed-in tariffs*, where they purchase electricity at a fixed price and for a long period of time (c. 20 years) from energy producers providing green energy. Alternatively, governments also offer *Contracts for Difference* (CfD), where they top up the price at which the project company sells power to a pre-agreed level.[3]

6.1.5   Rate Risk

It is key for parties in project finance to eliminate any risk of variation in interest rates. With large amounts of debt typically involved, there is a risk that the profitability of the project is sharply reduced in case of a rise in interest rates. The longer the project, the higher the risk.

The need to hedge interest rate risk comes from the fact that banks lend at floating rates. The cost of debt for a project company (and for anyone) is normally the sum of a reference rate (which is the liquidity cost of the bank) and a margin (which is based on the credit risk of the borrower – the higher the risk, the higher the margin). The margin is established explicitly in the contract (200bps, 300bps, etc.)[4] but the reference rate is floating and varies constantly depending on the supply and demand of liquidity for banks.[5]

To hedge this risk, sponsors usually swap a fixed rate for the floating rate due under the loan. This is done via an Interest Rate Swap (or IRS), where the project company pays a fixed rate to a financial institution and receives a floating rate in return. This floating amount is calibrated to match the floating rate payments due by the SPV under the project loan. On the whole, it is as if the project company had transformed a floating-rate loan into a fixed-rate loan.

---

[3]Governments usually organize public tenders to award these feed-in tariffs or CfD. The winner of the tender is the consortium bidding with the lowest level of feed-in tariffs or CfD (i.e. bidding for the lowest amount of governmental subsidies).
[4]As a reminder, one bp (basis point) is equal to 0.01%. So 300 bps = 3%.
[5]See Appendix A (How Banks Set Interest Rates) for more information.

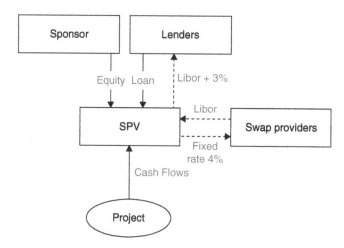

FIGURE 6.1   Interest Rate Swap in Project Finance

Figure 6.1 illustrates this contractual arrangement. In this example, a project company borrows at LIBOR + 300bps for a 20-year period. In parallel, it enters into an IRS where it pays 4% and receives LIBOR.[6] The total synthetic cost of debt comes to a fixed rate of 7% (4% + 3%).

The hedging counterparties to a project finance transaction are generally the banks that have acted as lenders in the transaction. This is a way for them to secure additional revenues that will not be too capital intensive (IRSs do not translate into high RWAs). However, this is a market practice that is not mandatory and other institutions can also provide swaps.

Unlike banks, infrastructure debt funds are more likely to offer fixed rates to project companies. They have a different business model, in which they collect funds from limited partners who are looking for fixed returns (to pay pensions, for instance). These funds do not have the funding constraints that banks do and usually prefer to offer fixed-rate loans.

6.1.6   Foreign Exchange Rate Risk

Exchange risk appears when the revenues and (operating or financial) expenses of the SPV are denominated in different currencies. This is the case, for example, if a project company sells its output in US dollars but has to pay lenders, suppliers or subcontractors in a local currency. Any fall in the dollar leads to a decrease in the profitability of the project company.

---

[6]The fixed rate (that we have set here randomly at 4%) is in reality determined when the IRS is signed on the basis of market expectations for LIBOR over the IRS period: 20 years in this case. This fixed rate is the weighted average of the expected floating rates over the next 20 years. In this example it means that at the time the IRS is signed, the market considers that receiving a fixed rate of 4% over 20 years equals to paying the expected floating rates over that same period.

The best way to limit this risk is to align as much as possible the currency of the construction with the currency in which project revenues are denominated. This is usually done both during the construction and the operations phase:

- *During the construction phase*: The alignment of currencies is done either through direct negotiations with suppliers (the SPV can request to pay in the project's currency) or by using currency hedging instruments during the construction. Eliminating FX risk during the construction provides certainty about the amount of debt to be raised by the project company.
- *During the operational phase*: Debt is usually raised in the same currency as that for which the product or service is sold. Neither lenders nor sponsors want to face a mismatch risk over a period of 15 or 20 years. Since currency hedging over such a long period is too costly, the only solution is generally to have debt and output denominated in the same currency. There are exceptions when projects (i) are located in countries where the local currency is pegged to the US dollar, and (ii) sell their output in that currency (in some Middle Eastern countries, for instance). In that case, sponsors want sometimes to raise debt in US dollars and not in the local currency, because there is more liquidity in dollars and margins are lower. This increases the sponsors' IRR. This creates, nonetheless, additional risk for the lenders as some countries have in the past abandoned the peg to the US dollar (Argentina).

6.1.7   Operational Risk

Operational risk is inherent in the construction and maintenance of projects. Lenders mitigate this risk by working mainly with sponsors that have a strong track record or have successfully completed similar projects. Sponsors do exactly the same when selecting suppliers. The contracts between the SPV and its various subcontractors are analyzed by lenders during the due diligence phase. These contracts contain professional guarantees and stringent obligations in terms of insurance.

6.1.8   Technological Risk

There is technological risk if the success of the project depends on technology that is particularly novel or at risk of becoming obsolete. In such a case, the project can generally not secure project debt. Financing new technology is more a domain for venture capitalists than for project finance specialists.

6.1.9   Political Risk

Political risk refers mainly to the threats of a political nature that can jeopardize the profitability or even the existence of a project. This risk is high in countries with recurrent political instability and a history of violence. A project can be destroyed during a war or a wave of social unrest or by an act of terrorism. The sponsors can also be expropriated, or the project nationalized by a government. To limit these risks, lenders can negotiate political risk insurance. This insurance can cover all or some of the afore-mentioned risks but also risks like the legal impossibility of the sponsor transferring cash out of the country where the project is located.

To some extent, political risk also exists in mature markets in the sense that polit-ical decisions, unforeseen at the time of financing, can have a strong impact on a project's profitability. This sub-set of political risk, which is very different from the risks we have already mentioned, is referred to as *change in law risk*. Like those risks, it also emanates from the public sphere, but pertains more to specific democratic deci-sions than political events. To mitigate change in law risks, lenders generally require that the legal documentation stipulates that additional costs incurred due to a legisla-tive change come at the expense of sponsors.

6.1.10   Environmental Risk

All projects involving the construction of infrastructure have an impact on the envi-ronment. This impact can be minor but has to be precisely assessed before the project starts. Penalties and reputational damage can be extensive for sponsors and lenders involved in projects that ultimately do environmental damage.

Lenders must ensure that the parties involved in the construction and mainte-nance of the asset are capable of respecting high-quality standards and that all neces-sary environmental licenses have been obtained by the SPV. The risk of a change in regulation that could increase these costs in the future is difficult to assess but can be limited by making sure that the infrastructure uses state-of-the-art equipment.

In some cases, costs to decommission the infrastructure have to be factored into the financial projections as well, as is the case in renewable energy projects. Wind and solar farms are generally awarded for a given period of time that corresponds to the expected lifetime of the infrastructure. After that period, the sponsors have to dis-mantle the equipment, and lenders must ensure that these costs have been taken into account.

6.1.11   Force Majeure and Other Risks

6.1.11.1   Force Majeure

The force majeure risk is a risk of prolonged business interruption due to an event outside anyone's control. Although there is no clear definition of force majeure, it is generally acknowledged that such events must be (i) unforeseeable, (ii) external to the parties to the contract, and (iii) unavoidable. Natural disasters like earthquakes, fires, floods, etc. fall into this category. Strikes or riots do as well.

Lenders generally insist on being protected against any risk of loss caused by a force majeure incident. Most of these risks (fire, earthquake, etc.) are covered by appropriate insurance policies. The loan agreement between the SPV and the lenders include the obligation by the SPV to have these risks insured.

6.1.11.2 Other Risks

The obligation to insure the SPV against various risks is not limited to force majeure. It includes a wide range of risks that are generally covered by two main insurance policies:

- *property insurance*, which covers the loss and the total or partial destruction of the infrastructure (and where force majeure risks are covered), and
- *third party liability insurance*, which provides indemnification in case the infrastructure is found to be responsible for damage caused to third parties (for instance, in the case of a leak in a factory that would damage the property of a neighbor).

The benefit of these insurance policies is generally assigned to the lenders. In other words, if an event requires the insurance company to indemnify the SPV, the indemnity may be directly paid to the lenders if they have suffered a loss following this event. This gives lenders an additional level of comfort as the cash will not transit via the SPV.

6.2   PROJECT FINANCE LEGAL STRUCTURE

Legal documentation in project finance is extremely detailed. Its role is to govern the relations between all the parties during the life of the project. Given the length of a project finance transaction and the level of risks involved, many potential issues have to be envisaged and dealt with.

6.2.1   Establishment of the SPV

6.2.1.1   Characteristics of the Project Company

The use of a project company to build, finance, own, and operate an infrastructure is the cornerstone of project financing.

From a legal perspective, the role of the SPV is to isolate the project from the other assets of the sponsor. In case the project fails, the sponsor is not financially liable beyond its initial equity investment. Lenders to the project company have no recourse on the other assets of the sponsors.

From a financial point of view, isolating an asset that generates steady revenues over a long period allows lenders to provide matching long-term debt to the project. Offering a long-term loan would not be possible if these revenues were mixed with the other assets and liabilities of the sponsor, i.e. with other more volatile cash flow and non-predictable expenses.

An SPV has a very narrow and restricted social object, namely the construction, financing, and operation of a project. It cannot change its strategy and has very limited scope to make decisions without prior consent of the lenders.

6.2.1.2 Employees

The project company subcontracts generally to external entities all the main aspects of the project. Subcontracting agreements involve the deployment of personnel (for the construction, the maintenance, and the operation) but these employees are usually not directly hired by the project company. They are employed by the companies acting as subcontractors.

An SPV can nonetheless have employees. In this case, they are usually seconded from one of the sponsors and their role is generally to monitor all the projects' sub-contractors and report on the performance of the asset to sponsors and lenders. If any, the number of direct employees is typically very limited.

Exceptions to the rule exist but are rare. Notable exceptions include large assets that need a lot of personnel. Eurotunnel[7] and Disneyland Paris, two major projects of the 1990s, had their own staff from the start. However, both companies were slightly more than just SPVs. They were in charge of complex projects that were offering a high level of service to clients. They were also both publicly listed and had to demonstrate to their supervisory authority that they could act autonomously without resorting extensively to employees seconded by other companies.

6.2.2 Loan Agreement

6.2.2.1 Main Features of a Project Finance Loan

Like LBOs, project finance transactions can be structured as club deals or include an underwriting.[8] The loan agreement signed between the lenders and the SPV is the main legal document in project financing. It contains the amount that each lender commits to lending as well as the expected drawdown schedule. Project finance loans are not drawn at once, but in stages over the progress of construction (unless the loan is used to refinance a brownfield asset).

Construction is usually divided into several phases. Each phase is clearly identified in the loan agreement, associated with a specific cost, and ends with a predetermined milestone, generally the completion of a part of the project. Once a milestone is reached, the SPV is allowed to draw on the loan so that the SPV can pay the construction company.

Drawdowns on the loan are also subject to *conditions precedent* unrelated to the construction of the project. A condition precedent (or CP) may be the receipt of a

---

[7]Groupe Eurotunnel, now Getlink, is the name of the company that was in charge of building the Channel Tunnel. It is now in charge of managing and operating this infrastructure. Getlink is listed on Euronext (and was listed on the London Stock Exchange until 2012).
[8]See Appendix B (Syndication and Club Deals) for more details.

construction permit, administrative approval, and satisfactory environmental or technical audits. Drawdowns can also be subject to the completion of actions by third parties. In some projects, for instance, infrastructure can only be used if the government builds a road to access the project. Building that road may be a CP to start drawing on the loan.

A project finance loan can include a second tranche of debt in addition to the main facility. This second tranche is not necessarily drawn upon but can be used by the project company in case of project overruns. It is meant to cover unforeseen additional costs and gives some flexibility to the SPV in case of a hiccup during construction. The amount of this second tranche is obviously capped at a pre-agreed amount. The margin on this tranche is usually higher than the one applicable on the main tranche.

6.2.2.2   Reserve Accounts

We have seen in Part I of this book on leveraged buyouts (section 2.3.2.2) that borrowers in a loan agreement have to make a certain number of commitments to the lenders. These commitments are called *covenants* and are essentially a guarantee from the borrower that (i) certain activities will or will not be carried out, or (ii) some actions will or will not be taken. Covenants are elements of protection for lenders. A breach in these covenants triggers sanctions for the borrower, including, in some cases, the obligation to repay the loan if the breach is not remedied within a pre-agreed cure period.

The setting aside of cash reserves in specific accounts at the SPV level is one of the most common covenants in project finance. Cash in these accounts can be used by the project company to cover large outflows. Thanks to this mechanism, these payments can occur without disrupting the project or affecting the SPV's debt repayment obligations.

There are generally two reserve accounts, each with a specific and well-identified purpose:

- The debt service reserve account (DSRA) is used if the project company is unable to repay its debt (in case the asset has temporarily ceased operating due to a specific issue, for instance).
- The maintenance reserve account (MMRA) ensures that cash is regularly put aside by the SPV in order to fund future major unavoidable and clearly identified capital or operating expenses (resurfacing of a highway or an airport runway, for instance).

The maximum balance in these reserve accounts is subject to negotiations between lenders and sponsors. The amount in the DSRA is a multiple of the average monthly debt service of the SPV (6, 12, 24 months, etc.). The amount in the MMRA is generally set as a percentage of the total project capex. The SPV stops making payments to these accounts once the maximum balance has been reached. If funds from these accounts are used at some point during the project, the balance has to be reconstituted.

The funding method for the establishment of the DSRA and MMRA is usually stated in the loan agreement and is one of the following:

- the reserve accounts are funded in full on the last day of construction
- they are partially funded on the last day of construction, then built up from the project's cash flow
- they are completely built up from the project's cash flow.

These cash reserves can sometimes be replaced by bank guarantees. In this case sponsors counter-guarantee the risk taken by the banks.

6.2.2.3   Debt Service Coverage Ratio

The loan agreement also includes covenants that ensure that the project company maintains certain minimum predetermined financial ratios. If the project company is not able to keep these ratios above the level agreed in the loan agreement, sanctions can be taken against the SPV.

One of these key ratios is called *Debt Service Cover Ratio* (DSCR). The DSCR is calculated as the total annual net operating cash flow divided by the total annual debt repayment obligations. Mathematically:

$$DSCR = NOCFt/(P + I)t$$

with

NOCF = Net Operating Cash Flow
P = Principal to be repaid
I = Interest to be paid
and t = a given year

The project documentation usually requires that the SPV maintains this ratio above a certain level. Several DSCRs can be calculated for the same transaction:

- The target DSCR is the DSCR determined in the base case for the project. It is the ratio expected by the parties if the project performs as expected.
- The lockup DCSR is lower than the target DSCR. If this ratio is reached, no payments can be made by the project company to the shareholders. It is meant as a protection for the lenders in case a project underperforms.
- The default DSCR is even lower than the lockup DSCR. It is the ratio that can trigger an event of default by the lenders (see section 6.2.2.6).

The DSCR required by lenders varies depending on the type of transaction. It is much higher for a project exposed to merchant risk than for a PPP in Western Europe with a creditworthy counterparty. The level of a DSCR is also impacted by market conditions applicable at closing. When liquidity is abundant, lenders tend to be more aggressive and compete not only in terms of margin and maturity, but also in terms of total leverage offered to the sponsors.

6.2.2.4   Loan Life Cover Ratio

Maintaining the Loan Life Cover Ratio or LLCR above a certain level is another common covenant in project finance. In contrast with the DSCR, which is simply a measure of a project's capacity to make its scheduled bank repayments at a given moment t, the LLCR provides a picture of the ability of the SPV to make repayments in the future. It measures the coverage rate of future cash flow available during the financing period in relation to the total debt of the SPV. It is calculated as follows:

$$LLCR = (\Sigma(OCFt/(1+i)^t) + DRt)/Dt$$

with

OCF = Operating Cash Flow

i = the discount rate

DR = amount available in the debt reserve account

D = total debt amount

and t = a given year

To calculate the numerator, the LLCR adds the present value of future net operating cash flow and the cash currently available in the reserve account. This sum is then divided by the amount due by the SPV to the lenders. The minimum LLCR required by lenders varies depending on the type of transaction. It is higher for projects exposed to merchant risk than for PPP with a creditworthy public entity.

6.2.2.5   Other Covenants

In addition to the covenants mentioned already (reserve accounts and financial ratios), loan agreements include other covenants that are more obvious and easier to negotiate. Like all covenants, they can be drafted in an affirmative or negative manner:

- Affirmative covenants: maintaining an adequate level of insurance, sharing the SPV's financial statements with the lenders, complying with applicable laws, etc.
- Negative covenants: commitment (i) not to use the proceeds of the loan to finance anything else than the project itself, (ii) not to perform actions that are not directly or indirectly linked to the project, and (iii) not to take any additional loan without the prior unanimous consent of the lenders, etc.

6.2.2.6   Events of Default

As explained earlier in the book when discussing LBOs (Chapter 2, section 2.3.2.3), an event of default is a predefined circumstance where lenders have the right to demand the early repayment of a loan. In a project finance loan, these events are not limited to the insolvency or bankruptcy of the project company. A breach of a covenant can trigger an event of default. If, for instance, the DSCR or the LLCR falls below a certain level or if the SPV performs actions that are forbidden under the loan agreement (like using its funds to acquire properties unrelated to the project), lenders can request immediate repayment of the loan.

Since the project company does not usually have the funds to do so (all revenues have been put towards debt repayment or dividends distributions), lenders do not automatically request an early repayment of the loan in case of default – even if they are entitled to do so. They may be more interested in seeking a compromise with the sponsors to remedy the default.

The objective of the lenders is, after all, to maximize their chances of getting repaid. If they believe the best option is to find an agreement with the sponsors and restructure the debt, they may decide to choose this path. This was the case with Disneyland Paris. Banks thought it made more sense to work hand-in-hand with The Walt Disney Company rather than exercise their rights under the security package to repossess the SPV. In this situation, the debt was rescheduled over a longer period, and the sponsor forwent dividend distributions for a certain number of years.

Restructuring the debt is not always possible or may simply be unsuccessful. In that case, lenders can always acknowledge default and exercise their rights under the security package (see section 6.2.3 on the security package). This occurred in the case of the M6 toll mentioned earlier. Banks repossessed the asset from Macquarie following an event of default and later sold it to IFM.

6.2.2.7 Junior Loan

The junior loan (if any) is documented in a separated agreement, signed between the borrower and the junior lenders. The mechanisms governing the junior loan are very similar to the rules applicable to the senior loan. There are covenants and events of defaults. The main difference is that senior lenders rank first in terms of repayment and securities (see section 6.2.3). Interactions between junior lenders and senior lenders are governed by a document called an *intercreditor agreement*.

6.2.3 The Security Package

6.2.3.1 Description of the Security Package

In consideration of their financial commitment to the project company, lenders obtain a certain number of securities. They can exercise these securities in case of an event of default. Commonly referred to as a *security package*, it generally includes the following elements:

1. A pledge on the shares of the SPV: This allows lenders to take control of the project company in case of default. They can then freely restructure the project, sell the project company to another sponsor or sell only parts of the project.

2. Step-in rights: These are rights given to lenders to "step in" to the project company's shoes and take control of the SPV – temporarily – without obtaining legal ownership. This allows lenders to force important decisions when needed, even if the board of the project company is unable or unwilling to make them. Step-in rights mechanisms are more flexible to exercise than a pledge over the shares of the SPV. They can be used to solve a temporary issue.

3. A pledge over all the SPV's bank accounts: This mechanism allows lenders to take control of the project company's bank accounts and the cash that sits in them. It gives lenders quick and direct access to the cash of the SPV in case of default.

4. A direct assignment of all the payments due to the project company: This allows lenders to benefit directly from all the payments due by the debtors of the defaulting project company.

5. A mortgage over the project itself (if legally possible, as explained in Chapter 4, section 4.4, Table 4.1): This security implies that the project company cannot legally sell its assets without the prior consent of the mortgage holders (i.e. the lenders).

In case a junior loan is signed at the SPV level between the borrowers and another group of lenders, these lenders also receive a security package. Logically, this security package is lighter than that of the senior lenders. It generally includes a second priority pledge on the shares of the SPV and a second priority mortgage on the asset itself. The term "second priority" means that junior lenders can exercise their rights but rank second to the senior lenders. In the case of a default and subsequent exercise of the pledge over shares of the SPV by lenders, the proceeds of the sale of the shares of the SPV are first assigned to the senior lenders and then to the junior lenders. In other words, junior lenders cannot be indemnified before the senior lenders have recovered their full investment.

6.2.3.2   Analysis of the Security Package

The assurances of a security package should not mask the delicate position lenders fall into when an SPV defaults. All the elements of the security package are directly linked to the infrastructure and its performance, meaning that in case of default (usually triggered by underperforming assets) there is a high probability that the value of the securities is seriously dented. It does not mean that the security package has no value, only that it might not be enough.

To minimize losses in the case of default, lenders have to act swiftly. They have to make the right call on whether to exercise their pledge on the shares of the SPV, restructure the debt, or negotiate with the sponsors or the offtaker (or the public entity in the case of a PPP). They can also push to replace the operation and maintenance (O&M) operator if poor performance is the reason for default.

From a conceptual perspective, lenders in project finance are in the same position as a senior lender in an LBO: they have no recourse to the sponsors. The only difference is that the type of business they finance is usually more resilient and has higher barriers to entry. Their security package is perceived as stronger.

6.2.4   Other Financial Documents

6.2.4.1   Intercreditor Agreement

The intercreditor agreement is a document signed by all lenders and swap providers to the project company.[9] It governs their relationships and describes how they are supposed to interact among themselves and with the SPV. If the project has several debt facilities, it sets out the ranking between them and how payments are made. These tranches of debt can have different ranking (junior and senior loans) or be pari passu (i.e. having the same ranking). A project can have two tranches of senior debt with different maturities, for instance (say, one 18-year tranche and one 30-year tranche).

An intercreditor agreement is necessary, as many decisions have to be taken by lenders and swap providers during the life of the project. Even a minor delay in the construction schedule may require a modification to the loan schedule. The project company in this case must ask the lenders for a change in the loan profile. An intercreditor agreement will typically deal with this type of situation and explain the steps to be taken by the SPV and the lenders to modify the loan agreement.

6.2.4.2   VAT Facility

A credit line called a *VAT facility* is usually necessary to finance the VAT applicable to expenses incurred during the construction of the project. Given that the SPV does not generate revenues during this phase, it does not invoice VAT and cannot offset the VAT due to its suppliers with the VAT collected from its clients. The SPV has a VAT credit.

The VAT credit is repaid by the government where the SPV is established. The repayment usually only occurs after three to six months, and during this period, a VAT facility is needed to bridge this outflow.

In practice, VAT is due on each payment made during construction. This implies that the VAT facility must be structured in such a way that it can be drawn and repaid several times during the construction period.

---

[9]Swap providers are creditors of the SPV in the sense that they expect financial flows from the project company (fixed rate flows to be paid under the IRS signed with the SPV). They are also at the same time debtors to the project company (they have to pay floating to the SPV). See section 6.1.5 (on rate risk) for more information. When the IRS is signed, the series of flows to be paid by the SPV and the ones to be paid by the swap providers are equivalent. However, as rates continue moving, the value of the series of floating flows evolves over time. If rates go up, swap providers become net debtors of the project company (they owe more to the SPV than the SPV owes them). If the IRS is terminated at that time (due to a bankruptcy of the SPV and subsequent termination of the IRS), they will owe money to the project company (and will have to pay the SPV). In case rates go down, the swap providers are net creditors to the SPV (and the SPV will have to pay them if the IRS is terminated). For all these reasons, swap providers must be part of the intercreditor agreement.

6.2.5   Project Documents

The project documents are agreements that are necessary for the project but are not financial documents.

6.2.5.1   Construction (or EPC) Contract

Our reader is now well aware that a project is only bankable if the counterparty in charge of the construction is a reputable party. This gives comfort to sponsors and lenders and minimizes risks. As already mentioned, the construction is sometimes carried out by the sponsor or one of its affiliates. This is often the case for core infrastructure like highways or airports. The same group can invest in equity and build the project. Major European construction firms like ACS or Sacyr (Spain), Atlantia (Italy), or Vinci and Eiffage (France) are all active on both the construction and the investment sides.

However, there are situations where the construction is done by a party that has no link to the sponsors. This is the case, for example, in the energy sector. Renewable energy developers do not build their wind or solar farms themselves. They rely on traditional construction firms (like the ones mentioned earlier).

The construction company usually commits to delivering the project within a predetermined schedule and pre-agreed budget. Indemnities have to be paid in case of failure to do so. This is a key element of the contract, as many projects awarded following public tenders have to be completed within a certain timeline to be eligible for subsidies or an offtake contract. For this reason, sponsors prefer to work with creditworthy construction companies that have extensive expertise.

We have already explained that a construction contract can be integrated into a full EPC contract, i.e. an agreement including all the engineering, procurement, and construction aspects of a project. An EPC contract greatly simplifies the construction process and allows the SPV to transfer a series of risks to one single construction company.

But an EPC contract is not always possible or desirable. EPC contracts are, indeed, quite expensive (after all, the construction company gets paid to coordinate the whole process and take additional risk). Furthermore, an EPC contract does not always make sense from an industrial perspective. It is sometimes more efficient to have the sponsor directly planning and arranging the construction. When a wind farm is built, it is common to have the turbine supply agreement totally separate from the rest. This other contract is called the BoP contract (balance of plant). It is sometimes even separated into two contracts, one for the civil works and one for the electrical works. To secure attractive financing terms, all parties to these contracts have to be reputable firms.

6.2.5.2   Operation and Maintenance Contract

The O&M contract is the agreement where the SPV delegates to a third party the O&M of the project. This entity is often related to the sponsor (or one of the sponsors). The cost of this contract is known in advance and indexed to inflation. It is disclosed to the lenders so that they have full knowledge of the project cash flow.

6.2.5.3   Offtake Agreements (and other Contracts through which an SPV Generates Revenues)

The contract that provides visibility on the SPV's revenues is a key element of the contractual set. It is the main driver of the financing and, as such, the cornerstone of every project finance structure. Depending on the nature of the project, various contract types may apply.

  - An offtake agreement is the contract through which the SPV sells all or most of its production under a pre-agreed price and conditions. Ideally, it covers a long period and involves a creditworthy counterparty. The contract tenor and the credit quality of the offtaker have a direct impact on the financing conditions of the project (margin, maturity, total leverage, etc.).
  - In a PPP, a PPP contract is signed between the project company and the public entity involved in the PPP. A PPP contract sets the availability payments to be paid and the cases in which these payments are reduced.
  - When a contract is awarded as a concession, a concession contract is signed between the project company (i.e. concessionaire) and the conceding party. Concession contracts can take various forms. An SPV can be fully exposed to merchant or traffic risk or can benefit from subsidies. It can pay for the right to operate the concession upfront or via an annual (or regular) payment during the life of the project. The nature of the cash flow can vary but is, as always in project finance, the key element in sizing the debt.

6.2.5.4   Lease Agreement

The lease agreement is the contract whereby the SPV obtains the right to use a specific site to locate its project. Lenders must ensure that the lease maturity is at least equal to the expected life of the project. The lease agreement can be signed with a government-controlled entity or with a third party willing to generate revenues from an unused parcel of land.

Lenders must also verify that the project company has obtained from the relevant authorities the right to build the project. Getting a construction permit free of appeal is a prerequisite before putting together the financing package.

6.2.5.5   Agreement(s) with the Host Country

Thanks to their contribution to economic development and job creation, some projects (not all, obviously) carry a strong political dimension. When this is the case, these projects involve a master agreement between sponsors and the government of the country where the project is located. This agreement contains the general framework and the specific regulations applicable to the project.

These specific regulations can include some advantages granted to the SPV: subsidies, tax incentives, bespoke regulations, free site allocation, etc. Sponsors are often required in exchange to commit to hiring a predetermined number of employees locally and/or to contract with local suppliers. A typical example of a contract of this kind is the agreement signed between the French government and The Walt Disney Company before the construction of Disneyland Paris (case study 6).

6.3 FINANCIAL STRUCTURE

6.3.1 The Financial Model

6.3.1.1 Building a Financial Model

One of the most complex steps in project finance is finalizing the financial model that will be used as a reference for the project. This exercise is extremely important and cannot be neglected. It is the business plan of the project company. All revenues and expenses of the SPV have to be identified and fed into the model to see if the project makes sense from a financial perspective given the sponsors' IRR requirements and the market condition for the debt.

Compared to a traditional business plan – or, more precisely, compared to the business plan of a traditional company – the project finance model raises the following challenges:

- Debt being relatively high, any error in the calibration of future revenues can have a material impact on the repayment capacity of the SPV and can threaten the continuity of the project.
- The maturity of the financing being relatively long, the cash flow of the project company has to be modelled for a longer period than for traditional business plans (rarely more than five years), which increases the risk of inaccuracy.
- The company's objective and its asset life being limited, it is complicated and often even impossible to materially change the strategy of the company in case of difficulties. In other words, there is no plan B. If the project company does not deliver on its business plan, shareholders and possibly lenders, will have to take a loss.

Building a sound project finance model requires experience. The model is built step-by-step and focuses successively on three main elements of the project: (i) identification of the revenues and operating expenses of the SPV, (ii) investment necessary during the construction phase, and (iii) debt sizing.

6.3.1.2 Identifying Operating Cash Flow

Developing a finance model begins with the identification of the operating cash flow. The financial modelers feed into the model all the positive and negative flow irrespective of financing considerations. This phase is mostly driven by industrial considerations. The construction schedule, the capital expenditure (capex), and the operating expenses (opex) are all based on inputs provided by the sponsors' technical teams. These elements form the backbone of the financial model. They cannot be optimized by financiers. The financial modeler has to use the assumptions provided by engineers.

Modeling the revenues of the SPV is slightly more complex. The way to feed them into the financial model depends on the project's legal framework. Projected revenues can either be an assumption or an output of the model.

- If the project is fully exposed to merchant risk, the calculation of revenues is based on data provided by the sponsors and their advisors. Revenues are an assumption of the model.
- If the project is a PPP with availability payments, the project is awarded to the sponsor that has bid for the lowest amount of availability payments. In this case, revenues are an output of the model. They are determined by the financial model considering debt conditions and the targeted sponsor's IRR.
- If the project relies on a mix of availability payments and merchant risk, part of the revenues is an output while another part is based on assumptions made by the sponsors.

The difference between projected revenues and expenses is equal to the operating cash flow of the project. Table 6.1 summarizes how the net operating cash flow is calculated.

TABLE 6.1 Simplified Calculation of Net Operating Cash Flow in Project Financing

Net Operating Cash Flow	
+	Revenues
−	Cost of raw materials (if any)
−	Operating and maintenance costs
−	Insurance
−	Levies and taxes
=	Gross operating cash flow
−	Increase/decrease in working capital requirement (WCR)
=	Net operating cash flow

A project starts generating operating cash flow once the construction is over. There are of course situations in which construction and operating periods partially overlap each other. This is the case, for instance, with mega projects like offshore wind farms, for which the production of electricity can start before all the wind turbines are installed. In this case, there can be revenues during the construction period (called *pre-completion revenues*).

6.3.1.3 Role of the Financial Advisor

Financial models being very complex, they are often built by a financial advisor acting on behalf of the sponsors. The role of this advisor is to model and structure the transaction, identify willing lenders and ensure a smooth execution of the transaction. Relying on advisors is extremely common for very large or complex transactions, especially when several investors are working together in a consortium. It is a way for all shareholders to ensure that the financial model is done by an independent party and that the debt raising process is optimized and handled by experts.

Having a financial advisor is also very common when several sponsors or consortiums compete against each other for a large concession or PPP. The financial advisor (which is a bank or a boutique) brings value to the bid in the same way an M&A advisor adds value in an acquisition process. It provides expertise, market knowledge, and additional resources to optimize the client's offer. Table 6.2 shows the global project finance advisory league table for 2019.

TABLE 6.2 2019 Global Project Finance Advisory League Table

Rank	Company Name	Value (m$)	Deals
1	Macquarie	11.302	17
2	Santander	9.383	62
3	State Bank of India	9.375	3
4	Citi	9.020	4
5	Morgan Stanley	7.378	2
6	Société Générale	6.768	7
7	SMBC	5.381	6
8	Rothschild	5.133	7
9	EY	4.627	13
10	MUFG	4.232	6

Source: Dealogic.

Advisors usually accompany their clients during the various phases of the process. During the bid phase (in which various consortiums compete for a concession, a PPP, or any other project) advisors help their clients put together a financial offer. They build the financial model, optimize the debt structure, and sound out the market to determine the financing conditions for this project. If their client's bid is successful, advisors then have to execute the transaction and select the final lenders based on final negotiations with the borrower.

6.3.2 Debt Sizing

6.3.2.1 How to Determine the Total Debt Amount

Calculation of the total debt needed for a project is one of the main topics of discussion between lenders and sponsors. For lenders, the equity contribution of the sponsors is a necessary buffer against losses. The more equity in a project, the less debt is required and the more cash flow there is to service the debt. Equity investors have the exact opposite interest. All things being equal, more equity in a project means a lower return on investment.

Whatever the discussions between lenders and equity investors, a fundamental principle applies to all projects: net operating cash flow must be higher than the debt repayment obligations of the project company (principal and interest). It is always explicit in the loan agreement that the ratio of net operating cash flow to debt service obligations (i.e. the *DSCR* defined in section 6.2.2.3) has to be higher than a predetermined figure. If the project company is not able to maintain a certain level of DSCR, it may trigger a default, meaning that lenders are – among other things – in a position to request an early repayment of their loan.

6.3.2.2 Legal Form of a Sponsor's Contribution

Although the amount invested by a sponsor is generally referred to as *equity*, it very rarely takes the legal form of share capital only. The contribution is often a mix of share capital and a shareholder loan, i.e. a form of loan granted by a shareholder to a subsidiary.

Investing via shareholder loans gives sponsors more flexibility when it comes to revenue distribution. From a legal point of view, paying a dividend is more complex than paying interest:

- Although modes of payment vary from one country to another, there are strict rules governing dividend distribution. Dividends are usually only paid once a year after a formal decision by shareholders on the basis of annual financial statements (generally available only several weeks after the end of the fiscal year). On the contrary, interest and principal repayment on a loan can be paid on a regular basis (monthly, quarterly, etc.) depending on the loan agreement. Using a shareholder loan makes it easier for an SPV to distribute cash to its shareholders. Cash flow can be paid to the sponsor almost at the same time they are generated by the SPV – which has a positive impact on the IRR of the equity investor.

– In addition, dividend payments can legally only be made by a company if it is profitable. In project finance, the first years of a project are generally loss-making from an accounting standpoint. These losses do not mean that the project is underperforming, they only exist because accounting depreciation of the project's assets during the first years is extremely high. Cash flow to the SPV remains positive, nonetheless. Using a shareholder loan in this situation allows sponsors to benefit from interest and principal payments while dividend distributions are off limits.

The fact that a sponsor's investment is made in the form of a shareholder loan does not change the lender's risk profile. Their loan remains senior to the sponsor's contribution whether in the form of share capital or shareholder loan. Whatever the legal form of the sponsor's contribution (i.e. capital or shareholder loan), this investment is referred to as equity.[10]

6.3.2.3   Is There an Ideal Debt-to-Equity Ratio?

All things being equal, the higher the risk in a project, the higher the contribution required from the sponsors. There is therefore no ideal debt-to-equity ratio. It depends on the type of project, the underlying risks, the location of the infrastructure, and market conditions. DSCR is usually the main driver of the debt-to-equity ratio. In order to meet a certain DSCR over time, the debt amount cannot exceed a certain percentage of the asset cost.

Project loans also include the maximum net debt-to-equity ratio (or maximum gearing) that the project company is allowed to have (70/30 or 80/20, etc.). This gearing sets a cap to the relative maximum debt amount in a project. The gearing is an important element of protection for lenders. If a project does not just perform well but performs extremely well, and cash flow exceeds initial financial projections, the SPV will have excess cash flow to repay the shareholder loan, meaning that the total leverage of the project can become (relatively) higher than at the beginning of the project. The gearing ensures that sponsors keep sufficient skin in the game over time, even if a project performs very well.

In practice, the debt amount is capped either by the DSCR or the gearing. While the DSCR generally sets the maximum loan amount at the beginning of the deal (and the gearing is more an element of protection for the lenders), it can also happen that the debt amount is capped by the gearing from the start. This is notably the case if the project benefits from a very generous offtake contract.

The debt-to-equity ratio of a project can also evolve following a refinancing. If a project has performed well and market conditions allow it, the project company can typically take out a new loan for a larger amount. The proceeds of this loan are used to repay the existing debt and pay an extra dividend to shareholders. The refinancing of brownfield assets is common in project finance and the norm when there is abundant liquidity in the market.

---

[10]This means that when we refer to "equity" in the rest of the chapter, we think of the total investment by the sponsors (capital and shareholder loans).

The debt-to-equity ratio of a project can also be modified if the project underperforms and needs to be recapitalized. Although sponsors have no obligation to do so, they may decide to reinvest in an SPV rather than letting the project go bankrupt. This is how The Walt Disney Company chose to save Disneyland Paris (case study 6).

6.3.2.4   Timing of a Sponsor's Equity Investment

Depending on the project and the negotiations between sponsors and lenders, equity providers can invest at different stages:

- Equity investors can be drawn in priority. In that scenario, the first payments due under the construction contract are financed by equity only. The senior loan is drawn only once the total amount of equity has been fully deployed.
- Equity investors can also invest jointly with loan drawdowns as the construction progresses. In that case, if the debt-to-equity ratio for the project has been fixed at 80/20, each payment under the construction contract will be financed with 20% of equity and 80% of senior debt.
- In some other cases, equity is only invested at the end of the construction period (the equity is said to be *back-ended*). In this case, each payment during the construction is financed by a given amount of debt (80% in our example) while the rest is financed by a bridge loan. Bridge loans are fully guaranteed by the sponsors and are repaid at the end of the construction with an equity injection from the sponsors. The use of bridge loans delays the equity investment and improves the sponsors' IRR. This solution is, however, only possible for large and creditworthy sponsors because banks providing the bridge loan take a credit risk on the sponsors during the construction phase.[11]

6.3.3   Waterfall

6.3.3.1   Debt Repayment and Dividend Distribution

Lenders and sponsors agree before the project starts on how the cash flow is to be split between them during the operating phase. The manner in which this flow is distributed is referred to as a *waterfall*, meaning that the cash flow falls from the top (revenues) to the bottom (dividends) according to a specific arrangement.

Details of the waterfall are left to the discretion of the interested parties. They are nonetheless ranked by the following priorities (from the most important to the least):

1. Priority to capital and operating expenses necessary for the project.
2. Priority to lenders: the principal and interest of the loans are repaid before dividends are distributed to sponsors.

---

[11]Alternatively, the back-ended equity contributions can be structured without bridge loan. In this scenario, the debt is drawn first and equity is simply drawn last. In case of default of the SPV during the construction period, the lenders have a recourse to the sponsors for an amount equal to their equity contribution (pro rata the progress of the construction until that date).

3. Priority to senior lenders: if several loans are granted, senior lenders are repaid first. As a result, the more junior a debt, the higher its cost (interest rate) for the project company.

4. After repayment of the loans, and before dividend distribution, a portion of the revenues is allocated to the reserve accounts.

5. Payments of dividends as well as interest and principal payments on share-holder loans come last, once all the other payments have been made.

This type of distribution offers a relatively high level of comfort to lenders while giving ultimate priority to the smooth operation of the project. Table 6.3 illustrates a typical waterfall in project finance.

TABLE 6.3   Waterfall in Project Finance

Illustrative Waterfall Possible During the Operating Phase
+   Net operating cash flow
−   Interest on senior debt
−   Principal of senior debt
−   Interest on junior debt (if any)
−   Principal of junior debt (if any)
−   Payment to the debt service reserve account
−   Payment to the major maintenance reserve account[12]
=   Cash flow available for the sponsors

6.3.3.2   Is There a Risk of Conflict of Interest?

Some sponsors get remunerated for a project both as a shareholder of the SPV and as a subcontractor in charge of the construction or the operation of the project. This could in theory open the door to potential conflict of interest, given that sponsors may prefer to be remunerated as a contractor rather than as a shareholder: a shareholder gets paid at the bottom of the waterfall while contractors are paid during the construction period or in priority during the operation phase.

In reality, this risk is limited because lenders monitor this possibility in their due diligence (i.e. lenders want to ensure that the project company pays the market price for the construction, operation, and maintenance of the asset). The risk is also mitigated by the fact that several sponsors usually bid together for a project. If a partner wants to artificially increase construction or maintenance costs, the other sponsors can choose to walk away or partner with another company.

---

[12]Sometimes the funding of the reserve accounts comes prior to payments to junior lenders.

Summary

Project Finance: What Have We Learnt?

- Project finance is a financing technique that facilitates the construction of large infrastructure projects (pipeline, wind farm, highway, stadium, etc.) through a company established with the sole purpose of financing, constructing, and operating the asset.

- The company – also called a project company or SPV – is constituted by a shareholder or a group of shareholders called sponsors. These sponsors can be industrial or financial players. Industrial sponsors are companies that have an economic interest in the completion of the project (e.g. a construction company), while financial sponsors are private equity firms specialized in investing in infrastructure assets.

- The project company is financed by a mix of equity (provided by sponsors) and debt (provided by lenders). The debt is repaid only through the cash flow generated by the project. It is said to be non-recourse, meaning that lenders have no recourse to the sponsors in case the project cash flow is not sufficient to service the debt. As security, lenders generally receive a pledge on the shares of the SPV and its bank accounts.

- Thanks to this technique, large infrastructure assets designed to be used for long periods can be financed with long-term loans (possibly 25 to 30 years or more). This maturity is generally not achievable in the case of projects financed directly by sponsors. Project finance is therefore a tool that facilitates the financing of infrastructure by the private sector.

- Given the steady and regular cash flow provided by this type of project, SPVs can be highly leveraged. The main constraint is that the net operating cash flow of the project has to be higher than the debt service obligations. The buffer between these two flows depends on the risk of the project: the riskier the project, the lower the leverage.

- Lenders conduct a detailed analysis of the project before committing to lend to the SPV. They analyze the technical feasibility and the economic viability of the project and ensure that long-term cash flow is sufficient to repay the debt. The margin on the loan is based on the risks of the project.

- Each project financing is divided in two phases: construction and operation. During the first phase, the SPV uses the investment from sponsors and lenders to pay for the construction of the infrastructure. During the operating phase, the net operating cash flow is distributed to those who have funded the SPV by order of priority, first the lenders and then the sponsors.

PART III

ASSET FINANCE

Asset finance is a set of financing structures designed to fund the acquisition of large movable assets such as ships, aircraft, or trains. It emerged as a distinctive group of financing techniques in the early 1970s when ILFC, Polaris, and GPA, the first modern aircraft leasing companies, were set up.

Although asset finance – in its most modern form – dates back only 50 years, the first transactions of this kind were structured in the seventeenth century, when Dutch bankers began to finance vessels for shipowners willing to trade with Asia. Given the risks involved, asset finance at that time looked more like venture capital than structured finance. Bankers providing funds for the vessels were not simply offering a loan, they required a significant share of the profits that the ship would generate.

In the centuries that followed, the decrease in risk and the growth of maritime trade gradually impacted financing structures. Asset finance moved slowly, from a model in which the repayment of a loan was linked to the sale of a cargo, to transactions in which lenders would finance a shipowner whilst accepting a collateral over a ship. In other words, asset finance moved from a shipment-based type of financing to financing relying on the quality and value of the asset itself.

Unlike the other financing techniques analyzed in this book (LBO, project finance, and securitization) asset finance does not refer to one type of financing structure only. It describes a set of techniques whose purpose is to finance large movable assets. Amongst these structures, some are rather simple while others are obviously more complex. Although only the latter match the definition of structured finance seen in the Introduction, we suggest analyzing them all. This should give readers a better understanding of what asset finance really is.

CHAPTER 7

Definition of Asset Finance

7.1 THE SCOPE OF ASSET FINANCE

7.1.1 What is an Asset?

In the large family of structured transactions, asset finance is probably the most confidential technique. It is difficult to know exactly why, but a plausible explanation could be the lack of clarity that exists in English around the term *asset*, This word has such a broad meaning that it defines almost everything in finance, from a building (a real estate *asset*) to a security (a financial *asset*). One thing is sure, the expression *asset finance* can lead to confusion.

The word *asset* (in the expression asset finance) refers to assets that have the following features:

- they are physical assets
- they are movable assets
- they are very expensive assets.[1]

Asset finance techniques are mainly used to finance the acquisition of aircraft, ships or trains – and more rarely of some smaller assets like helicopters, containers

---

[1] Even if there is no official floor set to define what "very expensive" exactly means, it is usually agreed that asset finance techniques are more likely to be used to finance a $100 million asset than a photocopier or a water machine – both of which are physical and movable assets. It is often said that asset finance is used to finance large ticket assets. Alternatively, asset finance techniques can be used to finance portfolios of smaller assets, like containers or buses for instance. Taken individually, containers are not expensive ($200,000) but when a large number of them are bundled together, the amount can be significant.

or cranes. These assets constitute the bulk of the assets being at the same time physical, movable, and expensive. The vast majority of firms that rely on asset finance are, therefore, airlines, or shipping and railway companies. Occasionally, companies that use aircraft or ships in their operating cycle can also benefit from these techniques. A bank can finance an aircraft for Fedex or a supertanker for Shell or Chevron.

The aforementioned physical assets can be used over a long period. The lifespan of a commercial aircraft is between 25 to 30 years, about the same as a container ship or a bulk carrier. Some helicopter types can fly even longer if they are properly maintained. This remarkable lifespan explains why there is an organized secondhand market for these assets. Some clients want to use brand new assets while others are happy to buy less expensive ones.

The demand and the liquidity that exist for these assets make them relatively easy to finance. Lenders can take pledges on them and sell them or find new users in case of default of their clients. In a way, these movable assets have some similarities with real estate: they are long-term assets that have an intrinsic value independent from their current user.

7.1.2 Three Types of Structures

Unlike the techniques already seen in the earlier chapters, asset finance covers various sub-types of financing structures. While LBOs and project finance transactions are always a variation of the same model, asset finance structures are split between three different categories:

  (i) mortgage loans,
 (ii) finance leases, and
(iii) operating leases.

As already explained, we will take the time to analyze them all, even if the three of them do not perfectly match the definition of structured finance given in our Introduction.

7.2 HOW TO FINANCE ASSETS

7.2.1 Mortgage Loans

7.2.1.1 Definition

A mortgage loan is a relatively simple financing option. It is a tool that is probably already well known by most of our readers. A mortgage loan in asset finance is not so different from the loans granted to individuals buying a property. The way it works is simple: a client takes out a loan to finance an asset; in exchange for this loan, the bank is given a mortgage on the asset, i.e. the right to take possession of the asset if the client does not repay the loan.

Mortgage loans are very common in aircraft or shipping finance. They are made possible because aircraft and merchant ships have a market value that is not linked to the creditworthiness of the client. In other words, the asset keeps a certain value even if the client defaults. This is what makes the lien over the asset valuable for the lender. If the client goes bankrupt (whether this is an airline or a shipping company), the lender can foreclose the asset and sell it to minimize its loss. Figure 7.1 shows a simplified mortgage structure in asset finance.

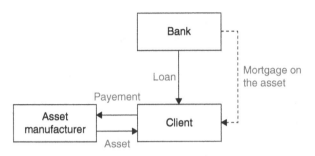

FIGURE 7.1   Simplified Mortgage Loan Structure

7.2.1.2   In Case of Default

In case of the client defaulting, the bank that has a mortgage on the asset can repossess the asset and sell it. Depending on the sale price and the exposure of the lender when the client actually defaults, the proceeds of the sale can be lower or higher than the amount due to the bank. If the sale price is higher, the proceeds of the sale are used to repay the debt and pay the costs incurred by the bank in relation to the repossession and sale of the asset. The surplus is given back to the client. If the sale price is lower, the client is still liable to the bank for the amount that has not been repaid via the sale of the asset. The bank is nonetheless in the same position for this portion of the loan as the other unsecured lenders.

7.2.1.3   Debt Sizing

Given that the mortgage on the asset is a strong element of comfort for the lender, the value of this asset is taken into consideration when sizing the loan. If the main driver of the credit decision for the bank remains (or should remain) the ability of the client to repay the loan, the market value of the asset sets the maximum amount that can be borrowed. A mortgage only makes sense if the exposure of the lender is not considerably higher than the value of the asset. A mortgage is supposed to bring additional comfort to lenders. If the value of a mortgaged asset is significantly lower than the amount lent to the client, the mortgage brings limited value.

With the size of a loan being based on the value of the asset, the concept of Loan-to-Value (LTV) has emerged to measure the amount of a loan compared to the value of the asset being financed. The LTV is generally set at a maximum of 80% but can obviously be lower depending on the credit quality of the borrower. This buffer of

20% (or more) is meant to absorb the costs linked to the repossession and sale of the asset in case the client defaults. It is also meant to give some comfort to the lender if the market value of the asset does not evolve favorably. The market value of the asset (aircraft, vessel, etc.) is usually determined by an independent party (broker, appraiser)[2] to ensure that the loan is correctly sized.

7.2.1.4 Maturity

Given the long lifespan and the liquidity of the assets being financed, a mortgage loan can be provided for a rather long maturity. It is not uncommon to see transactions of 10 to 12 years. Maturities obviously shorten if transactions are to finance a secondhand asset or refinance an existing loan. This is only logical as the asset has, in this case, a shorter lifespan.

Loans with a 10–12-year maturity are generally fully amortizing installment loans, meaning that all repayments made by the borrower are equal until the loan is entirely repaid. Loans with a shorter maturity can be structured with a balloon. In that case, the loan is partially repaid via equal installments but includes a significant final payment at maturity (generally between 20% and 40% of the total loan amount). Given that the client rarely has the cash to pay for this final balloon, it means that the loan has to be refinanced before maturity.

Loans with balloons are similar to the hard mini-perms available in project finance (Chapter 5, section 5.3.1.2). Unlike project finance lenders, though, a lender in asset finance is not exposed to project risk. Whether the asset being financed is an aircraft, a vessel, or a train, the repayment of the loan is not directly linked to the profitability or the performance of the asset taken independently. The loan is a corporate loan with an additional collateral on the asset. Repayments are due even if the asset is not used by the client.

Mortgage loans in asset finance are generally structured as club deals. Assets are usually financed separately and there is therefore no need for an underwriting[3] given the amounts at stake. Loans rarely exceed $150 million unless a batch of assets are financed together.

7.2.2 Finance Lease

7.2.2.1 Definition

A finance lease (also sometimes called capital lease) is a lease under which the owner of an asset recovers the total investment (plus interests) made when buying the asset through the rentals paid by the lessee during the original lease period. A finance lease

---

[2]Appraisers and brokers are two different occupations. An appraiser is an expert in valuing assets who has usually obtained a professional certification to do so. A broker is a specialist in the sale and purchase of secondhand assets.
[3]See Appendix B (Syndication and Club Deals) for more details.

is therefore a lease in which the discounted value of the rentals paid by the lessee is equal to the investment made by the owner.

Put differently, a finance lease is a lease in which the lessee (i) operates the asset, (ii) has full control over the asset, and (iii) pays for the total value of the asset during the leasing period. The owner (also called *finance lessor* or *lessor*) gives total freedom to the lessee to use the asset as it wishes.[4] The lessor does not plan to lease the asset further after the original lease period. For the finance lessor, the payback comes only from the original leasing period. At the end of the lease, the asset is generally either scrapped or acquired by the lessee via the exercise of an extremely attractive purchase option (e.g. $1 or $1,000).

It is often said that a finance lease is a lease that substantially transfers all of the risks and rewards of ownership of the asset to the lessee. Given that (i) the lessee has the economic ownership of the asset and (ii) the lessor is not exposed to the risk of finding a new lessee after the original lease period, the owner is mainly exposed to the lessee's credit risk. The lessor is not exposed to the profitability of the asset taken independently: rentals are due whatever the use of the asset by the lessee. Finance leases are, for this reason, a corporate financing technique. They are usually offered by banks, directly or via subsidiaries, acting as finance lessors.

A lessor in a finance lease is only exposed to the value of the asset in case of default of the lessee. Since the leasing term of a finance lease tends to be relatively long term (to fully pay for the asset), this asset exposure is not negligible. Finance lessors will have a preference to focus on solid credits so that they reduce the likelihood of dealing with the asset, following a default. In that case, the finance lessor must indeed sell the asset to a third party and try to recover its investment through this sale. Alternatively, the lessor can also look for a new lessee. Since the finance lessor is a financing entity and not an asset expert, it is seldom equipped to deal with these situations.

7.2.2.2 Use in Asset Finance

There are two main reasons why finance leases are used in asset finance. It can be a way to (i) finance up to 100% of the purchase price of an asset or (ii) structure a tax efficient transaction.

7.2.2.3 Finance Lease Structure

In a finance lease, banks do not finance clients directly. They set up an SPV with a nominal amount of equity (e.g. $1,000) and provide a senior loan to this SPV so that it can acquire an asset and lease it to a client. The leasing period is generally set between 10 to 12 years.

At the end of the lease, the lessee can purchase the asset for a symbolic purchase option (e.g. $1,000). Considering the lifespan of an asset like an aircraft or a large vessel and its market value after 10 to 12 years, this amount is negligible and

---

[4]As long as the lessee does not intentionally damage the asset.

extremely attractive. Even if the lessee has no use for the asset after the original lease period, it should buy the asset and sell it to a third party to make a profit.

As a security for the loan, the banks obtain from the SPV a mortgage on the asset. This senior loan is sized like any mortgage loan. A conservative LTV is calculated so that banks have a buffer in case of default by the client – that would necessarily cause a default of the SPV (as the SPV is set up for the purpose of the transaction and has no other source of income). Depending on the lessee's credit risk, the senior loan can be equal to c. 70% or 80% of the total asset cost.

The remaining 20% to 30% is provided to the SPV under the form of a junior loan. This junior loan can be provided either by (i) the lessee itself or (ii) another lender. The rentals paid by the lessee cover the repayment of the senior and the junior loans. The SPV therefore distributes to lenders the totality of its cash flow. Figure 7.2 represents a simplified finance lease diagram.

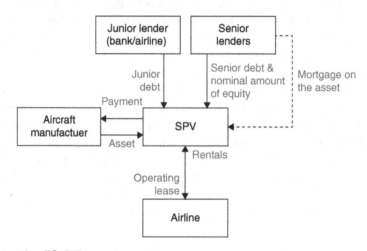

FIGURE 7.2 Simplified Finance Lease Structure

When the junior loan is provided by a bank, the margin of the junior loan reflects the risk taken by the junior lender. The pricing is higher than the senior loan. The junior lender benefits from a security: a second ranking mortgage on the asset. In case of default of the SPV (triggered by a non-payment of rent by the lessee) and subsequent exercise of their securities by the lenders, the asset is sold and the proceeds of the sale are directed in priority to the senior lenders and then to the junior lender (once the senior lenders have fully recovered their loan). When the junior loan is provided by a third-party lender, a finance lease allows the lessee to fully fund the original asset price with external debt. The user of the asset does not need to make any down payment.

If the junior loan is provided by the lessee itself, the applicable margin is not a concern as payments made by the lessee are ultimately redirected to the lessee. The junior loan is, in this case, more of a buffer designed to maintain a conservative LTV for the senior lender.

7.2.2.4 Tax Lease

Why would banks and clients enter into a finance lease to finance an aircraft, a vessel, or a train? If the client provides the junior loan, the structure is, in fact, no different from a mortgage loan, and the possibility of financing 100% of the cost of an asset does not necessitate a finance lease: a junior loan can be structured without the use of an SPV.

A finance lease is generally structured to allow for a tax arbitrage. This arbitrage exists because large physical assets must be depreciated and consequently generate tax allowances for their owners. In the case of a finance lease, it is the SPV and not the user of the asset that depreciates the asset from a tax perspective. That is a major difference from a mortgage loan.[5]

Let us try to summarize the extent of this tax arbitrage.

The amount of tax due by an SPV involved in a finance lease is calculated as follows:

+ Rentals

– Interests (on the senior and junior loans)

– Asset depreciation

= Tax result

If the depreciation period is no longer than the lease period then, over the leasing period, the sum of the rentals is necessarily equal to the sum of [Interests + Asset depreciation]. This is the case for two reasons: (i) the value of the asset is equal to the sum of the loans and (ii) the rentals cover the repayment (plus interest) of the two loans.

That said, if the equation [Rentals – Interests – Asset depreciation = 0] is true over the leasing period, it does not mean that it is true every year. If the depreciation period is shorter than the lease period, then the tax result of the SPV will be negative when the asset is being depreciated and positive thereafter. Assuming the lease period is 12 years while the depreciation period is eight years, then the SPV will have a negative tax result for the first eight years and a positive tax result from year 9 to year 12.

As explained before, the SPV is generally established and fully owned by a bank. It therefore belongs to the same tax group as the bank. This tax grouping means that

---

[5]We are discussing here tax depreciation and not accounting depreciation. Given that a finance lease is a structure in which the lessee keeps the risks and rewards linked to the ownership of the asset, accounting standards (notably IFRS and US GAAP) consider that an asset under a finance lease must be depreciated by the lessee from an accounting perspective. Tax and accounting rules are nonetheless two different frameworks and do not follow the same rules. In sum, in a finance lease the asset can well be depreciated by the lessee from an accounting perspective but depreciated by the legal owner from a tax perspective.

the bank and the SPV are considered as a single entity for tax purposes. The tax results of the two companies are added up to calculate the tax due by the tax group.[6]

Given that the SPV has a negative tax result during the first eight years of the lease and a positive tax result thereafter, it means that the tax group formed by the bank and the SPV pays less tax than what the bank would have paid on a standalone basis during the first eight years. After this, the tax group formed by the bank and the SPV pays more tax than what the bank alone would have paid on a standalone basis.

Although the total tax saved during the first eight years is equal to the tax paid from years 9 to 12, the transaction has a real value. Considering the time value of money (a concept that we have explained in Chapter 3), it is better to save taxes now and pay taxes in the future than the opposite. In other words, there is a real value for the bank in forming a tax group with the SPV.

Given the benefit that it obtains through the lease, the bank is willing to make a payment upfront to form a tax group with the SPV. This payment takes the form of an equity investment in the SPV. This investment reduces the amount to be financed by the lessee and explains why asset users rely on finance leases. The bank does not expect any dividend from its equity investment. The only purpose of this investment is to benefit from the tax advantage created by the finance lease. For this reason, the bank acting as investor in a tax lease is referred to as a *tax investor*.

Tables 7.1 and 7.2 show what would be the tax result of the SPV considering the following assumptions:

- asset cost: $100 million
- senior loan: $80 million (provided by the bank as lender)
- junior loan: $18 million (provided by the lessee)
- equity investment: $2 million (provided by the bank as tax investor via the SPV)
- interest on the senior and junior loans: 5.5% (fixed rate)
- lease period: 12 years
- depreciation of the asset: eight years on a linear basis
- discount rate: 5.5%[7]
- corporate tax rate applicable in the country where the SPV is located: 30%[8]

Tables 7.1 and 7.2 show that a tax lease allows for the user of an asset to transfer the tax benefit linked to the ownership of an asset to a third party – in this case a bank. The lessee does not benefit from the tax depreciation of the asset (as it would have with a mortgage loan), but obtains in exchange a discount on the down payment to be

---

[6]The concept of tax grouping is explained in more detail in Chapter 1, section 1.2.2. Alternatively, to avoid creating a tax group, the SPV can be established as a tax transparent entity. The end result is the same, as the SPV has no tax entity and the tax is paid by its parent, in this case the bank.
[7]See definition of discount rate in Chapter 3, section 3.1.2.2.
[8]These numbers are randomly selected for easy reading. The tax depreciation period for an asset is set independently in each country. Some countries adopt a tax depreciation period in line with the lifespan of the asset, some others implement a shorter period to incentivize investment.

TABLE 7.1 Calculation of Rentals

| | Senior loan | | | | Junior loan | | | | Rentals |
	Loan amount	(a) Interests	(b) Principal repayment	(c) Debt service (DS1)	Loan amount	(d) Interests	(e) Principal repayment	(f) Debt service (DS2)	(c)+(f)=(g) Total rentals (DS1+2)
Start date	80 000 000				18 000 000				
Year 1	75 117 662	4 400 000	4 882 338	9 282 338	16 901 474	990 000	1 098 526	2 088 526	11 370 865
Year 2	69 966 794	4 131 471	5 150 867	9 282 338	15 742 529	929 581	1 158 945	2 088 526	11 370 865
Year 3	64 532 630	3 848 174	5 434 165	9 282 338	14 519 842	865 839	1 222 687	2 088 526	11 370 865
Year 4	58 799 586	3 549 295	5 733 044	9 282 338	13 229 907	798 591	1 289 935	2 088 526	11 370 865
Year 5	52 751 224	3 233 977	6 048 361	9 282 338	11 869 025	727 645	1 360 881	2 088 526	11 370 865
Year 6	46 370 203	2 901 317	6 381 021	9 282 338	10 433 296	652 796	1 435 730	2 088 526	11 370 865
Year 7	39 638 226	2 550 361	6 731 977	9 282 338	8 918 601	573 831	1 514 695	2 088 526	11 370 865
Year 8	32 535 990	2 180 102	7 102 236	9 282 338	7 320 598	490 523	1 598 003	2 088 526	11 370 865
Year 9	25 043 131	1 789 479	7 492 859	9 282 338	5 634 704	402 633	1 685 893	2 088 526	11 370 865
Year 10	17 138 165	1 377 372	7 904 966	9 282 338	3 856 087	309 909	1 778 617	2 088 526	11 370 865
Year 11	8 798 425	942 599	8 339 739	9 282 338	1 979 646	212 085	1 876 441	2 088 526	11 370 865
Year 12	0	483 913	8 798 425	9 282 338	0	108 881	1 979 646	2 088 526	11 370 865
Total			80 000 000	111 388 062			18 000 000	25 062 314	136 450 376

185

TABLE 7.2   Calculation of the Profitability for the Tax Investor

		Tax			Tax investment	
	(h)	(g)–(a)–(d)–(h)=(i)		30%*(i)	Equity investment	Discounted flows
	Depreciation	Tax result		Tax		
Start date					2 000 000	–2 000 000
Year 1	12 500 000	–6 519 135		1 955 741		1 853 783
Year 2	12 500 000	–6 190 188		1 857 056		1 668 477
Year 3	12 500 000	–5 843 148		1 752 944		1 492 831
Year 4	12 500 000	–5 477 021		1 643 106		1 326 343
Year 5	12 500 000	–5 090 757		1 527 227		1 168 534
Year 6	12 500 000	–4 683 249		1 404 975		1 018 952
Year 7	12 500 000	–4 253 328		1 275 998		877 168
Year 8	12 500 000	–3 799 761		1 139 928		742 776
Year 9		9 178 752		–2 753 626		–1 700 720
Year 10		9 683 584		–2 905 075		–1 700 720
Year 11		10 216 181		–3 064 854		–1 700 720
Year 12		10 778 071		–3 233 421		–1 794 259
Total	100 000 000	–2 000 000		600 000	2 000 000	1 252 445

made when buying the asset. In our example, the discount on the asset cost is equal to the equity investment made by the bank ($2 million). In other words, the total asset cost for the lessee is $98 million and not $100 million.

The transaction is not only positive for the lessee, it is also profitable for the tax investor. Although the bank does not receive any dividend or interest on its investment, it is still making a profit. As shown in Table 7.2, the net present value of this deal is $1.2 million.[9] This profit arises because the transaction creates tax losses in the first years of the lease (years 1 to 8) while tax is only payable during the second part of the deal (years 9 to 12).

The decision to enter into a finance lease or sign a mortgage loan depends on the financial strategy of the asset user. In our example, for instance, the client has chosen a finance lease to benefit from a $2 million discount on the asset cost. It will, however, not benefit from the eight-year tax depreciation of the asset. Instead, finance lease rentals will be deductible but over a longer period, in this case 12 years, which is less advantageous.

More precisely, in this example, the airline as lessee benefits from the tax deductibility of the rentals but is taxed on the interest received on the junior loan. Compared to a situation where it would buy the asset with an 80% mortgage loan, the airline benefits therefore from the depreciation of the sum of columns (b) and (e) in Table 7.1 (i.e. depreciation of $98m over 12 years) but does not benefit from the depreciation of the asset shown in column (h) of Table 7.2 (i.e. depreciation of $100m over 8 years). In both cases, the interest payable on the $80m loan are deductible (column (a) of Table 7.1), either because they are interest (case of the mortgage loan)

---

[9]The net present value (NPV) of an investment is the difference between the discounted cash flows generated by this investment minus the cost of the investment.

or because they correspond to the portion of the rental affected to the repayment of the interest of the senior loan (case of the finance lease).

In sum, a client chooses a tax lease over a mortgage loan if it considers that it will not fully benefit from the asset's tax depreciation in the future. This is the case if the asset user has regular tax losses and if the tax rules applicable in the country where it is registered limit the ability to carry forward tax losses.[10] In this situation, the client may want to structure a tax lease to monetize part of its tax advantage when it buys the asset.

At this stage, readers will probably note that if the tax investor invests $2 million in the deal, then the equation mentioned earlier [Rentals – Interests – Asset depreciation = 0] is wrong. The result is negative, not nil. The sum of the rentals is indeed lower than the sum of [Interests + Asset depreciation]. This is because the rentals are calculated on loans that amount in total to $98 million, while the asset cost is $100 million. This does not change our reasoning, it only makes the tax lease more powerful as tax losses are greater.

7.2.2.5 Tax Lease Industry

A tax lease is a powerful tool to finance large movable assets. It is also an attractive tax investment opportunity that banks have refined over the years. Many variations have been added to the basic structure described earlier. We will not mention them all, but will focus on two of them.

> First, *third party tax investors*. Although banks remain the vast majority of tax investors, they have also structured tax leases to offer the opportunity to other companies to invest in finance leases as tax investors. In this case, the tax investors invest equity in the SPV so that they can form a tax group with the SPV. For these companies, investing in a tax lease is a way to optimize their taxes. Banks charge structuring fees to these tax investors and remain lenders in the transaction. The tax investors come from a large variety of sectors.
>
> Second, *lease tails*. The profitability of a tax lease comes from the tax losses that the SPV generates during the first years (in our example, the years 1 to 8). As such, the profitability of a tax lease is greatly enhanced if the tax investor sells the SPV once it generates a positive tax result. In this case, the tax investors would benefit from the tax losses in the first eight years but would not pay tax on the profits generated from years 9 to 12. This investment would be hugely profitable.
>
> What type of company could, however, acquire an SPV that must pay taxes but generates no cash flow? This situation is counterintuitive, but potential buyers exist nonetheless. They are companies with huge carry forward losses (because they have made bad investments in the past) or companies that are structurally loss-making from a tax perspective (because they have, for instance

---

[10]In many countries, companies are legally allowed to carry forward their existing losses. This means that firms can use past or present tax losses to offset future profits (and therefore decrease their future taxes payable). There may be limits in terms of amount of losses that can be carried forward. Time limits may also apply. Companies can, for instance, only carry forward their losses for three or five years. The specifics of this mechanism (when it exists) are different in each country.

large non-taxable revenues but also deductible expenses). For this type of buyer, forming a tax group with the SPV is neutral as it does not trigger tax payments. A sale of the SPV to this type of buyers is called a *lease tail*.

A lease tail is obviously difficult to structure. Although the original tax investor sells its equity interest in the SPV, it has to pay for the transaction (which is rather unusual for a seller). As a matter of fact, to avoid paying taxes in the future the seller is ready to pay a buyer to acquire the SPV. The amount paid by the seller obviously has to be lower than the amount of tax due by the SPV in the future. For the company acquiring the SPV, a lease tail is a way to monetize tax losses. It receives a payment from the seller but does not pay taxes on the profits generated by the SPV.

As it is generally legally complicated to pay a buyer to acquire a company, lease tails are usually bundled with other transactions to mask the tax optimization structure. Lease tails are extremely profitable but have come under great scrutiny from tax authorities worldwide since the mid-2000s. Many governments have introduced laws or regulations that forbid these transactions. As a consequence, lease tails have almost entirely disappeared.

7.2.2.6   Tax Leases Today

An attentive reader probably understands from the figures in Tables 7.1 and 7.2 that the efficiency of a tax lease is linked to three major elements: (i) the asset depreciation period, (ii) the level of interest rates, and (iii) the applicable corporate tax rate:

(i) *Asset depreciation*: The shorter the depreciation period, the more powerful a tax lease is. Having a short depreciation period creates large tax losses at the beginning of the transaction. This is optimal for the deal, given the concept of time value of money. In theory, the most profitable tax lease is the lease of an asset that can be depreciated over 12 months but leased over a long period: the tax savings are generated upfront in year 1 while taxes are paid over many years.[11]

(ii) *Interest rates*: The higher the level of the interest rate, the more profitable the tax lease is. High interest rates create large tax deficits at the beginning of the transaction. This because the rentals paid to the SPV mirror the repayment of two installment loans (senior and junior loan). As explained before, the tax result of the SPV is calculated as follows: [Rentals – Interests – Asset depreciation]. Given that the rentals are strictly equal the repayment due under the loans, the tax result is also equal to:
[Principal + Interests – Interests – Asset depreciation]
or simply [Principal – Asset depreciation].

---

[11] Although the possibility of depreciating a large movable asset over 12 months is rather unlikely in any jurisdiction, there are countries where depreciation rules are (or were) more advantageous than the eight years in the example mentioned before.

When interest rates are high, an installment loan with fixed interest rate amortizes rather slowly at the beginning and quickly at the end. This means that the equation [Principal – Asset depreciation] is more negative at the beginning of the deal and more positive at the end when interest rates are high than when they are low. Consequently, high interest rates create larger deficits at the beginning of the transaction. All things being equal, a tax lease with a loan yielding 8% creates more value for the parties than when interest rates are set at 2%.

(iii) *Corporate tax rate*: The higher the corporate tax rate, the more negative the tax results are at the beginning of the deal. A high corporate tax rate is therefore positive for the parties.

The tax lease market today is more limited than it was in the late 1990s or early 2000s. The main reason is that the evolution of interest rates and corporate tax rates have negatively affected the profitability of tax leases. Given the accommodating monetary policies followed by central banks since 2008, interest rates have come down significantly. This has greatly reduced the possibility of creating large tax losses during the first years of a lease.

Many OECD countries[12] have also decreased their corporate tax rates with the aim of fostering investment. France, the United Kingdom, and the United States, which were all important tax lease markets, now have corporate tax rates 15 to 20 points below what they were in the mid-1990s:

- In France, the corporate tax rate was above 40% in the late 1990s. It was 28% in 2020 and will be 25% from 2022 onwards.
- In the United Kingdom, the corporate tax rate was more than 50% in the early 1980s and was still 33% in the mid-1990s. It is now below 20%.
- In the United States, the federal corporate tax rate went from 35% in the mid-1990s to 21% in 2020.

In addition, several governments have introduced more stringent regulations around tax leases. While it was possible in the 1990s to structure a tax lease in the United States (a *US tax lease*) to lease assets to a client in Europe, this type of transaction is now forbidden. US lawmakers have indeed considered that creating tax losses in the United States to subsidize investment in Europe was probably not the best use of the US taxpayers' money.

In general – and at the risk of oversimplifying – tax optimization schemes have come under greater scrutiny since the 2008 crisis. Governments have limited the possibility for banks to optimize their financings and many structures, including tax leases, have been affected. Since 2020 and the introduction of the DAC 6 directive in the European Union, companies must declare to their respective tax authorities

---

[12]For readers unfamiliar with the OECD, please see the definition provided in footnote 15 in Chapter 5, section 5.2.3.2.

all cross-border transactions that could be considered as aggressive from a tax perspective. The directive also allows for the automatic exchange of this information among EU member states.

7.2.2.7 Tonnage Tax

Despite all this, there is still a market for tax leases, especially in the shipping industry. In some countries, tax leases can be structured to take advantage of the tonnage tax system. The tonnage tax is an alternative taxation method that allows shipping companies to be taxed on the tonnage of their fleet instead of being taxed on their profits. In countries where this system exists, shipping companies must decide how they want to be taxed: a certain percentage of their tonnage (tonnage tax) or a certain percentage of their profits (corporate tax). The tonnage tax is usually the option chosen as it is extremely advantageous, the tax payable being extremely low. This is indeed the reason why this system exists. Governments want to foster the development of their local shipping industry by decreasing their tax burden.

Tax leases can use the tonnage tax system to optimize the financing of vessels. The transaction starts generally like a normal tax lease. The asset is acquired by the SPV and leased to a shipping company. The SPV, as owner of the vessel, opts to be taxed based on its profits and not on the tonnage of its ship. As a consequence, the SPV registers negative tax results while the vessel is being depreciated. The tax investor benefits from this structure and pays less tax. Once the tax result becomes positive (for instance, in year 9 in our example in Table 7.2), the transaction is restructured so that the shipping company – which has chosen the tonnage tax system – becomes the owner of the vessel. In other words, the transaction is terminated when the SPV becomes liable to pay corporate tax. At this point in time, it is the shipping company, as owner of the vessel, which pays taxes. Given that it has selected the tonnage tax option, the tax payable is extremely low.

The specifics of a tax lease that relies on the tonnage tax system obviously varies from one country to another. Indeed, all countries have different taxation rules and banks must structure transactions so that the acquisition of the vessel by the shipping company does not trigger a negative tax impact for the SPV nor the investor. The economics of a tax lease using the tonnage tax system are, in essence, not so different from a lease tail. The parties benefit from tax allowances during the first years but find a way to minimize the tax burden when the tax result of the SPV becomes positive.

7.2.3 Operating Lease

7.2.3.1 Definition

An operating lease is an extremely straightforward version of leasing. The asset (aircraft, vessel, railcar, etc.) is acquired by a leasing company and leased to a client for a given period of time. At the end of the lease, the asset is returned by the lessee to the lessor (or operating lessor). An operating lease does not include a purchase option.

Operating leases can be signed for very variable durations, from a few months to several years. The lease period is in any case significantly shorter than the lifespan of the leased asset. In aircraft finance, for instance, operating leases can be contracted for a period of several months (to cover the summer – the busiest period for airlines) and up to 12 years (the usual lease duration for new assets). Some deals have been signed for 15 years for a newly delivered aircraft, although it is far from being the norm.

Unlike a lessor in a finance lease, a lessor in an operating lease takes a real asset risk: (i) the lessee does not acquire the asset at the end of the lease, and (ii) the sum of the rentals paid during the original lease period does not cover the investment made by the lessor. The lessor must therefore find a new lessee or sell the asset at the end of the lease. This risk is referred to as a *residual value* risk. It means that the lessor takes a risk on the expected value of the asset. If the lessor is unable to release the asset (or sell it at a given price), the lessor takes a loss. However, the lessor does not take any project risk. Rentals are due by the lessee irrespective of whether the aircraft is full or not.

7.2.3.2 Clients Need Flexibility

Clients favor operating leases when they need flexibility. We will see in case study 7 on Virgin Atlantic, how it can concretely benefit an airline. Lessors offer this advantage but require in exchange relatively high rental payments to cover their risk. For this reason, the cost of operating leases is usually relatively higher than other asset finance techniques.

Operating leases exist in several sectors but are especially popular in the air transport industry. Almost 50% of the world's commercial aircraft fleet belong to leasing companies and are leased to airlines under operating leasing.

These operating leases can take several forms. In the vast majority of cases, the leasing company provides an aircraft without crew to its clients. This concept is known as a *dry lease*. The leasing company remains the legal owner of the asset but the aircraft is fully operated by the airline. This type of leasing contract is generally signed for several years. They are a real alternative to the acquisition of an aircraft.

Wet leases are a form of leasing agreement whereby the owner of the aircraft also provides crew members, maintenance, and insurance to its client. Wet leases are generally signed for a short period and are usually only used to cover a punctual temporary need (during peak season, for instance). Wet leases are also a good way for airlines to manage their excess capacity, by wetleasing out their fleet and crew to another airline: for example, wet leasing from a European carrier after the European summer to an airline in the southern hemisphere for their summer season. Wet leases represent a very small portion of the leasing market compared to the more traditional dry leases – although they were popular in the early years of the aircraft leasing industry, as shown in case study 8 on Guinness Peat Aviation (GPA).

It may seem strange that railway companies, shipping firms, or airlines want to lease assets that are so inherently part of their business model, but a similar trend can be found in many sectors. An extremely large number of companies do not own the premises they occupy, they rent them from specialized real estate companies. Owning real estate is extremely capital intensive so firms prefer to rent their offices. They use their resources to focus on what they know best. The same is true notably for airlines: transporting passengers does not require owning an aircraft. Emirates, for instance, one of the airlines best known for the quality of its service, is the largest user of operating leases globally.

7.2.3.3   A Few Words on Lessors

Leasing companies are firms specialized in the ownership of large and expensive movable assets, they do not operate assets themselves. Their only purpose is to acquire assets and lease them to clients. They are usually specialized by asset types (aircraft, vessels, trains, etc.), although some companies lease a wide range of assets.

Leasing companies should not be confused with banks. They are not financial companies and are not regulated nor subject to the Basel Accords. If some of them are subsidiaries of banks, it is only a minority. Others are listed, privately owned, or part of larger conglomerates.

Unlike a mortgage loan or a finance lease, an operating lease is a financing solution that can only be offered by an entity that has a strong knowledge of the sector. Operating leasing requires real industry expertise. A leasing company must ideally invest in in-demand assets so that it can easily find a new lessee once a lease terminates. We will discuss this point in detail at a later stage (see Chapter 9, section 9.1.2).

That said, operating lessors must have a real credit risk analysis – similar to those of banks – when they enter into an agreement with a lessee. Lessors specialized in large ticket assets are not car rental companies and do not get paid upfront. They sign leases for periods up to 12 years and are generally paid monthly. They take a real credit risk on their lessees. Leasing an asset to the right lessee is key if they want to avoid taking back an asset before the end of the lease.

7.2.3.4   Lessors' Financing Strategies

The acquisition of an asset by a lessor is generally financed via an SPV. This SPV is financed by a mix of equity (coming from the lessor) and debt (provided by lenders). The debt is generally non-recourse, meaning that in case of default of the lessee, the lender has no recourse on the lessor. Banks benefit in exchange from a mortgage on the asset. Figure 7.3 represents a simplified operating lease structure for an aircraft.

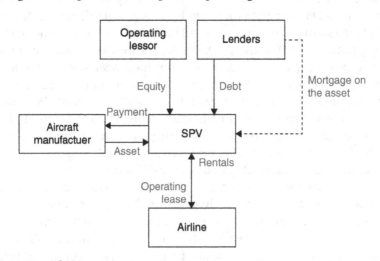

FIGURE 7.3   Simplified Operating Lease Structure

Alternatively, lessors can fund the SPV directly and entirely with equity and shareholder loans and raise funding at corporate level. This is a solution adopted by large lessors, especially when they are investment grade. This significantly brings down their cost of debt as the risk for the lender is not on the airline, but on an investment grade lessor. Lessors can also have other financing strategies that we will detail later (see Chapter 8, section 8.3).

7.2.3.5 JOLCOs

Some tax efficient transactions must sometimes be structured as operating leases. This is the case of the Japanese Operating Lease with Call Option (JOLCO), a type of lease that offers specific tax allowances to Japanese investors. A JOLCO is very different from a traditional operating lease. It is not provided by the same types of investors: an operating lease is offered by a leasing company while a JOLCO is done by a banks and a Japanese tax investor. The JOLCO is, in essence, a finance lease that must be structured as an operating lease to allow the investor to benefit from specific tax allowances available to taxpayers in Japan. JOLCOs are very popular in aircraft finance.

In a typical JOLCO, an SPV established in Japan is financed with (i) equity coming from Japanese tax investors for 20% to 30%, and (ii) a fully amortizing senior loan provided by Japan-based banks for 80% to 70%. The SPV acquires the asset – in most cases an aircraft – and leases it to a lessee under an operating lease. At the end of the lease (generally 10 to 12 years), the lessee benefits from a call option on the asset for a value strictly equal to the equity amount in the SPV. Figure 7.4 shows a simplified JOLCO structure.

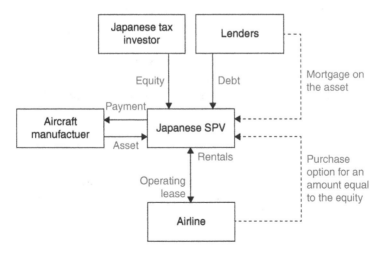

FIGURE 7.4 Simplified JOLCO Structure

The rentals paid by the lessee during the lease cover the debt service of the senior loan and the payment of a coupon for the tax investor. This coupon is extremely low, as Japanese tax investors benefit in parallel from local tax allowances. These tax allowances are granted by the Japanese government to foster investment by Japanese firms overseas. They represent the bulk of the profitability of the tax investors. The coupon paid by the lessee on the equity portion is only an add-on.

The tax allowances are granted to Japanese tax investors only if they take a real equity risk. It implies that the lease is structured as an operating lease. The SPV (and hence the investors) must face a real residual value risk. In reality, this risk is minimal if not non-existent. A JOLCO is structured in such a way that the call option amount is always significantly lower than the expected value of the asset at the end of the lease. If an asset is expected to have a market value of $45 million when the lease terminates, a call option of $20 million will always be exercised by the lessee. The lessee can always buy the aircraft and sell it if it does not want to use it.

This structural feature explains why JOLCOs are especially popular for financing aircraft. A tax investor must indeed be sure that the call option will be exercised when the lease ends. Given that aircraft values depreciate rather slowly and remain quite stable and predictable over time, investors have with aircraft the certainty that the call option will be in the money.[13] The value of vessels being more volatile, there is no real JOLCO market in shipping finance. The investors have no certainty that there will be a significant buffer between the call option and the asset price. They cannot take the risk of being truly exposed to residual value risk.

A JOLCO is an extremely powerful financing tool. It provides lessees with a 100% financing of the asset, including a bullet tranche (i.e. the equity) at a price lower than the senior debt. In that sense, if a JOLCO is legally an operating lease, it is in essence a finance lease.

7.2.4 How the Three Options Compare to Each Other

Table 7.3 summarizes the various solutions that can be used to finance an asset. From the three options, only operating leasing matches the definition of structured finance given in our Introduction. It is on this specific structure that we will focus in the following chapters.[14]

---

[13]A call option is in the money if the market price of the asset on which the option exists is higher than the price set in the option.

[14]That being said, due to the high level of accounting and tax structuring involved in arranging a tax lease, many bankers and financiers consider that finance leases are also part of the structured finance world.

TABLE 7.3   The Different Financing Options

	Mortgage Loan	Finance Lease	Operating Lease (excluding JOLCOs)
Duration	Often between 8 to 12 years	Often between 8 to 12 years	Extremely variable, from a few months to 12 years
Legal ownership of the asset	Airline	SPV	SPV
Payments from the client	Repayment of the mortgage loan	Rentals paid to an SPV. These payments are used by the SPV to repay the loans taken out to buy the asset	Rentals paid to an SPV to repay the equity investment of a lessor and the debt raised to finance the acquisition of the asset
Corporate risk on the user of the asset	Yes	Yes	Yes
Option to buy	Not applicable	Yes, a very attractive price at the end of the leasing period	No
Economic ownership of the asset	Airline	Airline	Airline (dry lease) or operating lessor (wet lease).
Depreciation of the asset from a tax perspective	Airline	SPV	SPV
Advantages	Ideal financing solution for asset users that want to buy an asset and use it until it is scrapped	Reduction of the asset cost thanks to the sharing of the tax advantage between the lessee and the lessor	Flexibility
Constraints	Require upfront investment of at least 20% of the asset cost	No flexibility	Relatively high rentals

Case Study 7: Richard Branson and the Beginnings of Virgin Atlantic

How do you launch a successful airline with only £2 million when the Boeing 747 you need costs more than £200 million? This apparently insoluble problem was the question Richard Branson had to confront while launching Virgin Atlantic in 1984.

Virgin Records

Born in south-east London in 1950, Richard Branson showed from a very young age a strong interest in business. He started his first venture – a magazine named *Student* – when he was not even 18. Three years later, at the age of 21, he opened a store in London selling records bought directly from manufacturers. Thanks to agreements with the labels, Branson was able to sell products for considerably less than the High Street outlets. His first shop on Oxford Street was an immediate success. Within a few months he was able to open several other stores in London.

Riding on this success, in 1972 Branson along with Nick Powell, founded the record company that would make him famous – Virgin Records. *Tubular Bells* by Mike Oldfield, an album without drums and lyrics, was the first album released by the label. It was a colossal success. The sales started slowly but accelerated suddenly in December 1973, when the horror movie *The Exorcist*, whose soundtrack was the opening theme of *Tubular Bells*, became a hit.

In the wake of this first success (for a first album!), Virgin signed controversial band the Sex Pistols. The album *God Save the Queen* was another huge financial success and allowed the label to become very profitable. Thanks to its financial muscle, Virgin went on to sign major artists in the following years: The Rolling Stones, Peter Gabriel, Paul Abdul, UB40, and Culture Club.

In the 1980s, Virgin gradually diversified its activities. The company invested in a night club and a video production and distribution company. Business opportunities outside the music and entertainment industry were generally turned down, but Branson was hooked when one Friday evening he found on his desk the business plan of a start-up airline looking for investors.

An Airline, Really?

Branson knew very well that he was not the first potential investor to be contacted by the authors of the business plan. He was in the record industry, not in the air transport sector. He could therefore easily imagine that many business angels before him had disregarded the project and refused to invest. But Branson was tempted. An airline. It sounded cool. It sounded fun.

The idea of Alan Hellary and Randolph Fields, the entrepreneurs behind the proposal, was to launch a 100% business class transatlantic airline. Branson agreed with the transatlantic part of the project but immediately rejected the concept of a company without economy class. How would one fill the aircraft on public holidays and during vacations?

To get an idea of the market, Branson tried to book a ticket for New York the same night. It proved impossible as the phone lines of all the airlines were constantly busy. His attempt the next day brought the same results. Branson simply could not get a ticket to New York. Guided by intuition, he concluded that either all the airlines were inefficient or that the demand was such that the phone lines were always jammed. Either way, it was a sign that there was room in the market for an efficient airline.

Branson's partners at Virgin were far more skeptical than him. The air transport industry was a sector with very high fixed costs in which historical players had access to the largest airports and the best time slots. Moreover, if the project in question was still on track, it was simply because Laker Airways had been declared bankrupt two years earlier. The defunct airline vacated daily slots for flights between London and New York, which still had not found any takers.

Lease with Boeing

Branson did not get disheartened. He loved the idea of owning an airline. He knew nothing about the sector but believed that it was possible to succeed if costs remained under control. He promised his partners that the investment would remain minimal and swore not to put more than £2 million into the business, irrespective of the outcome.

Given this constraint, the new airline was in no position to purchase an aircraft. Leasing a plane over a short period was the only option. Branson directly called the Boeing Headquarters in Seattle. After being transferred from one department to another, he managed to speak to an engineer who told him that Boeing did not usually lease aircraft. That said, it so happened that Boeing had just been returned a secondhand 747 for which they had no use.

Taking an aircraft on an operating lease was still quite uncommon in the early 1980s. More than 90% of the world's fleet was at that time still directly owned by airlines themselves. The rest belonged mainly to the three leading lessors of that time: International Lease Finance Corporation (ILFC), Polaris Aircraft Leasing, and GPA.

Boeing's representatives revealed to Branson that it was the first time that they had to negotiate a contract of this type. They usually sold aircraft, they did not lease them. Despite tough commercial discussions (Boeing wanted a long-term lease while Branson did not want to commit to more than a year) both teams got along well. Soon discussions that were held first in Virgin's offices moved to Branson's houseboat, moored near Regent's Park in the north of London.

After several weeks of negotiations, a 96-page agreement was finally signed between the parties. The deal looked like a short-term lease but was not legally one. Virgin purchased the 747 on credit and agreed to pay a fraction of the purchase

(continued)

(*continued*)

price every month over several years. After one year, though, Virgin had the option to sell back the aircraft to Boeing for a price equal to the portion of the purchase price, which would still not have been paid by Virgin at that date. If the market value of the aircraft (as determined by independent experts) was higher than the price set in advance under the put option, Boeing committed to buying back the asset at market price.

The deal negotiated by Branson was excellent for Virgin:

- If the project did not work out as expected, the deal could be terminated after one year. Virgin Atlantic could, in this case, return the aircraft and Branson limited his losses as instructed by his partners.
- If, at that time, the market for secondhand 747s performed better than expected, the airline would sell the aircraft at a profit. This would partly offset the losses.
- Finally, if Virgin Atlantic proved to be a success, the airline could choose not to exercise its put option and keep the aircraft.

During the dinner held to celebrate the deal, the Boeing team revealed to Branson that this was by far the most enjoyable deal that they had ever worked on. They also confessed that it was probably also the toughest one. They all jokingly admitted that it was more difficult to close a one-year deal with Branson than to sell an entire fleet of aircraft to PanAm or United Airlines.

The Launch of an Airline

Virgin Atlantic Airways was established in 1984. Branson and his partners wanted to launch their airline in June to benefit in full from the summer period, the most profitable period of the year in this business. The initial days were epic: singers under contract with Virgin Records came to boost the morale of the staff and were present on the maiden flight from Gatwick to Newark.

A small incident with one of the engines almost ruined the event. Out of sympathy for the young airline, the journalists who had taken the flight decided not to report it in the press. They knew that the issue was minor and totally out of Branson's control. Mentioning it would have killed the airline before it had even started.

After the First Flight

This first flight marked the beginning of a long love story between Branson and the air transport industry. After a profitable first year, Virgin Atlantic began to expand and opened new routes to Miami and then to Boston, Los Angeles, and Tokyo. By the end of the 1980s Virgin Atlantic had become the second largest UK airline and competed directly with British Airways on some international routes.

This direct competition led to a major commercial dispute between the two airlines, a fight that triggered large losses for Virgin Atlantic in the early 1990s. To save the airline, Richard Branson decided (reluctantly) to sell his record business to EMI in 1992 and invest the proceeds into the ailing company.

As of March 2020, Virgin Atlantic owned a fleet of more than 40 aircraft. Its two major shareholders are Delta Airlines (49%) and Virgin Group (51%). It is famous for having introduced amenities such as walk-up bars and seat-back entertainment systems, two innovations that are now extremely common in international air travel.

Epilogue

After his success with Virgin Atlantic, Branson started many other ventures in the airline industry. In 1996, Virgin acquired Euro Belgian Airlines and renamed it Virgin Express, before merging it with Brussels Airlines and selling it to Lufthansa. Virgin launched then Virgin Blue (now Virgin Australia) in 2000, Virgin Nigeria in 2005 (sold to Nigerian investors in 2010 before ceasing operations in 2012), and finally Virgin America in 2007 (acquired by Alaska Airlines in 2016).

CHAPTER 8

The Stakeholders

8.1 CLIENTS

8.1.1 Asset Users

8.1.1.1 Who are They?

Firms that heavily rely on operating leasing are active in a very limited number of sectors. They are mainly airlines, shipping firms, or railway companies. Of these three sectors, the airline industry is probably the most interesting to analyze. The high percentage of commercial aircraft leased globally via operating leases (almost 50%)[1] demonstrates the value that structured finance represents for the sector as a whole.

Railway companies do not use operating leasing as frequently as airlines. Many railway companies throughout the world are government-owned and sometimes enjoy monopoly status. They often benefit from very competitive funding sources and do not need operating leasing. Seen globally, operating leasing is only a niche product for the railway sector. It mainly exists in Europe and North America, where markets have been open to competition and new entrants look for a variety of financing options.

Operating leasing is also a niche product in the shipping sector, but for a different reason. Vessels are simply less standardized than commercial aircraft. While all airlines use similar aircraft (mostly manufactured by Airbus or Boeing), shipping companies use a large variety of asset types (tankers, bulk carriers, container ships, LNG carriers, etc.). These vessels are built by a large number of shipyards. The market is therefore more fragmented, which means that the pool of potential lessees for each asset is more limited. This makes operating leasing relatively less attractive for lessors.

---

[1]Numbers as of December 2019.

For all these reasons, these next two chapters will focus mostly on airlines and their usage of operating leasing. We will try to understand why this financing solution has become so popular and the value that it brings to lessees. The specific case of shipping and railway companies will be discussed at a later stage.

8.1.1.2 The Case of the Airline Industry

Without even considering the Covid-19 crisis, financing the airline industry is a challenging task. The following elements have to be considered by a lender:

1. The cost of an aircraft is significant. Depending on the asset type, the cost of a new Airbus or Boeing aircraft varies between approximately $50 million and $250 million.[2] For a bank – whichever it may be – agreeing to finance such an amount is an important decision.

2. When it buys an aircraft, the return on investment for the airline is particularly long. The revenues generated by each flight are extremely low in comparison to the cost of the asset. In other words, the acquisition of an aircraft is a long-term investment. If an airline finances a new aircraft by a traditional corporate loan (with, say, a five- to seven-year maturity), this airline is, in fact, financing long-term assets with short- to medium-term liabilities. This is not a strategy recommended by financial orthodoxy. If the loan is bullet, the airline is taking a refinancing risk. If the loan amortizes completely within the five- to seven-year period, the revenues generated by the aircraft are not sufficient to repay the loan.

3. Due to aircraft cost and fuel price, an airline's fixed costs are significant. In other words, an airline's break-even point is generally very high. The break-even point is the level of revenues for which the total revenues generated by a company cover its expenses. At this level of activity, the profit of the company is nil. A high break-even point means that a company has to generate a high turnover to be able to cover its expenses.

4. Lastly, the airline industry is cyclical. Airlines are exposed to the economic performance and the events of the countries where they operate. Any local economic slowdown implies a decrease in revenue for airlines. Air travel is an expense that households and companies can easily limit.

---

[2]The prices mentioned here are very low when compared with prices officially presented by Airbus and Boeing. This is because substantial discounts are generally granted off the list price by the two manufacturers. We are not talking about 5% discounts, but more like 40% to 60% discounts. This practice may seem surprising, but it is used by the two manufacturers to have the maximum leeway when they negotiate with their clients. It is also a strategy used to ensure that real prices granted to a customer are not known by the competitors. The official prices are never the prices paid by the clients. John Leahy, the charismatic former chief commercial officer of Airbus, used to say jokingly that, during his career, only one customer ever paid the full list price, a billionaire who had requested his aircraft to be customized into a business jet.

8.1.1.3   A Long History of Defaults

Because of the reasons we have just mentioned, it comes as no surprise that most airlines are sub-investment grade.[3] Some of the most famous airlines have gone bust over the years, highlighting the difficulties of managing a business with high fixed costs in a competitive environment. Pan Am, once the world's most prestigious airlines, went bankrupt and ceased operations in 1991. In 2001, TWA, the airline owned successively by billionaire Howard Hughes (from 1939 to 1966) and corporate raider Carl Icahn (from 1985 to 1992) went bankrupt for the third time in 10 years (after 1992 and 1995), and was finally acquired by its rival, American Airlines.

Some major European airlines have also disappeared. Swissair, the pride of the Swiss nation and symbol of the country's excellence in the business sector ceased operations in 2001 due to its staggering level of debt. The list of airlines more recently affected due to the Covid-19 crisis is also long: LATAM Airlines, Avianca, Aeromexico, etc. No one summarized the difficulty of running an airline better than Richard Branson, founder of Virgin Atlantic: *"If you want to be a millionaire, start with a billion dollars and launch a new airline"*.

Although they have not ceased operations, other airlines could be added to this list. Several US airlines have filed for protection under Chapter 11 of the Bankruptcy Code in the last 20 years, thereby gaining time to restructure their debt and streamline their business. In the United States, when a company is no longer in a position to pay its creditors, it can file a petition to be granted protection by a federal judge under Chapter 11. This protection suspends repayment of loans by the debtor. In the meantime, the company can prepare a restructuring plan that implies generally a large debt rescheduling and debt waivers from lenders. When the federal protection stops, the company returns to its normal course of business. If the restructuring is not possible, the company is simply liquidated: its assets are sold off to pay the creditors.

Table 8.1 covers the list of the major US airlines that have been under Chapter 11 since 2001, a particularly difficult year for air transport given the tragic events of 9/11. The mergers that have taken place since then highlight the fragile nature of the sector and the need for restructuring.

This focus on the post-2001 period (or the analysis of the 2020 Covid-19 crisis) should not hide the fact that the airline sector is, in essence, an industry with high fixed costs and low margins. This is a difficult business to be in, even under normal circumstances. Unlike many sectors with high fixed costs, this is indeed not necessarily an industry with high entry barriers. The example of Virgin Atlantic in case study 7 shows that the two main elements to secure in order to set up an airline are (i) the asset (which can be leased) and (ii) the slots (which can be easily obtained in a second-tier airport). Setting up a profitable airline is difficult, but creating an airline is not complicated.

---

[3]This paragraph is written in the midst of the Covid-19 events. It is likely that after this crisis all airlines will be non-investment grade and the general situation of the sector will be calamitous. That said, even if we ignore this crisis and focus on the long-term trend, airlines have generally been non-investment grade. Only a handful have reached investment grade status over the years.

TABLE 8.1 Major Bankruptcies Among US Airlines Since September 2001

Airline	Protection Under Chapter 11	Release	Comments
US Airways	August 2002	March 2003	To curtail costs, the airline put an end to its generous pension scheme for pilots
United Airlines	December 2002	February 2006	Merger with Continental Airlines in 2010
US Airways	September 2004	September 2005	US Airways came out of bankruptcy by merging with America West
Northwest Airlines	September 2005	May 2007	Acquisition by Delta Airlines in 2008
Delta Airlines	September 2005	April 2007	During this period, US Airways offered to buy out Delta but the banks finally decided to support an independent project with Delta
American Airlines	November 2011	December 2013	Merger with US Airways approved in 2013. The name American Airlines was retained by the new group

Source: author.

These factors explain the relative financial weakness of the sector. Table 8.2 shows the list of airlines that ceased operations in 2019, a year that was not marked by any specific global or regional economic slowdown. The diversified origin of the names in the list shows that operating an airline remains a difficult task, regardless of the country.

8.1.2 Valuable and High-Demand Assets

Although readers may now believe that financing airlines is an impossible task, there are still several reasons to remain positive:

- Demand for air travel has grown steadily since 1950. There have been hiccups, but the long-term trend is unequivocal. The rise in spending power of a large part of the population, notably in Asia, has led to more people flying.
- The airline industry has not been a victim of technological disruption. It cannot be compared with sectors such as the press or record industry, which both have been deeply shaken by domination of the internet.
- The success – even relative – of some low-cost airlines (EasyJet, Ryanair, Southwest, AirAsia) proves that it is possible to generate profits in this sector. The industry is simply extremely competitive. Given the high fixed costs, any strategic mistake can rapidly jeopardize an airline.

TABLE 8.2   Airlines that Ceased Operations in 2019

Airline	Country of Origin	Fleet Size (Including Leased and Owned Aircraft)
Adria Airways	Slovenia	10
Aerolineas de Antioquia	Colombia	4
Aigle Azur	France	10
Air Philip	South Korea	3
Al Naser Wings Airlines	Iraq	1
Asian Express Airlines	Tajikistan	3
Astra Airlines	Greece	1
Avianca Argentina	Argentina	2
Avianca Brasil	Brazil	43
California Pacific Airlines	US	2
Far Eastern Transport	Taiwan	7
Fly Jamaica Airways	Jamaica	1
Flybmi	UK	17
Germania	Germany	31
Insel Air	Curacao	3
Jet Airways	India	99
New Gen Airways	Thailand	3
Peruvian Airlines	Peru	6
Silverstone Air	Kenya	11
Tajik Air	Tajikistan	7
TAM Bolivia	Bolivia	6
Taron Avia	Armenia	1
Thomas Cook	UK	34
Via Airlines	US	3
Wisdom Airways	Thailand	Not Available
WOW Air	Iceland	15
XL Airways	France	4
Total		**327**

Source: KPMG.

An interesting takeaway of Table 8.2 is that although the number of bankrupt airlines in 2019 was significant, only very few aircraft have been grounded. Operating lessors have repossessed and redeployed their assets successfully while other airlines have taken the opportunity to buy available airplanes.

Aircraft are sought after for several reasons:

1. A commercial aircraft is a standard asset. The majority of the fleet operating worldwide is produced by two manufacturers only, Boeing and Airbus. This enhances the usable value of an asset. In addition, aircraft do not have any convincing substitute. The other means of transport (train, bus, car) are not real alternatives.

2. Airplanes are assets with a long lifespan. It is possible to operate an Airbus or a Boeing aircraft for more than 25 years. Some even fly for almost 30 years. After that, spare parts can be sold and used on other aircraft.

3. For the two previous reasons, aircraft are assets for which a real secondary market exists. This secondary market is highly structured. There are players specialized in valuing aircraft (appraisers) and others acting as intermediaries in the sale and purchase of aircraft (brokers). The secondary market is all the more organized as it is possible to have a very precise knowledge of the condition of each aircraft thanks to its technical record.

8.1.3 Traditional Financing Options

8.1.3.1 Mortgage Loans

The strong capex needs of airlines is obviously the main reason why they look for funding. Given the relative weaknesses of the sector, on one hand, and the features of the assets they use, on the other, the easiest option for airlines is to use their aircraft to raise funding. Aircraft, being very liquid, represent a valuable collateral for lenders.

Mortgage loans are a popular tool amongst airlines. They represent a simple financing option. Lenders take a risk on companies operating in a cyclical sector with high fixed costs but obtain a mortgage on a liquid asset with a relatively stable value.

Table 8.3 summarizes the risks and opportunities that financing airlines represents. Risks are linked to the sector while opportunities derive from the intrinsic qualities of aircraft. In this context, mortgage loans are one of airlines' favorite financing solutions. They allow the raising of long-term funding (i.e. 10 to 12 years), despite the inherent fragilities of the sector.

8.1.3.2 Tax Leases

Tax leases are also a traditional source of funding for airlines. If, in many countries, tax leases are now less efficient than in the past,[4] some structures keep a certain appeal. That is the case of the Japanese tax lease structure, the JOLCO.[5]

---

[4]See Chapter 7, sections 7.2.2.4, 7.2.2.5, and 7.2.2.6.
[5]See Chapter 7, section 7.2.3.5.

TABLE 8.3   Financing Airlines – Risks and Opportunities

Risks	Opportunities
Extensive funding requirements	Standardized asset without any substitute
Industry with high fixed costs	Long life of the asset
Cyclical industry	Secondary market for the asset

JOLCOs are very popular among airlines. They are an extremely competitive solution to obtain a 100% financing for an aircraft. The market remains, nonetheless, limited as the pool of Japanese tax investors interested in these transactions is not infinite. For this reason, JOLCOs are generally structured for tier-one airlines. Japanese tax investors prefer to be exposed to airlines that have the best credit metrics.

8.1.3.3   Other Corporate Financing Options

If we exclude operating leasing, mortgage loans are the most popular financing option for small airlines. Major players have obviously more solutions. They can use the financing tools generally available to large companies: bonds, loans, hybrid debt, etc. These instruments allow big airlines to optimize their funding mix and diversify their pool of lenders: mortgage loans are generally provided by banks but bonds, and other hybrid instruments, are acquired by asset managers. This is an element of comfort for airlines as it reduces their dependency on banks.

Although these instruments are appealing to airlines, mortgage loans remain for them the most common financing tool. Figure 8.1, shows Air France-KLM's debt repayment profile as of December 2019 (i.e. pre-Covid-19). The weight of mortgage loans' repayment obligations compared to other instruments indicates that this is by far the company's favorite financing option.

Lufthansa Group, one of the largest airlines globally, also has a diversified pool of lenders. In its 2019 annual report, the company states that it has issued (i) several borrower's note loans[6] for an aggregate amount of €1.4 billion, (ii) a five-year bond for €500 million, and (iii) a 60-year hybrid bond[7] for €500 million. It also has several unsecured loans with a volume of €100 million. The case of Lufthansa should, however, not be generalized. The company before the Covid-19 crisis was one of the very

---

[6]Borrower's note loans are instruments similar to bonds that are extremely flexible in terms of coupon payments (fixed or floating) or maturity.

[7]A hybrid bond is a subordinated bond with very long maturity. It is generally issued by companies that have very strong capex. A hybrid bond sits somewhere between traditional unsecured debt and equity in the capital structure. Non-payment of coupons does not trigger an event of default, although they remain due and have to be paid later (having said that, not paying a coupon is a big decision for an issuer as it can negatively impact its reputation). Hybrid bonds are structured with a call option at par at the hand of the issuer after 5 or 10 years. Rating agencies consider that they are 50% debt and 50% equity.

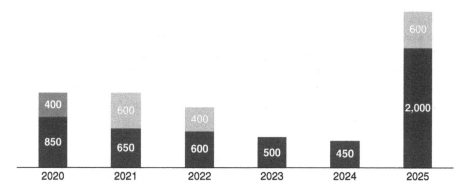

FIGURE 8.1   Air France-KLM's Debt Reimbursement Profile at 31 December 2019
Source: Air France-KLM.

few airlines to enjoy an investment grade status (BBB outlook stable by S&P and Baa3 outlook stable by Moody's) allowing the company to use a large array of financing instruments.

8.1.4   The Appeal of Operating Leasing

Despite the simplicity of mortgage loans and the existence of alternative corporate funding options, operating leases have become over the years the most popular financing instrument for airlines. They now account for around 45% of the global commercial aircraft fleet in operation.

Leasing is not confined to small airlines, all airlines in the world lease. National flag carriers in Europe, legacy carriers in the United States, or low-cost airlines: they all lease. As already mentioned, Emirates is the world's largest user of operating leases today: 54% of its fleet is made up of leased aircraft. Considering that Emirates operate only wide body aircraft such as the A380 or B777,[8] it is by far in value the number one client of operating lessors globally.

Why do airlines use operating leases? There are mainly three reasons.

8.1.4.1   Cash Flow

As already mentioned, the air transport industry has enormous capital expenditure needs. It is an industry with high fixed costs and a constant need to upgrade airplanes. Airlines are generally simply unable to purchase all their aircraft outright. Most of

---

[8]Wide-body aircraft (or twin-aisle aircraft) are aircraft large enough to accommodate two aisles with at least six or seven seats to a row. They are typically used for long-haul flights. The A350, A380, B777, and B787 are examples of wide-body aircraft. By comparison, narrow-body aircraft such as A320 or B737 only have one aisle and are designed for short-haul flights.

them are, in fact, sub-investment grade and not only do they not have the cash to pay for these assets, they do not have the ability to raise the cash needed. The aforementioned examples of Lufthansa or Air France-KLM are exceptions. These two airlines are amongst the largest in the world, they have strong brands, a prestigious standing in their respective countries, access to the best airports, the best landing slots, and have the type of shareholders that gives additional comfort to financiers. As a result, they have special access to the banking and capital markets. Most airlines do not have this luxury.

Smaller airlines sometimes even find it difficult to rely on mortgage loans. This financing method remains a simple and powerful financing tool; however, it usually requires an initial investment by the airline of 20% to 30% of the total aircraft cost (see Chapter 7, section 7.2.1). For many airlines, using mortgage loans to finance all their aircraft is, for this reason, simply impossible.

Operating leases offer the opportunity to obtain usable aircraft without massive cash outflows upfront. Rentals are paid monthly and if the business plan has been correctly designed, the cash generated by the aircraft is higher than the rent to be paid by the airline.

8.1.4.2   Residual Value Risk

The second reason why airlines prefer operating leases over the outright purchase of airplanes is that leasing allows them to avoid being exposed to a residual value risk. The residual value of a purchased asset is the expected value of that asset at a given point in time in the future after deduction of the cumulative depreciation. Airlines are exposed to a residual value risk whenever they sell an aircraft. A sale can generate a large profit or a loss. The price at which they sell the aircraft then becomes a key component of the overall profitability of that asset. Even if the aircraft has been fully depreciated, the price at which the aircraft is sold is important: this represents actual cash for the airline. Since airlines are in the business of flying aircraft and not in the business of trading aircraft, they prefer to avoid this uncertainty.

Many airlines, especially the largest ones, want to maintain a young and modern fleet. They do not keep their airplanes for 25 years. The competition to attract business class passengers (the most profitable type of customer) is fierce and having new aircraft is a solid sales argument. In addition, newer aircraft are generally more efficient in terms of fuel consumption and are less noisy. They are therefore cheaper to operate: (i) they require less fuel and (ii) pay lower airport landing fees – as these fees are generally at least partly indexed to noise and fuel emissions.

Considering the need of many airlines to constantly upgrade their fleet, the residual value risk is significant. For this reason, operating leasing can be seen as a hedge for the airline against the obsolescence of the technology. It allows them to be able to return obsolete technology to a lessor in favor of new and more efficient aircraft.

Although it may appear more expensive on paper, operating leases offer airlines a safeguard against the residual value risk. The cost of the investment is known well in advance and is simply equal to the discounted value of the future rentals over the lease period. The profit on an aircraft is then solely dependent on how it is operated and not on how it is sold.

8.1.4.3 Flexibility

The third reason why airlines use operating leases is that they offer more flexibility. If an airline owns all the aircraft it operates, it cannot react efficiently to variations in traffic. A decline in the number of passengers must be addressed quickly. There is nothing costlier for an airline than flying an empty aircraft.

An airline that owned all its aircraft would face difficult times in case of a decline in traffic. It could be tempted to sell aircraft, but that would be very costly. Asset values would be low and losses inevitable. The only alternative would be to continue flying all the aircraft – another very costly option.

A well-managed lease portfolio for airlines must be like a debt maturity profile. A certain percentage of their fleet has to come off lease every year. If market conditions deteriorate, aircraft are handed back to lessors and are not replaced. This strategy provides airlines with the much-needed flexibility to react to traffic changes.

8.1.4.4 And Accounting?

In the past, it was sometimes argued that one of the reasons why airlines leased aircraft was that accounting rules allowed them not to disclose the full impact of leases on the balance sheet and the income statement. An operating lease, in effect, was an off-balance sheet transaction and lacked full transparency.

This argument was actually never very strong. Analysts had always found ways to account for the leases as debt in their analyses. There are two aspects to leases. Rentals are legally operating expenses (this is a leasing contract, not a loan) yet are also capex from an economic point of view (they are meant to pay for a long-term asset). For this reason, rating agencies and equity analysts have always readjusted airlines' level of indebtedness by considering operating lease rentals as debt-like obligations.

- *Rating agencies* such as S&P and Moody's treat operating lease obligations of rated airlines as debt. There are nuances between the approaches of the two agencies but the underlying methodology is similar: the present value of future lease payments is added to the total net debt of airlines. This methodology is widely used in the sector and is applied by bankers to non-rated airlines.
- *Equity analysts* are not fooled by the legal nature of leasing either. They calculate the operating profitability of airlines using the concept of EBITDAR (Earnings Before Interest, Taxes, Depreciation, Amortization and *Rentals*). Subtracting rentals from the traditional EBITDA metric excludes de facto rentals from an airline's operating expenses. It also means that rentals are considered a capex.

And since 2019, this argument is completely invalid. The US Accounting Standards Board and the International Standards Board issued ASC 842 and IFRS 16 respectively, which require that companies report their operating leases as both assets and liabilities on their balance sheets. These rules had to be implemented as of January 2019. In the case of ASC 842, specifically, publicly traded companies had to implement the new rules as of January 2019, while private companies must implement the rules in 2021. The new rules, broadly, require that leases be recorded as *right of use assets* to be depreciated over the useful life of the asset and that the present value of all future lease payments be recorded as a liability.

8.2 LESSORS

8.2.1 A Historical Approach

8.2.1.1 The Beginnings

Since its inception in the early 1970s, aircraft leasing has grown to represent c. 45% of in-service, commercial aircraft ownership. It is now an integral part of the aviation industry. The first aircraft leasing company, International Lease Finance Corporation (ILFC), was established in 1973 in Los Angeles by a trio of Hungarian immigrants: Steven Udar-Hazy, his friend Louis Gonda, and Louis's father, Leslie. ILFC had originally only one aircraft leased to Aeromexico. It became an incredible success story in the 1980s and was acquired by AIG in 1990. ILFC had a fleet of more than 1,000 aircraft in 2013. At that date, ILFC was sold for $5.4 billion to a rival (but smaller) leasing company, AerCap, as part of a move of AIG to divest non-strategic assets.[9]

Two other aircraft leasing companies were created around the same time as ILFC. Polaris Aircraft Leasing was established in San Francisco in 1974 by Peter Pflendler, a former US fighter pilot. GPA, the first European lessor, was set up in Ireland in 1975 by Tony Ryan, an ex-Aer Lingus executive.

Leasing took off in the 1970s for various reasons. The first one was probably the oil shocks of 1974 and 1979. The price of oil increased dramatically over the period (from $5 per barrel to more than $40), radically changing the economics of airlines and their profitability. Airlines perceived more vividly the advantages of operating leasing, fueling the growth of these newly established lessors, especially after 1980.

The US Airline Deregulation Act of 1978 also shook up the airline industry – at least in the United States. It removed stringent federal government control over the sector, which led to a sharp increase in the number of flights, a decrease in fares, and an increase in the number of passengers. Many airlines were established during that time.

---

[9]Although he sold the company to AIG in 1990, Hazy remained chairman until he left in 2010 to establish (at 64!) his second leasing company, Air Lease Corporation (another success story). Hazy is one of the most influential figures of the aviation industry today and has an estimated net worth of $4 billion.

For these new players, leasing was the only solution to start operations without major capital outlay.

Deregulation was the true fertilizer of the leasing industry. ILFC owned only 13 aircraft in 1979 and increased its leased fleet to 79 aircraft with an order book of 260 by 1989. GPA was another fortunate recipient of this new growth, going from six aircraft in 1979 to 152 aircraft 10 years later. Many lessors were set up in the early 1980s. Ansett Worldwide Aviation Services (AWAS) was, for instance, established in 1985 and owned 41 aircraft five years later.

By 1990, operating leasing represented around 15% of in-service commercial aircraft. The deregulation of the airline sector in Europe from 1987 onwards, combined with the growth in traffic in the Middle East and Asia, cemented the relevance of operating leasing. Ten years later, almost 25% of the world's commercial fleet was leased.

8.2.1.2 The Cape Town Convention and the Globalization of Leasing

One of the keys to success in the leasing business is the repossession of aircraft. Lessors must be able to quickly repossess the aircraft leased to their bankrupt clients to redeploy them in regions where demand exists. Repossessing aircraft must be done quickly to minimize both costs and loss of revenues.

Until the mid-2000s, many obstacles limited the ability of lessors to repossess their assets. Once an aircraft was registered in a country, it was bound by the laws of that country. A lessor had to know how to navigate the laws of the country to be able to regain possession of its asset. Over the years, many legal battles occurred between airlines and lessors, especially in countries where the law was vague or pointedly favored the airlines within the country. Only the largest and most sophisticated lessors considered placement of aircraft in such countries.

Repossessing an asset in these countries was ultimately very expensive. Lawyers had to be hired, either to negotiate with the airline or spend time in court to assert the lessor's rights. The aircraft could then be repossessed but was often in bad condition because it had generally not been properly maintained. The aircraft was then flown out of the country and prepared for a new lease. During all this, no revenues could be obtained.

In the late 1990s, a certain number of countries decided to develop a common legal framework to facilitate transactions involving movable property. A treaty was signed in the city of Cape Town, South Africa in 2001, that imposed common standards for deals involving rail rolling stock, space vehicles, and aircraft, including engines. This treaty, called the Cape Town Treaty, or the Cape Town Convention, created a common protocol between signatories' countries to register assets and bring speed and certainty to aircraft repossession.

The aircraft component of the Cape Town Convention became effective in 2006. In 2020, the treaty had been ratified by 80 countries and one regional organization, the European Union. The treaty gave lessors easier access to their assets in case of the bankruptcy of their clients. Table 8.4 compares a selected number of airlines that went bankrupt and the average number of days needed to repossess an aircraft. The speed of recovery is much higher in countries where the Cape Town Convention is effective.

TABLE 8.4   Average Number of Days Needed by Lessors to Repossess Their Aircraft from Bankrupt Airlines

Airlines	Country	Compliance with Cape Town Convention	Bankruptcy Year	Average Number of Days Needed to Repossess an Aircraft
VIM Airlines	Russia	Yes	2017	35
Transaero	Russia	Yes	2015	60
Mongolian Airline Group	Mongolia	Yes	2013	17
Mexicana	Mexico	Yes	2012	90
Kingfisher Airlines	India	No[10]	2011	+180

Source: Aviation Working Group, Boeing.

The comfort brought to lessors by the Cape Town Treaty had the dual effect of (i) bringing down the cost of operating leasing for airlines, and (ii) intensifying competition between lessors in several jurisdictions. This situation fueled the growth of the sector and by the mid-2010s lessors owned around 45% of the global commercial aircraft fleet. This number has remained steady until 2020.

8.2.2   The Leasing Market Today

8.2.2.1   Leading Lessors

Leasing is today more popular than ever. There are around 150 active operating lessors worldwide, although only 20 to 30 have a global footprint. Today's leaders are the start-ups of yesterday. The two leaders in the sector, GECAS and AerCap, are the only lessors to own more than 1,000 aircraft (i.e. twice the number of aircraft of the sector's number three, Avolon). They are the heirs of yesterday's pioneers. Polaris was acquired by General Electric in 1986 and became GECAS in 1990 when it acquired a large part of GPA's portfolio. AerCap includes the former GPA. It bought out ILFC in 2013. Table 8.5 shows the list of the world's largest lessors ranked by number of aircraft.

---

[10] Although India had ratified the Cape Town Treaty in 2008, it did not pass legislation to bring the treaty into effect.

TABLE 8.5 Top 25 Aircraft Leasing Companies (Ranked by Number of Aircraft)

Rank	Lessors	Number of Aircraft	Backlog[11]	Shareholders
1	GECAS	1,144	351	General Electric
2	AerCap	1,019	306	Listed on NYSE
3	Avolon	529	362	Bohai Leasing (70%) and Orix Corporation (30%)
4	BBAM	509	—	Onex (35%), GIC (30%), and management (35%)
5	Nordic Aviation Capital	487	62	Martin Møller (founder), EQT, GIC
6	SMBC Aviation Capital	416	254	SMBC
7	ICBC Leasing	402	123	ICBC
8	Air Lease Corporation	384	316	Steven Udvar-Hazy (founder), listed on NYSE
9	BOC Aviation	356	151	Bank of China (70%), listed on Hong Kong Stock Exchange – HKEX (30%)
10	DAE Capital[12]	354	—	Investment Corporation of Dubai (ICD)
11	Aviation Capital Group	318	153	Tokyo Century Corporation
12	Aircastle	275	25	Marubeni (75%) and Mizuho Leasing (25%)
13	CDB Aviation	227	185	China Development Bank
14	Carlyle Aviation Partners	225	—	Carlyle
15	Orix Aviation	223	—	Orix Corporation
16	Bocomm Leasing	212	30	Bank of Communication
17	Castlelake Aviation	210	—	Castlelake
18	Macquarie AirFinance	195	60	Macquarie, PGGM Infrastructure Fund, Sunsuper
19	Boeing Capital Corporation	193	29	Boeing
20	Goshawk	177	40	NWS Holding, Chow Tai Fook Enterprises Limited
21	Jackson Square Aviation	174	30	Mitsubishi UFJ Lease & Finance Company Limited
22	Avmax Aircraft Leasing	149	—	Avmax Group
23	AMCK Aviation	145	20	Cheung Kong Group, Mitsubishi Corporation
24	China Aircraft Leasing Group (CALC)	137	190	China Everbright Limited (35%), listed on Hong Kong Stock Exchange – HKEX
25	Standard Chartered Aviation Finance	129	—	Standard Chartered

Source: adapted from Ascend. As at 31 December 2019.

---

[11] Aircraft ordered from manufacturers but not delivered yet.
[12] DAE acquired AWAS in August 2017 from Terra Firma Capital Partners and the Canadian Pension Plan Investment Board (CPPIB).

8.2.2.2 Their Strategies

Lessors have three options in building their fleet. They can (i) buy aircraft from airlines and lease them back to these airlines, (ii) order assets directly from manufacturers, or (iii) purchase aircraft with leases attached to other lessors.

(i) It is very common for lessors to enter into *sale and leaseback* transactions with airlines. In this scenario, the airlines order their aircraft from manufacturers (also called *Original Equipment Manufacturers* or *OEM*) and sell them to a lessor before delivery. They enter in parallel into a leasing agreement with this lessor whereby they lease back the aircraft, generally over 10 to 12 years.

Entering into a sale and leaseback with a lessor allows airlines to fully benefit from the advantages of leasing (limited upfront cash outflow, hedge against residual value risk, and flexibility). For lessors, this is a solution to put capital at work and obtain an immediate return on investment.

(ii) Lessors can order aircraft directly from the OEMs. These orders are generally referred to as *speculative orders* because lessors place these orders without knowing to which airlines they will lease the aircraft when they are delivered (there are usually waiting lists of six to seven years – if not more – at Airbus and Boeing).

Placing speculative orders is the preferred investment strategy of large lessors. They negotiate directly with the OEMs and avoid having the airline making a profit on the sale of the aircraft in the middle. Large lessors can also order aircraft in bulk and benefit from significant discounts. This dramatically increases the profitability of lessors.

Speculative orders only work for large lessors, however. Only large lessors can (a) afford to make down payments required by manufacturers when an order is made, and (b) pay for sales teams that will talk to airlines and place the aircraft on lease before it is actually delivered. While a sale and leaseback can be done by any lessor willing to deploy capital, placing speculative orders requires a good operating leasing platform.[13] In addition, OEMs are generally reluctant to sell aircraft to lessors with unproven track records as they do not want to end up having *white tails*, i.e. aircraft that have been built but remain unsold (which happens when the company that has ordered the aircraft defaults before delivery).

Contracting a lease with a lessor that has made a speculative order is very convenient for airlines. They do not have to make a down payment to an OEM nor plan the configuration of their fleet too long in advance. For many airlines, it is simply impossible to know six or seven years in advance which aircraft will be needed. Business is too volatile and unpredictable. For

---

[13] Asked about AerCap's placement capabilities during an Investor Day in September 2015, AerCap's chief commercial officer said that the company had 70 customer-facing people in EMEA, 31 in the Americas and 25 in Asia. This type of set-up is simply unaffordable for small lessors.

this reason, having a lessor capable of making an order in advance is extremely useful. It ensures that aircraft will be available when needed without committing to buy it. Lessors generally place aircraft with an airline two or three years before delivery.

(iii) Finally, lessors can purchase aircraft from other lessors. The aircraft is always sold with a lease attached, ensuring that the new lessor buys a cash flow-generating asset. These transactions are very attractive to newly established lessors who can in this way quickly build a large and diversified portfolio.

The lessors selling these aircraft are generally willing to decrease their exposure to a specific client, region, or aircraft type. It is also a strategy for them to generate additional profits as these aircraft are generally sold at a premium.

8.2.2.3 Their Relevance

The largest lessors today own more assets than the total number of aircraft operated by the largest airlines. Table 8.6 shows the fleet size of the world's biggest airlines. This number includes aircraft that are owned or leased.

Given that the largest lessors now have so many aircraft, they have become key clients for aircraft manufacturers. While they were sometimes seen as an annoyance by the OEMs in the early days of operating leasing, they are now well-respected

TABLE 8.6 The World's 10 Largest Airlines by Fleet Size

Rank	Airline	Country	Fleet Size
1	Delta Airlines	United States	884
2	American Airlines	United States	871
3	United Airlines	United States	808
4	Lufthansa Group (Lufthansa, Swiss, Austrian, Brussels Airlines, Eurowings)	Germany, Austria, Switzerland	752
5	Southwest Airlines	United States	739
6	China Southern Airlines	China	620
7	China Eastern Airlines	China	527
8	International Airlines Group – IAG (British Airways, Iberia, Aer Lingus, Vueling)	United Kingdom, Spain, Ireland	598
9	Air France-KLM	France, Netherlands	539
10	Air China	China	429

Source: author.

customers. Boeing, Airbus, and the other manufacturers know their weight in the market and listen to them carefully.

The most famous example of the influence of lessors is probably the reaction of Steve Hazy, back then CEO of ILFC, to the first design of the Airbus A350. Invited as a guest speaker to a conference in March 2006, Hazy said openly that the program – launched a year before – was a *"band-aid reaction to the 787"* that Boeing was working on. Airbus took this statement to heart, went back to the drawing board, and created an entirely new fuselage and not one based on the A330. In July 2006, the newly redesigned aircraft received its first orders.

If Hazy's comments were probably not the only reason why Airbus decided to redesign the entire aircraft (many airlines were also skeptical), his observation was widely seen as a sign of the growing influence of lessors in the market. Hazy had become the spokesman for the whole industry. He was able to publicly advise a leading OEM on its investment strategy and push them to make an $8-billion decision, the final cost of the A350 program.

8.2.2.4   A Fragmented Market

From a macroeconomic point of view, the strength of leasing comes from the fact that it is a global business. While airlines are highly dependent on a local context and can suffer from a recession in their home market, leasing companies can compensate for the difficult situation of clients in some parts of the world by placing aircraft in more dynamic regions.

If a lessor has a well-balanced portfolio, it should, in theory, remain rather immune to local jolts. It should be exposed to the growth of the air transport market globally. And as we have seen before, this market is in expansion. Over the last 50 years, the market has doubled every 15 years, driven mostly by the global increase in purchase power (especially in Asia), deregulation, mass tourism, and the decrease of fares.

For all of these reasons, leasing has attracted over the years a wide range of investors. The number of lessors increased by more than 50% between 2002 and 2018, creating a more fragmented market. The relative weight of leading lessors has decreased and several leading lessors have been established during this period. ICBC Leasing was created in 2007, and Avolon and Air Lease in 2010. Figure 8.2 indicates the growing fragmentation of leasing since 2002. The impact of the Cape Town Treaty – which came into force in 2006 – is clearly visible.

8.2.3   Dynamics at Work in the Aircraft Operating Leasing Market

The leasing market has deeply changed in the last 20 years. A closer look at the last column of Table 8.5 in section 8.2.2.1 shows that there is a wide variety of investors active in the sector. While some are historical players, others have only recently discovered the industry. Their background says a lot about the specificities of the leasing market, a sector that has attracted investors with a background in real estate or infrastructure.

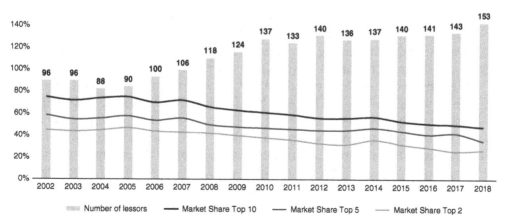

FIGURE 8.2   Lessor Fragmentation 2002–2018
Source: Ascend, Boeing.

8.2.3.1   A Business with High Entry Barriers

Although the leasing sector is more fragmented than ever, the pioneers of the 1970s remain the market leaders of today. They are at least twice the size of their competitors. As already explained, Polaris became GECAS and acquired a large part of GPA's portfolio in the early 1990s; AerCap is the result of several mergers and includes the old GPA and the former ILFC (see case study 8).

The domination of historical players almost 50 years after their establishment demonstrates the need to have an efficient platform to be successful in the sector. Operating leasing is an industry that requires (i) a lot of capital and (ii) a strong expertise. Avolon, the third largest lessor by fleet size, fully embodies this reality. It was established in 2010 by combining these two ingredients; the former management team of RBS Aviation[14] brought the expertise while four major investors brought the capital: Cinven, CVC, Oak Hill Capital Partners, and the Government of Singapore Investment Corporation (GIC).

Leasing requires a lot of capital (to buy airplanes) but it also needs a solid know-how. The right aircraft have to be purchased at the right price and leased to the right airlines. Lessors must also be capable of repossessing aircraft quickly in case of default by their clients. Following the bankruptcy of Kingfisher Airlines in 2011, leading lessors got their aircraft back in two weeks while some others had to wait for more than a year: the figures shown in Table 8.4 in section 8.2.1.2 are only an average.

8.2.3.2   The Rise of Chinese Lessors

The second take away of the analysis of Table 8.5 is probably the weight of Chinese lessors amongst the world's largest leasing companies. Four subsidiaries of Chinese

---

[14]RBS Aviation was sold in 2012 by RBS to SMBC to become SMBC Aviation Capital as a move by the British bank to divest non-core assets following the 2008 crisis.

banks rank in the top 20: ICBC Leasing (7), BOC Aviation (9), CDB Aviation (13), and Bocomm Leasing (16). Several other Chinese banks are also active in the sector: CCB Leasing and CMB Leasing, respectively subsidiaries of China Construction Bank (CCB) and China Merchants Bank (CMB), both own around 70 aircraft.[15]

The activity of these lessors is the direct result of the growth of the Chinese air transport market. This growth has been phenomenal over the last 30 years and is set to continue in the next two decades due to (i) the increase in spending power of the local population and (ii) the investments made by the Chinese government in airport infrastructures. This situation has triggered the appetite of Chinese investors, notably Chinese banks, whose role it is to participate in the development of the country.

Some non-bank-related Chinese investors are also active in the leasing sector. Bohai Leasing, a subsidiary of HNA Group, a Chinese conglomerate involved notably in the airline and tourism sectors, bought out Avolon in 2016. Avolon then acquired CIT Group's aircraft leasing business for $10 billion to form the third largest lessor globally.

More broadly, leasing is a key component of China's aviation strategy. Chinese lessors are, for instance, alongside Chinese airlines the first clients of the Comac C919, the new Chinese narrow-body aircraft, which is expected to enter commercial service in 2022 and compete with the Airbus A320 and the Boeing 737.

8.2.3.3   The Growing Interest of Hong Kong Investors

The opportunity that aircraft operating leasing represents in China – and more generally in Asia – has also been identified by Hong Kong-based investors. Three lessors in the top 25 list – Goshawk (20), AMCK Aviation (23), and CALC (24) – are owned by investors coming from the city. Interestingly, two of them, Goshawk and AMCK Aviation, are partly or totally controlled by shareholders that have a strong background in real estate: NWS Holding, Chow Tai Fook Enterprises (CFTE), and Cheung Kong.

The similarities between aircraft leasing and real estate may explain the interest of these companies for the sector. In both markets, investments are made in real assets whose supply is limited and whose market value fluctuates quickly based on demand. From a portfolio perspective, revenues come from a variety of final users who can legally not use the assets if they do not pay their rents. For this reason, some equity analysts sometimes refer to aircraft leasing as "flying real estate".

8.2.3.4   Japanese Lessors

Japanese investors are another driving force in the aircraft leasing industry. Several of them (Orix, SMBC, Tokyo Century Corporation, Marubeni, Mizuho, and Mitsubishi) own or control some of the world's largest lessors. One of them, Orix, even has interest in two different lessors. It owns 100% of Orix Aviation (15) and has a minority stake of 30% in Avolon (3).

---

[15] According to Airline Business Finance & Leasing Report 2019.

Japan is the third largest aviation market in the world (after the United States and China) and Japanese banks and investors have always shown interest in the sector. If they withdrew from the market after the local real estate crash of 1991, they have come back strongly since 2010. Some of the largest recent M&A transactions in the sector have involved Japanese investors: SMBC acquired RBS Aviation in 2012, Orix took a 30% interest in Avolon in 2018, Tokyo Century Corporation purchased US lessor Aviation Capital Group in 2019, and Marubeni and Mizuho bought out Aircastle in 2020.

This takeover frenzy reveals the strong appetite of Japanese investors for aircraft leasing. They are interested in the steady cash flow and the sector's high entry barriers. It represents for them an opportunity to make a long-term investment outside Japan in a resilient but growing market. Unsurprisingly, these investments are made by companies that are also active in the infrastructure sector, a business that shares a lot of commonalities with aircraft leasing (real assets, steady and recurrent cash flow, high entry barriers). Some of these Japanese lessors are notably subsidiaries of the most active banks in project finance: SMBC, MUFG, and Mizuho (see Chapter 5, section 5.3.1.1, Table 5.4).

8.2.3.5 Long-term Infrastructure Investors

Japanese banks are not the only ones to see the similarities between aircraft leasing and the traditional infrastructure sector. Several international investors holding stakes in brownfield infrastructure assets have an interest in leasing companies. GIC for instance, one of the shareholders of Heathrow Airport (see Chapter 5, section 5.2.2.3, Table 5.1) and an investor in many other infrastructure assets globally, has a stake in two of the world's leading lessors, BBAM (4) and Nordic Aviation Capital (5).[16] If leasing companies are not true infrastructure assets, they somehow belong to the family of infra-like assets that we have already mentioned (see Chapter 5, section 5.2.5).

Other infrastructure investors that have stakes in operating lessors are Macquarie, PGGM, and Sunsuper. The trio jointly controls Macquarie Air Finance, a lessor that owns almost 200 aircraft. While Macquarie is one of the leading investors in infrastructure finance, PGGM and Sunsuper are two major pension funds. They both look for long-term yield for the benefit of their clients.

These investors – to which could be added ICD, the sovereign wealth fund of Dubai, sole shareholder of DAE Capital – are generally here for the long term. They see a growing market, with strong fundamentals and high entry barriers. If running an airline is a difficult business, owning a stake as a well-managed lessor is supposed to be less volatile. Assuming people continue to travel more by air, aircraft will be needed, whatever the final customer.[17]

---

[16]In this case, conflict of interest is avoided as BBAM and Nordic Aviation are active in two different market segments. Nordic Aviation specializes in regional aircraft (ATR, Bombardier, Embraer), while BBAM owns mainly Airbus and Boeing aircraft.

[17]The Covid-19 situation may invite some of these investors to revise their views but we still believe that their analysis was right.

8.2.3.6   Private Equity Firms

Aircraft leasing has also attracted in the last decade the interest of traditional private equity firms. These investors have generally a shorter investment horizon than pension funds or traditional infrastructure investors. They have nonetheless invested in the sector for very similar reasons. Onex corporation, shareholder of BBAM, and EQT, shareholder of Nordic Aviation, both fall into this category.

Private equity firms can also directly manage their own operating leasing platforms. This is the case of Carlyle and Castlelake, which run respectively the fourteenth and seventeenth largest lessors globally. These private equity players manage portfolios of aircraft like others manage portfolios of stocks or bonds. They perceive an operating lease as a loan to an airline secured by an aircraft. A lease is, in essence, a high-yield loan backed by a real asset. In this regard it is no surprise that Carlyle Aviation Partners is integrated into Carlyle's credit business, and not into their equity division.

Carlyle and Castlelake should not, however, be perceived as financial investors with no aircraft expertise. Both are active in the mid- to end-of-life commercial aircraft segment. In other words, they mainly acquire and lease assets that are at least 15 years old. This is a market segment where assets are less liquid and where lessees tend to be smaller airlines. Returns are better but risks are intrinsically higher. Carlyle and Castlelake have raised several aircraft funds, some specialized in end-of-life aircraft where the investors' return comes partly from the capacity of the general partner to dismantle the aircraft at the end of its lifetime and sell spare parts in the market. This strategy obviously requires a strong industrial know-how.

8.2.3.7   Sidecars

Joint ventures between major lessors and third-party investors are another feature of the operating leasing market. The expansion of the air transport industry and the positive prospects for the next 20 years have attracted a lot of capital in the market, notably – as we have seen – from Asian investors or private equity specialists. Investors who do not want to invest in a platform or have not been able to acquire an interest in a leasing company or take control of a lessor have formed joint ventures (or *sidecars*) with existing players.

In a typical sidecar transaction, the lessor and the third-party investor form a new company whose purpose is to buy aircraft and lease them to customers. Both parties contribute to the equity of the joint venture (JV) but the lessor also acts as servicer to the structure. It is responsible for originating deals, buying and selling aircraft, negotiating with airlines, handling payments and back office work, and, if necessary, repossessing and redeploying the assets. The lessor receives for all this a series of fees, fixed and variable, depending on the shareholder agreement between the parties. Fees can be paid, for instance, for originating a deal (origination fee), selling an aircraft (sale-based fee), and negotiating a rental (rent-based fee). The precise mechanic of these fees varies from one sidecar to the other, but the objective is always to ensure that the lessor is paid for each step of the work done on behalf of the JV. Figure 8.3 shows a simplified diagram of a sidecar transaction.

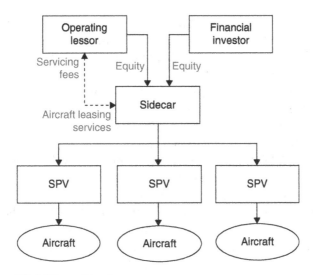

FIGURE 8.3 Simplified Sidecar Structure

The JV is a fully independent company. It has its own Board of Directors and its own decision-making process. It is not managed by the lessor. The leasing company is often a minority shareholder in the structure and does not control the JV. As such, it accounts for its share of ownership in the sidecar using the equity method. The sidecar is not consolidated by the lessor.[18]

Capital contribution to the sidecars is made progressively by shareholders as aircraft are added to the JV. Profit distributions can be structured in many ways. They can be split according to each shareholder's stake in the sidecar or similar to a private equity approach. Under this model, once both shareholders have been repaid their capital contributions and have reached a certain level of return, the lessor receives a higher share of profits than its percentage of ownership in the JV.

A sidecar's investment strategy is clearly defined at the outset in the JV's investment guidelines. The parties have to decide what type of aircraft to target (new or mid-life, freighter or passenger), the minimum lease period offered to clients, the customer base, and the concentration limits by airline, airline type, or country. The investment guidelines must also ensure that there is no conflict of interest between the lessor and the JV.

Some aircraft specialists are skeptical about this point. Sidecars are obviously a way for lessors to lease more aircraft with an airline than what their own concentration rules allow for. There could therefore be a risk of conflict of interest when, following

---

[18]Under the equity method, the investment made by an investor in a company is recorded as a non-current asset in the balance sheet of the investor. Profits arising from this investment are added to the value of this non-current asset at year end but are also in parallel recognized in the income statement of the investor. An investor must apply the equity method when it does not control the company it has invested in but exercises, nonetheless, a significant influence over it. Note that there are several rules that define significant influence such as equity interest, voting rights, influence on the board, etc. We give an illustration of this equity method in Chapter 5, section 5.2.4.3.

a default, several aircraft (some belonging to the JV and some to the lessor) have to be redeployed simultaneously by the lessor. A way to partly deal with this issue is to have the lessor and the JV focusing on two distinct market segments (new vs. end-of-life assets, different customer bases, etc.).

Despite the intrinsic potential risk of conflict of interest, the sidecar structure is relatively common in the industry. It is a way for a lessor to increase revenues without committing a lot of capital: AerCap has a sidecar with Chinese investors, Air Lease set up a sidecar with Napier Park called Blackbird Capital I in 2014 (in which Air Lease has a 9.5% interest), GECAS and CDPQ created their own vehicle in 2017, and CALC established one with three Chinese state-owned enterprises in 2018.

These sidecars allow financial investors to have access to the leasing market without having to buy an existing player or set up their own platform. They team up with a leading lessor and benefit from its platform. For the lessor, the fees paid by the JV represent an additional and stable income stream that does not come with additional debt (as the sidecar's debt is not consolidated).[19]

8.3   LENDERS

Operating lessors have several options to finance their assets. They can decide to finance each asset independently and rely on commercial banks or ECAs. They can also decide to raise funding at corporate level or finance together a portfolio of assets.

8.3.1   Mortgage Loans

8.3.1.1   Structure

As explained in Chapter 7, mortgage loans are a common financing structure in operating leasing. The asset is acquired by an SPV that is financed by a mix of equity and debt. The equity is invested by the lessor and the debt is brought by commercial lenders. The debt is non-recourse to the lessor but the lenders obtain a mortgage on the asset. A simplified mortgage loan structure involving an operating lessor is shown in Figure 7.3 in Chapter 7.

Mortgage loans are a very convenient financing option for lessors. Just like airlines, they can raise long-term funding to finance a long-term asset. The maturity of the loan matches the lease maturity so that the debt is fully repaid at the end of the lease. Rentals are calculated to cover the debt repayment obligations of the SPV and pay a dividend or a coupon to the lessor. Rentals are generally paid monthly and are

---

[19]Due to the use of the equity method.

used in priority to repay the lenders and then the lessor. This type of waterfall is now well-known to our readers.

The investment by the lessor in the SPV remains conceptually an equity investment but is legally a shareholder loan. The equity investment is generally limited to the minimal amount of equity required to set up a company. The rest of the investment is made in the form of a shareholder loan and is repaid monthly. This structure allows for the lessor to receive a monthly coupon regardless of the constraints applicable to dividend distributions (which can occur only once a year). This financing strategy gives more flexibility to the lessor. It increases its IRR and allows it to receive a payment even if the SPV is loss-making from an accounting perspective – which can happen depending on the depreciation profile of the aircraft. This technique is similar to what we have seen in project finance.[20] It only exists to optimize dividend distributions to the equity holder.

8.3.1.2 Mortgage Loans Seen by Banks

The mortgage loan option is very attractive for banks. Although they provide long-term funding, the loan is not too costly for them in terms of RWAs. The fact that they benefit from a mortgage on an aircraft is positive and many banks have obtained a favorable treatment from their regulators under the Basel advanced approach.

For banks and regulators, this treatment is justified by the fact that lenders are over-collateralized by a liquid asset. In addition, the long-term LTV improves over time (i.e. decreases), which gives lenders another element of comfort. This improvement in the LTV is especially true for the financing of new aircraft. The assets have a 25- to 30-year lifespan while they are generally financed by an amortizing loan of 10 to 12 years. In other words, it takes 25 to 30 years for the value of the aircraft to reach zero, while loans amortize down to zero in 10 to 12 years.

Let us take an example to illustrate this. If a $100-million aircraft has a 25-year expected lifespan, then the value of the aircraft will depreciate by $4 million every year (assuming, to simplify, a linear depreciation of the asset). If banks finance this asset through a 10-year fully amortizing $80-million loan, their exposure will decrease by c. $8 million a year (simplifying as well). The exposure of the banks therefore decreases much faster than the market price of the aircraft. This is one of the marvels of asset finance: the LTV improves over time, meaning that the risk taken by the lenders decreases.

Table 8.7 presents the LTV calculation for the following transaction:

- aircraft cost: $100 million
- senior loan amount: 80% of the asset value, i.e. $80 million
- interest rate: 4%
- loan maturity: 10 years without balloon payment

---

[20]See Chapter 6, section 6.3.2.2.

- estimated values of the aircraft: calculated on the basis of data provided by different appraisers[21]
- LTV: calculated as the ratio between the loan amount and the expected value of the aircraft.

TABLE 8.7   Calculation of The LTV of a 10-year $80-million Loan with a $100-million Aircraft as Collateral

Year	Loan Amount	Payment of the Principal Amount	Payment of Interest	Total Repayment	Estimated Market Value of the Aircraft	LTV
	80 000 000				100 000 000	80%
1	73 336 724	6 663 276	3 200 000	9 863 276	92 500 000	79%
2	66 406 918	6 929 807	2 933 469	9 863 276	86 487 500	77%
3	59 199 919	7 206 999	2 656 277	9 863 276	80 865 813	73%
4	51 704 640	7 495 279	2 367 997	9 863 276	75 609 535	68%
5	43 909 550	7 795 090	2 068 186	9 863 276	71 072 963	62%
6	35 802 657	8 106 894	1 756 382	9 863 276	66 808 585	54%
7	27 371 488	8 431 169	1 432 106	9 863 276	63 134 113	43%
8	18 603 071	8 768 416	1 094 860	9 863 276	59 661 736	31%
9	9 483 919	9 119 153	744 123	9 863 276	56 380 341	17%
10	0	9 483 919	379 357	9 863 276	53 279 422	0%

Table 8.7 shows clearly that the LTV of the transaction improves over time. The first years of the financing are the riskiest for the lenders. In case of default of the lessee, they have a lower protection buffer from their collateral. This situation is caused by two complementary phenomena:

- During the first years, the value of an aircraft decreases sharply. This is simply due to the fact that the aircraft is no longer new. The demand for one- or two-year-old assets is relatively limited, as potential buyers would always choose a new aircraft if the price range is similar. A big discount is required to ensure a quick sale.

---

[21] Data aggregated by the author: the changes in the price of the aircraft take into account a decline in the market value of the aircraft by 7.5% in the first year, 6.5% in the second, third, and fourth years, 6% in the fifth and sixth years, and then 5.5% every year after that. Needless to say, nobody is capable of determining future prices and the appraisers' estimates are no exception. These projections are nevertheless useful, since they are based on past statistical data with calculations involving a large number of aircraft. Even though these figures are only an approximation, they are relevant as there is limited volatility in the used-aircraft market.

- Inversely, an installment loan amortizes rather slowly at the beginning of the financing. Interest payments are significant at the beginning but minimal at the end ($3.2 million in year 1 and $0.3 million in year 10).

The lenders' position improves as time passes. The LTV improves only by one point in year 1 and two points in year 2 but improves by 11 points in year 7 and 12 points in year 8.

From a risk perspective, the gradual improvement in the LTV means that there are two distinct phases in the transaction:

- In the first phase, lenders accept a corporate risk. During this period, the banks have a high LTV. In case of default by the lessee, they are exposed to sharp price swings in the aircraft secondary market. In other words, the protection offered by their collateral is real, but limited. Lenders enter into the transaction mainly because they do not anticipate a default by the lessee during this phase. Considerations as to the asset are secondary.
- The transaction enters then into a second phase. Who can actually claim to have a view on the development of an airline over a period of 10 or 12 years? This uncertainty – that grows with time – is partly offset by an LTV that, in contrast, improves gradually. Lenders compensate for the lack of visibility as to the future of the lessee by a loan that becomes more and more collateralized.

8.3.1.3 Non-recourse Financing

Although the debt provided to the SPV is conceptually non-recourse to the lessor, there are usually additional elements of comfort for the lenders. A lessor can, for instance, offer to guarantee debt repayments for a given period (usually six months) following a lessee's event of default. This mechanism gives a lessor, in theory, enough time to find a new lessee and brings value to both parties:

- It is positive for the lessor, as otherwise lenders would exercise their rights under the mortgage, take control of the asset, and sell it – whatever the market conditions.
- It is also beneficial for lenders. They are not specialized in repossessing assets and prefer to have the lessor do it and find a solution with another lessee.

Once a new lessee has been identified and takes the asset on lease, a new loan is taken out (generally provided by banks more familiar with the new lessee) and the first loan can be repaid.

All things being equal, this structuring feature means that it is more comfortable for banks to provide a loan for an operating lessor than to directly offer a mortgage loan to an airline. While banks originally saw lessors as unnecessary intermediaries, they now perceive their value. The figures mentioned in Table 8.7 would also be true in the case of a bank lending directly to an airline. With a lessor, however, banks benefit from a financial and logistical support in case of default of the airline. This increases their chances of optimizing the value of the collateral, as lessors are better equipped than banks to repossess and sell or release an aircraft.

8.3.1.4   Export Credit Agencies

Lessors can also finance the acquisition of their assets with the support of export credit agencies. If a lessor purchases an asset that is not manufactured in the country where it is established, there is indeed an export contract and the lessor is potentially eligible for an ECA cover.[22]

Transactions in which ECAs are involved are not so different from other deals in which an SPV is set up and funded in equity by a lessor and debt is provided by commercial lenders. The only difference is that the debt is guaranteed by an export credit agency. In exchange, the banks assign the ECA the benefit of the mortgage.

The decision to provide a cover is taken by the export credit agency in the light of the robustness of the structure, the experience of the lessor, the quality of the lessee, and the credit limits of the ECA. Depending on its own policy and its final credit approval, an ECA can require lenders to take a residual risk. The premium paid to the ECA is adapted to the risk of the structure.

8.3.1.5   Asset Finance vs. Project Finance

Although project finance and asset finance may look very similar, there are some key differences between a project finance loan and a mortgage loan designed to finance an operating lease. Table 8.8 recaps how these two types of loans compare with each other.

TABLE 8.8   Project Finance Loans vs. Mortgage Loans for a Lessor

	Project Finance Loan	Mortgage Loan for an Operating Lease
Use of an SPV	Yes	Yes
SPV funding	Mix of debt and equity	Mix of debt and equity
Financing of a real asset	Yes	Yes
Purpose of the financing	Fixed infrastructure	Movable asset
Construction risk	Yes, if it is a greenfield asset	Never. The asset is only financed once delivered
Credit risk	Project risk: cash flow generated by the project	Corporate risk: capacity of the lessee to pay rents. The lessee pays rents whatever the profitability of the asset taken independently

---

[22]See Chapter 5, section 5.3.5 for a definition of export credit agencies and a more detailed explanation of how they operate.

TABLE 8.8 (*continued*)

	Project Finance Loan	Mortgage Loan for an Operating Lease
Lenders	Banks, infrastructure debt funds, bond investors (if PF bonds), ECAs, DFIs	Banks only, sometimes backed by ECAs
Maturity	Up to 25 to 30 years	Mostly 10 to 12 years
Loan profile	Depends on the project cash flow and project risk. Can be a mini-perm or a fully amortizing loan	Installment loan
Equity investor	Financial or industrial sponsor	Operating lessor

8.3.2 Unsecured Funding

8.3.2.1 Bonds

Due to the growth of the leasing market over the last 20 years,[23] some lessors are now large enough to raise significant funding at the corporate level. Lessors with a diversified portfolio, a well-established platform, and conservative credit metrics have even been able to secure an investment grade rating. This rating allows lessors to tap the traditional bond market and access a large pool of liquidity.

Having an investment grade rating is positive, as coupons applicable in this market are significantly lower than those of high-yield bonds. In an industry where competition between lessors has intensified and in which product differentiation is minimal, this is a significant advantage. Table 8.9 shows the list of unsecured bonds issued by lessors in 2018. The price of the coupons paid by Avation or Intrepid Aviation, two smaller lessors, clearly shows the advantage that large or investment grade lessors have over smaller ones.

Securing an investment grade rating has become a key target for large lessors. The decision to welcome Orix Corporation as a minority shareholder in Avolon in 2018 was notably driven by the desire to increase Avolon's credit rating. This move was perceived positively by Moody's, which upgraded the lessor's rating shortly after the transaction, from Ba2 to Ba1, one notch below investment grade.

Several lessors have strongly improved their credit metrics in recent years and even successfully maintained an investment grade rating despite the Covid-19 crisis. Although we remain very cautious, the fact that Fitch affirmed an investment grade rating for eight of them on 9 July 2020, five months after the beginning of the worst crisis in the history of the aviation industry, is significant (see Table 8.10 in section 8.3.2.2). That said, the average rating of lessors could very likely be downgraded, especially if airlines' credit metrics further deteriorate. In its report, Fitch underlined that the sector outlook was negative.[24]

---

[23]From 25% to almost 50% of the world's commercial fleet.
[24]Source: Fitch.

TABLE 8.9   Unsecured Bonds Issued by Lessors in 2018

Lessor	Issue Date	Amount ($m)	Coupon	Maturity
Air Lease	02-Jan	550	2.500	2021
Air Lease	02-Jan	700	3.250	2025
AerCap	16-Jan	550	3.875	2028
AerCap	16-Jan	600	3.300	2023
BOC Aviation	25-Jan	300	3.500	2023
Avolon	01-March	500	5.500	2023
BOC Aviation	23-April	500	Floating	2021
Aviation Capital Group	24-April	650	3.875	2023
Avation	15-May	300	6.500	2021
AerCap	05-June	600	4.125	2023
Intrepid Aviation	23-July	500	8.500	2021
SMBC Aviation Capital	23-July	500	4.125	2023
Aviation Capital Group	25-July	500	4.125	2025
Aviation Capital Group	25-July	300	Floating	2021
AerCap	14-Aug	600	4.450	2025
Avolon	06-Sept	1,000	5.125	2020
BOC Aviation	19-Sept	500	Floating	2023
Aircastle	20-Sept	650	4.400	2023
Air Lease	09-Oct	700	3.500	2022
Air Lease	09-Oct	500	3.875	2023
DAE	01-Nov	500	5.750	2023
DAE	01-Nov	500	5.250	2021
Air Lease	06-Nov	500	4.625	2028
Aviation Capital Group	28-Nov	300	4.373	2024
Aviation Capital Group	28-Nov	500	Floating	2021
Total		13,300		

Source: FlightGlobal.

8.3.2.2   Bank Facilities

In addition to raising bonds, large lessors have bank facilities like any other company. They have bilateral lines, term loans and revolving credit facilities (RCF). As opposed to a term loan, an RCF is by default undrawn. It is a back-up facility that can be drawn when the client needs it. If it remains undrawn, the borrower only pays commitment fees. Commitment fees are usually equal to 35% of the applicable margin. Lessors drew

TABLE 8.10 Long-term Rating of a Selected Number of Lessors

Lessors	Long-Term Rating by Fitch as of 9 July 2020
AerCap	BBB-/Outlook negative
Aircastle	BBB/Outlook stable
Air Lease Corporation	BBB/Outlook negative
Avation	B/Outlook negative
Aviation Capital Group	BBB-/Outlook negative
Avolon	BBB-/Outlook negative
BOC Aviation	A-/Outlook stable
Dubai Aerospace Enterprise	BBB-/Outlook negative
SMBC Aviation Capital	A-/Outlook negative
Voyager Aviation[25]	BB-/Outlook negative

Source: Fitch Ratings.

on their RCFs during the Covid-19 crisis, which gave them access to short-term liquidity when most of their clients were facing difficulties and trying to renegotiate their leases. AerCap, for instance, drew $4 billion on its RCF in the first quarter of 2020. During the second quarter, the company raised $3 billion of funding, including $2.5 billion of unsecured bonds, allowing AerCap to repay its RCF.[26]

The growing importance of unsecured funding in the leasing industry is certainly no surprise to real estate specialists. The evolution in the financing strategies of lessors follows in many ways the path shown by real estate companies. While small real estate owners finance their assets independently on a non-recourse basis, large real estate companies raise most of their funding via corporate debt or bonds. It allows for more flexibility and simplicity, both on the asset and liability sides. According to Table 8.9, AerCap raised $2.3 billion of unsecured debt in 2018 in four transactions only. This would have been more complex and costlier to raise the same amount via a series of mortgage loans. Amongst aircraft lessors, Air Lease is at the forefront of this trend. As of March 2020, 98.7% of its funding is unsecured (vs. 72% for AerCap).[27]

Although lessors increasingly rely on corporate funding, aircraft are still acquired via separate SPVs. Each SPV is then financed by a shareholder loan. This is the best solution to distribute a regular coupon to the lessor but, also, to segregate risks. If for some reason the owner of an aircraft becomes liable for indemnification due to a loss caused by the aircraft to a third party, the liability of the owner is de facto limited to the value of the assets owned by the SPV.

[25]Voyager Aviation is the former Intrepid Aviation, mentioned in Table 8.9.
[26]Source: S&P.
[27]Source: companies.

8.3.3   Other Structures

8.3.3.1   Securitization

Securitization is a structure that allows lessors to finance a portfolio of assets via the issuance of instruments similar to bonds. In a typical aircraft securitization, several aircraft are sold by a lessor to an SPV, which in turn issues securities backed by the rentals generated by the portfolio of aircraft. These securities, called *Asset-Backed Securities* (or ABS), are acquired by investors willing to be exposed to a diversified portfolio of aircraft leases.

The revenues of the ABS stem only from the revenues generated by the assets sold to the SPV. Depending on the transaction, the lessor can invest in the ABS or not. The lessor usually remains in charge of the management of the portfolio sold to the SPV. It ensures that rentals are duly paid and has the responsibility of repossessing and releasing an aircraft in case of default of one of the lessees. It is said that the lessor acts as a *servicer*.

Securitization will be discussed extensively in Part IV of this book. It is in itself a type of structured transaction: The ABS holders acquire securities issued by an SPV and have no recourse to the original seller of the portfolio of aircraft. In 2018, the total amount of aircraft ABS issued was $6.1 billion, roughly half the size of the amount of unsecured bonds issued by operating lessors (see Table 8.9).[28]

8.3.3.2   JOLCOs

Although they are not a major source of funding for them, JOLCOs can be used by lessors to finance the acquisition of aircraft. In this case, the SPV set up by the Japanese tax investors leases the asset to an SPV owned by a lessor, which in turn subleases the aircraft to an airline.

Case Study 8: The Rise and Fall of GPA Group, the First Giant Aircraft Leasing Company

The story of Guinness Peat Aviation (GPA), the first giant aircraft lessor is singular in many ways. Born in a small city on the west coast of Ireland, the company grew to become a global leader and a firm admired by many. Despite its tragic destiny, GPA captured the collective imagination of the leasing industry and marked a generation of pioneers. Almost 30 years after its fall, it still remains a reference in the sector.

---

[28] Source: FlightGlobal.

The Early Days

GPA was established in 1975 by Tony Ryan, an ex-Aer Lingus executive convinced by the potential of the aircraft leasing business. Ryan was born in 1936 into a very modest family. He left school at the age of 15 and started working for Aer Lingus at 19 as a dispatcher at Shannon Airport. He then progressed through the ranks and obtained a series of senior positions within the airline, in Ireland and abroad.

The events in Northern Ireland in 1972 (Bloody Sunday) opened a difficult period for Aer Lingus. The airline was forced to revisit its strategy and Ryan was given the task of finding a solution for a Boeing 747 that the airline no longer had use for. Instead of selling the aircraft, Ryan decided to lease it with all its crew to Air Siam, an airline unable to purchase such an aircraft but eager to operate one.

Realizing the large profits that could be made in leasing, Ryan decided to leave Aer Lingus and start his own business. He was backed in his new venture by two strong shareholders, Aer Lingus and the Irish bank Guinness Mahon. GPA was established in Shannon, in the west of Ireland, in a tax-free zone created by the government to incentivize investment.

The successive oil shocks offered a fantastic opportunity to GPA as major airlines trimmed their fleet in the wake of the global crisis. GPA bought aircraft from national flag carriers in the northern hemisphere and leased them to newly created airlines in the southern hemisphere. Many governments of recently independent countries in Africa or Asia were only too happy to start or develop a national airline with minimum investment.

To serve these clients, GPA even started its own airline, Air Tara, whose only purpose was to *wet lease* aircraft to start-up airlines in emerging markets. A wet lease means that the leasing company provides all or some of the flight crew, cabin staff, maintenance, and insurance to its client in addition to the aircraft. Air Tara, whose pilots were mainly Aer Lingus alumni, leased its first aircraft (a B737-200) to Nigeria Airways and played an instrumental role in the development of Air Lanka, the national airline set up by the government of Sri Lanka in 1979.

An Innovative Product

GPA was from the start a very profitable venture. It offered a product that was at that time very rare on the market: the opportunity for an airline to benefit from an aircraft without massive investment upfront. Aircraft financing solutions were still very basic. Aircraft were usually purchased by airlines directly from the manufacturers and were kept by the same owner for their entire lifespan, i.e. 25 to 30 years. Aircraft were generally financed by a mix of cash from the airline (20%) and a loan provided by a bank. In exchange for the loan, the bank benefitted from a mortgage on the aircraft.

GPA's solution modified this paradigm. It enabled airlines with limited access to bank or capital markets to operate modern aircraft. The airline only had to pay a

(continued)

(*continued*)

monthly rental and maintenance reserves.[29] A three-month deposit was also generally required but this amount was nowhere near the 20% aircraft cost that airlines had to pay when they bought an aircraft.

Leasing is, however, not only a product for young airlines or airlines from emerging markets, it offers flexibility to all airlines in their fleet management. In case of economic downturn and a decrease in traffic, an airline is not stuck with an oversized fleet. It can simply decide not to renew the leases of its aircraft. This minimizes the financial impact of a crisis, an advantage well understood by airlines in the wake of the oil shocks of the 1970s.

The Cash Machine

The advantages offered by leasing obviously do not come cheap. Rentals paid by a client are much higher than the loan repayment obligations due by an airline that would have bought the same aircraft. This reflects the additional risk taken by the lessor.

This situation probably explains the incredible success of GPA. The company was profitable year after year and distributed hefty dividends to its shareholders. GPA became the Irish success story of the 1980s and Tony Ryan was probably at that time the most revered business figure in Ireland alongside Tony O'Reilly, the former Irish international rugby player who became the first non-Heinz family member to become chairman of Heinz.

The success of GPA was such that by the mid-1980s the company was able to attract a series of foreign investors: Air Canada, GE Capital (the financial arm of General Electric), Prudential, and Long-Term Credit Bank of Japan (now Shinsei Bank). Tony Ryan owned 9% of the company and became around that time, one of the wealthiest men in Ireland.

Capital increases were, however, not reserved to institutional investors. The company remained private and employees were invited to subscribe to the shares that were regularly issued. The confidence in GPA's strength was such that banks provided loans to employees so that they could participate in these capital increases. The value of those shares increased spectacularly in a few years, from their original price of $1 when the company was established to $650 at their peak. In addition, the shares paid a dividend of well above $200 for several years. Those dividends allowed GPA's employees to repay their loan in a few years. Many executives of the company (who collectively owned 6% of the company) had loans well above $1 million, taking a new loan to subscribe for each new issue of shares.

---

[29]Maintenance reserves are a monthly additional payment by the lessee meant to cover the maintenance costs of the aircraft.

GPA's employees formed some kind of royalty in Ireland. In the small town of Shannon (8,000 inhabitants) they were seen driving sports cars and wearing the same expensive suits as Wall Street bankers. They were the new Irish elite and only the top graduates in the country could join the company. Salaries were astronomical and even secretaries made substantially more than the average salary in Ireland.

Ryan invited to the board of GPA some prominent international figures, such as the former Irish prime minister Garrett FitzGerald, the chairmen of Air Canada, The Economist and Allied Irish Bank, the president of Mitsubishi Corporation, and the former chairman of Rolls Royce. They brought a lot of seniority to the board and many political contacts, especially in emerging markets where most of GPA's clients were located. Many of these board members also became shareholders of the company.

In 1989, GPA was valued by analysts at $1.5 billion. It owned 164 aircraft leased to 62 airlines in 20 countries. It was one of the three largest aircraft leasing companies in the world. Tony Ryan's wealth was estimated at $250 million. He owned properties in Ireland, Mexico, Ibiza, and Monte Carlo and was reported to earn around $13 million a year.

ILFC and Polaris

If it was one of the forerunners in the field, GPA was nonetheless not the only aircraft leasing company at that time. Its main competitor, ILFC, was established in 1973 in Los Angeles, California by two American citizens of Hungarian origin, Louis Gonda and Steven Udar-Hazy.

Just like Ryan after them, Gonda and Hazy – who met while studying at UCLA – realized that aircraft leasing had huge potential. Leasing brings notable flexibility to airlines, a much-needed feature in an industry with high fixed costs. Gonda and Hazy each put $50,000 in the business. Louis's father, Leslie, who made a fortune in real estate in Venezuela before moving to the United States in 1963, backed the pair and became ILFC's third shareholder. ILFC's first deal was the lease of an old DC-8 to a Mexican airline.

ILFC was also instantly extremely profitable. The company was rigorously managed and paid extreme attention to the quality of its lessees. ILFC had strong lease contracts and withdrew aircraft as soon as an airline showed signs of weakness. The company operated under a strong cost control policy and went public in 1983. At that date, the three original shareholders still owned 58% of the company.

Competing with ILFC and GPA, Polaris Aircraft Leasing was the third main lessor of that period. Founded in San Francisco in 1974 by Peter Pfendler, a Harvard law graduate and US fighter pilot Vietnam veteran, Polaris enjoyed the same growth as its competitors. It was bought out by GE Capital in 1989, which saw it as the perfect instrument to support the sales of aircraft powered by GE engines.

(continued)

(*continued*)

Although many other lessors sprang up in the 1980s, leasing remained a niche product despite its growth. In 1986, operating lease companies represented only one-tenth of the sales of Boeing and McDonnell Douglas combined. At that time, manufacturers still preferred to sell aircraft directly to airlines. They saw lessors as a necessary annoyance.

Strategic Mistakes

In this context, from the mid-1980s, GPA was in a position to order new aircraft directly from manufacturers. To find lessees for these assets, Ryan relied on an extremely well-paid sales force. Marketeers were measured based on the number of deals they signed and were encouraged to travel extensively to meet potential lessees. Ryan believed in physical presence with clients and put extreme pressure on his team. The whole country knew about the Monday morning meetings in which he gathered GPA's sales team, slaughtered those who were believed to under-perform, and urged everyone to travel and *"bring back the bacon"*.

Placing large speculative orders with aircraft manufacturers became a key component of GPA's strategy. The company made significant orders to benefit from strong price discounts and then relied on its sales force to have these aircraft leased before they were even delivered. In 1989, GPA announced a series of orders for hundreds of aircraft, on firm order and on option, worth $15 billion.

Not everyone within GPA agreed with this aggressive strategy. Many employees thought that the company was over-ordering. Some also criticized the types of aircraft that were purchased. GPA ordered, for instance, the yet uncertified Fokker 100 jets instead of Boeing 737s. To benefit from significant discounts, the company ordered 50 firm aircraft and 50 options. Unfortunately the Fokker 100 suffered from the competition of the A-319 and the smaller version of the B-737. It was unable to attract sufficient clients and GPA was forced to cancel deliveries and to pay high penalties, losing on the way the pre-delivery payments already made to the manufacturer. The same thing happened with MD-8s. GPA ordered many of them, but the aircraft was old and consumed too much fuel compared to its competitors.

The situation worsened with the US economic slowdown of 1990 and the global recession that followed. GPA struggled to place even its best aircraft. Many airlines went bankrupt or were simply unable to pay their rent: Aerocalifornia in Mexico, German Wings in Germany, Transbrasil and VASP in Brazil, Spantax and Hispania in Spain, etc. The number of aircraft that GPA had on the ground (i.e. parked without lessee) reached a record high. The company had simply over-ordered at the worst possible time.

To many observers, GPA was less well equipped than its peers to survive the downturn. Polaris's shareholders cashed out before the crisis in 1989, and the company was now part of General Electric, one of the largest firms in the world.

Its other main competitor, ILFC, was perceived as a leaner organization. It had fewer employees than GPA and a lower cost line. It also had aircraft that were more in demand. And while Hazy and Gonda sold their company to AIG in 1990 for $1.3 billion, GPA's future as an independent company looked extremely uncertain.

The failed IPO

In this new environment, raising additional capital seemed like the right option for GPA. The management decided in the early days of 1992 to go public and a string of prestigious advisors was hired to coordinate the IPO. Road shows with potential investors were coordinated by Goldman Sachs and Salomon Brothers in the United States, by Schroders and Hambro Magan in the United Kingdom, and by Nomura in Japan. The IPO was planned for 17 June 1992 and was meant to raise $850 million.

Against all odds, the IPO was pulled. The price demanded by GPA for its shares was too high and there were not enough investors to build the book. The Irish press – long tired of GPA's arrogance – lashed out at the company. The whole market, starting with clients, lost faith in GPA. Employees were worried. Many of them had taken loans to buy shares and realized that they might lose everything. Tony Ryan himself had a $35-million loan by Merrill Lynch pledged with GPA shares.

Under these circumstances, and to avoid bankruptcy, GPA was forced to renegotiate its debt. It claimed to still have $500 million in cash at the bank but this amount was, in fact, the sum of maintenance payments made by lessees in the past. This could not be used to repay debt. It had to be used to pay for the aircraft's future maintenance costs. In 1993, GPA's credit rating was downgraded to CCC. Its bonds traded at 22 cents and the company hired the bank Donaldson, Lufkin & Jenrette to negotiate a repayment deferral with bondholders.

In the meantime, the situation of many lessees did not improve. In a period in which leasing still only represented a niche in the market (c. 10% to 15% of the world's aircraft fleet), GPA's client base consisted mainly of second-tier and third-tier airlines. These players were seriously hit by the economic slowdown of the early 1990s and many of them were close to bankruptcy. Amounts due by lessees reached astronomical levels and GPA had to let go a substantial part of its workforce. The financial year ending March 1993 showed a loss of $998 million, the first loss in GPA's history.

The Rescue by General Electric

Although GPA found a temporary agreement with banks and bondholders to restructure its debt, the company was still in need of a new partner. There were not many potential buyers. GE Capital seemed for many reasons the only logical candidate: (i) the company was already a shareholder of GPA, (ii) it was a major

(continued)

(*continued*)

aircraft engine manufacturer and could use GPA as a tool to support sales, and (iii) GE Capital had already acquired Polaris four years before and could merge it with GPA, creating substantial synergies between the two.

An agreement was reached in July 1993 between GE, GPA, and the banks. GE did not take control of GPA directly but played a key role in the restructuring of the company. The rescue plan revolved around four pillars:

1. Aircraft: GPA drastically reduced its future aircraft purchase obligations. The number of orders decreased from 242 aircraft to 57. This reduction triggered the payment of penalties of more than $400 million but diminished the overall financial burden of the company.

2. Lenders: existing lenders agreed to defer for up to three years the repayment of $750 million. Additional short-term liquidity lines were also granted by GPA's core banks.

3. GE: GPA sold 44 aircraft (with leases attached) to a newly established subsidiary of GE Capital, GE Capital Aviation Services (GECAS). GPA remained the owner of the remaining aircraft but the management of these assets was transferred to GECAS. In the process, GE transferred the ownership of Polaris to GECAS but the two lessors were not merged. GECAS benefitted nonetheless from an option to acquire GPA.

4. Existing shareholders: The company raised an additional $150 million through bonds and convertible notes subscribed by existing shareholders. Tony Ryan and the employees were not concerned in this new capital issue. Only institutional shareholders took part in the transaction.

After the Restructuring

The restructuring was brutal. A large part of the workforce was made redundant and those who still owned shares in GPA at that time knew for sure that they would never become millionaires. Among the employees who had taken loans to buy shares, only those who had structured non-recourse loans (i.e. non-recourse to their other assets) could truly limit their losses. The others had to sometimes sell their homes to repay their loans. The former Irish prime minister, Garrett FitzGerald, who sat on GPA's board, was one of them.

Tony Ryan left GPA in October 1994. He joined the budget airline Ryanair, created (with his money) by his three sons in 1984, as non-executive chairman. Merrill Lynch was rumored to have written off their $35-million loan although Ryan remained a shareholder of GPA.

Despite the company restructuring, GPA's long-term future remained uncertain. The management still needed to find ways to repay future debt obligations and rebuild a solid cash buffer. It was decided that the company would sell a large part of its aircraft portfolio to third-party investors via securitization.[30] GPA was to remain the operating manager of the aircraft but the revenues generated by the leases attached to these assets were to be redirected to the new owners. In March 1996, GPA succeeded in selling a portfolio of 222 aircraft leased to 89 airlines in 40 countries to a consortium of investors. This was the largest aircraft securitization ever closed.

This transaction marked the end of a long and painful journey for GPA. The company – albeit smaller and very different than in the past – was back on its feet. In November 1998, private equity firm TPG Capital, former owner of Continental Airlines, acquired 62% of GPA with GECAS, dropping its option to buy the company to become only a minority shareholder. In December 1999, GPA merged with Swedish lessor Indigo Aviation, and was renamed AerFi.

Epilogue

Although the Tony Ryan years seemed to be history, the Irish entrepreneur remained at that time a shareholder of GPA. In November 2000, AerFi was acquired by Dutch lessor Debis AirFinance, part of Daimler Chrysler. Tony Ryan received a payment of $55 million for the sale of his shares. He was still at his death, in 2007, one of the wealthiest men in Ireland.

In May 2005, Cerberus acquired Debis AirFinance and renamed it AerCap. The company was IPOed the following year and ended up acquiring ex-GPA arch rival ILFC in 2013 as part of a move by AIG to sell non-core assets. In a way, 40 years later, the market was still being dominated by the three pioneers of the aircraft leasing industry. AerCap and GECAS are now the world's largest lessors. And even if Tony Ryan and Peter Pfendler have passed away, Steve Hazy is still doing business. He established another company, Air Lease Corporation, in Los Angeles in 2010. As of 2020, Air Lease is the eighth largest lessor globally.

---

[30] For more details on aircraft securitization, see Part IV of this book.

CHAPTER 9

Behind the Scenes

9.1 INSIDE A LEASING COMPANY

9.1.1 Choosing a Location

9.1.1.1 Ireland as a Global Hub for Aircraft Leasing

One of the most important legacies of GPA is probably its impact on the leasing industry in Ireland. The country is today the world's major hub in aircraft finance. According to PwC, Ireland has a 65% share of the global leasing market and 14 out of the 15 largest lessors in the world have a base in Dublin.

GPA has trained countless leasing experts and many of them have remained in the country after the collapse of the company. New lessors have been established and several banks have set up leasing subsidiaries in Ireland to benefit from the local know-how. Many CEOs of top lessors are still today GPA's alumni: Aengus Kelly, CEO of AerCap; Domhnal Slattery, CEO of Avolon and former CEO of RBS Aviation; Peter Barrett, CEO of SMBC Aviation Capital; and Colm Barrington, CEO of Fly Leasing.

The domination of Ireland in this sector is also partly due to tax aspects. Aircraft leasing is a sector where the competition is truly global and where product differentiation is very limited. In these circumstances, tax considerations are extremely important for lessors. It is a key element of their profitability.

The growth of the industry was nurtured by Ireland's tax incentive regime, which was first introduced in the 1950s. Tony Ryan took advantage of this regime when he established GPA in Shannon in 1975 and the lessors that have followed have done the same. After merging with California-based lessor ILFC in 2014, Dutch lessor AerCap moved its headquarters to Dublin, a decision worth €200 million of annual tax savings.

The tax advantages offered to leasing companies by Ireland can be broken down into several pillars:

- *Low corporate tax rate.* Since 2003, Ireland's corporate tax rate has been set at 12.5%, ensuring that profits are taxed at a rate significantly lower than in most OECD countries. While this rate is not specific to leasing and applies to all companies taxed in Ireland, it is a real competitive advantage for Irish lessors.
- *Relatively high capital allowances.* The treatment of capital allowances (i.e. tax depreciation) is crucial in any capital-intensive operation. Leasing is no exception. The standard rate of capital allowances for aircraft in Ireland is 12.5% calculated on a straight-line basis over eight years. In other words, lessors can depreciate over eight years an asset that has a 25- to 30-year lifespan. This system ensures that the first eight years of a lease do not generate a taxable income as, during this period, rentals paid by the lessee are lower than capital allowances.
- *High number of tax treaties.* Ireland has been very active in signing double tax treaties with foreign governments. Most of these treaties stipulate that if rentals paid by an overseas airline to an Irish lessor are subject to a withholding tax (i.e. are partly taxed in the country where the airline is established), then the Irish lessor is granted a tax credit equal to the amount of tax withheld. In addition, Irish domestic law also provides for foreign tax credit relief for irrecoverable withholding tax suffered on lease rentals from countries that do not have a double tax treaty with Ireland. Since 2013, these tax credits can be carried forward, meaning that they can be used to offset future taxes, in case the taxes to be paid during the year in which the tax credit arises are lower than the tax credit amount.
- *Unilateral tax credit.* In 2007, Ireland included tax provisions to allow unilateral credit relief for foreign tax suffered by a company that has a trading branch or agency in a country with which Ireland does not have a double tax treaty. This favorable inclusion allows Irish lessors to reduce their Irish corporation tax liabilities by the foreign tax levied on the profits of any branch or agency they may have overseas.

Beyond their technicalities, these measures demonstrate the importance of aircraft leasing in the Irish economy and show that the government has the desire to support the sector. That is also a strong element of comfort for lessors as they know they can count on a government that understands their concerns.

9.1.1.2 Other Geographies

Other countries have obviously also put together sets of specific rules to attract leasing companies. In Singapore, the tax rate applicable on income derived from the leasing of aircraft or aircraft engines is 8%, a significant discount compared to the normal corporate tax rate of 17%. The country has also introduced some measures to limit the impact of withholding taxes. Thanks to that, Singapore is today the major aircraft leasing hub in Asia.

After a long and intense lobbying period, Hong Kong financiers also obtained in 2017 a legal leasing framework favorable to aircraft leasing activities. In a city where asset owners cannot benefit from tax allowances on aircraft leased to an overseas lessee, the government introduced a set of measures meant to attract aircraft lessors. The tax rate applicable to aircraft leasing is half the normal corporate tax rate (8.25% vs. 16.5%) and the taxable amount of rentals derived from leasing of an aircraft to a non-Hong Kong aircraft operator by a Hong Kong lessor is equal to 20% of the gross rentals minus deductible expenses (a decision taken to overcome the impossibility under Hong Kong tax law to benefit from tax allowances on assets used abroad).

Mainland China also has its own leasing framework. If the corporate tax rate applicable to the sector remains at 25%, several zones can benefit from various tax incentives, notably in Shanghai, Shenzhen, or Tianjin. The use of a Chinese lessor is especially attractive for Chinese airlines as otherwise withholding taxes may apply. In addition, any agreement between a Chinese lessor and a Chinese airline must be governed by Chinese law. This hinders the capacity of Mainland China to attract foreign lessors. Establishing a leasing presence in China is best for Chinese lessors targeting the Chinese market.

9.1.2   Building a Portfolio

Choosing the perfect location is not the main task of a lessor. A leasing company is indeed like any financial institution, it must build a balanced portfolio that generates maximum returns.

9.1.2.1   Credit Considerations

As mentioned at the beginning of Chapter 8, most of the airlines are non-investment grade. Managing a portfolio of aircraft leases is therefore, in essence, like managing a portfolio of high-yield bonds: they pay a fixed coupon until maturity. The main difference is that the loan is backed by a liquid asset (or "*backed by metal*" as is often said in leasing jargon).

Given the risks inherent to their market, lessors must have a strong credit management culture and risk teams that are aware of the specificities of the aviation market. All major listed lessors usually underline this aspect in their roadshows or in communications with investors. Lessors also have teams chasing airlines when they do not pay on time.

Lessors obviously enjoy the benefit of their collateral. Airlines know that they can lose their aircraft if they do not pay rents. Other mechanisms are included in the lease contracts to ensure that the owner of the aircraft is protected in case of default by a lessee: payments of rentals in advance, security deposit, maintenance reserves, etc. (see section 9.2.2).

Lessors also mitigate their risks by building portfolios of diversified lessees. This diversification is based on geographies but also by airline types within regions. A leasing company typically wants to be exposed to low-cost carriers, full-service carriers, or charter carriers. Large lessors have in this respect another advantage over smaller ones. They are exposed to a variety of airlines and suffer less in the case of default by one of their clients. Their revenue streams are steadier than smaller lessors. They can take advantage of the structural growth of the air transport market without being overly exposed to one name in particular.

9.1.2.2 Assets

A lessor must ideally own in-demand assets so that it can easily place them or find a new lessee in the case of default by a client. Selecting the most liquid assets is not an easy task. Each airline has obviously different needs: Emirates operates only wide body aircraft (A380, B777, etc.), while low-cost carriers like Southwest or Easyjet only fly smaller narrow bodies (A320 and B737).

Although airlines have different strategies, they all look primarily for modern, fuel-efficient assets. These aircraft consume less fuel and are significantly cheaper to operate. They may be more expensive than older aircraft but are a good investment over a long period. Considering that most airlines lease new aircraft for 10 to 12 years, lessors mainly target these types of assets when they do sale and leaseback or place speculative orders. They know that demand will be strong. Aircraft that belong to this category are all the recently launched aircraft (generally referred to as "*new technology types*"): the A220, the A320 NEO family, the B737 MAX, the A350, the B787, and the new generation of Embraer aircraft.[1]

Technology is not the only choice that lessors have to make. Lessors must also decide which aircraft type they should purchase. They can indeed buy wide-body, narrow-body or regional aircraft. Table 9.1 shows the top 10 busiest scheduled air routes in the world in 2017. All the flights in this list qualify as short hauls.

With a few exceptions, this type of route is operated with narrow-body aircraft. This is a (sometimes) counterintuitive conclusion of the aviation market. People fly, they fly more and more, but they do not fly long hauls. They stay within a region, or even a country. Out of the top 100 busiest routes in the world, only 18 are international.[2]

This conclusion advocates for investing in narrow-body aircraft. The backlog of Airbus and Boeing confirms that this is where demand exists. As of May 2020, Airbus reported a backlog of 7,621 aircraft, of which 88% are A220 or A320, two narrow-body aircraft.[3] The trend is similar at Boeing. Out of the 5,301 unfilled orders, 80% are B737s, the only narrow-body aircraft produced by Boeing.[4]

---

[1]The A320 NEO and the B737 MAX are new versions of the A320 and the B737. They have more efficient engines, better technology, different cabins, and slightly larger capacity than the older versions.
[2]Source: OAG Schedules Analyser.
[3]Source: Airbus.
[4]Source: Boeing.

TABLE 9.1   The Top Ten Busiest Scheduled Air Routes in the World in 2017

Ranking	Route	Passengers	Flight Duration
1	Jeju–Seoul Gimpo (CJU-GMP)	13,460,306	1h10
2	Melbourne–Sydney Kingsford Smith (MEL-SYD)	9,090,941	1h25
3	Sapporo–Tokyo Haneda (CTS-HND)	8,726,502	1h35
4	Fukuoka–Tokyo Haneda (FUK-HND)	7,864,000	1h45
5	Mumbai–Delhi (BOM-DEL)	7,129,943	2h10
6	Beijing Capital–Shanghai Hongqiao (PEK-SHA)	6,833,684	2h15
7	Hanoi–Ho Chi Minh City (HAN-SGN)	6,769,823	2h10
8	Hong Kong–Taiwan Taoyuan (HKG-TPE)	6,719,030	1h30
9	Jakarta–Juanda Surabaya (CGK-SUB)	5,271,304	1h30
10	Tokyo Haneda–Okinawa (HND-OKA)	5,269,481	2h35

Source: OAG Schedules Analyser.

If, accordingly, the obvious strategy for a lessor is to mainly invest in new technology narrow-body aircraft, some players have adopted a different view. These lessors specialize in niche segments and target different types of assets and clients. As explained in Chapter 8, section 8.2.2.2, lessors like Castlelake or Carlyle are active in the end-of-life segment. They serve smaller and riskier clients and part of their revenues come from the sale of spare parts of the assets they dismantle. Some other lessors are active in very specific segments. Nordic Aviation Capital invests, for instance, only in regional aircraft.

Owning the right assets is only part of the journey. Aircraft have to be bought at the right price. Large and experienced lessors have an advantage in this respect compared to their peers. They can make speculative orders and buy directly from OEMs. This is a riskier play, but it is more profitable than entering into a sale and leaseback with an airline. There is no one to make a profit in the middle. Large lessors can also take advantage of their size to make bulk orders. This allows them to benefit from significant discounts from manufacturers.

At the other end of the spectrum, lessors can also increase their profitability by selling the right assets at the right time. If a lessor assumes that the price they can get from a buyer is better than the present value of the rents attached to this aircraft, they should sell it. Actively managing a portfolio of aircraft leases is again, in that sense, not so different from managing a portfolio of high-yield bonds. The buy-and-hold strategy is the easiest but not always the most profitable. Selling aircraft is also a solution to decrease an exposure to a specific name.

Large lessors generally sell their aircraft to optimize their returns and invest in new assets. This is a strategy followed by top lessors in recent years to make room in their portfolio for all the new technology aircraft already mentioned. These lessors have sold mid-life aircraft to new entrants willing to build large portfolios of assets quickly. To maximize the value of these sales, aircraft are obviously always sold with leases attached. No one wants to buy a mid-life aircraft that is off lease. In the course of the 2019 financial year, AerCap sold 88 aircraft with an average age of 15 years, which represents a total net gain of $188.8 million.[5]

9.2 LEGAL CONSIDERATIONS

9.2.1   Rents and Maintenance Reserves

Rents and maintenance reserves are defined in the lease agreement. The lease agreement is the main contract between the SPV and the lessee. It governs the relation between the parties for the duration of the transaction. It is a complex document of 200 to 300 pages. It is binding for both parties and does not offer options to exit the transaction before its term. The lessee cannot return the asset before the end of the lease. Inversely, the lessor cannot terminate the lease early, except in case of default.

9.2.1.1   Aircraft Specifications and Configuration

The lease agreement contains a description of the aircraft, including (i) the specifications and (ii) the configuration of the asset. The *specifications* are all the technical options that can be chosen when buying an aircraft. They include the type of engines, the weight, the maximum range, etc. The *configuration* is the internal arrangement of the aircraft, i.e. the types and number of seats, the in-flight entertainment (IFE), the design of the overhead bins, etc.

In case of sale and leaseback, this section of the lease agreement is pretty simple. The specifications and configuration of the aircraft have already been negotiated between the airline and the OEM. The lessor buys an aircraft that has been fully designed.

Things are more complicated when the lessor buys the asset directly from the manufacturer. In this case, the lessor will only specify and configure the airplane once a lessee has been identified:

- Most of the specifications will be based on requirements by the lessee. As the lease agreement is signed before the construction of the aircraft has started, the document must be drafted in such a way that it leaves room for the lessee and the lessor to jointly select the final specifications of the aircraft.
- When a lessor makes a speculative order, the configuration of the asset is also obviously not yet defined. The lessee has generally a special allowance granted by the lessor to select what it wants. If the cost of the configuration exceeds the allowance, the lessee must pay for the difference. This difference can be paid to the lessor before delivery or by increasing future rents.

---

[5]Source: AerCap.

9.2.1.2   Rents

Rents are paid monthly in advance by the lessee. They are set as a fixed figure in the lease agreement but are adjusted at delivery based on several elements:

- *Adjustment to the final cost of the aircraft.* These adjustments are linked to the final specification and configuration of the asset but also to the price of the aircraft adjusted by inflation. Aircraft are indeed purchased well before they are delivered. The buyer and the OEM agree on a purchase price on the acquisition date but this price is always to be adjusted to inflation at delivery. This mechanism allows for the OEM to reflect the increase in costs between the purchase date and the delivery date, a period that can sometimes last five years or more.

  This situation means, however, that the lessor does not know the exact final price of the aircraft when the lease agreement is signed (as the contract is always signed before delivery, and very often several years before). Rents must be adjusted to inflation to ensure that the lessor does not bear any inflation risk. The formula used to calculate inflation in the aircraft purchase agreement is also the formula used to adjust rents in the lease agreement.

- *Adjustment to interest rate.* Rents are also to be adjusted in case interest rates go up. This mechanism protects the lessor in case of variation of interest rates and significant increase in its funding cost.

These adjustments only occur at delivery. Once the rents are set, they do not vary during the lease term.

9.2.1.3   Maintenance Reserves

Lease agreements are said to be net leases, meaning that the costs associated with the ownership of the aircraft are borne by the lessee. This includes expenses related to the operation and maintenance of the asset. Maintenance expenses are mandatory: an aircraft loses its airworthiness certification if inspections are not done on a regular basis or if some parts of the airframe or the engines are not frequently changed or repaired.

The lessor can impose the creation of maintenance reserves on the lessee. Maintenance reserves are cash reserves that are built up monthly by the airline. These payments cover the anticipated maintenance costs of the aircraft. They are sometimes referred to as "supplemental (or additional) rent". Maintenance reserves ensure that cash will be available when inspections of the aircraft take place or when the asset has to be repaired. Maintenance reserves are the property of the lessor.

The supplemental rent is, in fact, the addition of several maintenance payments, each meant to fund a specific maintenance reserve account. There are five reserve accounts. They cover for the cost of:

- (i) the airframe inspections,
- (ii) the landing gear overhauls,

(iii) the restoration of the engines,

(iv) the replacement of some specific parts of the engines, and

(v) the restoration of the auxiliary power unit.[6]

At the end of each month, the lessee must tell the lessor how many hours the aircraft was used. Based on the information, the lessor invoices the lessee and receives maintenance payments for each of the five reserve accounts.

As operator of the aircraft, the lessee is responsible for the payment of the costs of the inspections and maintenance checks. Under the control of the lessor, it can use the cash sitting on the maintenance reserve accounts to pay for them. If the cost of a specific inspection or maintenance check is higher than the amounts available in the reserve account, the lessee must pay for the difference. The money in a specific reserve account can generally not be used to pay for expenses related to another reserve account. In other words, if, for instance, the airframe inspections cost more than anticipated, the cash sitting in another reserve account cannot be used to cover for the difference.

Maintenance payments are generally a topic of intense discussion between the lessee and the lessor. They represent an important additional cost for the lessee but are an extremely valuable collateral for the lessor. In case of default of the lessee, the cash in these reserve accounts is used to put the aircraft back in optimal condition.

Maintenance reserves are not mandatory. When they enter a lease with a leading airline (state-owned, investment grade, etc.), lessors generally do not require maintenance reserves. Alternatively, lessors can also accept a Letter of Credit (LOC), i.e. a bank guarantee issued by an institution ready to assume the lessee's credit risk.

9.2.1.4   Maintenance Reserves and Value of an Aircraft

Assuming an aircraft is properly operated, two major factors influence its value. The first one is age. Like any movable asset with a limited lifespan, aircraft decrease in value over time. The second one is the cost needed to bring the asset back to its optimal maintenance status given its age. To put it simply, two aircraft of the same age do not necessarily have the same value. If one has recently undergone a full heavy maintenance check and the other one has not, the difference in value between these two aircraft should be equal to the cost of the heavy maintenance check.

Aircraft that have just undergone heavy maintenance checks achieve what is referred to as *full-life status*. This status implies that the airframe and the landing gears are fresh from an overhaul, that all engines (including APU) have been restored and that the specific parts of the engines that have to be changed regularly are brand new.

Full-life status is a theoretical reference. All maintenance events have different frequencies and it is therefore impossible for an aircraft to have an optimal maintenance status in each field. Airframe heavy checks must, for instance, occur every six

---

[6]The auxiliary power unit (or APU) is the turbine that allows the aircraft to move on the tarmac.

TABLE 9.2   Different Types of Maintenance Events

	Fixed or Predictable Interval	Interval Based on Number of Hours of Use
Fixed cost	Engine Life Limited Parts (or Engine LLPs)[7]	
Variable cost	Airframe heavy maintenance checks	Engine performance restoration and overhaul
	Landing gear overhaul	APU overhaul

Source: IATA.

years, while APU and engine restorations are to be done every time an aircraft has reached a certain level of flying hours. Table 9.2 summarizes the various maintenance events that exist and whether they have to be done on fixed or variable intervals.

The *half-life status* is another reference used in the aviation sector. It defines aircraft that are midway between each of the five regular maintenance events. For the same reasons as those already mentioned, this is also a theoretical status.

Although they are only theoretical references, full-life and half-life statuses are useful benchmarks when it comes to aircraft valuation. Everybody understands that a full-life aircraft has more value that a half-life asset. When they value aircraft, appraisers propose two price assumptions for each asset type and year of construction: one for a full-life aircraft and one for a half-life aircraft.

In this context, the payment of maintenance reserves is important for the lessor. These supplemental rents are meant to cover the maintenance costs that the use of the aircraft for that specific month will trigger in the future. In theory, the sum of the value of the aircraft on lease plus the sum of the maintenance reserves paid equals the full-life value of the aircraft, i.e. the optimal value for an aircraft of this age.

9.2.2   Security Package

The lease documentation contains a number of elements that are meant to protect the lessor in case a lessee defaults.

9.2.2.1   Rents and Supplemental Rents

The rent structure just described is the first element of protection for the lessor. As explained, rents are paid monthly in advance. This is a major difference compared to a loan, which is usually repaid quarterly or semi-annually in arrears. This payment mechanism means that the client is billed as regularly and as early as possible so that the credit risk taken by the lessor is minimal. The payment of supplemental rents, if any, is also an element of comfort for the lessor.

---

[7]Some parts of an engine, called Engine Life Limited Parts (or Engine LLPs or simply LLPs), must be removed from an engine and replaced after a precise number of flights.

9.2.2.2 Security Deposit

The lessee must generally pay a security deposit before the delivery of the aircraft. This deposit is typically equal to three times the monthly rent.[8] This deposit is supposed to cover the cost that the lessor could incur in case of default by the lessee and subsequent repossession of the asset. The payment of a deposit is usually a condition precedent (or CP) to the lease, meaning that it must be paid by the lessee before the lease actually starts. In some cases, this security deposit can be replaced by a bank guarantee.

9.2.2.3 Other Elements of Comfort

In addition to these main elements of comfort, the lessor can benefit from the following safeguards:

- Documents are usually governed by UK law. Disputes between the parties have to be settled under the jurisdiction of the court of England and Wales. This gives certainty to the parties, and especially to the lessor, as to how the various clauses of the lease agreement will be interpreted in case there is a need to go to court. More rarely, a lease agreement can be governed by US law.
- When the lessee is very small or has a complicated credit history, lessors can require a security over the bank accounts of the airline. This security is exercised in case of default of the lessee.
- If the airline is part of a larger group, a parent guarantee can be required by the lessor.
- Aircraft are generally registered in the country where the lessee is based. Lessors can nonetheless require airlines to register their aircraft in another jurisdiction if there are difficulties in repossessing or deregistering an aircraft under the law of this country. Offshore registration is common for Italian or Russian airlines. In this case, the offshore register is often Ireland or Bermuda.
- The lessee has to return the asset to the lessor in accordance with the redelivery conditions set out in the lease agreement. These return conditions ensure that the aircraft is returned in good condition. This is a point that we shall discuss in more detail in section 9.2.3.

9.2.3 End of the Transaction

9.2.3.1 End of the Lease without Events of Default

At the end of the lease, the aircraft must be returned to the lessor in accordance with the return conditions set in the lease agreement. Most lease agreements typically contain stringent redelivery requirements that can be broken down into four categories:

---

[8]It can sometimes go up to six months for start-up airlines.

- *Physical requirements.* The aircraft must be in as good condition as when orig-inally delivered to the lessee, minus normal wear and tear. Over time, the def-inition of wear and tear has become increasingly documented, as lessees and lessors want to avoid disputes over the condition of the aircraft. The aircraft usually has to be stripped from its original livery and painted in white or in a livery according to the lessor's requirements.
- *Certification requirements.* The aircraft has to comply with the standards defined by a reputable airworthiness authority, generally the Federal Aviation Admin-istration (FAA) in the United States or the European Aviation Safety Agency (EASA) in Europe. This is a key legal requirement as the lessor cannot lease the aircraft to another lessee if the aircraft is not authorized to fly.
- *Records requirements.* The lessee must provide the lessor with all the technical records of the aircraft, i.e. all documents that have been drafted after inspect-ing or repairing the aircraft. The purpose is to ensure that the aircraft has been properly maintained and that all potential issues have been addressed.
- *Performance requirements.* Parties agree on the precise maintenance status of the aircraft. For each of the elements of the aircraft that are subject to a main-tenance event (defined in Table 9.2), the lease agreement sets a precise level of expected performance.

The redelivery of an aircraft is usually planned six to nine months in advance. During a pre-redelivery meeting, the parties agree on a precise redelivery schedule and together set the date at which the lessee must share the aircraft records with the lessor. The parties also set a date for the physical inspection of the aircraft and the final redelivery.

9.2.3.2   After the Lease

Once the aircraft has been returned, the lessor must adapt the configuration of the asset to the new lessee. The seats, the IFE, the carpet, the overhead bins, and all the elements of the configuration of the aircraft must generally be changed.

The new lessee has usually been identified well ahead of the physical redelivery of the aircraft. This way, the lessor minimizes the time between two leases. In most cases, the delivery requirements under the new lease mirror the redelivery conditions imposed on the previous lessee.

9.2.3.3   End of the Lease Following an Event of Default

Events of default in a lease agreement typically include all the situations in which the lessee fails to make a rent or supplemental rent payment. Bankruptcy of the lessee as well as failure to properly maintain or insure the aircraft are other traditional events of default. Defaults under other lease agreements for other aircraft leased and oper-ated by the lessee also generally qualify as events of default. They are referred to as *cross-defaults.*

Including cross-defaults in a lease agreement represents an additional protection for the lessor. Without a cross-default clause, a lessor would remain potentially exposed to a lessee struggling financially, and therefore decide selectively not to pay for some of its leased aircraft. This would allow for the lessee to decrease its monthly rental burden but it would mean that the lessor who has not included a cross-default clause in its lease agreement is leasing an asset to a lessee in a precarious position.

As in any other structured finance transaction, the occurrence of an event of default only triggers the termination of the deal if the financier – in this case the lessor – wishes to do so. In some situations, a lessor may decide to negotiate with the lessee instead of taking back the aircraft. This was the strategy chosen by many lessors during the Covid-19 crisis.

While it is usually more logical to repossess an aircraft and lease it to another airline, the specifics of the Covid-19 crisis have strongly affected the liquidity of aircraft. In a world in which very few people travel, aircraft have almost no value. Assuming that this situation is only transitory, many lessors have offered rental payment deferrals to airlines severely hit by the crisis. Leases have generally been extended for a period equal to the number of months during which rentals have decreased. Alternatively, some lessors have simply increased the expected post-crisis rentals without extending the lease maturity.

9.2.3.4   Repossession of Aircraft

Repossession of an aircraft following an event of default is most of the time consensual. When a default occurs and is not remedied by the lessee, the lessor contacts the lessee to arrange for the repossession of the aircraft. The parties agree to have the aircraft parked in a certain location at a certain date and the lessor's team usually takes over. Large lessors deal frequently with these issues. It famously took AerCap only a few weeks to repossess two Airbus A320s from Yemenia and lease them to other airlines after the civil war broke out in Yemen in 2015.

Repossession requires a real know-how. One of the main logistical problems is that aircraft are sometimes equipped with engines that were not originally on the aircraft. Engines must be frequently inspected and airlines use spare engines to equip their aircraft while the original engines are being restored. These original engines are then sometimes put on another aircraft while the engines of this second aircraft are themselves being repaired.

Because of the maintenance requirements that apply to engines, they can usually be easily traced. However, in case of default, the lessor must act swiftly to ensure that it not only gets its aircraft back but also the engines attached to it. Failure to do so would mean that the lessor is taking someone else's property.[9]

---

[9]Engines are one of the most valuable parts of an aircraft and airlines must have spare engines to ensure that they can properly operate their fleet. Engines can be leased by airlines from aircraft lessors or specialized engine lessors.

9.2.4 Interaction with Lenders

9.2.4.1 Timing: When to Structure the Loan

In case an airline wants to structure a sale and leaseback, a competitive process is generally organized so that various lessors can bid for the aircraft. The lessee can in this way optimize its rentals and push prices down. During this competitive process, lessors engage with lenders to see what type of financing conditions they could obtain in the market. Depending on the lessor's strategy, a lessor may want to bid for the aircraft with a fully committed financing or only with price indication from lenders. In this second situation (which is the most common) the SPV is fully financed via a shareholder loan and then refinanced a few weeks later with senior debt.

When the asset is acquired via a speculative order, the lessor generally enters into negotiation with lenders only a few months before the delivery of the asset. Even if the lessee has been identified a few years before, there is no need for the lessor to structure financing too far in advance. Banks would be unable to set margin and upfront fees or would do so at a cost that would be uneconomical for the lessor.[10]

While debt funds are now extremely active in the LBO and project finance sectors, the aviation market is still largely dominated by banks. Funds interested in the sector mainly invest via ABS structures (i.e. securitization, see Part IV). Traditional asset managers can also take an exposure to the sector when they buy bonds issued by leasing companies.

9.2.4.2 Loan Structure

As already mentioned, the loan is generally a fully amortizing loan with fixed installments. Its maturity is equal to the lease duration. The loan is non-recourse to the lessor, although the lessor can guarantee rent payments for a given period in case of default of the lessee (see Chapter 8, section 8.3.1.3).

In exchange for the loan, lenders obtain a mortgage on the asset and are assigned the maintenance reserves linked to this asset. They are also assigned any insurance proceeds that would be paid to the SPV in connection with the aircraft. This is similar to what we have seen in project finance: in case lenders suffer a loss due to a damage caused to the asset, they are paid directly by insurance companies. The cash does not transit via the SPV.

9.3 THE DYNAMICS OF LEASING MARKETS

9.3.1 Aircraft

One of the reasons aircraft leasing is popular is that aircraft are standard and aircraft values rather predictable. This is due to the steady growth of the air transport market[11]

---

[10]To mitigate the risks of interest rates going up between the signing of the deal and the start of the deal, the rent level is usually adjusted to interest rates (see section 9.2.1.2).

[11]In that sense, the Covid-19 crisis represents a profound change in the air transport market. This is the first time the market has decreased since 1945.

and the fact that the production of aircraft has always matched this growth. There is no oversupply and the risk of this happening is very low. There are only two major OEMs and neither of them have any interest in flooding the market.

Airbus and Boeing form a duopoly. Given the high entry barriers in the sector, no serious competition is expected in the short term. China is developing its own OEM (Comac) but it will take time for the company to level with the two giants. Other initiatives, in Russia or Japan, may be successful at some point but do not threaten the duopoly for the moment.

Many economists have analyzed the behavior of firms in a duopoly. Their conclusions are sometimes contradictory but a general point of convergence is that duopolies produce less and sell at a higher price than markets in which many players compete freely. In other words, Airbus and Boeing do not have to collude to recognize their interdependence and adjust their production and their prices. This protects both players against the risk of oversupply.

Clients do not buy aircraft off the shelf, they have to order them. And although Airbus and Boeing are really good at pushing airlines to over-order, they have no reason to deliver aircraft that their clients do not need. When an airline cancels orders, they require penalties or increase the price of the aircraft that the airline has not cancelled. Given their huge backlogs (see section 9.1.2.2), cancellations do not affect their prospects. This is even part of the business model, as cancellations mean a higher average sale price per aircraft in the end. This is one of the reasons Airbus and Boeing push airlines to over-order.[12]

9.3.2 Shipping

There are numerous similarities between airlines and shipping companies. Both sectors are highly capital intensive and correlated to global growth. A major part of international trade is done through ships and any economic slowdown is reflected in the freight charges and revenues of shipping companies – and vice versa.

As already explained, merchant ships are frequently financed through asset finance techniques. Just like aircraft, they (i) are generally highly expensive, (ii) have a long lifespan, (iii) are pretty standardized, and (iv) can be traded on a secondary market. The standardization of ships is nonetheless lower than those of aircraft. While the number of aircraft types is limited, ships are very specialized: bulk carriers are different from oil tankers, LNG carriers, or ro-ros.[13]

Although the growing focus on environmental norms and the generalization of size standards[14] have had a positive impact on the standardization of vessels, the

---

[12]One way to push for this is to offer very significant discounts on aircraft or propose earlier delivery dates.

[13]LNG carriers are ships designed to transport liquefied natural gas. Ro-ros (or roll-on/roll-off ships) are ferries designed to carry cars or trucks. They have a built-in ramp that allows the cargo to be easily rolled on and off when in port.

[14]These standards emerge to a certain extent from port restrictions (port in deep waters or not) but also from the limits imposed by the width of the most famous crossing points. *Suezmax* or *Panamax*

merchant ship market remains very fragmented. The technology is less complex than in the aviation sector and there are globally many more shipyards than aircraft OEMs. This has a negative impact on ship values as there can easily be an oversupply in some market segments.

For this reason, operating leasing is not extremely common in the shipping sector. Vessels are usually financed via traditional mortgage loans or possibly, when they exist, via tax lease structures relying on the tonnage tax system (see Chapter 7, section 7.2.2.7). In other words, financiers are happy to have a pledge on a vessel but are more reluctant to take a residual value risk.

9.3.3   Rail

9.3.3.1   Corporate Funding and Tax Lease Structures

Given the dominance of government-owned companies in the rail sector, many firms secure funding at a corporate level and buy assets directly from manufacturers. They usually obtain very competitive financing conditions, thanks to the implicit or explicit credit support of their shareholders (i.e. the governments). In some countries, national rail companies are even directly financed by governments.

In the 1990s, large rail companies also financed many of their assets via tax leases. For monopolies with a public service purpose, tax leases were an optimal financing solution. These companies do not have to generate profits and can sometimes not take full advantage of the deprecation of their assets – due to their intrinsic low tax results. Entering into a tax lease was for them a solution to obtain an upfront discount on the cost of their asset (see Chapter 7, section 7.2.2.4). Amtrak in the United States or SNCF in France structured many tax leases until the early 2000s. For these players, the extinction of the tax lease market means that they now mainly rely on corporate funding to finance their assets.

9.3.3.2   Operating Leasing Market

Locomotives and railcars are in theory good assets for operating leasing. They are indeed very standard and often have a lifespan of more than 40 years. They also have a major advantage compared to aircraft: they do not require a high level of maintenance. This is especially true for railcars used in the freight business.

Operating leasing remains an attractive financing solution for the sector if two factors are combined:

- *No monopoly*. If the rail market is dominated by a state-owned monopoly, the use of operating leasing does not make any sense. Operating leasing creates value if and only if several railway operators are allowed to compete in the same

---

ships are, for instance, ships that have the maximum size allowed for crossing, respectively, the Suez or Panama Canal.

market. It can therefore solely exist in countries (or regions, like the European Union) that have partly or totally liberalized the rail sector.

- *Large market*. Just like aircraft lessors, locomotive and railcar lessors must have the flexibility to redeploy their fleet. The rail business is, however, different from the aviation industry. Assets cannot be moved globally. The global rail market is therefore more the addition of several local markets than a truly integrated market. These markets must, however, be large enough to offer operating lessors the flexibility to redeploy their fleet at the end of a contract.[15]

Operating lessors in the rail business are mostly regional players. Firms active in the sector generally have a focus on a specific market. Companies like VTG, Akiem, or Ermewa are, for instance, solely active in Europe. Inversely, US lessors RGCX or Trinity Industries are only present in North America. Cross-network economies of scale are limited. In 2008, British lessor Angel Trains spun off its continental European business to establish Alpha Trains. In 2017, US lessor CIT Rail sold its European business to German company VTG.

The leasing business in the rail sector is divided into two segments. In the *freight market*, leasing companies lease their assets to operators who, in turn, offer a service to firms that want to move goods from one point to another. The contracts can be short or long term but the contractual arrangement is entirely up to the parties. Operating lessors provide capacity to operators based on demand. Railcars can easily be added or removed, depending on the clients' requirements. They can also be quickly redeployed to another part of the network and leased to another customer. In case of economic slowdown, the railcars that have not been contracted over a long period remain unused.

The dynamics of the *passenger market* are different. Private operators provide a public service and must generally commit to a public authority to offer a certain level of service to passengers (including frequency and size of trains). This means that the trains they operate in a given region usually have some very specific characteristics. When the contract between the operator and the public authority terminates, there is therefore little incentive to change the trains. The new operator usually continues to lease the trains that are already in place. There are sometimes even incentives from the public authorities to keep the existing trains. For this reason, the leasing of passenger trains is stickier than leasing in the freight sector. Once a lessor leases trains in a region, it enjoys a privileged position.

Unsurprisingly, many of these lessors are owned by private equity firms specialized in infrastructure. These investors like the long-term nature of these assets and the resilience of the activity. They see it as an infra-like business,[16] with high entry barriers, strong cash flow generation, and limited downside. Out of the three leasing companies established after the privatization of British Rail in 1994 (the infamous

---

[15]Although track gauges are not identical in all countries, some international standards have emerged. This facilitates the redeployment of locomotives or railcars. The most widespread gauge (called the "standard gauge") is 1.435mm. It is used in North America, China, South Korea, Australia, most of Europe, and large parts of South America and Africa.

[16]See Chapter 5, section 5.2.5.

Roscos, or Rolling Stock Companies), two – Porterbrook and Angel Trains – are owned by investment firms specialized in infrastructure. The third one, Eversholt Rail, is a 100% subsidiary of Cheung Kong, a Hong-Kong-based infrastructure conglomerate that also owns aircraft lessor AMCK Aviation (see Chapter 8, section 8.2.2.1, Table 8.5).

Summary

Asset Finance: What Have We Learnt?

- Asset finance is a set of financing techniques designed to finance large, movable, and expensive assets like aircraft, trains, or vessels. These assets all have a long lifespan, are fairly liquid, and can be traded on a secondary market.
- There are several asset finance techniques: mortgage loans, finance leases, and operating leases.
- A mortgage loan is a loan in which the lender benefits from a pledge on the asset. In case of default of the client, the bank can repossess the asset and sell it to recover its investment. Given the liquidity of the assets that are financed via mortgage loans, lenders can provide attractive financing conditions to their clients. The pledge mitigates the risk taken by the bank.
- A finance lease is a lease in which the owner of the asset (the lessor) recovers from the user of the asset (the lessee) its investment – plus interest – during the original lease period. At the end of a finance lease, the client has a bargain purchase option on the asset.
- Finance leases are often – but not always – structured as tax leases. A tax lease is a lease in which the lessee gives a tax investor the right to benefit from tax allowances on the depreciation of the asset. In exchange, the lessee benefits from a discount on the asset cost, which is equal to the amount invested by the tax investor to benefit from the depreciation.
- Operating leasing is a straightforward version of leasing. It is a simple lease without purchase option or tax trade-off. Operating leasing is very frequent in aviation finance. Almost half of the global commercial aircraft fleet is owned by operating lessors.
- Operating leasing brings several advantages to airlines: (i) they do not have to make any upfront payments to obtain an aircraft, (ii) they are not exposed to the risk of having to sell the asset if they want to change their fleet, and (iii) they have more flexibility to adapt the size of the fleet to their needs.
- Large lessors are generally investment grade (at least pre-Covid-19) and have various options to finance their assets. They can issue bonds, take out corporate loans, or securitize part of their fleet. They can also finance their assets independently. In this case, they raise non-recourse debt from banks via an SPV. The lenders are exposed to the rentals paid by the airline to which the asset is leased. The banks also benefit from a mortgage on the aircraft granted by the SPV.

PART IV

SECURITIZATION

Of all the financing tools presented in this book, securitization is undoubtedly the most controversial. The 2008 financial crisis has clearly damaged the reputation of this technique for a long time, erasing in the minds of many the positive aspects of this structure.

Securitization was born in the United States in 1977. The first transaction was structured by Lewis Ranieri and his team of traders at Salomon Brothers.[1] The story has all the ingredients of a US movie. Lewis Ranieri – the banker behind what is undoubtedly the most significant post-World War II financial innovation – started his carrier in the mail room of Salomon Brothers. He then gradually climbed up the ladder and became head of the fixed income trading desk – a surprising journey when compared to the resumés of the traders working nowadays in the largest US investment banks.[2]

Beyond provocative headlines and endless debates on the origins of the subprime crisis, securitization is today a major financing instrument in the global economy. It is also for banks and companies a fantastic tool for managing risks and transferring assets. For this reason, it is probably a technique that illustrates, more than any other, the financial revolution that started in the 1970s.

---

[1]Salomon Brothers is a former US investment bank established in 1910. It was well known for its fixed-income platform. Salomon Brothers was acquired in 1997 by financial conglomerate Travelers Group, which merged it with another of its subsidiaries, the broker Smith Barney, to create a full-fledged investment bank, Salomon Smith Barney. After the merger of Citibank and Travelers Group in 1998, Salomon Smith Barney became Citigroup's investment bank. The name Salomon Smith Barney ceased to exist in 2003 to simply become a division of Citigroup.
[2]A description of the people and internal dynamics of the department headed by Lewis Ranieri at that time can be found in Michael Lewis, *Liar's Poker* (New York: WW Norton & Company, 1989).

CHAPTER 10

The Securitization Process

10.1 TRANSFORMING ILLIQUID ASSETS INTO LIQUID SECURITIES

10.1.1 Definition

Securitization is a financing technique that converts illiquid assets into marketable securities. It is a sale of assets that generate cash flows (corporate loans, mortgage loans, receivables, etc.) by an entity (bank or company), called *originator*, to an investment vehicle established for sole the purpose of acquiring these assets (SPV).

The SPV finances the purchase of these cash-flow generating assets by issuing securities called *Asset-Backed Securities* (ABS). These ABS are generally acquired by institutional investors (insurance companies, assets managers, pension funds), banks or hedge funds.[1] The returns generated by the ABS are derived only from the cash flows generated by the assets. Since it issues debt securities, the SPV is also often referred to as *issuer*.

10.1.2 Example

To help get a better understanding of what securitization is, take the example of a bank that decides to securitize a portfolio of mortgages loans. In such a transaction, the bank selects the loans that it wants to transfer and sells them to an SPV. The acquisition of the loan portfolio by the SPV is financed through the issuance of securities. These securities (also called *notes*) are acquired by various types of investors.

---

[1] A hedge fund is a fund that seeks to achieve absolute returns by using leverage and taking short as well as long positions in a variety of financial instruments (stocks, bonds...).

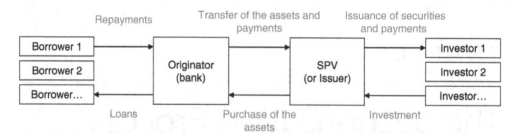

FIGURE 10.1   Simplified Securitization Structure

Once the loans have been transferred to the SPV, the payments (including principal and interest) due by the borrowers to the bank are redirected to the SPV. The bank does not retain any revenue from the payments made by the clients whose loans have been sold to the SPV. All the revenues flow to the SPV, which then distributes the revenues collected from these loans to the investors who have acquired the securities (see Figure 10.1).

When the bank sells these loans to the SPV, it not only transfers the revenues generated by these assets but also hands over their complete ownership. The SPV becomes the new legal owner of the loans. The bank is not affected if one of the original borrowers fails to make a payment. The loss is solely borne by the SPV – and ultimately the investors. Neither the SPV nor the investors can claim any form of financial compensation from the bank. Lawyers qualify this type of sale as *true sale* to clearly indicate that the legal ownership as well as all the risks and rewards attached to the ownership of the assets have been transferred to the SPV.

The entity selling the assets also transfers all the securities or guarantees attached to these assets. In the example shown in Figure 10.1, the bank not only passes on to the SPV the ownership of the loans, it also transfers all the mortgage deeds signed for these loans. In case of a default of one of the original borrowers whose loan has been sold to the SPV, the SPV can exercise its rights under the mortgage, foreclose the property, and sell it to pay off the amount due.

The ABS issued by the SPV are freely transferable in market. They become tradeable securities. If the ABS market is clearly less active than this of listed securities, securitization has nonetheless allowed a portfolio of mortgage loans, each of them individually illiquid (because too small), to be transformed into liquid financial securities that can attract a wide range of investors.

10.2   TRANCHING OF SECURITIES

10.2.1   Different Levels of Return and Risk

10.2.1.1   Different Tranches

The notes issued by the SPV and acquired by the investors are usually not all identical. They are generally divided into sub-categories called *tranches*. The number of tranches varies from one deal to the other. They are comprised of between one (see case study 9 on the Bowie Bonds) and a world record of... 24(!) for a transaction set up in 2007 in the midst of the credit bubble.

The market is, however, nowadays pretty standardized. The number of tranches depends on the type of collateral (mortgage loans, corporate loans, auto loans, credit card receivables, etc.). Each market segment has its own references. When it comes to portfolios of corporate loans and bonds, for instance, it is common to have an SPV issuing six or seven tranches of notes. There is, however, absolutely nothing from a legal, technical, or financial standpoint that prevents the setting up of a transaction with a higher or a lower number of tranches.

The tranches issued by an SPV all come with a different risk and return tradeoff. Some tranches pay a high coupon but expose their owners to a high level of risk. Others, ranking senior to the latter, represent a safer investment opportunity: they offer a lower yield and a lower level of risk.

10.2.1.2   Waterfall

The cash generated by the collateral, either via payment of a coupon or repayment of principal, is distributed to investors according to a single specific golden rule: the lower the return of the securities, the higher their priority in the order of distribution. In other words, the tranche with the lowest return is paid first. Then comes the tranche with the second lowest return, and so on and so forth. The payments continue according to this system until the most junior tranche. This cascade effect is known as *waterfall*, a term the reader is already familiar with, having discovered the concept earlier in this book.

The holders of the securities of the most junior tranche do not receive their coupons until the holders of the securities of the other tranches have received theirs. They can potentially obtain the highest return but face the risk that there is not enough cash available to pay out their coupons or repay their principal (due to defaults in the underlying portfolio).

Table 10.1 reflects a real-life case in which the SPV owned a diversified portfolio of corporate loans and bonds, mostly denominated in US dollars. It shows the split into six tranches of securities worth $700 million. The tranche with the lowest level of risk is the one with the lowest coupon.

As highlighted in Table 10.1, the riskiest tranche does not offer a fixed return. The investors simply receive all the revenues that have not yet been distributed by the SPV. This tranche is generally referred to as *subordinated notes* in contractual arrangements but is called *equity tranche* amongst professionals. Its return looks indeed more like a dividend than an interest payment.

Table 10.1 also highlights that the various tranches do not have the same size. The most senior tranche is generally by far the largest one. It represents usually around 50% to 70% of the total balance sheet of the SPV. The other tranches are generally much thinner.

TABLE 10.1   Tranching of a $700-million Securitization

Name of the Securities	Amount in $	Amount in %	Rate of Interest Applicable to the Tranche	Order of Distribution of Profits	Credit Rating
Class A Notes	479,500,000	68,50%	USD Libor 3m+0.63%	1	AAA
Class B Notes	52,500,000	7,50%	USD Libor 3m+1.00%	2	AA
Class C Notes	42,000,000	6,00%	USD Libor 3m+2.00%	3	A
Class D Notes	35,000,000	5,00%	USD Libor 3m+3.25%	4	BBB
Class E Notes	35,000,000	5,00%	USD Libor 3m+5.70%	5	BB
Sub. Notes	56,000,000	8,00%	Not applicable	6	Not rated
Total	700,000,000	100%			

10.2.1.3   Risk-based Approach

Another way to describe the tranching of the notes is to work it out in terms of risks rather than returns. Instead of stating that the priority tranches have the lowest coupon, it can be said that in case of defaults in the underlying portfolio, the tranche bearing the highest level of risk is the first to be affected. If the extent of defaults is so high that the SPV cannot distribute any income to the holders of the equity tranche, the other tranches are affected, in the opposite order to the priority of distribution of coupons.

10.2.1.4   Comparison with other Structured Finance Transactions

An attentive reader will instantly notice that the concept of tranching is very similar to what we have already seen earlier, especially in the chapters on leveraged buyouts and project finance. In all three cases (LBO, project finance, and securitization), an asset (or a portfolio of assets) is transferred to an SPV whose sole purpose is to acquire this asset (or a portfolio of asset). The SPV is financed with a mix of equity and debt. The cash flows received from the asset (or from the portfolio) are allocated according to a predetermined order, in which the equity holders figure last. These features are typical from structured finance transactions and coincide with the generic Figure I.1 in the Introduction.

10.2.2   Rating of the Various Tranches

10.2.2.1   Principle

To attract investors and improve liquidity of the notes in the primary and secondary markets, ABS are usually rated by one or two credit rating agencies. The role of these institutions (Moody's and S&P obviously, but also smaller ones like Fitch

Ratings, DBRS, Kroll Bond Rating Agency, or Scope Ratings) is to evaluate the probability of default of each of the tranches.

When an SPV owns a collateral of corporate loans and bonds and issues six tranches, as shown in Table 10.1, the split is usually the following:

- four tranches have an investment grade rating
- one tranche is sub-investment grade
- one tranche remains unrated, the equity tranche.

The rating of each tranche is based on its intrinsic default risk. The tranches that are least exposed to a potential default of the underlying portfolio have the best rating. The tranche with the highest priority in terms of distribution and the lowest risk of default is rated AAA, the next tranche is rated AA, the following one is rated A, and so on until BB. Note that when the SPV issues seven tranches, there is usually one additional sub-investment grade tranche. It is rated B.

The tranche rated AAA is called *senior* tranche, while the other debt tranches are together called *mezzanine* (tranches AA, A, BBB, BB, and, if there is one, B). As explained earlier, the most subordinated tranche is called *equity* tranche. The balance sheet of the SPV established for the purpose of a securitization can be represented in a simplified manner as in Figure 10.2.

As mentioned earlier, the various tranches do not have the same size (see Table 10.1, for instance). The size of each tranche is driven by rating considerations.

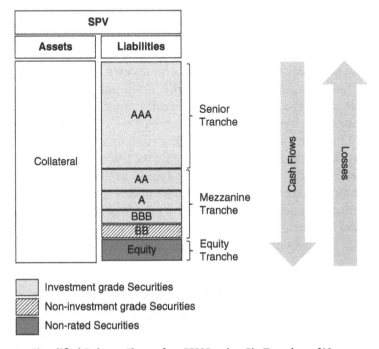

FIGURE 10.2 Simplified Balance Sheet of an SPV Issuing Six Tranches of Notes

When the collateral is made of corporate loans or bonds (as in this example), the AAA tranche usually represents the bulk of the notes issued by the SPV (around 60%).

10.2.2.2   Rating Upgrades and Rating Downgrades

Just like any other credit rating, the ratings originally given to the notes can evolve over time. Market events can affect the performance of the underlying portfolio and rating agencies may revise down the rating assigned to the different tranches.

This is exactly what happened in 2008. The sharp decline in the economic activity led to a dramatic increase of defaults of both households and companies under the payment obligations of the mortgage and corporate loans that they had taken out. Rating agencies sometimes lowered by several notches the ratings given to ABS tranches that were collateralized by this type of assets. They use harder assumptions for stressing the collateral portfolios, leading to downgrades of ABS tranches. When the situation improved and rating agencies realized that in some cases the defaults anticipated did not entirely materialize, they revised up their ratings.

10.2.3   Different Products

Although we have so far focused most of our analysis on (i) mortgage loans and (ii) corporate loans and bonds, securitization is a tool that can be used by financial institutions and corporates to finance a wide range of assets. Almost any asset that generates cash flow can be used as a collateral for securitization: mortgages loans, obviously, but also commercial loans, high-yield bonds, corporate bonds, long- or short-term client receivables, intellectual property rights, rights to perceive future revenues, aircraft leases, auto loans, etc.

Behind the generic term of ABS, there is therefore a series of different products with different markets and different investors. From one collateral to another, the maturity of the notes and the number of tranches can differ. As mentioned earlier, it is rather standard to have six or seven tranches for a collateral of corporate loans and bonds, but there are, for instance, only three or four tranches for aircraft leases.

Given that they form specific market segments, the notes issued in a securitization have different names, depending on the type of assets the collateral consists of. Table 10.2 shows the names of some of these securities. These names generally have a double meaning in financial jargon. They are used to define the securities issued by an SPV involved in a securitization as well as to refer to the SPVs that issue this type of securities.

10.2.3.1   Residential Mortgage-backed Securities

Residential Mortgage-Backed Securities (RMBS) are a type of securities backed by a large portfolio of residential mortgage loans. They are probably – alongside CLOs and CDOs (see section 10.2.3.3) – the most common type of ABS. They are also certainly

TABLE 10.2 Different Names of Securities

Type of Collateral	Name of the Securities
Residential real estate loans	Residential Mortgage-Backed Securities (RMBS)
Commercial real estate loans	Commercial Mortgage-Backed Securities (CMBS)
Corporate loans	Collateralized Loan Obligations (CLO)
Bonds, corporate loans, and various debt obligations	Collateralized Debt Obligations (CDO)
CDOs	CDO-squared (CDO^2)
Credit cards, student loans, auto loans, auto leases	Consumer ABS

the most iconic of these instruments, as the first ever loan portfolio securitized by a bank was a pool of US residential mortgage loans.[2]

RMBS can be issued by private institutions like banks or by public or semi-public bodies whose role is to facilitate the financing of affordable housing for low- and moderate-income households. Banks also use this type of transaction as a way to decrease their exposure to the residential mortgage loan market.

10.2.3.2 Commercial Mortgage-backed Securities

Commercial Mortgage-Backed Securities (CMBS) are a type of mortgage-backed securities that are backed by commercial real estate loans. These commercial real estate loans include a variety of instruments, such as loans for condominium developments, apartment complexes, factories, hotels, warehouses, office buildings, and shopping malls. Like RMBS, CMBS are created when a lender takes a group of loans outstanding on its books, bundles them together, and then sells them in securitized form as a mortgage-backed security.

The performance of these securities is generally considered less predictable than the one of RMBS. Commercial real estate loans are indeed usually more exposed to economic downturn than residential mortgage loans. In addition, RMBS have generally a larger number of assets and a more geographically diversified loan portfolio.

10.2.3.3 CLOs and CDOs

A Collateralized Loan Obligation (CLO) is a security backed by a pool of corporate loans. These loans are usually a mix of investment grade and leveraged loans. A Collateralized Debt Obligation (CDO) is similar to a CLO, but bonds or other type of debt

---

[2]The first securitization was structured in 1977 and involved the sale of a $100-million securitized portfolio of mortgage loans to Bank of America.

instruments can also be included in the collateral. CDO is also used as a generic word for all types of securities backed by a pool of debt instruments. In the end, CLOs and CDOs are sometimes indifferently used, although the majority of transactions in the market are CLOs.

10.2.3.4 CDO-squared

If all the terms mentioned so far are quite easy to understand, the concept of CDO-squared might be rather puzzling for a reader unfamiliar with structured finance. The instrument is identical to a CDO, except that it is not backed by a pool of loans and bonds but directly by ... CDO tranches (which are themselves obviously backed by traditional credit instruments). The logic of securitization is in this case pushed to an extreme insofar as bankers securitize securitization instruments.

CDO-squareds can in turn be pooled and then securitized – at least in theory. These instruments are called CDO-cubeds. The generic term of $CDO^{\wedge n}$ is sometimes used to refer to these complex securities. Although they have been popular in the past, especially before 2008, CDO-squareds and CDO-cubeds do not exist anymore.

10.2.3.5 Other ABS Types

Securities that are not referred to by a specific name are by default usually called ABS. The term ABS can be thus slightly misleading since it can be used both (i) as a generic term to define all type of securities issued through a securitization and (ii) as an abbreviation to refer to securities that do not have a specific name (i.e. that cannot be classified as CDOs, CLOs, RMBS, etc.). Among the latter, certain categories of ABS form liquid and distinctive market segments and offer well-known investment opportunities to investors: student loans, aircraft leases, auto loans, and credit card receivables are used respectively as collateral for student loans ABS, aircraft ABS, auto ABS, and credit card ABS. We will present some of these instruments later (see Chapter 12, section 12.3.3).

Case Study 9: The Securitization of David Bowie's Intellectual Property Rights

The securitization of David Bowie's intellectual property rights is one of the most original financial deals ever closed. Referred to alternately as scandalous or genius, the Bowie bonds are the evidence that it is possible to securitize a wide range of assets.

The Context

Negotiations over the *Bowie Bonds* started towards the end of 1996. The origin of the idea is still uncertain. The banker David Pullman, who arranged the transaction, claimed to have come up with the idea, but Paul Trynka, author of a biography on the singer, explained that the idea was William Zysblat's, David Bowie's financial advisor at the time.

In 1997, David Bowie was 50 years old. Born in London after the war, he was one of the most successful British singers of his generation. His songs include hits such as "The Man Who Sold the World", "Heroes", "Let's Dance", and "China Girl". Despite his astonishing success, Bowie was not as financially well off as one might have expected. There were multiple reasons for that: an extravagant lifestyle, a costly divorce... and a contract with his former manager, according to which Bowie had to share with him 50% of the revenues derived from the songs released during their collaboration.

The Deal

To stabilize the financial situation of their client, Bowie's advisors decided to terminate the agreement with his ex-manager. To that end they proposed to buy him back his rights with a lump sum payment. If all the parties agreed in principle with this mechanism there was one major hurdle to executing the deal: Bowie did not have the cash to pay for this indemnity.

To resolve the issue, Bowie's advisors took inspiration from the securitization structures created by banks to refinance their mortgage loans. They decided to sell to a third party the rights attached to the songs released during the collaboration of the two men. The deal was possible because, in contrast to most singers, David Bowie was the legal owner of both the copyrights and the original recordings of most of his work. Unlike many other artists, he had not sold the rights of his songs in exchange for future royalties. He had only granted his label the right to use his songs under a certain set of rules and for a given period of time.

The deal moved forward in 1997. The rights attached to 287 songs, owned and written by Bowie, were transferred for 10 years and $55 million to an SPV. Half of this sum went to Bowie and half to his ex-manager, who in exchange accepted to put an end to the agreement that bound them. At the end of the 10-year period, the rights of the songs were meant to return entirely to Bowie.

The acquisition of the rights by the SPV was financed by the issuance of ABS with a 10-year maturity. Given the rather small size of the deal, Bowie's advisors decided to keep the transaction simple. Only one tranche of securities was issued: the *"David Bowie Class A Royalty-Backed Notes"*.

The deal was structured in such a way that the SPV would receive for 10 years all the revenues generated by the 287 songs: sale of discs, royalties from broadcasts or concerts, use for commercial purposes, licenses, etc. The SPV also benefitted from a pledge on the legal ownership of the songs. The notes were acquired by US insurance company Prudential. They were rated Aaa by Moody's[3] and paid a

(continued)

---

[3] Equivalent to S&P's famous AAA.

(*continued*)

7.9% coupon. In case of default, Prudential – through the SPV – could exercise its rights under the pledge and take possession of the original recordings and the rights attached to them. Figure 10.3 represents a simplified structure of the deal.

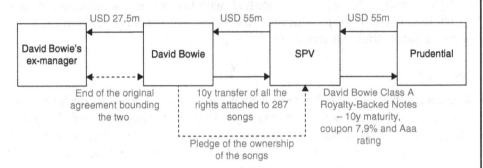

FIGURE 10.3   Simplified Transaction Structure

After the Signing

Despite being criticized by some journalists,[4] the deal was a success. The timing was perfect. CDs were still at that time the most popular conduit for listening to music and record labels sold them at outrageous prices.

The creation of Napster by Sean Parker in 1999 and the generalization of free mp3 downloads radically transformed the music industry. Revenues derived from the sale of CDs decreased significantly in the following years. The Bowie deal was affected and the notes issued for the transaction were downgraded by Moody's from Aaa to Baa1 (equivalent to BBB+) in 2004. The downgrade, however, did not have much impact on the deal. Prudential had adopted a buy and hold strategy and had no intention of selling the bonds.

Despite the rating downgrade the securities kept paying their coupon. The whole deal came to an end as planned, without any hitches, in February 2007. At this date, David Bowie had transferred back to him all the rights sold 10 years earlier and no longer owed anything to his former manager.

Epilogue

For David Pullman, the banker behind the deal, the *Bowie Bonds* were the beginning of a lucrative period. He structured several similar transactions, coming up

---

[4]The journalist Mark Steyn famously quipped: "Once upon a time, rock stars weren't rated by Moody's. They were moody."

with the concept of *Pullman Bonds* to describe the securitization of future flows derived from intellectual property rights. Within a few years Pullman arranged deals for many other singers and songwriters, dead and alive – including James Brown for whom Pullman closed a $30-million deal, allowing the artist to repay a $2-million tax debt to the US government.

Despite these successes, this market shrank after the year 2000 due to the internet revolution and the fact that people got used to downloading music for free. The deal carried out by Bowie and Pullman remains nonetheless a landmark transaction, as it opened up the possibility of structuring instruments backed by non-financial assets. In May 1999, Morgan-Stanley and West-LB arranged a similar deal on the television broadcasting rights of Formula 1. For a sum of $1.4 billion, the issue of the *Bernie Bonds*[5] was worth over 25 times the amount of the Bowie deal.

Case Study 10: What is a Covered Bond?

Covered bonds are debt securities issued by banks or financial institutions and collateralized against a pool of assets. They are sometimes wrongly confused with ABS.

Definition

Covered bonds appeared for the first time in Prussia in 1769 during the rule of Frederick the Great. Originally known as *Pfandbriefe*, covered bonds are bonds that can only be issued by banks or regulated financial institutions. Compared to traditional bonds, they offer bond holders an additional recourse to a specific and clearly identified collateral in case of default of the issuer.

This collateral (known as *cover pool*) is a portfolio of loans owned by the issuing bank. Due to the additional security offered by the cover pool, covered bonds have an excellent credit rating. They are generally rated AA or above by rating agencies. They are perceived quite rightfully as extremely low-risk securities.

(continued)

---

[5]Bernie is Bernard Ecclestone, the Formula 1 business mogul and the negotiator of the deal with the banks. Bernie Ecclestone ruled over the Formula 1 business from 1978 to 2017. With a personal wealth of more than $3 billion, he is one of the richest persons in the United Kingdom.

(*continued*)

Although they are both secured by a pool of assets, covered bonds and ABS are radically different. The holder of an ABS has no recourse against the entity that has transferred the assets to the SPV in the first place. If some of the assets sold to the SPV default, the ABS holders do not have any claim against the company that has originally transferred the assets to the SPV.

A covered bond, on the other hand, has all the characteristics of a traditional bond. Its holder has a clear legal recourse against the issuer. The collateral is simply an add-on that enhances the risk profile of the bond. In case of default of the issuer, if the sale proceeds of the collateral are not sufficient to repay the bonds, the bond holders still have a direct claim against the issuer for the amount which has not been repaid (a concept known as *dual recourse*).

Unlike an ABS holder, the buyer of a covered bond is not directly exposed to the performance risk of the collateral. A covered bond works like any other bond. Its issuer has to pay a coupon as long as it does not default. The payment owed by the issuer to the bond holders remains due even if some of the assets posted as collateral default. The cover pool only exists to give an additional comfort to the bond holders. This collateral is also dynamic, meaning that if some of the under-lying assets deteriorate (or pre-pay), they have to be replaced by assets of a similar credit quality. In case of bankruptcy of the issuer, this dynamic is broken and the cover pool becomes static.

The pool of assets used as collateral for a covered bond remains the legal property of the covered bond's issuer. The cover pool is clearly identified and assets are usually put aside to facilitate a claim of the covered bond holders in case of bankruptcy of the issuer. In some countries, an issuer has the obligation to set aside the cover pool in an insolvency remote SPV. This SPV remains unaffected in case of a bankruptcy of the issuer.

The Covered Bonds Market Today

The covered bond market is the second largest debt market in Europe after standard bank bonds (i.e. bonds issued by banks without specific collateral) and before corporate bonds. After years of constant volume increases and a peak at €2,800 billion in 2012, the covered bond market has slightly decreased until 2015. It has since stabilized around €2,500 billion, at a level where bonds reaching maturity are replaced by new issues of roughly the same value.

Even if Europe is and remains covered bonds' core market, the product has become more and more international over the years. The leading markets are Germany, France, Spain, the United Kingdom, and the Nordics, but banks in countries such as Singapore, Canada, the United States, Australia, New Zealand,

and Turkey have also issued covered bonds. According to NordLB,[6] the proportion of non-euro denominated covered bonds reached a record high of 36% in 2015, confirming the trend that covered bonds are becoming increasingly international. Each market has certain country-specific characteristics but everywhere they exist, covered bonds are used by banks as an instrument to tap long-term investors looking for low-risk/low-yield investments.

The demand for covered bonds is partly explained by the rise in demand from certain conservative investors. Considering that they offer the double advantage of low risk and high liquidity, covered bonds are in demand by banks that wish to comply with regulatory obligations, and particularly the requirements of the Liquidity Coverage Ratio (LCR) imposed by Basel III.

Introduced as part of the Basel III Accords in 2010, the LCR requires banks to continuously maintain an amount of liquid assets higher than their cash requirements over the next 30 days. The LCR is a short-term liquidity ratio designed to ensure that banks can survive an extended liquidity disruption in the market. It was introduced in response to the bankruptcies of Bear Stearns, Lehman Brothers, and Washington Mutual. In the context of this ratio, covered bonds count as liquid assets, which explains the interest displayed by banks to invest in them.

Covered bonds are also attractive for insurance companies. Their regulatory framework in Europe (Solvency II) assigns covered bonds a preferential status in terms of capital charges.[7] In other words, they do not need to mobilize a lot of regulatory capital to fund the acquisition of covered bonds. Despite their low yield, covered bonds can be for them an attractive investment opportunity.

Overview of Assets Given as Collateral

Financial institutions issue covered bonds because it allows them to lend long term. Banks can refinance through covered bonds assets such as mortgage or public sector loans. They can therefore more easily offer long-term financing options to their clients, as they know they can use the loans granted to these clients as a collateral for covered bonds. Banks reduce in this way the structural mismatch between their long-term assets (20-year mortgage loans, for instance) and short-term liabilities (mainly customers' deposits).

Mortgage-backed covered loans are by far the most popular type of covered bonds. They make up roughly 80% of the total value of bonds outstanding, followed

(continued)

---

[6]NordLB Fixed Income Research, Issuer Guide Covered Bonds 2016.
[7]See Chapter 5, section 5.3.2 for a short description of Solvency II.

(continued)

by public sector bonds (c. 15%). The other collaterals remain niche products. They are made up of shipping loans,[8] aircraft loans, or portfolios of corporate debt.

Covered bonds are usually over-collateralized, meaning that the total value of the cover pool exceeds the notional value of the bonds. This over-collateralization is a requirement of both local regulators and rating agencies. In each country, legal frameworks set minimum levels of over-collateralization, with the aim of protecting the holders of covered bonds: 102% in Germany and Sweden, 105% in France, 108% in Denmark, and 125% in Spain. In addition, covered bonds can only achieve a credit rating higher than the rating of an issuer's unsecured bonds if the value of the collateral exceeds the notional value of the bonds by an amount of between 10% and 20%.

What are the Risks?

The long history of covered bonds sometimes creates the impression that they are simple and risk-free instruments. In October 2013, however, the asset manager PIMCO attracted the attention of investors on the risks inherent to covered bonds and the danger of assuming that certain securities are necessarily without risks.[9] PIMCO pointed out the obvious: although covered bonds have on average an excellent rating, their holders are exposed to a potential risk of loss.

As long as the issuer does not default, the coupons due on the covered bonds are paid from the operating income of the issuer rather than the income generated specifically by the collateral. If a bank that has issued covered bonds defaults, the assets posted as collateral for the bonds are removed from the issuer's balance sheet and continue to be operated independently by a trustee. If these assets are insufficient to cover the total amount due to the covered bondholders, the investors still have a direct recourse to the issuer for an amount equal to the portion of debt that is not covered by the value of the collateral. For this portion, the covered bond holders are in the exact same position as the issuer's unsecured debtors.

ABS and Covered Bonds

Table 10.3 summarizes the similarities and differences between ABS and covered bonds.

---

[8]Historically, German banks, which frequently issue covered bonds, have been very active in the shipping sector.

[9]Ana Cortes Gonzalez, Graeme C. Williams, and Ben Emons, *Viewing Covered Bonds Through a Structured Finance Lens*. PIMCO newsletter, October 2013.

TABLE 10.3   ABS and Covered Bonds

	ABS	Covered Bond
Issuer	An SPV established with the sole purpose of purchasing a pool of assets. The acquisition of the portfolio of assets is financed by the issue of ABS	Depends on local regulation but usually a bank or a mortgage institution
Type of collateral	Wide range of assets (mortgage loans, corporate loans, leverage loans, corporate bonds, student loans, receivables, lease payments, etc.)	Mortgage loans for the vast majority (80%) but also public sector (15%) or corporate loans
Credit risk taken by the investor	Full exposure to the pool of assets collateralized against the ABS	Issuer's risk – with the benefit of the collateral
Recourse	To the assets held by the SPV. The ABS holder has no recourse to the entity that has sold the assets to the SPV in the first place	Full recourse to the issuer. If the issuer is not able to meet its payment obligations, the collateral may be sold and the proceeds transferred to the bond holders
Tranching	Yes, in most cases	No
Maturity	Very variable but generally around 10 to 15 years	Up to 30 years
Main markets	United States, United Kingdom, and Western Europe	Western European and Nordic countries

CHAPTER 11

The Different Stakeholders

Before fully diving into the intricacies of securitization, readers are invited to discover the role of each party in a transaction. This should help you better understand how securitization works.

11.1 BORROWERS

The borrowers are the people or entities whose debt is transferred to the issuer. This category regroups all physical or legal entities that contribute to generating revenues for the SPV. These borrowers are the households or companies who have taken out loans and whose loans are being securitized (see Figure 11.1). They are the revenue providers of the transaction and are the people or entities on which the investors take a payment risk.

Please note that using the expression "borrowers" to designate this category of stakeholders is somehow erroneous. Not all securitized assets are loans. They can be any type of receivables. However, since loans (of all kinds – i.e. mortgage loans, corporate loans, commercial real estate loans, etc.) constitute most of the securitized assets, we prefer this term to any other to facilitate discussion.

11.1.1 Their Role

Securitization does not change anything for this category of stakeholders. Individuals and companies whose borrowings are the underlying assets of this type of deal are generally not aware of them being transferred to an SPV. They continue to repay their loans to the bank that has originally granted them that loan. The payments are then directly and automatically transferred to the SPV.

If the assets transferred to the SPV are not loans but commercial receivables, the situation is not much different. The clients keep paying their original supplier. They

272

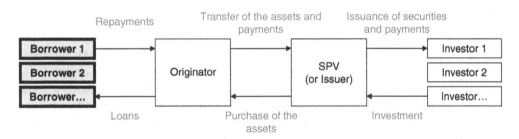

FIGURE 11.1 Overview of the Borrowers' Position in the Securitization Process

do not know that the new legal owner of the payments they have to make is a shell company. The example of the Bowie Bonds (case study 9) is similar: the clients who bought CDs of David Bowie from 1997 to 2007 had no clue the money was going to an SPV and then to Prudential – unless they worked on Wall Street or read the *Financial Times*.

11.1.2   Their Interest in the Transaction

Even if the borrowers rarely (or never) realize that their future payments are transferred to an SPV, securitization is paradoxically of importance for them. From a macroeconomic point of view, securitization increases the available credit supply. In the same way that the bond market provides companies with an alternative to bank loans, securitization brings another set of solutions to finance or refinance individuals, households, businesses, LBOs, etc. It creates a new pool of liquidity in addition to traditional tools.

Securitization is for this reason an integral part of the financial disintermediation process that we already discussed several times in this book, notably in case study 2 on Michael Milken. Securitization is a major driver of the change in the way the economy is financed. Whereas in the traditional economic model companies and individuals were only financed by banks, they can now be financed directly by a wide range of players (banks, pension funds, insurances companies, asset managers, etc.) through a large variety of instruments (loans, bonds, securities, etc.). The recourse to banks is today just one option amongst others.

Given the increasing regulatory constraints imposed on banks, securitization represents a solid alternative to traditional financing routes. All things being equal, regulation indeed limits the supply of bank loans available to finance the economy. Insofar as regulation demands that banks partly finance their loans by an increasing amount of capital,[1] banks have to be more disciplined in the way they use their balance sheet. This leaves room for investors who do not have the same regulatory constraints: pension funds, hedge funds, private equity firms, etc.

---

[1] Constraints imposed by the Basel Accords as our reader is now aware of (see the Introduction).

11.2   THE ORIGINATOR

The originator is the legal entity that originally owns the income-generating assets that are sold to the SPV (see Figure 11.2). The originator can be a bank or any other type of company. Banks are the most usual type of originator (and loans are the most frequently securitized assets) but any other kind of company or legal entity can use securitization: private or public corporations, public bodies, governments, etc. Even individuals can use securitization (see case study 9 on David Bowie). The only prerequisite for using this tool is to own a large portfolio of similar receivables or income-producing assets.

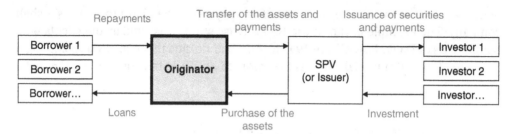

FIGURE 11.2   Overview of the Originator's Position in the Securitization Process

11.2.1   The Role of the Originator

One of the main tasks of the originator is to select the collateral to be transferred to the SPV. This choice is made jointly with the deal arranger, usually an investment bank. The objective is to create a portfolio that can be the basis for a successful securitization. The asset selection is made having in mind that the notes issued by the SPV have to obtain a certain credit rating to attract liquidity. The originator and its advisor have therefore to anticipate how rating agencies evaluate and rate securities. Rating agencies can be involved early in the process to help built the optimal portfolio.

The sale process of the assets to the SPV has to follow some basic rules. The value of these assets has to be agreed upon by the seller and the arranger, who both have to be able to demonstrate that the transfer is made on an arm's length basis. What looks on paper like an easy task is not necessarily straightforward. Rate variations and foreign exchange fluctuations can affect valuations. If, for instance, one of the bonds to be transferred to the SPV is rated AA and pays a fixed coupon, the transfer value of this bond will depend on the yield offered on AA-rated bonds by the market on the transfer date. If the average yield offered on the transfer date for bonds with a similar rating is higher than the coupon paid on this bond, the bond will be transferred at a discount. If it is the other way around, the bond will be sold at a price higher than the face value.[2]

---

[2]These price movements are due to the fact that financial investors make constant market arbitrages. If AA-rated securities issued two years ago pay a 2% coupon while new securities of this type are

There are usually three methods to value the price at which assets should be transferred from the originator to the SPV:

- Assets can be transferred at market price.
- They can be sold for an amount equal to their purchase price – if it can be evidenced that the value of the assets has not changed between the moment it was taken on its book by the originator and the transfer date. This method is mostly used when not much time has elapsed between the two dates and/or when it is difficult to precisely assess minor variations in the price of the assets (portfolio of client's receivables for instance).
- Assets can also be transferred at *fair value*, i.e. for an estimated market value of the asset. This method is used when the asset is particularly unusual or illiquid.

11.2.2   The Interest of Securitization for the Originator

There are several reasons why banks or companies are willing to pool together a group of assets and securitize them. These reasons are obviously not mutually exclusive.

11.2.2.1   Reason 1: Liquidity Requirement

A seller may want to securitize assets for liquidity purposes. It may have to repay debt or finance new capex. In a way, the Bowie Bonds described in case study 9 is a securitization triggered by liquidity purposes. David Bowie, acting as originator, was looking for a solution to obtain cash and maintain his lifestyle. Selling his intellectual property rights to an SPV financed by Prudential for a given period of time enabled him to achieve these objectives.

The securitization structured by GPA in 1996, and mentioned in case study 8, also falls into this category. GPA was at that time heavily indebted. Selling a large portfolio of aircraft through a securitization was a way for GPA, acting as originator, to generate cash and repay creditors.

11.2.2.2   Reason 2: Balance Sheet Optimization

The recourse to securitization is a way for companies to optimize their balance sheet. The sale of assets generates cash, which diminishes a company's net debt. For many companies, the regular sale of clients' receivables through securitization is a tool to maintain net debt below a certain level and secure a given credit rating.

Selling assets is also important for banks. It improves their position from a risk perspective, as cash – if it is a major currency – is always less risky than any other

---

suddenly issued (due to new market conditions) at 1.5%, investors will acquire securities issued two years ago because they are more profitable than the new ones for an equivalent risk. The demand for vintage securities will raise their price until their return equal the return of new securities – in this case 1.5%.

asset. From a regulatory perspective, the sale of loans can also be positive insofar as it reduces the RWAs of the bank. Cash has no weighting and accounts for zero RWAs (as long as it is an easily tradable currency). The downside of this strategy is obviously that the bank is also selling the future profits associated to these loans. We will see later the strategies of banks that securitize assets but then buy some of the securities issued by the SPV they have sold their assets to. If is for them a way to reduce their RWAs and increase their profitability (see section 11.4.2).

11.2.2.3   Reason 3: Risk Management

Securitization is a major tool of many companies' risk management policy. Regular ABS issuers like Sallie Mae (student loans) or Volkswagen Financial Services, the in-house bank of the Volkswagen Group (auto loans), have integrated securitization at the very heart of their financial strategy. It is a tool that allows them – despite the limited size of their balance sheet – to be constantly active in the lending market. They securitize a large number of loans as soon as their exposure reaches a given limit. For these companies, securitization means that they can continue to be active lenders in their original markets without keeping loans on their balance sheet. These issuers almost act as loan warehousing entities. They grant loans to a high number of borrowers before selling them to third party investors under a repackaged format.

The case of Volkswagen Financial Services has to be analyzed in the light of the global Volkswagen strategy. Volkswagen is indeed a major car manufacturer and its main objective it to generate profits through car sales. Offering financial solutions to customers through Volkswagen Financial Services is only a way to ensure that potential clients can pay for their vehicles. If Volkswagen Group as a whole was not selling part of its auto loans portfolio on a regular basis, the company would in the end be more exposed to the credit risk of its customers than to the success of its car production. The group would look more like a bank than a car manufacturer.

Traditional banks can also have recourse to securitization for the same reasons. If, for instance, a major UK bank considered itself overexposed to the local residential real estate market, it would securitize part of its portfolio of loans. This way, the bank could decrease its exposure to this asset class while remaining an active lender in the market. The alternative, i.e. not granting any more residential mortgage loans to customers, would be commercial suicide, as securing a real estate loan is the main reason why individuals select a bank or switch from one to another.

11.3   AROUND THE SPV: THE TRANSACTION'S LIFE

The establishment of the SPV (see Figure 11.3) is the central piece of the arrangement of the whole transaction. A wide range of stakeholders revolves around it: investment banks, lawyers, rating agencies, trustee, and servicer.

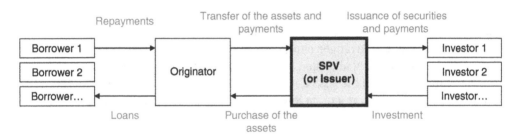

FIGURE 11.3   Overview of the SPV's Position in the Securitization Process

11.3.1   The SPV or Issuer

The company that acquires the collateral is a special purpose entity established for the sole purpose of the transaction. It is a company without staff whose only role is to (i) buy the assets transferred by the originator and (ii) issue securities for investors. Its by-laws are very restrictive. It cannot perform any action that is not related to the transaction itself. It is in a way in autopilot mode. The only permitted tasks are the ones necessary to set up the deal and ensure proper follow-up of the transaction: asset transfer, issuance of the ABS, reporting to investors, dividend distributions, etc.

The SPV is neither a subsidiary of the originator nor the investors (remember – even if they do not perceive a fixed coupon, the holders of the equity tranche are legally investors in a junior debt tranche: they do not own the SPV). The SPV is generally a trust or a similar type of entity and is entirely autonomous.

The SPV is said to be *bankruptcy remote*. This means that it is a legal entity totally separated from the originator. It is not financially impacted if the originator goes bankrupt or is insolvent. Creditors of the originator cannot access the assets held by the issuer.

11.3.2   The Arranger

The arranger is an investment bank (or more rarely a boutique) whose responsibility is to structure the deal. Its role is to assist the originator in selecting the assets to be transferred to the SPV. It must optimize the collateral to ensure that the various tranches will obtain the rating traditionally expected by investors for this type of transaction. As such, the role of the arranger includes the coordination of the interactions with rating agencies.

The arranger is also responsible for drafting, under the supervision of a law firm, the *offering circular*, i.e. the document that presents the transaction to potential investors. Having an offering circular is a legal obligation when securities are issued. It is a very formal document of 300 to 400 pages that explains the investment opportunity in detail: nature of the issuer, purpose and terms of the transaction, etc.

The role of the arranger is also to identify the investors who will acquire the notes issued by the SPV. There are sometimes several arrangers for the same transaction.

This is a way for the originator to optimize the placement of the securities insofar as banks may not have exactly the same investor base.

In some cases, the arranger can guarantee the placement of the securities. The bank underwrites the deal and then distributes the securities to investors. It takes the risk of getting stuck with the ABS if it is unable to sell them. It can also compute a loss if it is forced to sell them at a price lower than the original subscription price.[3]

11.3.3   Rating Agencies

Rating agencies contribute to the liquidity of the ABS market. Many investors – and amongst them the largest pension funds, asset managers or insurance companies – are only allowed to invest in debt securities with a credit rating. Obtaining a rating for the various tranches (except the equity tranche) is necessary to attract a large number of investors and support the liquidity of the securities in the secondary market.

Rating agencies are involved at a very early stage in a deal. They discuss their rating methodology with the arranger and explain what should be done or avoided to get a specific rating. There is generally an open and constructive dialogue between rating agencies and banks. The final ratings of the ABS are generally not a surprise. The choice of the assets included in the collateral and the way the securities are tranched are guided by the objective to obtain given ratings.

Although rating agencies were heavily criticized during the subprime mortgage crisis (see case study 11), they cannot be guilty of what they are not responsible for. Their role is to assign ratings to facilitate the transmission of financial information and support, indirectly, market liquidity. Even if analysts in rating agencies are professionals, they make mistakes like everyone else and their opinion is theirs alone. The existence of a rating does not dispense a qualified investor from making their own analysis.

11.3.4   The Trustee

The trustee is the entity responsible for the administration of the issuer. Its duties are the following:

- It ensures that the flows generated by the assets are properly paid to the SPV.
- It oversees payments from the SPV to the investors.
- It provides investors with regular reporting of the performance of the assets.
- It is in charge of managing all operating expenses of the SPV and coordinating the work of all the external service providers (accountants, lawyers, servicer).

The trustee is a company specialized in the administration of special purpose entities. Its role is to ensure that the interests of the investors are protected.

---

[3]See Appendix B (Syndication and Club Deals) for more details on the concepts of syndication.

11.3.5   The Servicer

The role of the servicer is to collect the payments generated by the portfolio of assets transferred to the SPV. Its role is not to be confused with the trustee's. While the trustee is in charge of the administration of the SPV, the servicer is a service provider. Its role is to actually collect the payments. The trustee only has to see that the payments are effectively made and that the interests of the security holders are protected.

The servicer is in most cases the originator itself, as it usually has the relevant expertise and the necessary set-up to play this role. The choice of a servicer is important, as an experienced servicer is key to attract investors. Rating agencies consider the track record of the servicer when rating securities.

If the originator of the deal is a bank, this bank is usually chosen as servicer. It receives payments from borrowers and channels them to the SPV. In case of non-payment or default by a borrower, it takes all necessary legal action to obtain, on behalf of the SPV and under the supervision of the trustee, the payment of the amounts due. In some cases, the servicer may have to enforce the securities attached to the asset (i.e. foreclosure of a property if the asset that has defaulted is a mortgage loan).

11.3.6   The Law Firm

The role of the law firm is to draft the legal documents necessary for the transaction. This includes notably the by-laws and the investment guidelines of the SPV, the asset transfer agreement, and all the documents related to the issue of the securities. As stated earlier, it also assists the arranger in preparing the offering circular. Moreover, the law firm ensures that legal formalities required by the legislation of the country where the SPV is established are complied with.

The law firm also plays a key role in ensuring that the transfer of the assets from the originator to the SPV cannot be legally challenged. As already mentioned (Chapter 10, section 10.1.2), the sale of assets has to qualify as a *true sale*. While the character of the transfer of the loans or receivables may seem straightforward, some of the commercial requirements of a transaction may result in doubt being cast on whether there has been a valid and effective transfer of title to the assets. If the transaction has certain characteristics, such as the originator receiving a servicing fee calculated by reference to a certain level of profit in the receivables pool, or having a right to repurchase the assets at the end of the transaction, the transfer may be recharacterized as a loan with a grant of security, rather than a true title transfer. This obviously creates issues if the originator becomes insolvent or if there are defaults in the collateral.

To clarify this point, or any other potential legal issues that the transaction could raise, the law firm can draft one or several legal opinions. The purpose of these legal opinions is to explain to investors how the sensitive clauses of the documentation should be interpreted in the light of existing legislation and previous case laws.

11.4   THE INVESTORS

ABS holders bring together a wide range of investors (see Figure 11.4). These investors are generally institutional investors or hedge funds but can also be family offices,[4] private banks,[5] or individual investors. The equity of some CLOs is even listed and accessible to modest investors.

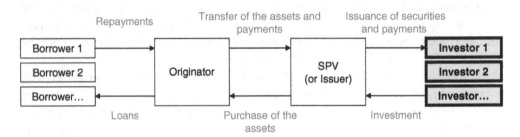

FIGURE 11.4   Overview of the Investor's Place in the Securitization Process

11.4.1   Their Interest

11.4.1.1   Diversification

Securitization offers investors the opportunity to invest in asset categories which are not otherwise accessible to them. Thanks to securitization, almost any investor (even the smallest one) can, for instance, easily invest in CDOs backed by US LBO loans. Without securitization, investors cannot have direct access to this market. At best, they can invest in stocks of a bank that is highly exposed LBO loans. This investment strategy, however, would result in exposing them to assets other than those they initially wanted to purchase – in this case all non-related LBO assets held by the bank (i.e. mortgage loans, project finance loans, corporate loans, trading activities, etc.). Even if the bank they invested in is a major LBO house, buying shares of a bank would make them equity investors and not just investors in the portfolio of LBO loans held by the bank.

    In short, securitization allows investors to have more direct control over their asset allocation. By having a much larger choice of investment opportunities, in terms of type of assets (CDOs, CLOs, RMBS, ABS, etc.) and risk profile (equity, mezzanine, or senior debt), investors – including the smallest ones – can create portfolios that most correspond to their market views.

---

[4]A family office is an investment company that manages assets of extremely wealthy families. If needed, see the definition of family office in Chapter 2, section 2.2.1.3.
[5]Private banks are banks specialized in managing the assets of wealthy or very wealthy clients. They are directed more towards well-off clients, compared to traditional retail banks, but much less so than family offices.

11.4.1.2 Extra Yield

Another reason why investors look actively at securitization is that it offers a spread pick-up compared to similar instruments with the same rating. This is especially true for CLOs and CDOs. Unlike many other ABS types, these products have a real equivalent in the non-structured finance market. Their collateral consists of corporate bonds and loans and these loans and bonds are generally freely tradable and can be acquired by investors (this is a major difference with RMBS for instance, which, from an investor perspective, do not have a direct equivalent as investors cannot buy individual mortgage loans directly in the market). In other words, save for the diversification effect caused by the pooling of assets, a CLO AAA is comparable to an AAA-rated bond.

CLO AAA pay, however, a higher coupon than AAA-rated bonds. This spread pick-up is due to the complexity of the instrument and its relative lower liquidity. The downside is that, for the very same reasons, the market is more volatile. Buyers need to be prepared for mark-to-market volatility, especially in mezzanine, where the market is not as deep as in senior debt.

11.4.1.3 Liquidity Purposes

While they still look for diversification and extra yield, some buyers want to maintain a liquid portfolio. These investors tend to favor investment in consumer ABS. These products have a short maturity and rely on a strong granularity.[6] They are therefore less volatile than CLOs. In a way, they can be seen as the money market lines of the structured credit sector.[7]

11.4.2 The Specific Case of Originators Who also Act as Investors

11.4.2.1 Regulatory Capital Trades

A bank can in some cases acquire some of the notes issued by the SPV to which it has transferred loans. As has already been explained (section 11.2.2.2), this is a strategy used by banks to optimize their balance sheet.

The recourse to securitization to sell assets – as opposed to the straight sale of a portfolio of loans to an investor – allows banks to invest in some of the notes issued by the SPV. With this structure, a bank can retain part of the revenue associated to the portfolio it wishes to sell. This may sound counterintuitive but it is a technique used by banks to maintain a certain level of revenues while increasing their profitability.

---

[6]A high level of granularity means that there are a lot of assets in the collateral. Consumer ABS (credit cards, student loans, auto loans, auto leases) offer a strong granularity to investors given the small size of each asset.
[7]The money market is the market of short-term financing instruments. Assets in this market have a maturity of less than a year. This is considered as a safe and low-yield investment segment.

The steps of such a transaction can be described as follows:

1. Let us assume that a bank decides to securitize its portfolio of high-yield bonds. These debt securities being non-investment grade, their equivalent in terms of RWAs is equal to 120% of their nominal value.[8]

   For ease of reference, we can consider that:

   - the value of the portfolio is $1 billion
   - its equivalent in terms of RWAs is $1.2 billion
   - the portfolio generates an average return of 5%, i.e. $50 million a year
   - the return on RWAs for this portfolio, also called RoRWA, is equal to 4.1% (50/1,200);[9]
   - the amount of capital that the bank must use to finance this portfolio is equal to $96 million (8% × 1,200 million)[10]
   - the return on regulatory capital for this portfolio is 52.0% (50/96).

2. An SPV acquires the bank's entire high-yield portfolio and issues six tranches of securities, including five tranches of debt (rated AAA to BB) and one of equity. The whole senior tranche (AAA) is acquired by the originating bank. The five other tranches are sold to third-party investors.

3. If we assume that the AAA tranche represents 70% of the deal value, it means that the bank keeps a total exposure of $700 million. If the senior tranche pays 1.5%, the bank retains a share of revenues of $10.5 million per year (1.5% × 700 million).

4. The senior tranche being rated AAA, it does not consume a lot of RWAs. It is equivalent to 20% of the nominal value of the credit exposure.[11] The total amount of RWAs for the bank is therefore now equal to $140 million (20% × 700 million).

---

[8] According to Basel II rules, revised by Basel III, corporate exposures to BB+ to BB- names translate, under the standard approach, into 100% of RWAs. Below BB- the weighting is 150%. For the sake of simplicity, we assume in this example the average weighting of the portfolio of high-yield bonds is 120%.

[9] The concept of RoRWA may be surprising for a reader unfamiliar with financial jargon. It is, however, a widespread concept in the banking sector. It measures the revenues generated by a bank based on the risk-weighted use of its balance sheet. It is a useful ratio to measure the profitability of a bank (or a transaction) based on risk. Banks usually set internal RoRWA targets. It is generally not permitted to close transactions yielding below the target RoRWA unless there is a strong commercial rationale.

[10] We have assumed in this example that the amount of regulatory capital required to finance an asset is equal to 8% of the total RWAs. We have used the same number in our Introduction. Please note, however, that in reality regulators do not require the same level of capital from all banks. Banks whose insolvency could jeopardize the stability of the global financial system are, for instance, required to maintain a higher level of capital (i.e. more than 8%). These banks are referred to as *global systemically important banks*. Their list is updated every year by the Financial Stability Board, an entity in charge of monitoring the financial system acting under the control of the G20. As of November 2020, there are 30 global systemically important banks.

[11] Basel II standard approach, revised by Basel III.

5. Thanks to the transaction, the RoRWA of the bank improves significantly. It is now equal to 7.5% (10.5/140) as opposed to 4.1% before the deal. This is due to the fact that the decrease in RWAs is relatively more important than the loss of revenues.

6. The amount of capital used for this AAA investment is now $11.2 million (8% × 140 million), meaning that the return on capital for this transaction is equal to 93.5% (10.5 million/11.2 million).

Table 11.1 compares the two situations (before and after securitization). It shows the advantages that a bank obtains in acquiring securities issued as part of its own securitization program. Even if the numbers have been simplified here for easier reading, this example underlines the role played by securitization in the optimization of banks' capital.

TABLE 11.1   Key Metrics Before and After the CLO Issuance

	Before CLO Issuance	After CLO Issuance
Credit exposure of the bank	$1,000m	$700m
Yield	5%	1.5%
Annual revenues	$50m	$10.5m
RWAs (in %)	120%	20%
RWAs (in $)	$1,200m	$140m
RoRWA	4.1%	7.5%
Required amount of capital (in %)	8%	8%
Required amount of capital (in $)	$96m	$11.2m
Return on capital[12]	52.0%	93.5%

11.4.2.2   Investors

Some hedge funds or traditional asset managers have set up funds specialized in acquiring the mezzanine or equity tranches of such CLOs. The objective of these players is to offer banks solutions to optimize their use of capital. This type of deal is variously referred to as *capital relief trade* or *regulatory capital trade* (or more commonly *reg cap trade*). For the same reasons, these specialized funds are called *reg cap funds*.

Given the regulatory constraints faced by banks, these deals have become more popular over the last few years. With these transactions, banks are only exposed to the risk of the underlying portfolio if defaults exceed a predetermined threshold. In our example, the bank suffers a loss only if more than 30% of the portfolio defaults. In other words, banks sell to *reg cap funds* the risk of *first loss* on a given portfolio.

---

[12]The return on capital shown here should not be confused with the bank's return on equity. It is a ratio that measures the revenues generated by a deal against the regulatory capital needed for this specific transaction. It does not consider the expenses of the bank (i.e. financing costs, salaries, rents, etc.). This number is given for illustrative purpose only. In real life, banks would tend to focus on RoRWA only.

Reg cap deals are extremely attractive to banks. In our example, the bank has greatly reduced its use of capital (from $120 million to $5.6 million). It has also improved its profitability as RoRWA and returns on capital have increased dramatically, respectively from 4.1% to 7.5% and from 52.0% to 93.5%. Finally, risks have been reduced, as the first loss on the portfolio has been sold to another investor.

These deals are also of interest for investors. In our example, these investors are making collectively an investment of $300 million. Their revenues are equal to $39.5 million, i.e. the difference between the total yield on the portfolio and the revenues kept by the bank (50−10.5 = 39.5). Their total return on investment is equal to 13.1%. This return is obviously a blended return. The equity holders earn much more while the AA holders earn significantly less.

11.4.2.3   Synthetic Transactions

Capital relief trades are in fact generally structured without an actual sale of the collateral to the SPV. The assets remain on the bank's balance sheet but the risks associated with these assets are synthetically transferred to investors via the combination of credit derivatives. Transactions relying on this mechanism are for this reason referred to as *synthetic* securitizations.

In a typical capital relief trade, the bank looking to optimize its capital remains the legal owner of the assets. It buys from an SPV a credit insurance against the default of these assets. This credit insurance is called *Credit Default Swap (CDS)*. Under this CDS, the bank pays the SPV a regular fixed payment (generally quarterly) called a CDS premium. In exchange, it is indemnified by the SPV if an asset of the underlying portfolio defaults. As such, the bank becomes a *protection buyer* while the SPV is a *protection seller*.

To finance the protection offered to the originating bank, the SPV issues notes called *Credit Linked Notes (CLNs)* that are sold to investors. The SPV deposits the proceeds of the sale of the CLNs in a bank account or invests them in risk-free instruments, typically US government bonds for a US dollar transaction. The bank receiving the deposit (the custodian bank) can be the originator itself. In any case, this deposit is segregated from the other assets of the custodian bank.

Over the life of the transaction, the SPV passes on the CDS premiums it receives from the bank to the CLN investors. If an asset of the underlying portfolio defaults, the originating bank makes a claim under the CDS sold by the SPV. In turn, the SPV draws on the amount deposited with the custodian bank to meet that claim. Depending on the transaction structure, the returns earned by the SPV on the amount deposited with the custodian bank can be transferred to the originator or the CLN investors.[13]

Only the risk of first loss is sold to third-party investors. The other tranches are acquired by the originator itself. Since the buyer of these CLNs and the protection buyer are the same entity, the amount corresponding to the sale of these CLNs is generally not transferred to the SPV. Table 11.2 summarizes a real transaction closed in the mid-2010s by a bank to cover the risk of first loss of a portfolio of project finance loans. Figure 11.5 is a simplified representation of the same transaction.

---

[13]Readers who are not familiar with the concept of CDS and CLNs can find a definition of these products in Appendix C (Credit Derivatives).

TABLE 11.2 Tranching of CLNs for a Synthetic Regulatory Capital Trade

Credit Linked Notes	Rating	Amount (in €)	Amount (in %)	Status
Class A	AAA	1.514m	66.03%	Retained by the bank
Class B	AA	132m	5.76%	Retained by the bank
Class C	A	212m	9.25%	Retained by the bank
Class D	BBB	143m	6.24%	Retained by the bank
Class E	BB	172m	7.50%	Sold to investors
Class F	Not rated	120m	5.23%	Sold to investors
Total		2.293m	100%	

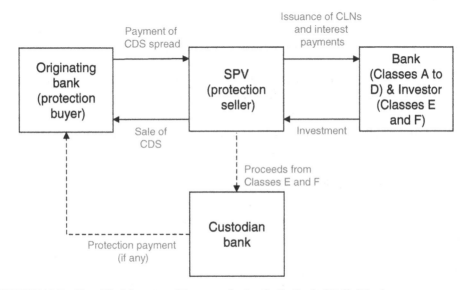

FIGURE 11.5 Simplified Structure Diagram of a Synthetic Capital Relief Trade

---

Case Study 11: The Subprime Crisis

The subprime crisis is one of the most traumatic examples of the bursting of a financial bubble – alongside, probably, the Great Depression in the 1930s and the Tulipomania in the seventeenth century.[14] Many economists claim today that this

---

[14]Tulipmania refers to a period of Dutch history from November 1636 to February 1637, when the price of tulip bulbs reached extraordinarily high levels (several times the average annual salary in the Low Countries at that time) and then dramatically collapsed. It is often analyzed as the first ever recorded speculative bubble. Some recent financial and economic research papers have, however, disputed the traditional interpretation of these events. They have shown that this bubble may not have had the magnitude that we once thought it had.

(*continued*)

dramatic crash was written in advance, that company valuations were too high and leverage too aggressive. They usually pretend that they had seen the crisis coming.

The truth is that even if many observers believed at that time that a double real estate and stock market bubble was forming, very few could actually tell where the crash would come from. It is easy to read the future with hindsight but it is far more complicated to understand the slow mechanism of the formation of a bubble. This is even more difficult to analyze in real-time interactions among stakeholders who, each in their own way, contributed to the crisis.

The FED Policy

The decade preceding the subprime crisis was marked by rapid credit expansion, encouraged by the accommodating monetary policy of the Federal Reserve (FED). To limit the risk of recession after the bursting of the dot-com bubble,[15] the FED decided in the early 2000s to drastically lower its rates over a very short period of time. Rates fell from 6.5% in May 2000 to 1.75% in December 2001. They reached 1% in 2003, their lowest point in 45 years. The FED's objective was to facilitate access to credit and encourage companies to invest more. Low interest rates were here to support investment and job creations and have, in the end, a positive impact on consumption.

The FED's policy achieved its objective. Demand for credit expanded and banks generally responded positively to companies willing to invest more. In parallel, however, many US households also took advantage of this new economic environment. Low interest rates facilitated the purchase of real estate and prices started to rise significantly in many parts of the country. Some states such as California, Arizona, Hawaii, and Nevada recorded several years of average price rise well above 10%. In 2007, Alan Greenspan, Chairman of FED from 1987 to 2006, confided that he had been aware of the existence of a bubble since the end of the year 2005.

Households

The increase in real estate prices in the early 2000s was also partly the consequence of the impact of the dot-com bubble on the saving habits of US citizens. Many

---

[15]The dot-com bubble (1997 to 2001) was a period of excessive valuation of internet-based companies that was fueled by the rapid growth of internet usage in developed economies. During that time, the NASDAQ index went from 1,000 to more than 5,000 before dropping rapidly by more than 50% when investors started to realize that most of these companies were not delivering the profits they had promised. A symbol of this period of "*irrational exuberance*" (Alan Greenspan) was the company pets.com, a company selling pet supplies online, which went from an IPO on the NASDAQ to liquidation in only 268 days.

households saw in the dot-com crash as an illustration that investing in stocks was risky. They switched to real estate, which was perceived to be a safer investment. This belief fueled the real estate bubble. It created a self-fulfilling prophecy. Many people bought real estate believing it was a good opportunity. This led to a rise in prices confirming the belief that it was indeed a wise investment strategy. In the end, prices went up steadily and people kept buying more and more.

The number and the percentage of US households owning a property reached historic levels during that period, as did the number of US citizens owning a second, a third, or a fourth property. Twenty-eight percent of residence purchases in the United States in 2005 were acquisitions of properties that did not qualify as a main residence. In some regions, and particularly in Miami and Southern California, purchases for speculative purposes (*flipping*) multiplied: buyers resold their assets soon after their purchase (without even living there or renting them out) with the sole objective of benefitting from a rise in prices.

American Housing Policy

It is in this very specific context that the US housing policy of that period is to be analyzed. With the intention of supporting very modest households, the Clinton (1993–2000) and Bush Administrations (2001–2008) required Fannie Mae and Freddie Mac[16] to be more actively involved in the financing of real estate loans granted to low-income families.

In 1997, the US government officially authorized the two companies to acquire CDOs collateralized with subprime loans. In other words, Fannie Mae and Freddie Mac were invited to refinance loans granted to households presenting a high risk of default due to their low income or difficult job history. This measure was obviously taken with the objective of increasing the liquidity available for real estate acquisitions by the poorest citizens. Banks and mortgage societies – which lend to households in the first place – could distribute part of their subprime loans to these two companies.

In 2004, the US Department of Housing and Urban Development revised upwards the targets set in 1997, creating a new cash inflow towards subprime borrowers. The decision was positive for low-income US citizens but was only made possible by the weakening of Fannie Mae's and Freddie Mac's credit profile. The situation, however, did not really seem to be an issue, as both institutions benefitted from a guarantee from the US government. It even looked like a very positive step as the two companies had very low funding rates (due to the

(*continued*)

---

[16]Fannie Mae and Freddie Mac are two private companies that had the benefit of an implicit guarantee from the Federal State in lieu of conducting public service projects in the housing domain.

(continued)

guarantee of the Federal State) but were recording high profits thanks to the hefty interest rates charged to poor families.

Negative Amortization Adjustable Rate Mortgages

The growing US real estate bubble was also characterized by the generalization of very aggressive loan structures. From the mid-2000s onwards, banks only rarely required down payments from clients for buying a house. Households with extremely limited resources could borrow amounts equal to the value of the property they wanted to buy. In many cases, loans were even granted for a higher amount as they covered all costs incurred by the acquisition of a property: taxes, registration fees, and refurbishment works. This situation created de facto for banks an additional level of risk as they accepted weaker security packages. In case of default of their clients and foreclosure and sale of a property, they did not benefit from any buffer to minimize their loss.

Some even more aggressive types of loans were offered to customers, especially to the poorest households. Banks proposed loans that gave the possibility to defer for two years the repayment of the principal and a large part of the interest. For extremely modest households (i.e. subprime borrowers), these *negative-amortizing adjustable-rate mortgages* (ARMs) were extremely attractive. They offered the opportunity of becoming a home owner rapidly without a down payment and without paying much during the first two years.

From 2005 onwards, these ARMs became the norm in the subprime lending segment. A household with limited resources could borrow a large amount of funds over a long period. Only a small part of the interest was due during the first two years. The deferred interest was added to the principal amount of the loan, to be paid later.

These loans were in essence debt with *adjustable rates* (rates were lower during the first two years) and *negative amortization* features (interest not paid during the first two years was added to the borrowed amount, meaning that the outstanding amount of the loan did not amortize but increased during the first two years – hence the term *negative amortization*).

Let us take a numerical example to illustrate how these loans worked:

- A household borrows $500,000 for 15 years at 10% to buy a property valued at $500,000. Given its limited resources, the household chooses a negative amortization ARM to finance the acquisition of their home.
- The loan is divided into two phases. During the first two years, no repayment of principal is due. The household only pays a small portion of the interest, i.e. 2%. The remaining 8% is added to the outstanding balance of the loan. The second phase of the transaction works as a fully amortizing loan with fixed installments.

- During the first year, the household only pays 2% of interest on $500,000, i.e. $10,000 per year or $833 per month. In parallel, the outstanding balance of the loan increases by 8%, i.e. by the value of interest due and deferred. At the end of the year, the total debt amounts to $540,000 (500,000 + 8% × 500,000).

- During the second year, the household continues paying 2% of interest on the outstanding amount of the loan. Given that the total debt amount has increased to $540,000, the annual payment due from the couple is $10,800 (or $900 per month). The balance of the loan increases by 8% and reaches $583,200 (540,000 + 8% × 540,000).

- After the first two years, the loan ceases to offer attractive features. The amount of $583,200 is supposed to amortize fully over the next 13 years. Considering the 10% interest rate, the debt service reaches, in theory, more than $6,600 per month – an amount that a couple with limited resources is generally unable to afford.

- The bank and the borrowers are aware that it is impossible to repay the loan after the first two years. They generally agree to envisage a refinancing after the first period. In this scenario, the $583,200 loan must be replaced after two years by a loan of the same amount. This new loan is another ARM that includes a two-year period during which only part of the interest is due. Thanks to this refinancing strategy, poor families can continue living in their homes.

- After another two years, a new refinancing offer can be made, involving again another ARM. The story can then in theory continue forever or until the situation of the household improves – in which case a more conservative and traditional form of loan can be structured.

A Pernicious System

The whole system was extremely pernicious. It could only exist because all participants believed – or wanted to believe – in a constant rise in real estate prices. In this very optimistic scenario, three very aggressive assumptions were made by the parties:

1. *Assumption 1*: the economy is so strong that people losing their jobs will quickly find another one. Defaults under the loans granted by banks are therefore unlikely to happen. Banks do not need to require a down payment. They will not have to foreclose properties. If a residence has a value of $500,000, this very same amount can be lent to the household buying the property.

(continued)

(*continued*)

2. *Assumption 2*: real estate prices will continue to rise. Since real estate prices go up incessantly, properties can be used two years later as a collateral to raise a new financing for a higher amount. The new loan will refinance the first one and offer the same features: discount interest rate with no principal repayment during the first two years.

3. *Assumption 3*: real estate prices will not only continue to increase, they will rise at a rate higher than the portion of deferred interest. In our example, if real estate prices rise more slowly than 8% per year, it becomes impossible to refinance the property in two years' time. Its market value will be lower than the amount needed for the new loan. No financial institution will accept lending more than the value of the collateral. The borrower will therefore not be able to refinance their loan and will default, as they do not have the revenues to repay an amortizing loan with fixed installments.

This final assumption shows the extent to which these ARMs were fragile. The whole system was vulnerable, not only to a fall in prices, but also to a *decline in the rise*. If real estate prices rose at a rate lower than the rate of deferred interests, households with limited revenues became unable to refinance their loans.

Despite their obvious flaws, ARMs became the cornerstone of the US subprime lending market. In 2005 and 2006, nearly one in ten mortgage loans granted in the United States was an ARM loan. The combination of these structures with the relative slow rise in prices in the second half of 2006 and first half of 2007 was one of the main triggers of the crisis. ARMs suddenly became impossible to refinance and defaults of households multiplied.

ARMs were, however, only one part of the problem. In a euphoric context, many loans were granted to customers without proper credit analysis. Mortgage documentation standards declined and loans were offered to low-income households without proper analysis of the value of the property (the famous *No Income No Asset* – or *NINA* loans). Some more aggressive types of loans were even dubbed *NINJA* loans (*No Income, No Job, No Asset*) to illustrate the fact that paperwork was extremely reduced and credit decisions were based on a very limited set of information.

Securitization as a Distribution Channel

The generalization of ARMs and the indirect support of the Federal Government (through Fannie Mae and Freddie Mac) gave a major boost to the US subprime market. It multiplied by more than 200 in 10 years. From $3 billion in 1995, it reached $130 billion in 2000 and $625 billion in 2005.

Securitization played a major role in this spectacular increase. Piles of bad loans were bundled together and distributed to investors worldwide. This new galaxy of lenders offered an impressive additional source of liquidity and fueled the growth of the subprime market. Investors in the United States, Europe, and Japan joined the party. Out of the $625 billion of subprime loans outstanding in 2005, $507 billion were refinanced through CDOs.

Albeit deeply rotten, the whole system appeared to be functioning perfectly. Poor families were finally able to afford a home, banks recorded growing profits, and investors globally found a new niche to diversify their investments.

The Role of Investment Banks

The distribution of subprime loans was orchestrated by large investment banks. Securitization was for them a major source of revenues, and by the late 1990s subprime loans had become a popular collateral for CDOs. Investment banks supported lenders in structuring their portfolios. They set up securitizations and distributed CDO tranches to investors worldwide.

In an industry where ratings are important, major banks were experts in navigating through the maze of Fitch, Moody's, or S&P requirements. They optimized loan portfolios to obtain the desired ratings for CDO tranches and knew how to take advantage of the flaws in the credit rating system for US households.

FICO was at that time the most popular credit rating process in the United States for individuals. It is named after the company that designed it (Fair, Isaac and Company[17]) and is used by all major lenders to gauge the credit quality of individual borrowers. A high FICO score demonstrates a high level of solvency while a low score indicates a high probability of default.

Leading investment banks were quick to understand that rating agencies based their own credit analysis on one parameter only: the average of FICO scores of all the borrowers in a loan portfolio. They did not take into consideration another important element, namely the dispersion of the borrowers' individual scores. In other words, a portfolio of loans granted to average-rated borrowers (portfolio A) and another portfolio in which half of the loans were granted to people with a high likelihood of default and the other half to borrowers with prime credit quality (portfolio B) were considered equivalent by rating agencies. This was obviously wrong, as defaults were more likely to occur – and affect CDO investors – in portfolio B.

To obtain acceptable FICO score averages and offload a maximum of subprime loans, investment banks put together portfolios mixing two categories of borrowers only: the ones with a very good credit quality and those who were clearly subprime. Bankers knew that the probability of default of these portfolios was high, but in a world in which subprime loans were the new big thing, their main objective was to find channels of distribution for these loans.

(continued)

---

[17]The company was founded in 1956 and renamed Fair Isaac Corporation in 2003 and then FICO in 2009. It went public in 1986 and is listed on the NYSE.

(*continued*)

Another flow of the FICO system was that highly rated households were not always prime borrowers. The rating process was such that people of a certain age who had never defaulted under a loan nor a credit card became necessarily creditworthy counterparties. Households without credit history in the United States were therefore generally able to obtain a decent FICO score, irrespective of their real repayment capabilities. Recent immigrants with very low income could get a decent score if they had never defaulted – which was likely to be the case since they were new to the country and had sometimes not been granted a credit card in the first place.

While they took full advantage of the flaws of the FICO system to build their portfolios, investment banks also bundled together several sub-segments of subprime loans. Their intention was to create artificially a relative diversity within their portfolios. Alt-A loans (alternative to A-rated borrowers), HEL (Home Equity Loan), HELOC (Home Equity Line of Credit), and mid-prime loans were some of the different categories of loans that could be found in portfolios structured by investment banks at that time.[18] This mix seemed to match the diversity required under the securitization doxa but merely hid the fact that all these loans were subprime loans.

Investment banks did not only play a role in the distribution of bad loans. Ironically, while some departments within investment banks structured riskier and riskier CDOs, other teams saw these assets as good opportunities. Many of them even set up in-house funds to invest in CDOs. Combined with the need to underwrite some of the CDO tranches that they would then distribute, these investments meant that banks' exposure to subprime loans increased significantly over the years.

The Responsibility of Rating Agencies

When S&P gives a AAA rating to a security, it considers that this instrument has a 0.12% probability of default within the next five years. Given that 28% of the CDOs rated AAA by S&P over the period preceding the crisis would finally default,[19] it was clear that S&P (and the others) had missed something. The number of defaults of these securities was indeed 200 times more than the assumptions made originally.

---

[18] A Home Equity Loan (HEL or simply *equity loan*) is a loan used to finance the down payment that households are traditionally supposed to invest from their own savings to buy a property. A Home Equity Line of Credit (HELOC) is a consumer loan provided to a household where the collateral is the borrower's equity in its mortgage. It differs from an equity loan in that the money is not lent upfront to purchase the property but at a later stage, usually to deal with unexpected expenses. Alt-A loans or mid-prime loans designate the upper category of subprime loans.
[19] Source: S&P.

Several reasons can be put forward to explain these errors. The continuous rise in real estate prices and the excitement of the pre-crisis period had probably put to rest the wariness of rating agencies. Be it negligence or incompetence, the Moody's model used to rate CDOs did not use any data on the US real estate market prior to 1980 – a reference period during which real estate prices had constantly risen. In addition, analysts who put the model together did not deem it necessary to study what had happened in other countries over the same period. The model only included limited gloomy scenarios and gave an optimistic floor to a potential fall in prices. It excluded the possibility of a major real estate crash like the one Japan experienced in the 1990s.

The views of rating agencies were also partly biased by the nature of the contractual relations they had with banks. A rating agency was indeed selected for a deal by the bank that structured the transaction. Surely, S&P, Moody's, or Fitch had a reputation at stake, but challenging every deal was to run the risk of not being commissioned for the next. In the midst of the greatest financial party of all time, pressure from management was intense and the financial stakes were extremely high. The profits of Moody's structured finance division (the one rating CDOs) rose by 800% from 1997 to 2007. Moody's was at that time one of the most profitable companies in the United States. It had for five years in a row (2002 to 2007) the highest profit margin of all S&P 500 companies – with a peak at 47.22% for the fourth quarter of 2006.

Another pernicious bias disrupted the work of rating agencies: the lure of money and the fact that many employees dreamed of joining a bank where salaries were notably higher. Many analysts at top rating agencies had for this reason already applied for a job on Wall Street at some point. They had been turned down but were often waiting to gain more experience before trying a second time. One of the famous expressions in New York at the time was, "*those who do not get a job at Wall Street take up a job at Moody's*". It was cruel but not totally inaccurate. Rating agency analysts were sometimes more occupied in discussing job opportunities with the bankers they worked with than in analyzing CDOs. Their personal job strategies did not make them challenge what banks proposed but, on the contrary, encouraged them to build personal relations with people who could one day be their future colleagues. This behavior, albeit shocking, was understandable: the average annual salary at Goldman Sachs was $520,000 in 2005 but only $185,000 at Moody's.

Bursting of the Bubble

The perfect picture of a new financial paradigm finally cracked in 2007. That year, a peak in defaults of home owners in the United States triggered major losses in the portfolios of many investors. The crisis spread rapidly, leading first to the bankruptcies of companies specialized in mortgage loans, then to the fall of Bear Stearns

(continued)

(*continued*)

in March 2008. Six months later, in September, the two largest bankruptcies in US history (Lehman Brothers and Washington Mutual) happened within 10 days.

The sum of lies, mistakes, and omissions made by politicians, bankers, brokers, and rating agencies had led to one of the most traumatic financial crises in history. Out of the six major US investment banks, five were in deep trouble. One was declared bankrupt (Lehman), two were acquired by other companies (Bear Stearns and Merrill Lynch), and two were bailed out by the US government (Goldman Sachs and Morgan Stanley). In the global crisis, the US economy was particularly hit. Several key variables such as job level, real GDP per capita, or household net worth would take several years to fully recover.

The ultimate irony of this period is that the very people who did not see the crisis coming – and who had sometimes indirectly played a role in triggering it – were the ones who had to find solutions to solve it. Henry Paulson, George W. Bush's Treasury Secretary, was the former CEO of Goldman Sachs (from 1998 to 2006), Timothy Geithner, who replaced Paulson after the election of Barack Obama as US president, was the former president of the New York Federal Reserve (and as such had the responsibility of supervising and regulating banks located in New York), and Ben Bernanke, chairman of the FED, had served on its board from 2002 to 2005, validating directly Greenspan's monetary policy.

Case Study 12: Michael Burry's Big Short[20]

It was at the beginning of 2004 that Michael Burry, a young 33-year-old fund manager suffering from Asperger's syndrome, decided to immerse himself in the intricacies of the US subprime market. Despite his limited knowledge of the sector, Burry had a strong sense that the real estate market was probably overvalued. Newspaper headlines mentioning that the market kept reaching record highs left him cold. It was for him a sign that a correction was about to happen.

Shorting the Real Estate Market

Driven by his obsession for detail, Michael Burry was probably the first investor at that time to carefully read the whole legal documentation of the countless CDOs and RMBS issued around this period. He discovered that the quality of

---

[20]The title of this case study is a tribute to the excellent book *The Big Short* by Michael Lewis, which has greatly inspired this case.

borrowers for mortgage-backed securities had steadily declined over the years and that recourse to ARM had been generalized.[21]

Michael Burry – who at the time was heading and managing his own fund, Scion Capital – decided to buy CDS[22] on the main companies involved in the US real estate market (i.e. property developers, real estate managers, building societies, banks, etc.). If a crash or a correction happened, he assumed that these companies would very likely be the first ones to suffer. Burry was obviously making this investment without lending to these companies. He was buying an insurance against a risk that he did not run. He was betting on the fall of these companies. He was paying an insurance premium to a CDS seller in the hope of seeing these companies default on their debt. If this happened, Burry would benefit from an indemnification from the CDS seller based on the amount covered under the CDS agreement. This was a way to short the debt of these companies: he paid a (negligible) amount to be insured and would be able to draw (maximum) compensation if his analysis was right.

Michael Burry quickly grasped that it would be better to directly short the CDOs or RMBS fueled with bad loans than the debt of the companies involved in the US real estate market. Even if he strongly believed that property developers, real estate companies, or banks were going to make losses due to the market correction he foresaw, he also knew that this did not mean that they would all default on their debt.

Buying CDS on CDOs

To fully benefit from the real estate crash that he anticipated, Burry contacted banks to buy CDS on CDO tranches collateralized by subprime loans. It was a first. The instrument did not exist and most of the banks ignored Burry's request. They considered the product to be too complex and the market limited. Of all the banks that Burry approached, only Goldman Sachs and Deutsche Bank showed interest. The three parties put together a master agreement, which governed, for all future transactions of this kind, (i) the payment mechanisms of CDS premiums and (ii) the indemnification rules between the CDS seller and the buyer, in case of default of the underlying CDO or RMBS tranches.

(continued)

---

[21] See case study 11 on the subprime crisis.

[22] A CDS, or Credit Default Swap, is a freely tradable financial instrument which works as a credit insurance. The buyer of the CDS pays a premium for protection in case of default of a debt security. The CDS buyer is indemnified by the CDS seller if the security eventually defaults. Readers not familiar with the concept of CDS should refer to Appendix C (Credit Derivatives) where a detailed explanation of this product can be found.

(*continued*)

A few months later, in June 2005, the International Swap and Derivatives Association (ISDA), the professional association in charge of providing standard contracts for derivative instruments, validated the document prepared by Burry, Goldman Sachs, and Deutsche Bank. The payment method agreed upon was pay-as-you-go, meaning that the CDS seller had to compensate the buyer progressively as defaults occurred on the underlying portfolio.[23] Thanks to this document, Michael Burry was finally allowed to buy CDS on CDO tranches.

In the following weeks, Scion Capital became a very good client of Goldman Sachs and Deutsche Bank. The two banks sold to Burry protection against the default of a large number of CDO tranches for a cumulative amount of several hundred million dollars. At the other end of the chain, they distributed part of the risk to institutions willing to sell CDS to Burry. Amongst them, AIG emerged as the entity with the most appetite and became Scion Capital's largest counterparty.

AIG was convinced that selling large amounts of CDS on AAA-rated CDO tranches was very good business. The traders of the insurance company believed that, given their rating, these securities had a very limited probability of default. It would emerge later that this investment was the direct cause of AIG's losses during the crisis. By 2008, AIG had insured through this mechanism a portfolio of more than $57 billion of subprime loans.

The Copycats

Among the bankers acting as brokers between Scion Capital and AIG, a senior trader at Deutsche Bank, Greg Lippman, refused to see Burry as an idiot. While many of his fellow traders did not really understand why Scion Capital was buying so many CDS, Lippman wanted to discover Burry's motivations. He asked his team to analyze these transactions and discovered that the CDO tranches Burry bought protection against were full of ARM to subprime borrowers.

These loans made the CDOs vulnerable not just to a collapse of the real estate market but to a simple slow down. Lippman summarized the situation by telling his bosses and clients that "zero means zero", i.e. a zero growth of the real estate market makes refinancing of these loans impossible and automatically leads to the default of many CDOs.

---

[23] Founded in 1985 and headquartered in New York City, ISDA is a professional organization with more than 800 members (mostly banks and brokers) whose purpose is to create industry standards for derivative instruments and provides legal definitions of terms used in contracts. The idea behind this standardization is that parties to derivative transactions should not have to renegotiate payment terms and definitions every time they enter into a new transaction. Having a single master agreement produced by ISDA and used by all parties throughout the world makes it easier for everyone to trade derivative instruments. Parties only have to add a few specifics to this master agreement in an appendix (notably notional amounts and dates) before closing their deal.

Willing to find additional clients, Lippman explained Burry's strategy to other investors. John Paulson bought CDS worth several million and ended up being the investor making the most money out of the crisis.[24] Other hedge funds followed suit: Cedar Hill Capital Partners, Elliott Associates, FrontPoint Partners, Harbinger Capital Partners, Hayman Capital, etc. Despite an intense marketing effort by Lippman, however, only a handful of investors decided to take the plunge. In total, the number of players that replicated Burry's strategy was limited – probably fewer than 20.[25]

The beauty of this bet was that the CDS buyers did not need to hold the CDO tranches they were buying protection against. A hedge fund could even get protection for the same tranche from different CDS sellers at the same time. Some of the worst CDO tranches available in the market were therefore insured several times by different parties. This market had in theory no limit. As long as someone (AIG or other) believed that a specific CDO tranche was worth AAA and was ready to sell a CDS, a hedge fund could take advantage of it.

Shorting the Whole Bank Market

Early in 2008, only very few investors were really aware of the crisis that was looming. And the more they dug, the more they discovered how tragic it would be. Realizing that many investment banks had heavily invested in so-called AAA tranches on CDO backed by subprime loans, some of them decided to buy CDS on these banks. Michael Burry himself bought CDS on Goldman Sachs and Deutsche Bank – without, obviously, owning shares of the two banks.

This was for these investors the beginning of a complicated game. As they understood that many banks would be severely hit, they wanted to buy CDS on many of these institutions. However, they faced a big problem: they needed to buy these CDS from counterparties that were not themselves too exposed to the CDO market. If they wanted to buy from Morgan Stanley CDS on Lehman Brothers, they needed to make sure that Morgan Stanley would not be bankrupt because of the crisis. Otherwise, they would not be indemnified and the whole structure would not make sense.

(continued)

---

[24] According to Gregory Zuckerman in his book the *Greatest Trade Ever: The Behind-the-Scenes Story of How John Paulson Defied Wall Street and Made Financial History,* Paulson's firm, Paulson & Co, made over $4 billion on this trade alone.

[25] Readers should bear in mind that most of the hedge funds were private companies and did not have to report their earnings other than to their investors, tax authorities, or regulators. It was consequently difficult to know for sure who had done what and for which amount. In addition, several hedge funds that decided to short the subprime market at that time also did it because they had themselves heavily invested in CDO tranches backed by subprime loans in the first place. This was a way for them to hedge their initial investment and limit their losses.

(*continued*)

Epilogue

Although he was the first fund manager to see that the US subprime market was leading the country to a major crisis, Burry was not the financier who would make the most money during the crisis. The size of a fund's investments is limited by the amounts that it has under management (the famous AUM, Assets Under Management) and, with only $500 million AUM, Scion Capital was a modest player in the world of hedge funds. In comparison, Paulson & Co, the fund that would record the highest gains due to bets against the subprime loan market, had over $12 billion AUM at that time.

Michael Burry was also somehow penalized by his genius. Being the first to buy CDS on CDO tranches, he was automatically the asset manager who paid CDS premiums for the longest period of time. This turned some of his investors against him. At the end of 2006, Gotham Capital,[26] a New York City-based hedge fund with an investment of $100 million in Scion Capital, asked to recover its investment due to the fund's poor performance. Burry refused to return the money and was on the brink of being sued before the subprime bubble finally burst and changed (surprisingly) the opinion of Gotham's management ... Scion Capital ultimately recorded returns of 489.34% (net of fees and expenses) between its inception in November 2000 and June 2008. The S&P 500 returned just under 3% including dividends over the same period.

---

[26]Gotham Capital is a fund established in 1985 by Joel Greenblatt, mostly with seed money provided by Michael Milken.

CHAPTER 12

Structuring a Securitization

12.1 COMPOSITION OF THE COLLATERAL

At this stage – especially after two case studies pertaining to the subprime crisis – discerning readers will have understood that the key element of a successful securitization is to carefully select the assets to be transferred to the SPV. The first thing to do is, obviously, to avoid pooling together flawed or bad assets as brokers, bankers, and asset managers had done too often from 2004 to 2008. Assuming this condition is met, the portfolio of assets held by the SPV has to comply with three main conditions: bundling together (i) a large number of (ii) similar and (iii) uncorrelated assets.

12.1.1 Granularity: Pooling Together a Large Number of Assets

12.1.1.1 Number of Assets

Pooling together a large number of assets is the first duty of an arranger in a securitization. Doing so ensures that earnings of the SPV are adequately diversified and that consequences of the default of a single asset remain limited.

If there were not a large number of assets in the underlying portfolio, the default of any of these assets would have a material impact on the note holders. In an extreme scenario, if there were only two loans of equal size pulled together in an SPV, the default of any of these loans would translate into a default of half of the portfolio. Several categories of note holders – if not all of them – would immediately be affected, making the tranching of the securities completely useless. If mezzanine or senior tranche investors are exposed to the same type of losses as equity holders, why would tranches be created in the first place? All note holders would invest in the riskiest tranche, as they would obtain a much higher return for a similar risk.

12.1.1.2   Size of Assets

To achieve an optimal granularity of the portfolio, arrangers must also ensure that the assets posted as collateral are all roughly the same size. It is one thing to have a large number of assets, it is another to verify that none of them is overweight. If, for instance, there were 10,000 loans in a portfolio with one single asset representing 20% of the collateral, this would create issues for the holders of the most junior tranches. They would not benefit from a proper granularity.

12.1.1.3   Granularity and Statistical Approach

The granularity in a portfolio obviously varies depending on the type of assets used as collateral. The average size of each loan in an RMBS is extremely small compared to the size of the transaction. This is the same generally for all consumer ABS transactions (student loan ABS, auto ABS, credit card ABS). Investors cannot perform a credit analysis on each borrower. They have to rely on statistics to measure their risks. Granularity is therefore extremely important in these transactions. Pooling together a very large number of assets is key to ensuring that the behavior of the collateral will not be polluted by outliers.

Granularity exists in all types of securitization but investors cannot always adopt a statistical approach. CLOs have, for instance, a lower number of assets than an RMBS. For a $500-million deal, there may be only 50 or 60 names in the collateral. Investors must analyze them all or, at least, focus on the most problematic ones to assess the probability of default. This name-by-name analysis is especially important for the holders of the most junior tranches, who are exposed to the risk of first loss.[1]

12.1.2   Similarity: Pooling Together the Same Type of Assets

A successful securitization should also focus on financing a portfolio of similar assets. If an SPV pools together European mortgage loans, corporate loans to Brazilian SMEs, Japanese client receivables, and US student loans, the analysis of the collateral becomes complicated and may repel investors. The portfolio would be illiquid, as it could only be of interest for investors who are comfortable with all the asset types represented in the portfolio. In addition, this would create a logistical issue: servicers are specialized entities. They do not cover all asset types or all geographies.

Bundling together a large variety of assets may appear at first as a good way of mitigating risks taken by note holders. However, as mentioned before,[2] investors active in the securitization market usually choose to carry out their own asset allocation themselves. They would usually rather invest in two separate securitizations, for instance, one with mortgage loans and one with project finance loans, than choose a single transaction whose collateral would be composed equally of these two asset

---

[1] The same is true with aircraft ABS as there are generally only around 20 aircraft per deal.
[2] See section 11.4.1.1.

categories. This is easier for them to manage their risks and monitor their investments in securitization.

In addition, if an SPV set up for a securitization holds loans of any sort, of any amount, and in any possible currency it becomes de facto a sort of a mini bank. It is not the best way to attract investors, as they would always prefer shares or bonds issued by real banks. For the same level of risk their investment would be significantly more liquid. Real banks can also be recapitalized and lay claim to the benefits of bankruptcy law provisions (or even take advantage of government assistance as in the late 2000s).

12.1.3 Diversification: Pooling Together Uncorrelated Assets

12.1.3.1 Definition

Even though the arranger of a securitized transaction has to make sure that it pools together a portfolio of similar assets, it must also verify that they are not correlated (or at least not too much). If all the assets in the SPV are perfectly correlated, this means that the default of one of them inevitably causes the default of all the others. In other words, if the coefficient of correlation between all the assets is 1 or 100%, it means that all assets behave identically. If one of them is defaulting, it means that the others are defaulting as well. It would be as if the SPV were holding one single asset.

A level of correlation of 100% would be reached if, for instance, all the assets held by an SPV were bonds issued by the same corporation – for instance, a portfolio of 1,000,000 IBM bonds. Such a portfolio would meet criteria (i) of granularity (high number of assets) and (ii) of similarity (identical assets), but it would fail to deliver any level of comfort to the note holders. The tranching of the securities would once again not make sense.

12.1.3.2 Idiosyncratic and Systemic Risks

Another way – probably a more scientific one – of explaining the concept of diversification is to say that the perfect portfolio should expose the ABS or CLO holders to the intrinsic risk of each asset (known as *idiosyncratic* risk) but should avoid exposing them to any risk that would collectively affect at the same time all the assets of the entire portfolio (known as *systemic* risk). Systemic risk was a major contributor to the 2008 financial crisis, as a correction in the US real estate market triggered one of the most spectacular economic upheavals of all times.

Systemic risk can in all fairness probably not be fully eliminated from a portfolio of financial securities. All financial assets are correlated one way or another – especially if they have to be somehow similar. They can, for instance, be denominated in the same currency (in which case they will be subject to the decisions of the same central bank), originate from the same geography, or be used to finance related industry sectors. Having said that, it is possible to keep systemic risk under control by carefully selecting the assets in the portfolio and ensuring that the correlation between them is limited.

12.2   MANAGED TRANSACTIONS

12.2.1   Static and Managed Transactions

12.2.1.1   Static (or Balance Sheet) Transactions

To help readers better understand the main tenets of securitization, we have so far somewhat simplified the mechanics of this technique. We have considered that the starting point of a securitization is always the willingness of a bank or a company to transfer a portfolio of assets to third-party investors. In Chapter 11, section 11.2.2, we outlined three main reasons why an originator usually opts for securitization:

- to optimize its balance sheet from an accounting or regulatory perspective,
- to transfer risks, or
- to obtain cash.

In this scenario, securitization can be seen as a static type of transaction. The assets acquired by the SPV are held until maturity and may not be sold before that date. The SPV is on autopilot mode. It cannot buy or sell new assets. As soon as an asset matures, the cash generated by the repayment of the asset is used to redeem part of the principal of the notes. The amount of this redemption is equal to the value of the asset that has reached maturity, minus applicable fees. In this context, the maximum duration of a transaction is the period between the deal starting date and the due date of the asset with the longest maturity. Once all the assets in the collateral have been repaid, the SPV can be wound up. *Static* transactions are also known as *balance sheet* transactions, to highlight their impact on the balance sheet of the company or the bank (i.e. the originator) that transfers the assets to the SPV.

12.2.1.2   Managed (or Arbitrage) Transactions

The existence of static (or balance sheet) transactions should not hide the fact that many deals arranged today are *managed* (or arbitrage) securitizations. In these structures, the SPV holding the collateral is not on autopilot mode. It generally buys the assets directly on the market from various issuers and has the possibility of reinvesting the cash generated by the repayment of the assets that have matured. It can also, in some cases, sell assets before maturity and buy some others in the market.

While these managed transactions seem similar to static securitizations, the financial logic behind them is nonetheless different. Static transactions are indeed based on an originator-oriented model. The purpose behind them is to solve an issue that the originator is facing (the need to optimize its balance sheet, to generate cash, or to manage risk). In contrast, managed transactions can be perceived as investor-oriented solutions. They are set up with the main objective to offer new investment opportunities to investors. Under the supervision of a collateral manager, the SPV of an arbitrage transaction pools together a variety of assets acquired from different sources with the sole purpose of offering the best risk/reward mix to the note holders.

12.2.1.3 The Collateral Manager

Unlike balance sheet transactions, arbitrage deals are not initiated by originators. They are set up by specialized asset managers (also called *collateral* or *portfolio managers*). Collateral managers are no different from the companies managing private equity funds. Their role is to raise cash from various investors to invest in assets they have identified. The only difference is that instead of offering opportunities to acquire private companies, they allow investors to have access to portfolios of debt securities.[3]

The main duty of a collateral manager is to select the assets to be acquired by the SPV. Its role implies being connected to all major banks and brokers to ensure it is in the loop each time an asset of interest is available on the market. In parallel, the collateral manager must also follow the market very closely to identify windows of opportunities to sell assets that it wants to divest. Depending on the type of assets that can be purchased by the SPV, arbitrage transactions can be referred to as arbitrage CLOs or arbitrage CDOs.[4]

The assets pooled by the SPV are not purchased from one single seller only. They are bought by the collateral manager from different sources, on either (i) the primary market or (ii) the secondary market:

(i) The primary market is the market of new issues of bonds and loans. CLOs are extremely active in this segment, especially with leveraged loans and LBO loans. They can acquire assets underwritten by banks but can also take part in club deals.[5]

(ii) The secondary market is the market for vintage assets. In this case, CLOs buy bonds and loans that other investors want to divest. The sale is done through a broker. Major investment banks have large trading desks and provide liquidity for buyers and sellers.

Figure 12.1 is a simplified illustration of an arbitrage CDO.

---

[3]Some very large investment firms are active both in the private equity space and in the CLO markets. The two categories of funds are nonetheless managed by two different departments. The most active collateral managers include notably PIMCO, Carlyle, Blackstone, Goldman Sachs Asset Management, etc. These asset managers can also manage separate funds specialized in private debt (see Chapter 2, section 2.3.4).

[4]A reminder to readers that the terms CDO or CLO do not only refer to the type of notes issued by the companies set up to acquire the debt securities, but are also used by extension to designate the issuers themselves (i.e. the SPVs).

[5]More on syndication and club deals in Appendix B (Syndication and Club Deals).

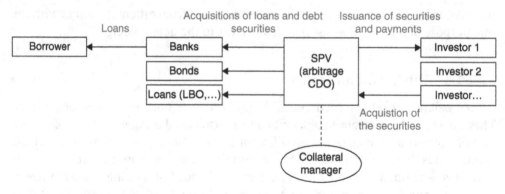

FIGURE 12.1   Concept of a Managed Securitization

12.2.1.4   The Investment Guidelines

The collateral manager has to manage the portfolio held by the SPV in compliance with the *investment guidelines* of the transaction. These investment guidelines can be seen as the road map of the collateral manager. They set out what the collateral manager is allowed to do, notably the types of assets he can sell or purchase. Given that the investment guidelines are designed by the collateral manager himself, they are to be seen as a sort of safeguard for investors. Having precise investment guidelines means that investors are not giving a blank check to the collateral manager. If a collateral manager was not to respect the investment guidelines of a transaction, it would be liable to investors.

There are three main concepts defining the investment guidelines: (i) the *eligibility criteria*, (ii) the *portfolio profile test*, and (iii) the *collateral quality tests*.

Eligibility Criteria

This factor defines the type of assets that the collateral manager is allowed to purchase on behalf of the issuer. It generally sets:

- the minimum rating of each eligible asset
- the currencies in which the eligible assets can be denominated
- the legal forms of the eligible assets: can it include leases? PIK loans? etc.
- the type of eligible asset that cannot be included in the collateral portfolio (e.g. project finance loan, sovereign bonds, etc.)
- the characteristics of the assets: can they be undrawn? what is their maximum or minimum legal maturity? etc.
- the maximum discount at which the eligible asset trades in the market; a collateral manager can, for instance, specify in the investment guidelines that it will not acquire loans or bonds that trade below 60% of their par value.

Portfolio Profile Test

This test specifies criteria for purchasing the assets that form the collateral. It is designed to ensure sufficient diversification of the reference portfolio. The portfolio profile test determines for each asset class, asset type and issuer a maximum and/or minimum limit that the SPV can hold. Table 12.1 gives an example of criteria taken from a real transaction (same transaction as the one described in Table 10.1, Chapter 10, section 10.2.12). These criteria may of course vary from one transaction to the other.

TABLE 12.1   Example of Portfolio Profile Test

Test	Limit
Senior secured loans	Min 85%
Second lien, senior unsecured loans, high-yield bonds	Max 15%
High-yield bonds	Max 10%
Zero-coupon bonds	Max 5%
Fixed-rate assets	Max 7.5%
PIK loans	Max 5%
Securities rated CCC+ or below	Max 10%
Issuer concentration	Max 2%
Industry concentration	Max 12%
Securities issued by issuers located outside the US	Max 20%
Securities issued by Canadian issuers	Max 15%
Securities issued by issuers from authorized European countries (per country)	Max 10%
Securities not denominated in US$	Max 15%

Collateral Quality Tests

These tests set a minimum level of quality criteria in the portfolio that the acquisition of new assets must not deteriorate: average rating, average life,[6] average spread, etc. These tests exist to ensure that the collateral manager maintains the average quality of the collateral portfolio over the life of the transaction, especially when an asset matures and is replaced by a new one. Given that rating agencies have their own collateral quality tests, investments guidelines usually import these tests. If the notes are rated by S&P, the tests of S&P will apply. If the notes are rated by two credit agencies, both series of quality tests must be satisfied.

---

[6]The average life of a loan (or a bond) is the average time until principal is repaid. The concept of average life is used to measure the risk associated with amortizing loans and bonds.

12.2.1.5   Shift from a Refinancing to a Financing Model

The investment rationale in a static or a managed transaction is quite different. In a static securitization (such as the Bowie Bonds, for instance), the quality of the underlying assets is central to the investment decision of the potential note holders. In an arbitrage transaction, the decision to invest in CDOs/CLOs is as much influenced by the kind of assets pooled in the portfolio as it is by the track record and reputation of the collateral manager. Investment guidelines – and more generally the whole documentation – are obviously a point of focus for potential investors, as they want to understand what the portfolio manager is allowed to do.

The emergence of managed transactions does change the nature of securitization. Whereas in a static model, securitization can be perceived as a mere refinancing tool, managed transactions are clearly offering direct financing solutions to borrowers. CLOs are active in the primary market and can lend to corporates, purchase bonds, or take part in LBOs without intermediaries.

The shift from a refinancing to a financing model changes the weight of securitization in financial markets. Today, CLOs represent, for instance, over 50% of the investor base in the leverage loan market. Having CLOs actively chasing investment opportunities means that there is more liquidity and more debt solutions available. If CLOs were not able to buy assets in the primary market directly, it would mean that banks would have to first underwrite these assets, sit on them, and bundle them together to sell them at a later stage to CLOs. It would be less efficient and consequently reduce the amount of liquidity available in the market via CLOs. We sum up in Table 12.2 the differences and similarities between static and managed transactions.

12.2.1.6   Could We Say That CLOs are Mini-banks?

In a way – and readers would probably have already thought about it by now – active CLOs could almost be viewed as small-sized banks. The way they operate is very similar as they provide loans and other type of debt securities to a wide range of counterparties. Their balance sheet is also comparable: they finance the acquisition of assets with a mix of debt and equity.

Payments available for equity holders in an active CLO are the difference between (i) the spread on the collateral and (ii) the cost of debt (senior and mezzanine), the management fees, and the various administrative fees.[7] This paradigm is no different from what can be found in banks where shareholders get paid the difference between revenues (mostly interest on loans and fees) and costs (financing costs and overheads).

In a simplified way, the economics of the equity tranche in a CLO work as follows:

+ Collateral Spread
− Cost of Debt (Senior and Mezzanine)
− Management Fees

---

[7] They include legal and accounting costs, payments to the servicer and the trustee.

– Admin Costs

= Equity Excess Spread

Assuming (i) the collateral earns 425bps over LIBOR, (ii) the cost of debt is LIBOR plus 200 bps, (iii) a 50bps management fee, (iv) and 5bps of other costs annually, the excess spread to equity would be 170bps per annum ($425 - 200 - 50 - 5 = 170$). If the equity is 10 times levered, the potential equity return would be 17%.

TABLE 12.2 Comparison of Static and Managed Transactions

	Static Transaction	Managed Transaction
Origin of assets	The assets are acquired by the SPV from a single originator	The assets are acquired in the secondary market from different originators (via brokers) and/or directly in the primary loan or bond markets
Type of assets	Theoretically, any type of asset generating regular cash flows	Mainly debt securities (loans or bonds)
Similarity of assets constituting the underlying portfolio	Yes	Yes
Transaction management	Passive	Active: when an asset matures, the collateral manager in charge of managing the assets of the issuer can acquire new assets The collateral manager may also have the right to freely sell and purchase assets
Duration	Defined in advance in the by-laws of the issuer: it is somehow based on the life-span of the SPV's assets	Defined in advance: it is mentioned in the investment guidelines applicable to the transaction
Criteria underlying the decision to buy ABS/CDOs	Quality of assets of the SPV	Quality of assets of the SPV at the time of buying the securities Track record/performance of the collateral manage Investment guidelines of the SPV
Focus of the transaction	Refinancing the assets of the originator Investment opportunities for institutional or alternative investors	Direct financing of the economy by non-banking players

There are, however notable differences between a bank – even a small one – and a CLO. A bank is a real company with a brand, manpower, and real assets. It is also an entity that is heavily regulated. A bank has to develop a strategy that must be approved by shareholders and that requires regular investments (in people, IT, real estate, etc.). Unlike CLOs' investment guidelines, this strategy can evolve over time. In addition, a bank is engaged in a variety of businesses that go beyond mere lending: cash management, credit cards, wealth management, M&A, debt and rating advisory, equity and debt capital markets, etc. A bank also offers a wide variety of loans, while we have seen that CLOs tend to focus on portfolios of similar assets. In sum, CLOs are not mini-banks, they are only an investment conduit that allows investors to invest in a diversified pool of loans and debt securities.

12.2.1.7   Remuneration of the Collateral Manager

The collateral manager receives a remuneration that is based on the performance of the securitization. The following fees are usually paid:

- *Administrative fees*: these fees are minimal and are senior to any interest payment. They are paid on each interest payment date.
- *Subordinated management fees*: these are paid on each interest payment date provided that interest on the various classes of rated notes have been paid.
- *Incentive fees*: which are payable on each interest payment date provided that the return of the equity holders reaches a pre-agreed level (12% for instance);
- *Additional incentives fees*: if the amount distributed to equity investors exceeds a predetermined level, the collateral manager generally receives a given percentage of the amount exceeding this level (20% above 15% for instance).

12.2.2   The Three Phases of a Managed Transaction

The lifecycle of an arbitrage transaction is usually divided into three phases:

- the ramp-up period
- the reinvestment period
- the post-reinvestment period.

Transactions last generally between 10 and 15 years, depending on the CLO's manager strategy and what is included in the investment guidelines.

12.2.2.1   Ramp-up Period

The ramp-up period is the initial phase of the life of the CLO. It includes in itself two sub-periods: (i) the warehouse period (which can also be divided into two phases: pre-pricing and post-pricing) and (ii) the first weeks of the transaction post-closing.

Warehouse Period (Pre-pricing)

The objective of this phase is to prepare the transaction, start building up the collateral and identify investors. The portfolio manager mandates a bank to arrange the deal and prepares all the steps necessary to launch the CLO: establishment of the SPV, selection of the law firm, servicer and trustee, drafting of the investment guidelines, etc.

As arranger of the transaction, the bank provides a loan (*warehouse facility*) to the collateral manager so that it can acquire loans in the primary and secondary market. The goal is generally to reach 50% of the targeted CLO size before pricing the deal, i.e. setting the margin of the debt tranches.

The warehouse facility is sized according to the advanced rate[8] that the bank is willing to offer. This rate is generally equal to 80% but depends obviously on the bank's decision and market conditions at the time of the transaction. Assuming a $500-million CLO, the structure usually looks as follows at the end of this phase:

- The deal has reached 50% of its targeted size, meaning that the value of the collateral is $250 million.
- It is financed by a warehouse facility of $200 million provided by the bank and a $50 million first loss investment from the collateral manager or third-party investors.

The role of the bank is key during this phase. Not only does it provide the warehouse facility and identifies assets for the collateral but it also markets the CLO to potential debt investors. The bank must indeed secure enough commitments from investors to launch the deal. Once the commitment of investors reaches 100% of the targeted deal size, the transaction is priced. At this stage, investors are not drawn. They do not finance the deal yet. They have only committed to do so.

Warehouse Period (Post-pricing and Pre-closing)

Once the transaction is priced and the investors committed, the bank can increase the size of the warehouse facility to allow the portfolio manager to buy additional collateral. The bank has no more execution risk at this stage and is hedged by the investors' commitments. It can therefore increase its advance rate. The amount of the equity tranche remains unchanged.

When the collateral reaches around 75% of the CLO targeted size (or more, depending on the deal), the transaction closes: notes are issued and the warehouse facility provided by the bank is repaid. This phase lasts around six weeks. At this stage, the transaction has reached its full size ($450 million of debt and $50 million of equity) but part of the funds deployed by investors is still in the form of cash.

Post-closing Phase

After the closing, the ramp-up period continues. The portfolio manager uses the cash available in the SPV to purchase additional collateral. Once the value of the collateral

---

[8]The advance rate is the value of a loan that a bank is willing to offer as percentage of a given collateral.

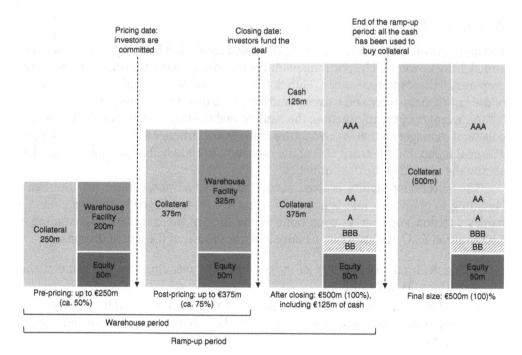

FIGURE 12.2   Example of a Ramp-up Period of a €500-million Arbitrage CLO

reaches the CLO target size, the ramp-up period is over. Figure 12.2 represents the various stages of a CLO ramp-up period.

12.2.2.2   Reinvestment Period

This period starts once the collateral of the transaction has reached its targeted size. During this phase, the collateral manager is usually free to manage the portfolio and buy new assets with the cash coming from the repayment of the loans that have matured. If this is permitted by the investment guidelines, the collateral manager can also sell some assets before they are due and buy others to replace them. In any case, the purchase of new collateral has to comply with the eligibility criteria, the portfolio tests, and the collateral tests as defined in the investment guidelines (see section 12.2.1.4). Depending on the CLO, this period can last between one and five years (but generally four to five).

12.2.2.3   Post-reinvestment Period

After the reinvestment period, the transaction enters the post-reinvestment period, a phase during which the collateral manager can no longer acquire new collateral. This period marks the end of the transaction. If, during this phase, an underlying asset matures, the amount is used to redeem the notes issued by the SPV, giving priority to the AAA tranche.

If some assets have not yet matured when the transaction reaches its term, they are liquidated and investors are paid what they are due, starting again with the most

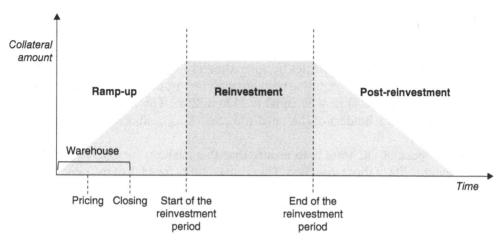

FIGURE 12.3 CLO Lifecycle

senior tranche. The excess cash available after repayment of the senior and mezzanine tranches, if any, is distributed to equity investors in its entirety. In case of shortfall equity investors receive nothing, and the next in line, the BB holders, can be affected. Figure 12.3 summarizes the lifecycle of a CLO in which collaterals are purchased, managed, and redeemed.

12.3 ADDITIONAL STRUCTURING CONSIDERATIONS

Readers have probably by now gained a good understanding of how securitization works. This is, however, a complex legal structure and a lot can be added. This section contains three sets of additional information on the topic. They are not key to understanding the main tenets of securitization but can be of interest for a motivated reader. First, we will discover the mechanisms that protect investors over the life of a transaction; second, we will describe some of the specific features that can be included in CLO and CDO structures; and finally, we will explain how lesser known deal types are structured: aircraft ABS, credit card ABS, whole business securitization, etc.

12.3.1 Coverage Tests

Coverage tests are an important element of comfort for investors in a securitization. Periodic interest proceeds (usually paid quarterly) are distributed to investors based on the outcome of these tests. In other words, interest cannot be paid to investors if these coverage tests are not met. The most common coverage tests – described in the deal documentation – are the *Overcollateralization* (OC) and *Interest Coverage* (IC) tests.

12.3.1.1 OC Test

OC of the debt tranches is a common feature in securitization. Its objective is to ensure that holders of the senior and mezzanine tranches are not directly impacted by defaults in the reference portfolio. It is an important structural protection granted to the debt investors.

The principal of the underlying pool of assets is generally greater than the principal amount of the rated securities by approximately 5% to 20%. The principal debt amount of the senior and mezzanine tranches may, for instance, be $100 million, while the value of the collateral may be equal to $120 million. The $20-million cushion is meant to protect the holders of the rated tranches. This cushion is financed via the equity tranche.

The purpose of OC tests is to ensure that this cushion (or OC) is maintained throughout the life of the transaction. There are OC tests for each of the rated tranches but there is no OC test for the equity tranche.

An OC test is calculated as follows:

$$\frac{\text{Principal amount of performing assets}}{(\text{principal amount of the respective class of notes} + \text{principal amount of the classes senior to the respective class})}$$

If an OC test for a tranche is not met (due to defaults in the collateral), payment of interest for this tranche cannot be made. Cash flow must be diverted from the most junior tranches to repay part of the most senior tranche and buy additional collateral. Once the minimum OC test set for this tranche has been restored, interest payment can take place.

12.3.1.2 IC Test

The IC test is another measure to protect senior and mezzanine note holders in the event of a reduction in the cash flows produced by the collateral. The IC ratio is calculated as the proceeds from interest payments on the collateral over a given period divided by the interest payments due on the deal's notes over the same period (see Table 12.4). The IC test is passed if the IC ratio exceeds a predefined level.

If a deal starts to fail its IC test, cash flows are diverted from more junior classes of notes to pay down the liabilities in order of seniority until the deal is back in compliance with the test. The IC test is in essence very similar to the OC test.

There are IC tests for each of the rated tranches but there is no IC test for the equity tranche. An IC test is calculated as follows:

$$\frac{\text{Interests perceived from the collateral}}{(\text{interest due on the respective class of notes} + \text{interest due the classes senior to the respective class})}$$

Figure 12.4 represents how the OC and IC work in a CLO. We have simplified the diagram and included only one test for the mezzanine tranche while there is in fact one OC and one IC test for each class of notes, except the equity tranche.

12.3.1.3 Importance of Tests in the Rating of Securities

Predetermined levels of OC and IC are not the only tests that the SPV has to comply with. There are several other tests that notably ensure that the new assets acquired

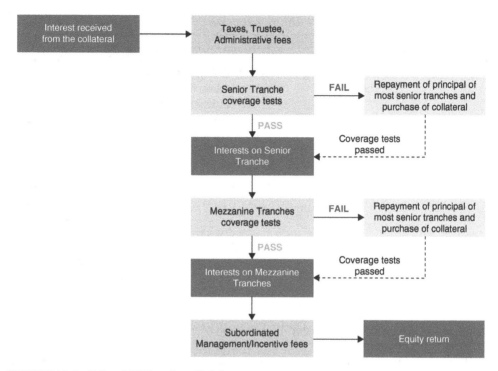

FIGURE 12.4   OC and IC Tests in a CLO Structure

by the collateral manager comply with the investment guidelines: these are the portfolio profile tests and collateral quality tests mentioned earlier in section 12.2.1.4 on investment guidelines.

These tests protect the investors but are also important for rating agencies. The continuous breach of a test can lead to a downgrade of the notes issued by the SPV. Table 12.3 gives an overview of the various tests that rating agencies look at when rating a securitization.

12.3.2   Other Specific Features of the Documentation

We have probably covered at this stage the most important features of the documentation of a securitization. Some other less important elements may nonetheless sometimes be included in a deal. They are not to be found in every transaction but are sufficiently common to be briefly mentioned here. Some of these features are favorable to equity holders, some to debt holders. Their inclusion depends on market trends, deal structure, and targeted collateral.

12.3.2.1   Call Option

Some managed transactions include a call option on the collateral for equity holders. The exercise of the call option triggers the termination of the transaction. The

TABLE 12.3   Tests Expected by Rating Agencies

	Coverage Tests	Portfolio Profile Tests	Collateral Quality Tests
Objective	Identify deteriorating collateral	Specify criteria for purchasing new assets (designed to ensure sufficient diversification of the reference portfolio)	Specify criteria for purchasing new assets (designed to maintain collateral characteristics)
Examples	OC and IC tests	Diversification of the portfolio is assessed based on country, industry, asset class, rating, currency, etc.	Collateral quality tests set a minimum level of quality criteria in the portfolio that the acquisition of new assets should not deteriorate (average rating, average life, average spread, etc.)
Impact on CLO or CDO if test is breached	Cash flows are diverted from the equity tranche (and possibly other tranches) Pay-down notes according to priority order Reduction of trading flexibility	Reduction of trading flexibility Each new trade should maintain or improve the breached test	Reduction of trading flexibility Each new trade should maintain or improve the breached test

collateral is sold by the portfolio manager and proceeds are used to repay the note holders, starting with the most senior tranche. Equity investors receive the sale proceeds available after repayment of the rated tranches.

A call option is a feature favorable to equity holders. It allows them to crystallize a gain if the transaction is doing extremely well. A call option is only exercised if the value of the collateral is greater than the investment originally made by investors. This can be the case when the portfolio manager has been extremely successful in managing the collateral. Let us take an example.

When a CDO receives an investment of $100 million (including $10 million of equity) it can acquire collateral for a total value of $100 million. If the portfolio manager believes that some assets are mispriced, it can buy them with a strong discount. When a bond trades at 20, for instance, it means that a bond originally issued at $100 is now worth only $20 on the market. This generally means that the company that has issued the bond has been severely downgraded by rating agencies.

However, whatever the rating or the value of the bond, the issuer is still legally obliged to pay back at maturity the amount borrowed originally. If the company does not default, bond holders will receive $100. A buyer that has acquired the bond for $20 makes a profit of $80.

The portfolio manager can invest (in theory at least, and subject to investment guidelines) the totality of the $100 million to buy assets that are severely downgraded. If these loans and bonds do not default, the value of the collateral increases significantly. It is therefore possible for a collateral manager to build a portfolio of bonds and loans trading all at 20. If none of them default, the CDO gets paid $500 million when the assets mature. The value of the equity is in this case equal to $410 million, i.e. the value of the collateral less the value of the senior debt and the mezzanine. If there is a call option in the deal, the equity investors should exercise it. They would make an immediate profit of $400 million. The example is obviously extreme but shows the value a call option can have for an equity holder.[9]

A call option is only exercisable if some criteria are met (OC and IC tests amongst others) so that the interests of the debt holders are preserved. The assets in the reference portfolio sold in case of exercise of the call option are typically ultimately purchased by CLOs that are still in their ramp-up or reinvestment periods.

A call option – if it exists – can also only be exercised after a predefined period, usually two years when the reinvestment period is comprised of between four or five years and one year when the reinvestment period is comprised of between one and three years. This is meant to protect the holders of the rated tranche and offer them at least some yield for a minimal period.

12.3.2.2 Turbo Tranche

In some cases, the documentation can specify that the most junior tranche of debt (generally rated BB) is a *turbo* tranche. This mechanism means that this tranche amortizes partially when the senior tranche does.

Turbo features are activated in two cases:

– At the end of the transaction: the collateral is sold by the portfolio manager to repay the note holders by order of seniority. If the deal includes a turbo tranche, a portion of the most junior tranche of debt is repaid in parallel to the most senior tranche.
– During the life of the transaction: if the OC or IC tests are not satisfied, the early repayment of the most senior tranche triggers also a partial repayment of the most junior debt tranche (see the earlier comments on OC and IC tests).

---

[9]This example is exaggerated but shows why an equity holder would choose to exercise a call option. In a real transaction, it would not be possible to buy only assets trading at 20 as it would probably go against the eligibility criteria or the portfolio profile test set in the investment guidelines. This extreme example shows, however, the value of having a top-notch portfolio manager.

A turbo feature is a counterintuitive structural element as it goes against the traditional waterfall principle. As a matter of fact, the most junior tranche is partially repaid before tranches that are more senior. A turbo structure is a form of protection for the holders of the most junior tranche of debt. It may be an element needed in a deal to ensure that this tranche obtains a given credit rating. Without a turbo feature, rating agencies could, for instance, assign an extremely low rating to this tranche or assume that there is no real difference in terms of risk between this tranche and the equity tranche.

12.3.2.3 Fixed-rate Tranches

While most CLO debt tranches are floating-rate and indexed to LIBOR (see Table 10.1 in Chapter 10, section 10.2.1.2, for instance), fixed-rate tranches are sometimes included in some structures. In many cases, these fixed-rate tranches are issued *pari passu* to some other floating-rate notes. The main difference is that they pay a fixed coupon at each payment period. These fixed-rate tranches are used to serve the needs of specific investors who want exposure to CLOs but prefer fixed-rate products (e.g. many insurance companies). Table 12.4 shows the tranching of a euro CLO that includes fixed-rate notes. The two fixed-rate tranches of this CLO (A-2 and D-2) rank *pari passu* with floating-rate notes (respectively A-1 and D-1) in the order of distribution of profits.

TABLE 12.4 Tranching of a €411-million Securitization Including Fixed-rate Tranches

Name of the Securities	Amount in €	Rate of Interest Applicable to the Tranche	Order of Distribution of Profits	Credit Rating Fitch	Credit Rating Moody's
Class A-1	216,000,000	Euribor 3m+0.96%	1	AAA	Aaa
Class A-2	30,000,000	1.50%	1	AAA	Aaa
Class B	41,000,000	Euribor 3m+1.80%	2	AA	Aa2
Class C	22,000,000	Euribor 3m+2.40%	3	A	A2
Class D-1	17,000,000	Euribor 3m+3.50%	4	BBB	Baa2
Class D-2	25,000,000	4.30%	4	BBB	Baa2
Class E	26,500,000	Euribor 3m+5.66%	5	BB	Ba2
Class F	11,500,000	Euribor 3m+7.21%	6	B	B2
Sub. Notes	42,000,000	Not applicable	7	Not rated	Not rated
Total	**411,000,000**				

12.3.3   Other Types of Securitization

12.3.3.1   Student Loans ABS (or SLABS)

Student loans form an important asset class in the securitization market. In the United States, the high level of tuition fees in universities mean that most students borrow money to finance their degrees. These loans are generally seized based on the expected future revenues of the borrower after graduation. All things being equal, it is easier to borrow money to finance an MBA program in an Ivy League university that an unknown degree in a sub-standard school.

Student loans usually include a grace period of several years due to the fact that borrowers are only expected to be able to repay their loans once they graduate and have a job. The repayment period starts in most cases six months to one year after the expected graduation. These loans are generally flexible, meaning that the grace period can be extended if the borrower decides to study for a longer period than originally planned.

Given the high number of student loans issued every year in the United States, it is no wonder that they have been a popular asset class for ABS investors. It is relatively easy to bundle them together and to structure a highly diversified portfolio of non-correlated and standardized assets. If the structuring bank pays sufficient attention to the quality of the borrowers, their geographical dispersion and the programs the students have chosen, the notes issued to refinance the portfolio of loans can achieve the level of credit ratings expected by investors.

In the United States, SLM Corporation (commonly known as Sallie Mae), a former government entity that is now publicly traded, is the largest lender of student loans and the main issuer of SLABS. Table 12.5 indicates details of the various securitization programs issued by SLM from 2014 to 2017.

12.3.3.2   Aircraft ABS

Aircraft ABS provide operating lessors with the opportunity to finance large portfolios of commercial aircraft with attractive debt pricing. As explained in Chapter 8, section 8.3.3.1, aircraft ABS are very common in the leasing industry. GPA was already using this instrument in the 1990s (see case study 8).

In an aircraft ABS, an operating lessor sells to a bankruptcy remote SPV a large number of aircraft (usually 15 to 25) leased to various airlines.[10] The collateral must be, in theory, as diversified as possible in terms of lessees, country of origin, aircraft type, etc. The SPV finances the acquisition of the portfolio through the issuance of a mix of rated and subordinated notes. There are generally two to three rated tranches

---

[10]But this can obviously be more, as shown in the GPA case study (222 aircraft). That said, the market has evolved since the 1990s and the GPA securitization deal. Transactions tend now to be smaller and executed more rapidly.

TABLE 12.5 Statistical Information on Securitized Pools of Sallie Mae Education Loans

	2014-A	2015-A	2015-B	2015-C	2016-A	2016-B	2016-C	2017-A
Dates								
Issue date	Jul.2014	Apr.2015	Jul.2015	Oct.2015	Apr.2016	Jul.2016	Oct.2016	Feb.2017
Balance (in $m)								
Principal balance	368	717	717	700	594	708	704	819
Capitalized interest	15	34	41	53	28	39	41	45
Pool balance	383	751	758	753	622	747	745	864
Loans & Borrowers								
Number of loans	34,253	68,117	65,540	65,494	54,409	64,331	63,952	76,957
Avg. outstanding principal balance	11,196	11,052	11,572	11,509	11,453	11,621	11,668	11,236
Numbers of borrowers	26,651	44,031	43,918	45,614	52,283	61,393	60,942	72,943
Average borrower indebtedness	14,389	17,097	17,269	16,525	11,919	12,177	12,244	11,854
Borrower / co-borrower								
Co-borrower	92.6%	92.0%	91.7%	92.4%	91.9%	91.7%	92.1%	91.9%
Borrower	7.4%	8.0%	8.3%	7.6%	8.1%	8.3%	7.9%	8.1%
	100%	100%	100%	100%	100%	100%	100%	100%
Borrower status								
In-School	73.8%	67.5%	63.2%	51.0%	63.7%	56.7%	48.5%	51.6%
Grace	14.8%	8.9%	11.5%	18.1%	8.0%	13.5%	17.5%	8.7%
Deferment	1.8%	2.5%	3.1%	4.3%	3.5%	3.5%	3.9%	4.6%
P&I Repayment	9.4%	19.5%	20.8%	24.1%	23.2%	24.5%	28.1%	32.9%
Forbearance	0.2%	1.6%	1.4%	2.5%	1.6%	1.8%	2.0%	2.2%
	100%	100%	100%	100%	100%	100%	100%	100%

Index								
LIBOR	85%	82%	82%	82%	82%	82%	80%	81%
Fixed rate	15%	18%	18%	18%	18%	18%	20%	19%
	100%	100%	100%	100%	100%	100%	100%	100%
Weighted average interest rate								
LIBOR	7.54%	7.87%	7.85%	7.93%	7.91%	7.92%	7.91%	8.08%
Fixed rate	9.44%	9.79%	9.82%	9.83%	9.66%	9.68%	9.67%	9.71%
	7.82%	8.21%	8.21%	8.27%	8.22%	8.24%	8.26%	8.39%
School type								
4-y institution	96.9%	94.4%	94.6%	95.3%	94.8%	95.0%	94.8%	94.5%
2-y institution	2.7%	4.3%	4.3%	3.8%	3.9%	3.7%	3.8%	3.7%
Proprietary/vocational	0.4%	1.3%	1.1%	0.9%	1.3%	1.3%	1.4%	1.8%
	100%	100%	100%	100%	100%	100%	100%	100%
Origination vintage								
2009	0.1%	2.2%	—	—	—	—	—	—
2010	5.7%	2.2%	2.3%	1.1%	1.1%	1.1%	1.1%	1.0%
2011	8.6%	9.3%	9.2%	15.1%	4.5%	4.4%	4.1%	3.6%
2012	16.7%	19.7%	18.4%	24.3%	9.8%	10.1%	9.6%	8.2%
2013	61.9%	32.6%	31.4%	33.2%	17.1%	17.6%	17.7%	15.3%
2014	7.0%	36.2%	38.9%	26.3%	28.3%	29.0%	30.6%	25.2%
2015	—	—	—	—	39.2%	37.7%	36.9%	36.8%
2016	—	—	—	—	—	—	—	9.8%
2017	—	—	—	—	—	—	—	—
	100%	100%	100%	100%	100%	100%	100%	100%

Source: Sallie Mae.

(called, by order of seniority, tranche A, B, and C – if any). The subordinated notes are usually referred to as E-notes.

The operating lessor generally acquires a portion of the equity. There are even cases where the operating lessor commits to hold a certain percentage of the equity until it is repaid (a documentation feature called *equity lock-up*). Our reader will note that aircraft ABS are another type of securitization where the originator can act as investor – this time, the investment is done at equity level.

The management of the aircraft portfolio is outsourced by the SPV to a company recognized and experienced in the management and remarketing of aircraft (i.e. the *servicer*). The servicer is usually the operating lessor itself. The role of the servicer is to provide aircraft and lease management and remarketing services for the aircraft portfolio. Subject to a limited universe of actions that require the SPV's board approval, the day-to-day decision-making regarding the aircraft portfolio is managed exclusively by the servicer.

If an airline to which an aircraft is leased defaults, the servicer is responsible for repossessing the asset, finding a new lessee, reconfiguring the aircraft (i.e. changing the seats, the livery, etc.) and passing it to the new client. It is also in charge of remarketing an aircraft when a lease comes to term.

Subject to the deal's investment guidelines, the servicer acting on behalf of the SPV can be given some flexibility to trade assets. The servicer's experience and reputation in the active management of aircraft is therefore a key component of the credit rating given by rating agencies. Table 12.6 shows the list of ABS deals issued in 2018. The transactions mentioned in this list include the first all cargo deal (with Vx Capital, on 35 freighters) and an all engine transaction (with Willis Lease).

The total value of aircraft ABS issued in 2018 compared to the total value of unsecured bonds issued the same year by operating lessors (see Table 8.9 in Chapter 8, section 8.3.2.1) shows the key role played by aircraft ABS in the financing of the aircraft leasing industry. Although aircraft ABS are a much more complex financing instrument than bonds, they account for roughly half of the size of unsecured bond funding ($6.1 billion vs. $13.3 billion). This demonstrates the value that securitization brings to lessors.

12.3.3.3   Auto ABS

Auto ABS are a form of ABS backed by a portfolio of leases or secured consumer loans used to finance new and used car purchases. Table 12.7 indicates the various types of assets that can be included in a typical auto ABS. These receivables carry a fixed interest rate and are usually originated for 36-, 48-, or 60-month terms, rarely longer. Clients can be individuals or households – but also SMEs, large companies, or governments, especially for leasing. The spectrum of credit profiles is consequently very broad.

Auto loans and leases can be originated:

- by the manufacturers themselves, through their in-house banks (called *captive finance companies*),

TABLE 12.6   Aircraft ABS Issued in 2018 (Excluding Equity Tranche)

Issue Date	Tranches	Amounts ($m)	Coupon (%)	Servicer	Average Asset Age	Average Lease Term
14 March	A	633	4.250	Avolon	9.7	5.0
	B	97	6.000			
	C	38	7.500			
26 April	A	352	3.800	Apollo Aviation	14.1	4.1
	B	59	5.437			
	C	32	6.143			
26 April	A	415	4.212	Merx Aviation	9.0	4.5
	B	55	5.193			
	C	37	6.413			
7 June	A	731	4.125	Castlelake	4.5	12.2
	B	115	5.300			
	C	66	6.625			
26 June	A	430	4.089	GECAS	8.0	4.2
	B	120	5.315			
	C	37	6.899			
19 July	A	375	4.147	Air Lease	8.0	4.7
	B	75	5.071			
18 Aug.	A	327	4.750	Willis Lease	NA	1.0
	B	47	5.438			
28 Sept.	A	337	4.610	Zephyrus Aviation Capital	12.9	3.1
1 Nov.	A	488	4.454	Apollo Aviation	13.9	3.6
	B	73	5.433			
	C	51	6.892			
20 Nov.	A	476	4.458	BBAM	9.8	3.4
	B	91	5.270			
	C	45	6.657			
20 Nov.	A	139	5.438	Vx Capital	23.1	4.3
	B	36	6.535			
	C	15	8.747			
11 Dec.	A	320	4.250	DAE Capital	8.9	4.5
	B	60	5.500			
Total		**6,171**				

Source: FlightGlobal.

TABLE 12.7   Types of Assets Pulled Together in Auto ABS

	Prime Auto Loans	Near-Prime Auto Loans	SubPrime Auto Loans	Auto Leases
Asset Type	Fully amortizing loan	Fully amortizing loan	Fully amortizing loan	Closed-end lease[10]
Car type	Predominantly new	Predominantly used	Predominantly used	New
Borrower credit	Excellent	Fair	Poor	Excellent
Coupon	+	++	+++	+
Originator	Captives, banks	Specialty finance companies, banks	Specialty finance companies, banks	Captives, banks or specialty finance companies

Source: JP Morgan.

- by banks, usually through their consumer finance division, or
- by specialty finance companies; these companies can be publicly listed companies like Element Fleet, subsidiaries of banks (Arval, a BNP Paribas subsidiary), or owned by private equity firms (LeasePlan, Fraikin).

12.3.3.4   Credit Card ABS

Credit card ABS refer to transactions in which the proceeds of the notes issued by an SPV are used to purchase credit card receivables. Credit card issuers (i.e. banks) take the credit card receivables of some customers and spin it off from the clients' accounts (referred to as the *designated accounts*). The bank retains ownership of the clients' accounts but sells the receivables to a SPV. The first Credit card ABS was structured in 1987.

Credit card securitizations differ from other ABS transactions for three main reasons:

1. The first specificity is that the credit card receivables have a relatively short life (generally between one and three months), while the notes issued typically have three-, five-, or ten-year maturities. As a result of this maturity mismatch, credit card ABS are structured in two different periods: (i) a *revolving period* and (ii) a *controlled amortization period* (or, more frequently, a *controlled accumulation period*).

---

[11] A closed end lease is a rental agreement that puts no obligation on the lessee to purchase the asset at the end of the agreement.

During the *revolving period*, ABS investors receive interest only. These interests are financed by the interest paid by the cardholders when they repay their debt. Repayments of principal made by the cardholders are used by the SPV to buy new receivables generated by the designated accounts. Cardholders use their credit cards regularly. As such, they constantly generate new credit card receivables. When these receivables are repaid at the end of each month, the proceeds of these repayments are used to purchase the receivables arising the following month. This first phase usually lasts for a period equal to the maturity of the notes less one year, when the *controlled amortization period* or the *controlled accumulation period* starts.

During the *controlled amortization* period, the principal collections are used to pay down the outstanding principal amount of the notes. This controlled amortization period takes roughly up to one year. Alternatively, if the *controlled accumulation* method has been chosen, the principal payments collected are deposited in a separate account and reinvested in short-term risk-free investments. These short-term investments become the collateral for the notes and increase as principal payments are received from the cardholders. When the total amount of these investments is equal to the amount due from the SPV to the noteholders, the short-term risk-free investments are sold and the proceeds are used to make a unique bullet payment to all investors. Most credit card ABS are structured using controlled accumulation and bullet payments.

2. The second complexity of credit card ABS is that due to cardholders' seasonal spending patterns, the total value of the receivables owned by the SPV during the revolving period varies greatly over time. To absorb these fluctuations, credit card ABS structures include an investment from the seller – called *seller's interest* – at SPV level. This seller's interest exists to ensure that there will be sufficient collateral available to support the amounts due to investors under the notes.

3. The third specificity of credit card ABS is that rather than setting up a new SPV for each deal, most banks or credit card companies use a single entity (master trust) for multiple issues. A master trust allows for various securitization programs to be included over time. Each new series of notes is identified by a specific issue date and has a specific maturity. All series are, however, collectively backed by the pool of credit card receivables held in the master trust. This structure is attractive to issuers as it is cheaper than to set up an SPV for each new transaction. Investors benefit as well from the structure as it means that the pool of assets gets more diversified over time.

Figure 12.5 shows a simplified credit card ABS structure.

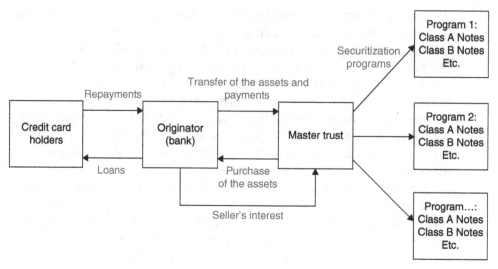

FIGURE 12.5 Simplified Diagram of a Credit Card ABS

Case Study 13: Whole Business Securitization

Whole Business Securitization (WBS) is a strange animal in the securitization world. It is a hybrid type of financing that sits somewhere between traditional securitization – where only a part of a company's assets such as loans or receivables are securitized – and secured corporate bonds, i.e. traditional bonds that are secured by a pledge on some of the company's assets.

The Specific Case of WBS

A WBS is a type of securitization backed by cash flows generated by a *business* more than by *assets* (hence the term *whole business*). The originator sells its cash flow generating assets to an SPV, which in turn finances the acquisition of these assets by the issuance of various tranches of notes. In most cases, the originator is required to (at least partially) fund the junior tranche.

The primarily purpose of a WBS is to achieve a better credit rating than the rating attached to the company's corporate debt. One of the most highly publicized transaction using WBS was the $1.7-billion franchise and trademark royalties securitization closed in 2006 for Dunkin' Brands Group, the parent company of US restaurant chains Dunkin' Donuts and Baskin-Robbins. The deal was implemented to refinance the LBO loan incurred when private equity firms Bain Capital, Carlyle and THL took over Dunkin' Brands Group the year before.

The refinancing of the LBO loan through a franchise securitization allowed the company to access the debt market with a dual tranche WBS rated Aaa for the senior tranche and Ba3 for the junior tranche. This was a significant improvement compare to the direct corporate debt of Dunkin' Brands Group which was rated B- at that time.

The rating uplift above the company's unsecured corporate credit rating was made possible because the note holders were directly exposed to the asset generating cash flows of the company. The royalty payments due from the franchisees did not transit via Dunkin' Brands Group. They flew directly to the SPV, offering a higher level of comfort to the lenders. To put it simply, note holders were, from a credit perspective, exposed to ability of the franchise system to generate cash flow and not to the profitability of Dunkin' Brands Group. The situation was all the more comfortable because, under a franchise system, franchisees pay a fixed percentage of store sale, not profits, therefore removing the risk of decreasing franchisee operating margins.

The result of this rating uplift was a dramatic reduction in borrowing costs for the company, estimated at $35 million per year. Following its IPO in 2011, Dunkin' Brands has continued to successfully raise financing through WBS (lately in 2015 and 2017). Figure 12.6 represents a simplified version of a standard WBS.

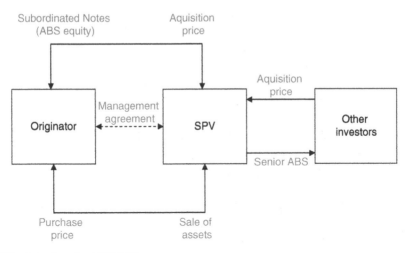

FIGURE 12.6   Standard WBS Diagram

The Interest of WBS

WBS is powerful financing tool for companies with stable and predictable cash flows operating in mature industries. The ideal candidate for a WBS is a company with a combination of (i) utility or utility-like characteristics (i.e. generating stable and steady cash flows), (ii) which has a strong underlying real assets element, essentially in the form of real estate or other fixed assets, (iii) which operates in

(continued)

(*continued*)

a market with high barriers to entry, and (iv) in which fundamental changes are expected to be limited.

Besides Dunkin' Brands, examples of WBS include a number of well-known US restaurant concepts: Domino's Pizza, Taco Bell, Sonic Drive-In, IHOP, Applebee's, and Wendy's. Due to the fact that these companies operate via a franchise system, they have structured transactions that are in essence similar to the Dunkin' Brands deal.

WBS is, however, not limited to restaurant chains. Other notable borrowers include players in the infrastructure or infra-like space, like London City Airport (the airport located in east London) or Alpha Trains (a European rolling stock leasing company).

WBS offers three types of advantages for an originator:

- *All in cost:* the improved credit rating enables companies to benefit from much more competitive terms than what they could obtain from other financing structures.
- *Leverage*: an originator can usually achieve a considerably higher financial leverage than otherwise possible through traditional forms of debt financing. Structuring a WBS can therefore facilitate a dividend distribution to shareholders.
- *Maturity*: an originator can obtain very long financing commitments. For the right asset, maturities can go over 20 years.

For investors, WBS is an opportunity to earn additional yield compared to traditional debt instruments. For the same rating, WBS tranches pay more than a vanilla product due to the structural complexity and the lower liquidity.

A unique feature of WBS is the sponsor's ongoing involvement in managing the business to generate expected cash flow, maintain asset value, and nurture the brand. An evaluation of the management team, growth strategy, and competitive position is thus central to the analysis done by the WBS investors.

Rating Uplift in Question

Insofar as a WBS is in fact a secured loan backed by the entire business of a company, some observers have argued that there is no real difference in terms of credit risk between a WBS and a corporate loan to this company. After all, lenders are in both cases exposed to the cash flows generated by the company.

Although this argument may seem appealing, it ignores some key features of a WBS:

- Firstly, the cash flow generating assets are legally isolated from the originator. They have been transferred via a true sale[12] to a bankruptcy-remote SPV. This decreases the likelihood that other creditors of the company can disrupt cash flow to the securitization following a bankruptcy of the originator.
- Secondly, the performance of the assets transferred to the SPV is generally not fully correlated with the profitability of the originator. A system of franchised restaurants for instance will likely continue to generate cash flow even in case of bankruptcy of the originator.
- Thirdly, WBS generally carry structural features that protect note holders against potential losses. In case the cash flow generated by the assets falls below a certain level, cash flow is usually redirected from the equity tranche to fund a debt reserve account or to repay the most senior ABS tranches.

Summary

Securitization: What Have We Learnt?

- Securitization is a financing technique that allows the conversion of illiquid assets into marketable securities.
- A bank (or a company) pools together a large number of loans (or receivables) and sells them to a Special Purpose Vehicle (SPV).
- The SPV finances the acquisition of these assets by issuing securities called Asset-Backed Securities (ABS). Interest paid on these notes solely derives from the cash flow generated by the assets.
- In financial jargon, the specific name of these ABS varies depending on the nature of the assets. The most frequent instruments are (i) CDO (Collateralized Debt Obligation) if the assets held by the SPV are debt instruments, (ii) RMBS (Residential Mortgage Backed Security) if they are mortgage loans, and (iii) CMBS (Commercial Mortgage Backed Security) if they are commercial real estate loans.
- An SPV generally issues various ABS tranches, offering each a different risk return profile. The profits of the SPV are paid out to investors according to a waterfall payment structure. Senior tranches have priority over junior tranches in terms of dividend distribution and principal repayment. To compensate

---

[11] See Chapter 10, section 10.1.2.

for the additional risk, junior tranches bear a higher interest rate than senior tranches.

- The riskiest tranche offers the best return but its holders run the risk that there may be no more cash flow to be distributed due to defaults in the reference portfolio. If the extent of defaults is so high that the SPV cannot distribute any income to the holders of the riskiest tranche, the other tranches are affected, in the opposite order to the priority of interest payment.

- Tranches (except the riskiest one) are rated by one or several rating agencies. This rating improves their liquidity. The safest tranche is called the senior tranche and the unrated tranche is called the equity tranche. The other tranches are collectively called mezzanine.

- In some cases, an SPV can be actively managed by an asset manager – called collateral manager. This collateral manager can buy and sell assets with the objective of optimizing the revenues of the SPV for the note holders. Assets can be acquired in the primary or in the secondary market.

- Such transactions are called managed transactions (or arbitrage transactions), as opposed to static transactions (or balance sheet transactions), where assets are purchased by the SPV from a single company or bank and held until maturity.

Conclusion

STRUCTURED FINANCE: WHAT HAVE WE LEARNT?

The reasons for using structured finance are extremely diverse, but six major financial and regulatory reasons explain its growing success:

1. *Structured finance solutions allow clients to isolate (or ring-fence) one asset from other assets*

   Each transaction is structured to finance only one asset or one portfolio of assets. Lenders have no recourse to the equity investors in an SPV but are not affected if other assets held by the equity investors default.

2. *Lenders can offer a higher level of leverage through structured finance*

   The possibility of a higher level of leverage is one of the main reasons for the success of structured finance. The total leverage of a transaction (measured as a multiple of EBITDA or loan to value) can reach levels well above what is recommended for a corporate loan. This is obviously true for LBOs but is also the case in project or asset finance. As for securitization, this is an instrument that uses liquidity coming from non-banking investors. From a macroeconomic perspective, this means that securitization brings additional leverage in the market.

3. *Lenders can directly select the risks they are most comfortable with*

   Structured finance has created a wide range of new debt instruments that allow lenders to directly select the risks with which they are most comfortable. Instead of funding large corporations performing different activities, each associated with a different level of risk, a lender can choose to finance one specific asset only. This logic applies to all structured finance transactions.

4. *Structured finance has created new investment opportunities*

   Structured finance has broadened the scope of investment opportunities for lenders. Before 1980, lenders could mostly invest in investment grade products. Now they can choose from a wide range of instruments, some of them high yield or non-rated. The same applies to equity investors. Buying publicly traded stocks is not the only investment strategy available to institutional investors. These investors are now also heavily invested in private equity.

5. *All types of risk/return combinations are available to investors*

Structured finance attracts a lot of liquidity because so many investment strategies are now available to investors. From buying project bonds benefiting from an investment grade rating to investing equity in a highly leveraged company, structured finance offers all types of risk/return combinations.

6. *Structured finance allows banks to optimize capital*

This is true for securitization, as the sale of assets is a way for banks to reduce their capital charges and optimize their return on equity. Also, generally, the security package given to lenders in structured transactions benefits from a favorable regulatory treatment.

A COMPARISON OF VARIOUS TYPES OF STRUCTURED FINANCE

	LBO	Project finance	Asset finance	Securitization
Underlying asset	Company (referred to as target company)	Infrastructure asset	Large movable asset (aircraft, train, vessel, etc.)	Portfolio of assets (loans, bonds, receivables, etc.)
SPV	Yes	Yes	Yes (except for simple mortgage loans)	Yes
Financial structure	SPV (Hold Co) funded by debt and equity	SPV (Project Company) funded by debt and equity	SPV funded by debt and equity	The SPV is funded by various tranches of notes. The most junior tranche is referred to as equity (as investors take an equity risk) but is legally a tranche of subordinated notes

(continued)

	LBO	Project finance	Asset finance	Securitization
Origin of SPV revenues	Dividends paid by the target company and sale of the target company	Project cash flow	Rentals paid by the user of the asset	Revenues generated by the portfolio of assets
Debt maturity	5 to 7 years	Mostly between 15 and 25 years for long term debt. 8 to 10 years with a balloon for mini-perm structures	8 to 15 years, depending on the credit quality of the user and the life expectancy of the asset	Depends on the maturity of the underlying assets but around 10 years for arbitrage CDOs
Debt tranches	There are usually one or two tranches of debt. In some cases, one tranche of debt (unitranche) can replace the senior and junior tranches	One senior debt tranche mainly (although a junior tranche can be added)	One tranche only in most cases but a junior tranche can be added	Variable but often five tranches rated from AAA to BB for CLOs
Debt investors	Banks for small LBOs and banks or CLOs for TLB. Debt funds providing unitranche funding	Banks or infrastructure debt funds backed by investors looking for long-term yield (like pension funds for instance)	Mostly banks	The investors in the rated tranches are asset managers, banks, insurances companies, family offices, hedge funds, pension funds

	LBO	Project finance	Asset finance	Securitization
Equity investors	Private equity firms (or sometimes individuals for very small LBOs)	Industrial sponsors interested in the construction and operation of the asset or private equity firms specialized in infrastructure	Lessors or, to a lesser extent, specialized funds (sidecars)	The investors in the subordinated tranche (the non-rated tranche) are usually hedge funds or asset managers
Equity return	Dividends paid out during the holding period and profit from the sale of the company	Project cash flow after debt repayment and potential sale of the asset	Rentals (minus debt service) and profit from the sale of the asset	The equity investors perceive the sum of the flows available after repayment of the other debt tranches

WHAT IS THE FUTURE FOR STRUCTURED FINANCE?

It is always perilous to predict what the future holds. We believe nonetheless that the changes at work since the end of the 1970s will not fade. Structured finance serves so many purposes and offers so many options for clients and lenders that it will continue to grow.

Financial markets in emerging countries are still in their infancy, but as they further develop, structured finance will become as important a financial tool to them as it is now to Europe and the United States. Project and asset finance are probably the two products that will flourish first. In many ways, they have been present in these markets for a good 10 years. Liquidity is indeed already available for a prime aircraft or an energy project with the right counterparty. It may take more time for LBOs to become mainstream. Some private equity firms are obviously already active in emerging countries, but the market is limited. Borrowers already pay a high-risk premium for corporate debt. Adding more leverage and complexity would only make the cost of debt in these markets prohibitively high.

Securitization is a different animal. It relies on large portfolios of diversified assets and an educated investor base. Given their size, China and India should in theory be the future new markets for this product. Both already have a legal framework in place. However, more investment-grade counterparties, additional financial stability and more sophisticated local players are still needed before these countries catch up with the United States and Europe.

Whatever happens to structured finance in emerging markets, these products have a bright future in the countries where they are already sought after. Unless banking regulation makes them unattractive, we do not see any reason why they would become less popular. Structured finance is, indeed, for us the final element of a long-term trend in the development of financial markets. A three-stage evolution that is summarized in what follows.

Stage 1: Traditional Financing

Figure C.1 below shows a traditional financing structure. Banks lend to their clients who in turn invest in the assets, projects, and companies they choose. The funds provided by banks come from shareholders (individuals, pension funds, asset managers, etc.) and depositors that are referred to as *liquidity providers*.

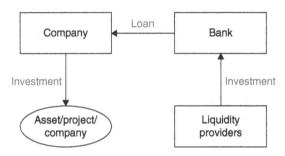

FIGURE C.1   The logic behind a corporate loan

Stage 2: Financial Disintermediation (Eliminating Banks as Intermediaries)

The traditional financing scheme shown in Figure C.1 has greatly evolved during the twentieth century. As shown in Figure C.2, a large part of the financing is now directly

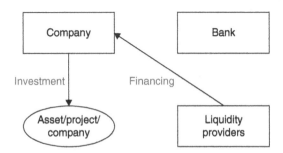

FIGURE C.2   Example of financial disintermediation

brought by the *liquidity providers* to companies, bypassing banks. These financings take the form of bonds or loans.

Financial disintermediation is not a new phenomenon but has been reinforced by successive measures imposed by the Basel Accords. By requiring banks to finance their loans with a growing part of capital (effects of Basel I, Basel II, Basel III . . .), the Basel Accords have indirectly reduced the profitability of banks. This has given more space to non-banking lenders.

Stage 3: Direct Financing of Asset

The third stage in the evolution of financial markets has been the liquidity providers directly financing the asset, project, or company that their clients acquire. This is the structure shown in Figure C.3.

In this new paradigm, liquidity providers focus on financing one specific asset or project only. This evolution is already underway and is the cornerstone of the development of structured finance in the coming years. LBOs are a good example. Lenders finance the acquisition of a company; they do not lend to a sponsor. These lenders are mostly non-banking entities: investors in TLB are mainly CLOs while a great number of mid-market LBOs are now financed by unitranche debt coming from alternative lenders. The trend is similar in other structured finance deals. In project finance, for instance, debt funds are becoming more active and directly finance many infrastructure assets without the involvement of banks.

We believe that this evolution will continue because it responds to a desire to segregate risk. In the traditional financing structure shown in Figure C.1, liquidity providers are exposed to three levels of risk: (i) the first is at the level of the bank to which they provide the funds; (ii) the second is at the level of the company in which the bank invests; (iii) the third is at the level of the project/asset/company itself in which the client invests.

Now, as shown in Figure C.3, liquidity providers are exposed only to risks on the project/asset/company they finance. This new financing model allows liquidity providers to more precisely select the risk they want to assume. They target directly the assets in which they want to invest instead of having to rely on a bank and/or a company to do so.

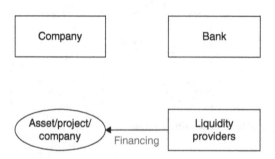

FIGURE C.3   Disintermediation thanks to structured finance

To be clear, we do not believe that corporate financing or corporate bonds will disappear. They will continue to exist because they offer advantages that structured finance solutions cannot provide. Corporate loans offer a lot of flexibility and are the cornerstone of a traditional, often long-term, relationship between a company and its banks. Corporate bonds are an extremely simple instrument that attracts a lot of liquidity, especially if it comes with an investment grade rating.

That said, we believe that the disintermediation of banks and corporations will continue and that the scope of structured finance will expand. Bonds are, for instance ever more present in project finance and asset finance structures. LBOs are becoming more common in Asia-Pacific and securitization is gaining traction with new asset classes like renewable projects and trade receivables.

The future is most certainly bright for structured finance.

How Banks Set Interest Rates

Interest rates charged by banks to their clients are the sum of two elements:

(i) the liquidity cost for the bank, and

(ii) the credit risk posed by the counterparty.

Interest rates are nothing other than the price paid by a client to borrow funds. This price is set like any other product as the sum of (i) the costs borne by the seller to obtain or produce the product or service sold plus (ii) a margin.

In a structured finance deal (as in any other financing), the interest rate to be paid by the borrower is clearly set in the loan documentation as the sum of these two components. They are both usually very precisely defined to avoid any confusion.

LIQUIDITY COST

Definition

The liquidity cost is the price paid by the bank to acquire the liquidity that it lends to a client. This cost is defined as the interbank rate, i.e. the rate at which banks lend to each other. This definition is an approximation as it does not fully correspond to the real liquidity cost for a bank (the real liquidity cost of a bank is a mix of its cost of equity, the rates applicable to the deposits of its clients, and the rates at which this bank borrows from other banks and at which it issues bonds). Using interbank rates to set the liquidity cost of a bank offers a reference that is easy to define in a loan agreement. It can be verified at any time by both the lender and the borrower.

For transactions in US dollars, the liquidity cost used as reference in the agreement between the lender and the borrower is usually LIBOR (*London Interbank Offered Rate*). There are various LIBOR rates. They are calculated every day in five currencies (euro, Swiss franc, British pound sterling, US dollar, and Japanese Yen) and for seven different maturities (one day, one week, one month, two months, three months, six months, and one year).

How is LIBOR Calculated?

Every day, a panel of banks is invited to share with Intercontinental Exchange (ICE), the parent company of the New York Stock Exchange (NYSE), the rate at which they believe they can borrow funds from other banks that very day before 11.00 a.m. London time. The number and the identity of banks in the panels varies depending on the currency. Only banks active in a currency can take part in a panel.

Eighteen banks are included in the panel for US dollar. They are all consulted for the seven maturities. The four highest and the four lowest responses are eliminated and an average is calculated by ICE with the other 10 responses (again for each of the seven maturities). This average rate is the US dollar LIBOR. It is published every day at 11.30 a.m. London time.

The way LIBOR is calculated in other currencies is similar to how LIBOR is calculated for US dollars. LIBOR for euro, Swiss franc, GBP and Yen is calculated as the average of the responses of the panel of banks (to which the highest and lowest responses have been excluded).

Other Reference Rates

LIBOR is not the only reference rate used throughout the world. There are several other interbank rates. EURIBOR *(Euro Interbank Offered Rate)* is set in continental Europe like LIBOR in London. It does exist in various maturities but only for one currency, the euro. EURIBOR is usually preferred as a reference rate over the euro LIBOR set in London for loans denominated in euros.

Other financial centers have their own reference rates: Hong Kong (HIBOR), Singapore (SIBOR), Shanghai (SHIBOR), etc. These rates are calculated for the local currency and various maturities. The documentation of each loan must specify the reference rate used by the parties as well as the maturity.

Day Convention

Depending on the reference rate, there are (i) 360 or 365 days in a year and (ii) 30 or the actual number of days in a month. EURIBOR convention is 30/360 while LIBOR convention is actual/360, except for GBP LIBOR where the convention is actual/365.

COUNTERPARTY RISK

Definition

The credit risk of the counterparty is analysed by the bank before the transaction. The higher the risk, the higher the margin required by the bank. This margin is expressed in *basis points* (bps) with 1bp being equal to 0.01%.

Example

As already explained, both the reference rate and the margin are defined in the loan documentation. Let us make the following assumptions:

- loan amount: €100 million
- maturity: 1 year
- format: bullet
- margin: 200bps
- reference rate: EURIBOR
- drawdown date: 15 January
- interest period: 3 months

Rates applicable on the drawdown date are the following:

- EURIBOR 3-month: 2.5%
- EURIBOR 6-month: 2.7%
- EURIBOR 12-month: 2.8%

Given that the reference rate is EURIBOR and that the interest period is three months, the rate applicable to calculate the interest rate is EURIBOR three-month rate set on 15 January (i.e. 2.5%). Interest will be paid on 15 April. The sum due by the borrower to the lender at that date is equal to $100 \times 4.5\%/360 \times 90^1$, i.e. $1.125 million. Another interest payment will be due on 15 June. The rate applicable to calculate that payment will be EURIBOR three-month as set on 15 April, etc.

If the interest period of that loan had been six months, then EURIBOR six-month would have been used (i.e. 2.7%). In that case, the borrower would have had to make a first interest payment on 15 June. That payment would have been equal to $100 \times 4.7\%/360 \times 180$, i.e. $2.35 million.

---

[1]Since the reference rate is EURIBOR, it is considered for the purpose of the calculation that there are 360 days in year and that each month has 30 days, i.e. 90 days for a quarter – see our earlier paragraph on day convention.

LIBOR SCANDAL

Facts

In April 2008, a few months before the Lehman bankruptcy, an article in *The Wall Street Journal* revealed that banks were manipulating LIBOR to hide their own funding issues. Many submitted a rate lower than the actual rate they knew was applicable to them. The former governor of the Bank of England, Mervyn King, even declared at that time in a public hearing that LIBOR was *"the rate at which banks don't lend to each other"*.

Investigations followed and showed that manipulations had been, in fact, common for years, allowing banks to make profits on capital markets instruments linked to LIBOR. Several banks were fined by regulators, and Barclays' chairman and CEO both resigned from their position in 2012 amid the scandal.

LIBOR was reformed in 2013 with an eye to improving its accuracy and making it less vulnerable to rigging. The main changes were as follows:

– Oversight of LIBOR was transferred from the British Bankers' Association (BBA) to the Financial Conduct Authority, the UK financial regulatory body.
– Panel banks were asked to keep data on how they determine the rates they submit.
– Deliberately making false statements on LIBOR became a criminal offence.
– From an operating perspective, the administration of LIBOR was taken over by ICE from the BBA.

Next Steps

Despite these improvements, The Financial Conduct Authority announced in 2017 that after 2021 it would no longer compel panel banks to submit the rates required to calculate LIBOR. This decision was seen as the first step to replacing LIBOR by a more reliable rate.

Following extensive reviews, several potential replacement rates have been identified. One option in the United States is the Secured Overnight Financing Rate (SOFR), which is based on the cost of overnight loans using repurchase agreements secured by US government debt. In the United Kingdom, the Sterling Overnight Index Average (SONIA) could potentially replace LIBOR. Like SOFR (and unlike LIBOR), SONIA is based on actual transactions. It reflects the average of the interest rates that banks pay to borrow GBP overnight from other financial institutions.

Overnight rates like SOFR and SONIA do not, however, have term structures. This is a disadvantage compared to LIBOR, which includes rates from one day to one year. This could create pricing issues for loans that have a longer maturity than overnight. Although regulators and industry groups are discussing options to overcome this, the main issue in switching away from LIBOR is the fact that trillions of loans and investments are already indexed to LIBOR. Using a new benchmark could create volatility and bouts of illiquidity during the transition period.

The FCA has taken these potential risks into account. Even if submitting the rates required to calculate LIBOR will not be mandatory after 2021, nothing prevents banks from continuing to submit the relevant data. That said, it is unclear what banks will do knowing the responsibility inherent to sharing judgment-based submissions that determine the value of such a high number of assets.

The post-LIBOR history is still to be written. In any case, even if LIBOR as a benchmark disappears, loans will still be defined as a sum of a reference rate plus a margin.

Syndication and Club Deals

DEFINITION

In a syndication, banks provide a loan to a client and distribute a large part of the debt to other financial institutions. Bank syndicates are typically formed to handle large structured finance transactions (LBO or project finance).[1] They allow banks to share the risk of a loan and work in a coordinated manner to offer a financing solution to a client.

Syndication processes are quite standardized. One or several banks (the *underwriters*) are selected by the client to arrange the loan. These banks then distribute part of the loan to other lenders. Some large transactions can easily have a total of more than 30 lenders. The bank syndicate that financed the construction of the Channel Tunnel in 1986 had more than 200 lenders for a total loan of £5 billion.

Underwriters get paid a *structuring fee* for arranging the transaction and an *underwriting fee* for distributing the loan, calculated as a percentage of the total loan amount (50bps, 100bps, etc.). The lenders brought in by underwriters are called *participants*. All final lenders in the transaction (whether underwriters or participants) receive *upfront fees* and a *margin* on the loan. Upfront fees are also calculated as a percentage of the final take for each lender.

There are two types of syndication: syndication with firm underwriting or best efforts syndication. If the syndication route is not chosen, a transaction can be structured as a club deal. This option is common for smaller transactions.

---

[1] Bank syndicates also exist for large corporate loans.

FIRM UNDERWRITING

Definition

Syndications with firm underwriting, the most common type, are those in which underwriters commit to provide the total loan amount. Firm underwritings are of real value for sponsors, offering two main advantages:

1. Although a sponsor may work on a large deal that will attract many lenders in the end, it only negotiates the terms of the transaction with the underwriters, i.e. a limited group of banks – generally one to three banks, depending on the deal size. It greatly simplifies the negotiation of the loan documentation.
2. It provides sponsors with the certainty that the full amount of necessary debt will be available by the time they execute their deals.

Underwriters do not keep the total underwritten amount on their books. They want to distribute a large portion of it to other lenders. Underwriters take the risk of not being able to distribute the loan or to do so but at a loss. They may also end up with a total credit exposure greater than what they had expected.

Underwriting as a Business Model

Banks have strong financial and competitive incentives to participate in firm underwriting. It brings real value to a client, especially when the deal is large, complex, or has to be executed quickly. Leading sophisticated investment banks typically offer these services to their clients. The various fees paid to the underwriters enhance the profitability of the transaction. For a given final credit exposure, the total profitability is higher for an underwriter than for a mere participant.

Fees paid to underwriters vary depending of the type of deal. Fees naturally increase with the complexity and the riskiness of the loan. Leveraged loans or project finance loans traditionally pay higher fees than corporate deals for large investment-grade companies. In many cases, these types of borrowers arrange the deal themselves and work with their core banks, so they have little need for real underwriting.

By contrast, underwriting deals for leveraged buyouts or project finance can be a lucrative business for institutions that have the proper setup. A bank willing to provide underwriting must have strong syndication and distribution teams. It has to be knowledgeable about the margins applied to similar transactions in the past and have built a strong network of lenders that can participate in these loans.

Market Flex and MAC Clauses

Underwritings can include *market flex clauses*. These clauses give flexibility to the underwriters to change some parameters of the transaction in case market conditions deteriorate and do not allow a successful syndication on the terms agreed with the client. An underwriter can obviously not totally change the deal. The possible changes are pre-agreed between the client and the underwriters when the deal is structured. Activating a market flex clause is always subject to previous discussions with the borrower. The elements that can be modified by a market flex are usually the upfront fees, the margin, and, sometimes, some financial covenants.

Reverse flex clauses can also be added to the documentation. They allow the borrower to benefit from improved terms if market conditions are better than expected or if the loan is significantly oversubscribed. The activation of a reverse flex clause usually means lower fees or lower margins for the lenders.

Market flex clauses are different from MAC (*Material Adverse Change*) clauses. A MAC clause can be used by the underwriters to pull out from the deal if market conditions are such that a deal can clearly not be syndicated, even under improved terms. While market flex or reverse flex clauses give flexibility to the parties to adapt a deal to new market conditions, MAC clause are an option to cancel the deal. MAC clauses usually refer to extreme situations (war, natural disaster, etc.) but, if they have not been well negotiated by the borrower, they can give room for underwriters to leave a deal that has simply been mispriced.

Syndication Process

A syndication process starts before an underwriting offer is sent to a client. The teams in charge of originating and structuring the loan present the opportunity to their syndication desk. This department is responsible for *reading* the market, i.e. finding out the margin active lenders would require to participate in the loan. This *market reading* can be done by presenting the deal to a limited number of lenders on a high-level and no-name basis. However, if comparable transactions exist and have been closed recently, there is no need to test potential lenders. The bank's syndication desk provides directly its market reading.

The market reading is used to set the margin and the various fees in the offer sent to the client. This offer can be done for 100% underwriting or less (usually a significant share, i.e. 50%, one third, etc.). The banks offering the best terms are chosen as underwriters and must then distribute the loan to other lenders. Depending how successful the syndication process is, underwriters can adjust the fees to be paid to the other lenders. They may have to share some of their underwriting fees if the process is difficult. If needed, they can also activate the market flex.

Who are the Participants?

A wide range of lenders participate in LBOs or project finance transactions. While large banks prefer to act as underwriters, there are many other lenders with different business models that only participate in loans. Traditional participants in a syndication are smaller banks, specialized lenders, or debt funds. The scope of lenders varies depending on whether the transaction is a PF or an LBO[2] but all these participants have in common: (i) funds to deploy (and therefore an appetite to lend), and (ii) relatively small teams (meaning they have limited origination capabilities).

It is not uncommon for a bank to distribute 100% of a loan that it has underwritten. An underwriter may, however, also keep part of the loan on its book. It all depends on the strategy of the bank and the size of its balance sheet. In this respect, there are differences between segments and geographies. LBOs are almost entirely distributed to investors, while underwriters in project finance usually keep a share of the debt. In Europe, where banks participate more actively in the lending market than in the United States, underwriters are generally more prone to keeping part of the loan.

BEST EFFORTS SYNDICATION

A best efforts syndication is a transaction in which the underwriters do not commit to provide the total loan amount. They only commit to make their *best efforts* to find lenders willing to participate in the transaction. Underwriters have an obligation of means, not results. If the loan is undersubscribed, the transaction may not close, or close with a smaller loan amount than anticipated.

Best efforts syndications usually have little value for clients. What sponsors look for when they select underwriters is the certainty that funds will be available – which a best efforts syndication does not provide. Best efforts syndications are generally only used for names with a complicated credit history or when market conditions become extremely difficult. They were the norm in Europe and the United States after the 2008 crisis and in Asia after the crisis of 1997–1999. When financial markets are booming, clients select as underwriters only banks that offer firm underwritings.

CLUB DEAL

A club deal is an alternative to a syndication. While in a syndication one or several underwriters negotiate the main features of a deal with a client (and sometimes sign the documentation) before distributing the loan, a club deal is a process in which all the final lenders negotiate directly with the borrower. Club deals are reserved for transactions with a limited number of lenders. Otherwise negotiations would be too long and complex.

Club deals are optimal for small to mid-sized transactions or for loans structured by parties that have a lot of experience of working together. In that case, parties can reuse loan documents they have already negotiated in the past. In structured finance, club deals are only possible with experienced lenders. Inviting a newcomer may slow down the execution of the deal.

---

[2]The variety of lenders in LBOs or project finance deals is detailed respectively in Parts I and II of this book.

Club deals are usually cheaper for borrowers than pure syndications because they do not have to pay fees to compensate the lenders for their extra work and the additional risk. If a borrower has a group of trusted financial partners and is financing a relatively standard asset for a limited amount, a club deal makes the most sense.

ARRANGERS' AND LENDERS' TITLES

Titles given to lenders for their role in a deal have grown in significance since the 1990s. The widespread use of league tables has led to title inflation and banks have been more careful in ensuring that they obtain a title in line with their role. Titles are a topic of negotiation and can be mentioned in the loan agreement, although this is not always the case.

There are no fixed rules around titles. The precise wording can vary from one transaction to the other. It is not rare that a bank with a large commitment is upgraded in terms of title compared to its real role in the deal.

The most common titles are generally the following:

- *Underwriter* (or *bookrunner*): this designates the banks that have arranged the deal and underwritten a large part of it. This is an optional title, even for transactions with firm underwriting.
- *Mandated lead arranger (MLA):* this is a significant title. An MLA is a major lender. It usually distributes part of its loan to other institutions. In some deals, distinction is made between senior MLAs and MLAs based on the size of their commitment. The title of MLA is also used to designate the arranger and underwriter in case the title of bookrunner or underwriter has not been given.
- *Lead arranger, arranger, and participant:* lenders with these titles play no role in structuring the deal. They are only providing the cash. If these different titles are used for the same loan, it suggests a difference in the size of the lenders' commitment.
- *Agent:* this title covers an administrative role and can be split into various sub-roles. The *documentation agent* is responsible for coordinating the legal negotiation process and selecting the law firm that will draft the deal. The *administrative agent* handles payments and channels discussion between the borrower and the lenders once the deal is closed.

THE POST-LAUNCH LIFE OF A LOAN

Secondary Sale

Banks acting as underwriters usually intend to sell the loans they have underwritten within a few weeks. This *primary syndication* starts either right after the loan has been drawn or in parallel to the finalization of the deal. In that case, the loan can be entirely distributed even before the transaction is closed and the loan is drawn.

Loans can also generally be sold at any point in time after the primary syndication is closed. The sale is in this case referred to as a *secondary sale* (or sale in the secondary market). Loans are tradable instruments and lenders can sell or acquire them depending on their strategy, credit appetite, balance sheet or RWA constraints, etc. Restrictions to trade can exist in the loan documentation but are usually limited. Borrowers know that lenders need some flexibility to manage their portfolios. A bank may decide, for instance, to reduce its exposure to a certain sector for strategic reasons or sell assets for liquidity purposes.

Restrictions notably take the form of a list of pre-agreed names of counterparties that lenders can sell their loans to. This list, known as *white list*, is defined in the loan agreement. The number of names in the white list depends on sponsors. Some give a lot of flexibility to lenders, while some like to limit the number of names in this list. These sponsors usually do not want to negotiate with lenders they do not know in case they need to restructure the loan in the future. The sale of a loan can also be restricted (i.e. forbidden or limited for a given period of time).

Amendments and Waivers

It is not uncommon that a borrower requests a change in the loan agreement, even after a deal is closed. These amendments are not necessarily major. They can be technical (change in a convention or a definition) or more structural (repricing, extension of the deal maturity, etc.). If the required changes imply an important modification of the deal, lenders charge a fee to the borrower. If not, lenders usually consent to the changes for free. Lenders obviously do not have to accept all amendment proposals.

A borrower may also ask the lenders for a *waiver*, i.e. their consent to relinquish a right under a clause of the loan agreement. A provision in the documentation may, for instance, stipulate that any change in the shareholding of the borrower triggers a repayment of the loan. If the shareholding is only slightly modified (i.e. a new minority shareholder takes 5% in the borrower), the borrower may not want to go through a full refinancing. In this case, it may simply ask the lenders to waive their right to repayment. Lenders may charge a *waiver fee* if they deem it appropriate.

APPENDIX C

Credit Derivatives

It is sometimes difficult for a bank to reduce its credit exposure by selling part of a loan on the secondary market. This is often the case when the loan documentation forbids any sell-down or when a sell-down is subject to prior approval from the borrower. A bank may indeed be reluctant to tell its client that it is looking to reduce its credit exposure, especially if the client has a longstanding relation with the bank. In that case, banks can reduce their exposure synthetically by means of credit derivatives.

CREDIT DEFAULT SWAPS (CDS)

CDS are financial instruments that allow for the transfer of credit exposure linked to a debt instrument (loan, bond, basket of securities, etc.) from one party to another. The buyer of the CDS is an institution that wants protection against the default of an asset. It pays a fee, called a CDS spread, to the seller and in turn receives payoff if the underlying asset defaults (see Figure C.1).

In sum, a CDS provides credit insurance. The value of the CDS spread is based on the credit risk of the underlying asset and is expressed in basis points. In case of default, the indemnity can be paid two ways:

- In case of *physical settlement*, the buyer of the CDS transfers the underlying asset to the seller and receives a cash amount equal to the notional value of the asset.
- In case of *cash settlement*, there is no asset transfer. The seller pays to the buyer an amount equal to the loss suffered by the buyer. This amount is equal to the nominal value of the asset minus the sums recovered after the bankruptcy/restructuring process.

Since the bankruptcy of Italian food industry giant Parmalat in 2003, when the physical settlement of a CDS contract ran into various practical obstacles, professionals prefer to use cash settlement.

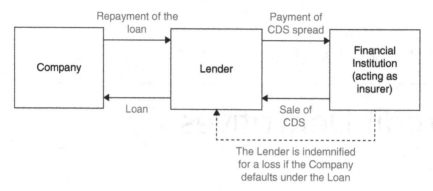

FIGURE C.1   Credit default swap

CDSs are governed by a standard document designed by the ISDA (International Swaps and Derivatives Association), the trade organization for participants in derivatives transactions. All CDSs exchanged in the market use this standard document, which clearly delineates the terms of a default and the indemnification process. The main credit events recognized by ISDA are the following:

– bankruptcy of the company that has issued the debt instrument subject to the CDS
– failure by the company to make a payment related to this debt instrument,
– restructuring of the debt of the company on unfavorable terms for the lenders.

Given their simplicity, CDS are a fantastic tool for managing risk. Some banks, acting as CDS buyers, can easily hedge their exposure, while other institutions (banks, insurance companies, hedge funds, etc.) can sell CDSs to take a synthetic exposure on assets whose risk they are comfortable with. It is also – as shown in case study 12 – a great speculative instrument if one wants to bet on the default of an asset.

A CDS, however, does not allow a seller to perfectly hedge a credit position. The buyer of the CDS is indeed exposed to a potential double default, i.e. a default of the CDS seller occurring simultaneously with the default of the underlying asset.

CREDIT LINKED NOTES (CLNS)

CLNs are another type of credit derivative. They take the form of bonds issued by an entity (issuer) looking to insure the risk of default of a particular asset (bond, loan, CDS, etc.). The CLN is acquired by an investor ready to accept the credit risk of that asset. Like any other bond, a CLN pays a coupon to the investor. The value of the coupon is linked to the risk and performance of the underlying asset.

The nominal value of the CLN is equal to the amount for which the issuer is looking for protection. The acquisition price paid by the investor is invested in

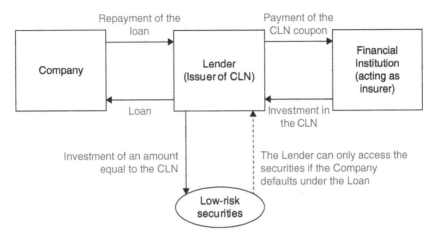

FIGURE C.2   Credit linked note

low-risk securities (US treasury bonds, for instance) in a segregated basket. The issuer cannot sell this basket except at maturity or when the underlying asset defaults (see Figure C.2).

If the underlying asset does not default, the investor receives a regular coupon and gets its nominal investment back at maturity. In case of default, two options are possible: (i) the issuer takes control of the low-risk securities and transfers the underlying asset to the investor (*physical settlement*), or (ii) a cash settlement has been agreed, in which case the issuer sells the low-risk securities and pays to the investor the amount of the CLN minus the loss suffered following the default of the underlying asset.

The main difference between a CDS and a CLN is that the CLN is a funded credit derivative, whereas the CDS is an unfunded one. A CLN widens the scope of potential insurers because some debt funds cannot buy unfunded instruments like the CDS (for legal reasons or because their investment guidelines forbid them to do so) but can invest in CLNs. As shown in Part III on securitization (Chapter 11, section 11.4.2), CLNs can also be used to structure synthetic capital relief trades.

Bibliography

BOOKS IN ENGLISH

Bierman, Harold Jr. (2003) *Private Equity, Transforming Public Stock to Create Value.* Hoboken NJ: Wiley.

Branson, Richard (1998) *Losing my Virginity, The Autobiography* (1st edn). London: Virgin Books.

Brown, Christopher (2009) *Crash Landing, An Inside Account of the Fall of GPA.* Dublin: Gill & Macmillan.

Bruck, Connie (1988) *The Predator's Ball. The Inside Story Of Drexel Burnham and the Rise of the Junk Bonds Raiders.* New York: Penguin Books.

Carey, David and Morris, John E. (2010) *King of Capital, the Remarkable Rise, Fall, and Rise again of Steve Schwarzman and Blackstone.* New York: Crown Publishing.

Choudhry, Moorad (2012) *The Principles of Banking.* Singapore: Wiley.

Cohan, William D. (2009) *House of Cards, a Tale of Hubris and Wretched Excess on Wall Street.* New York: Doubleday.

Ferguson, Alex and Moritz, Michael (2015) *Leading. Learning from Life and my Years at Manchester United.* New York: Hachette Books.

Fifer, Bob (1994) *Double your Profits in Six Months or Less.* New York: HarperCollins.

Finnerty, John D. (2007) *Project Financing, Asset-based Financial Engineering.* Hoboken NJ: Wiley.

Gatti, Stefano (2013) *Project Finance in Theory and Practice* (2nd edn). London: Academic Press.

Kadlec, Daniel J. (1999) *Masters of the Universe, Winning Strategies of America's Greatest Dealmakers.* New York: HarperCollins.

Kosman, Josh (2009) *The Buyout of America: How Private Equity is Destroying Jobs and Killing the American Economy.* New York: Portfolio.

Lewis, Michael (2010) *The Big Short: Inside the Doomsday Machine.* New York: WW Norton & Company.

Lewis, Michael (2011) *Boomerang. Travels in the New Third World.* New York: WW Norton & Company.

Marshall, Tim (2016) *Prisoners of Geography. Ten Maps that Tell you Everything you Need to Know about Global Politics.* London: Elliott & Thompson.

Pearl, Joshua and Rosenbaum, Joshua (2009) *Investment Banking. Valuation, Leveraged Buyout and Mergers & Acquisitions.* Hoboken NJ: Wiley.

Sliver, Nate (2012) *The Signal and the Noise. Why So Many Predictions Fail – but Some Don't.* New York: The Penguin Press.

Souza Homem de Mello, Francisco (2015) The 3G Way: *An Introduction to the Management Style of the Trio who's Taken Over Some of the Most Important Icons of American Capitalism.* 10x Books.

Stowell, David P. (2010) *An Introduction to Investment Banks, Hedge Funds, and Private Equity: The New Paradigm.* London: Academic Press.

Talbott, John R. (2009) *The 86 Biggest Lies on Wall Street.* New York: Seven Stories Press.

Trynka, Paul (2010) *Starman: David Bowie – The Definitive Biography.* London: Sphere.

Zuckerman, Gregory (2009) *Greatest Trade Ever: The Behind-the-Scenes Story of How John Paulson Defied Wall Street and Made Financial History.* New York: Crown Publishing Group.

BOOKS IN FRENCH

Gravereau, Jacques and Trauman, Jacques (2011) *L'incroyable histoire de Wall Street.* Paris: Albin Michel.

Larreur, Charles-Henri (2014) *Financements structurés, innovations et révolutions financières.* Paris: Editions Ellipses.

Le Fur, Yann and Quiry, Pascal (2015) *Finance d'entreprise 2015 – Pierre Vernimmen.* Paris: Dalloz.

Lyonnet du Moutier, Michel (2009) *L'aventure de la Tour Eiffel, réalisation et financement.* Paris: Publication de la Sorbonne.

ARTICLES, PROFESSIONAL REPORTS, AND CASE STUDIES IN ENGLISH

Athanassakos, George et al. (2008) *Harley Davidson Inc.* Ivey Publishing, 8 August, pp. 3–7.

Baker, Georges (2002) *K-III: A leveraged build-up.* Harvard Business Publishing, 15 May, pp. 1–6.

Baldwin, Clariss Y. and Quinn James W. (2012) *The auction for Burger King (A).* Harvard Business Publishing, 10 October, pp. 1–9.

Burger, Pieter et al. (2014) *Aircraft leasing in Ireland crossing borders.* Deloitte.

Carter, Bill (1990) New TV contracts for NFL's games total $3.6 billion. *New York Times*, 10 March.

Chad, Norman (1987) NFL's new TV deal is set: ESPN to get 8 Sunday night games Los Angeles Times, 13 March.

Chaplinsky, Susan (2003) *Formula one: intangible-asset-backed securitization* (revised edn). Darden Business Publishing.

Chung, Dawoon and Phalippou, Ludovic (2014) *Hilton Hotels: real estate private equity.* Private Equity Institute, Saïd Business School, University of Oxford, 5 April.

Clarke, Andrew (2007) Hilton's founding family agrees to $26bn buyout offer. *The Guardian*, 4 July.

Conn, David (2015) Glazers milk Manchester United with £15m dividend and football silent. *The Guardian*, 18 September.

Cortes Gonzalez, Ana et al. (2013) Viewing covered bonds through a structured finance lens. *PIMCO letter of information*, October.

Cros, Geraldine et al. (2017) *Guidance Material and Best Practices for Aircraft Leases* (4th edn). IATA, May.

Cuff, Daniel F. (1986) Polaris aircraft founder shifts company to GE. *New York Times*, 18 September.

De la Merced, Michael J. (2014) Ranking the biggest restaurant leveraged buyouts. *New York Times*, 7 January.

Engert, Herb et al. (2017) 2017 Global PE Watch – in-between days. *EY Annual Report on Private Equity*.

Eskenazi, Gerald (1982) NFL TV pact $2 billion. *New York Times*, 23 March.

Flint, Jo (2011) NFL signs TV rights deals with Fox, NBC and CBS. *Los Angeles Times*, 15 December.

Glaberson, William (1987) Life after Salomon Brothers. *New York Times*, 11 October .

Harris, Nick (2015) Premier League set for £3bn windfall from global TV rights as rival broadcasters slug it out to screen England-based superstars. *MailOnline*, 8 October.

Kester, Carl and Morley, Julia (1991) *Harley Davidson, Inc. – 1987*. Harvard Business Publishing, 15 December, pp. 1–8.

Landon, Thomas Jr. (2015) Robert F. Dall, mastermind of mortgage-backed bonds, dies at 81. *New York Times*, 18 November.

Lewis, Michael (2010) Betting on the blind side. *Vanity Fair*, April.

Leung, Clarence and Tsang, Catherine (2015) *Aviation Leasing: Leveraging Hong Kong's strengths*. PwC.

Mauboussin, Michael J. (2007) Anatomy of a market crash. *Forbes Magazine*, 25 October.

Moody's Investor Service (2010) *Structured Finance in Focus: A Short Guide to Covered Bonds*.

Morgan Stanley (2011) *Covered Bonds: A Primer*. Morgan Stanley Research, 10 February.

Ozanian, Mike (2017) Manchester United now biggest sport team in the world. *Forbes Magazine*, 19 January.

Perold, Andre F. and Singh, Kuljot (1994) *Lehman Brothers and the Securitization of American Express Charge-Card Receivables*. Harvard Business Publishing, 20 December, pp. 1–10.

Pope, Hugh (2004) Caspian pipeline financing solidifies U.S. policy. *Wall Street Journal*, 3 February.

Roan, Dan (2007) Premier League TV rights: Clubs set for "one of most important meetings". *BBC Sport*, 4 October.

Schlaman, William A. (2010) *Risk and Reward in Venture Capital*. Harvard Business Publishing, 3 December, pp. 1–4.

Schultz, Michael et al. (2016) Issuer guide covered bonds 2016. *Fixed Income Research NordLB*, 28 July.

Seagal, Sophie and Taylor, Ellis (2020) *Special Report. Finance & Leasing 2019*. Airline Business.

Sharf, Samantha (2016) Jonathan Gray: The man who revolutionized real estate investing on entrepreneurship in a big company. *Forbes Magazine*, 18 October.

Sorkin, Andrew R. (2007) Blackstone Group goes public. *New York Times*, 23 June.

Stewart, Larry (2004) New TV deal gives NFL the night shift. *Los Angeles Times*, 9 November.

Story, Louise (2007) Blackstone to buy Hilton Hotels for $26 billion. *New York Times*, 4 July.

Taylor, Daniel (2005) Ferguson seeks head to head with Glazer. *The Guardian*, 14 May.

Taylor, Daniel (2006) Ferguson heaps pressure on rivals after Gill confirms he will stay on. *The Guardian*, 8 April.

Tozer-Pennington, Victoria et al. (2020) *The Aviation Industry Leaders Report 2020. Steering the Supercycle. KPMG Aircraft Finance Report* 2020.

Treanor, Jill (2013) Barclays tax avoidance division generated £1bn a year – Salz review. *The Guardian*, 3 April 2013.

Vrooman, John (2000) The economics of American sports leagues. *Scottish Journal of Political Economy*, 47(4), pp. 391–394.

Ward, Andrew J. and Sonnenfeld, Jeffrey A. (2007) Firing back. How great leaders rebound after career disasters. *Harvard Business Review*, January, p. 8.

Wayne, Leslie (2007) Steve Hazy, aviation's low-profile giant. *New York Times*, 10 May.

EDITED TRANSCRIPT

AER (2015) *AerCap Holdings NV Investor Day*. 10 September.

ARTICLES IN FRENCH

Errard, Guillaume (2013) Manchester a bâti son modèle sur les succès de Ferguson. *Le Figaro*, 9 May.

Jacquillat, Bertrand (2008) Les rémunérations des dirigeants dans le capital-investissement. *Revue d'Économie Financière*, pp. 155–166.

Rolland, Sophie (2015) Les "yieldco" débarquent en Europe. *L'Agefi Hebdo*, 3 March.

Sabbah, Catherine (2018) *La tour Eiffel, future cash-machine de la Ville de Paris. Les Echos*, 12 February.

Acknowledgments

I am fortunate to have many friends and relatives with a background in finance. They have provided me with insightful advice and I am very grateful for their support. I read somewhere that writing a book requires extreme selfishness on the part of the author while demanding exceptional generosity from those around them. I could not agree more. I would not have found the time nor the energy to write this book if I had not benefited from the patience, the help, and the kindness of my friends and family.

My thanks go first to Cyril Demaria who connected me with Wiley and encouraged me to write this book. I do not forget the support provided by the whole Wiley team, especially Elisha Benjamin, Gemma Valler, and Purvi Patel.

I also would like to thank Andrew Vanacore, my assistant, for his help. Andrew found time to provide me with useful advice and spent hours reading the manuscript – all this while moving back from France to the United States and starting a very demanding job in consulting.

Thanks as well to the friends, students, and colleagues who helped me find useful information, anecdotes, and data on the topic of structured finance. In no particular order, I thank Atul Randev, Rishi Bajaj, Louis Beaux, Julien Wolff, Nicolas Sourin, François-Yves Gaudel, Julien Jugié, and Rodolphe de Lambertye.

The thanks continue to the various people who read all or some of the book as a work in progress, including Philippe Bergues, Carine Donges, Romain Larreur, Andrew Jones, Marcos Rueda, and Gonzague Touzé. They are all experts in the financing structures analyzed in this book and took time to make many worthwhile suggestions. This book would have looked very different without their input.

I obviously cannot forget the support of Frédéric Larreur and Kristina Borjesson. Their love of words and knowledge of the writing process helped me greatly in putting together the final version of the manuscript. They both patiently read entire parts of the book and shared with me countless relevant comments.

There are also many other people that helped me a lot in this journey, either directly or indirectly, through connections or moral support. I apologize for probably not listing them all but I would like to thank Jean-Xavier Bersot, Pascal Quiry, Lauren LaPage, Elodie Destruel, Pierre Lambrecht, and my brother Raphaël. Most of them probably do not realize how precious their support was.

This thank you list would be incomplete if I was not to mention here all the students I have taught over the years, in Europe or Asia. They are the main reason

I wrote this book. They have been an incredible source of inspiration. I hope they will find here the reference book on structured finance that many of them were looking for.

Finally, I could have not done this without the love and support of my family. I owe a great deal to my wife Tammy for her patience and kindness. Thanks also to my parents and my children who constantly encouraged me to get back to my desk when I wanted to have a break.

Index

Note: Page references in *italics* refer to figures and tables.